Jonathan Franzen and the Romance of Community

Jonathan Franzen and the Romance of Community

Narratives of Salvation

Jesús Blanco Hidalga

Bloomsbury Academic
An imprint of Bloomsbury Publishing Inc

B L O O M S B U R Y
NEW YORK · LONDON · OXFORD · NEW DELHI · SYDNEY

Bloomsbury Academic

An imprint of Bloomsbury Publishing Inc

1385 Broadway
New York
NY 10018
USA

50 Bedford Square
London
WC1B 3DP
UK

www.bloomsbury.com

BLOOMSBURY and the Diana logo are trademarks of Bloomsbury Publishing Plc

First published 2017

Library of Congress Cataloging-in-Publication Data
Names: Hidalga, Jesús Blanco, author.
Title: Jonathan Franzen and the romance of community: narratives of
salvation / Jesús Blanco Hidalga.
Description: New York: Bloomsbury Academic, 2017. | Includes bibliographical
references and index.
Identifiers: LCCN 2016025254 (print) | LCCN 2016040721 (ebook) | ISBN
9781501319839 (hardback) | ISBN 9781501319846 (ePub) | ISBN 9781501319853 (ePDF)
Subjects: LCSH: Franzen, Jonathan–Criticism and interpretation. | Salvation
in literature. | Redemption in literature. | Community in literature. |
BISAC: LITERARY CRITICISM / General. | LITERARY CRITICISM / American /
General. | LITERARY CRITICISM / Semiotics & Theory.
Classification: LCC PS3556.R352 Z65 2017 (print) | LCC PS3556.R352 (ebook) |
DDC 813/.54–dc23
LC record available at https://lccn.loc.gov/2016025254

ISBN: HB: 978-1-5013-1983-9
ePDF: 978-1-5013-1985-3
ePub: 978-1-5013-1984-6

Cover design: Daniel Benneworth-Gray
Cover image © wikimedia commons

Typeset by Deanta Global Publishing Services, Chennai, India
Printed and bound in the United States of America

To Lola, all my love and gratitude

CONTENTS

ACKNOWLEDGEMENTS

As is usually the case with projects like this one, the contribution of a number of people has been necessary for its ever becoming a reality. I am most indebted to Julián Jiménez Heffernan and Paula Martín Salván. It was my privilege to count on their exceptional insight and kindness during the process of writing this book. I must also thank Sonia Baelo Allué, Gerardo Rodríguez Salas and Juan de Dios Torralbo Caballero, who read through earlier versions of this text and made valuable suggestions that found their way to the final manuscript. I am also grateful to Mary Al-Sayed, my editor at Bloomsbury, for so deftly taking care of this project.

Likewise, this book would have never been possible without the unfaltering support I have enjoyed within my family. I wish to thank my parents, Manuel and María Ángeles, who raised me in a house full of books where the value of education was never questioned. Lola, of course, with her constant backing, is to be credited for the completion of this project, and Diego, no doubt, for filling our days with light.

PREFACE

I became first acquainted with the work of Jonathan Franzen in late 2010 through *The Corrections*, published nine years before. The thrill of meeting a major narrative voice for the first time is still vivid in my memory. In the subsequent months, as I went through the rest of Franzen's fiction, the possibility of bringing to bear my interest in the social dimension of literature to the analysis of those novels became readily clear. I was especially captivated by the way Franzen combined micro and macro lenses, his exploration of the intersection between familial and social concerns. The multivalent concept of community and the symbolic and ideological aspects of narrative quickly established themselves as the main axes of my study. The need to provide a map of the complex relationships between Franzen's work and its sociocultural context, with special attention to ongoing ideological struggles and communitarian concerns, also became apparent. Throughout the process, my intention was to integrate usually separated formal and ideological perspectives to cast new light on Franzen's stylistic choices. The result was the discovery of the inner logic that articulates Franzen's narratives. This logic relies on the concepts, typical of romance narratives, of salvation and redemption, and makes for a recurrent rhetorical strategy of ideological and psychological self-legitimation so far unaccounted for in the existing critical literature on Franzen. This strategy takes the form of an authorial metanarrative that reaches its closure in *Freedom*. Franzen's latest novel, *Purity*, which was released just as this study was achieving completion, departs in some respects from that metanarrative and shows the novelist confidently exploring new territories. It is my contention, however, that this novel confirms my main arguments about Franzen's fictional work and its underlying logic.

LIST OF ABBREVIATIONS

DZ   Jonathan Franzen (2006), *The Discomfort Zone: A Personal History*, London, etc.: Harper Perennial.

F   Jonathan Franzen (2010), *Freedom*, London: Fourth Estate.

FA   Jonathan Franzen (2012), *Farther Away*, London: Fourth State.

HA   Jonathan Franzen (2002), *How to Be Alone*, London: Fourth Estate.

KP   Franzen, Jonathan (2013), *The Kraus Project*, London: Fourth Estate.

P   Jonathan Franzen (2015), *Purity*, London: Fourth Estate.

SM   Jonathan Franzen ([1992] 2007), *Strong Motion*, New York: Picador-Farrar.

TC   Jonathan Franzen ([2001] 2010), *The Corrections*, New York: Picador-Farrar.

TS   Jonathan Franzen ([1988] 2010), *The Twenty-Seventh City*, New York: Noonday-Farrar.

1

Introduction: A formal and ideological approach to Jonathan Franzen's fiction

To read a plot – to take part in its work of recognition – is to imagine a transformation of life and its conditions, and not their mere reproduction.

IAN DUNCAN

1 Jonathan Franzen's relevance to contemporary American culture

Franzen's novelistic work raises a series of questions which are central to the understanding not only of modern-day American fiction but also of contemporary culture in the United States and elsewhere. Studying Franzen's work means coming to terms with pressing issues such as, in no particular order, the viability of the novel as a form of mass entertainment today; the cultural and political status of the socially engaged writer, and more specifically, of the white straight novelist in the face of the perceived compartmentalization of American culture; the possibility of exerting effective political critique in the age of late capitalism; the alleged exhaustion of postmodernist fiction and the pertinence – or mere feasibility – of an updated realist social novel in our postmodern times. Last but not least, Franzen's fiction is also concerned with the practicability, or even conceivability, of truly transformative political action in our age. Besides, the fact that Franzen sets his fiction in the present time, together with his calling for the inclusive social novel, also facilitates our discussion of the recent socio-historical development of the United States: its almost accomplished transition from *industrial society* into *advanced modernity*, to use Ulrich Beck's expressions, the so-called *culture wars* and, in short, the current state of American *Gemeinschaft* or community. These are all issues that are reflected in Franzen's work and I will be dealing with them in the course of the analysis of his novels. In fact, and this is another reason that makes Franzen an outstanding writer among his contemporaries, he has openly addressed some of these questions in quite outspoken essays. The discussion of these topics *per se*, however, is not the primary goal of this book. Rather, it is intended to be subservient to the main objective of this study as the necessary reconstruction of the cultural, historical and political context of Franzen's work. And this book's main objective is to offer a critical reading of Franzen's fiction that will focus on its formal and ideological aspects, drawing attention to the relationship between these two domains. My analysis of Franzen's novels includes the discovery and exploration of a complex, large-scale rhetorical strategy of persuasion and self-justification which unfolds through his novels in conjunction with some of his essays – a strategy so far unaccounted for in the existing critical literature on Franzen and which I have called, following remarks by Jeremy Green (2005) and Robert Rebein (2007), *the narrative of conversion*.

2 Narratives and metanarratives: The *conversion*

Franzen is still widely regarded as the novelist who – as Rebein (2007) put it – said 'No' to Po-Mo; the novelist who publicly abjured of postmodernism to embrace realism and subsequently attain massive success. To be sure, this is a more than adequate foundation for a story with religious overtones. The first critic to call attention to Franzen's frequent use of quasi-religious discourse was surely Green, who devoted a chapter to Franzen's work in his monograph *Late Postmodernism* (2005). In his text, somewhat derisively, Green interprets Franzen's famous act of recantation in his 1996 essay 'Perchance to Dream' (soon to be known as simply the *Harper's* essay) as a 'retreat from the political' (Green, 2005: 104) partially disguised under 'humanist platitudes' (2005: 95).[1] As Rebein later observed (Rebein, 2007: 209), for Green, Franzen's argumentation in that article evinced 'a deeply traditional notion of literature as quasi-religious solace' (2005: 96). It was Rebein, nevertheless, who specifically discerned a narrative in the way Franzen presented its literary evolution from postmodernism to realism. In the same way, it was also Rebein who perceptively drew the parallelism

---

[1]Franzen included an edited version of this essay, retitled 'Why Bother', in his 2002 compilation *How to Be Alone*. For practical reasons, in my discussion of the essay I provide reference to the latter.

between Franzen's move and a religious conversion. Rebein examined the already well-known *Harper's* essay, and also a 2002 piece published in *New Yorker* under the title of 'Mr. Difficult', where Franzen set out to criticize what he saw as 'needless difficulty' in much postmodernist fiction. As in the *Harper's* essay, in 'Mr. Difficult' Franzen predicated the existence of a community of solitary readers paradoxically united in their shared vital concerns and in their expectation to find these preoccupations reflected in literature. The satisfaction of these readers, Franzen argued, should be the novelist's aim, rather than a sterile pursuit of phony literary recognition by means of contrived obscurity. In his essay, Franzen proposed a twofold division of novelists: there were those who abided by a 'Contract' model, in which the writer is compelled by a sort of compact to provide a pleasurable experience to her readers; and there were 'Status' novelists who selfishly aspired to membership of an isolated literary elite in abstraction of – or even against – their potential readers. There is clearly an ethics as well as an aesthetics implied here. In 'Mr. Difficult', Franzen chose his declared former idol, the archetypal postmodernist writer William Gaddis, as the paramount example of self-sufficient, arrogant and ultimately vacuous Status novelist. As Rebein sharply recognized, Franzen was advocating a vision of literature as a cult in which he arrogated to himself the role of a reformer:

> It goes without saying that this, too, is a religion of sorts, that Franzen has cast himself not in the role of a faith-denier like Nietzsche, but rather in that of a faith-reformer, like Martin Luther. ... The dark, corrupt 'Catholicism' of postmodernism (the formulation is Franzen's, not mine) has given way to a lighter, more honest and forgiving 'Protestant'-style realism. It is a faith that will allow Franzen to pursue without guilt his interest in locale and character – to concentrate wholly, in his own words, on the business of 'peopling and arranging' his 'own little alternate world', trusting all along that 'the bigger social picture' he used to worry so much about will take care of itself. (Rebein, 2007: 212)

In any case, what both Green and Rebein stop short of realizing (they lacked the further evidence later offered by *Freedom*) is the fact that the narrative of self-justification that Franzen offers in his essays is also inscribed and replicated in his novels by means of a series of salvational narratives which indirectly support and legitimize Franzen's formal and political evolution. Indeed, from *Strong Motion* through *Freedom*, Franzen's protagonists go through vicissitudes that in some way or other mirror Franzen's own *Künstlerroman* or *artist narrative* in invariably legitimizing ways. In the *Harper's* essay and 'Mr. Difficult', Franzen presents his case as that of a young aspiring novelist who, partly out of admiration for a respected group of novelists, namely the classic American postmodernists, and partly out of a misguided notion of literary value, cultivates a kind of fiction completely alien to his literary self. In the end, the strain of writing against himself leads him to clinical depression, despair of the novel in contemporary culture and, in short, sheer inability to continue writing. As Franzen recounts in the *Harper's* essay, eventually he undergoes a sort of epiphany with the providential mediation of the linguistic anthropologist Shirley Brice Heath, a researcher of contemporary reading habits. Heath discloses her findings to Franzen: for readers, the point of reading is the sense of 'having company in this great human enterprise' (HA 83). With her help, Franzen discovers his real vocation for addressing and serving an extant *community of readers* of which he is himself a part. In that essay, he also brings to bear a reassuring letter from his admired Don DeLillo in which the older writer expresses his confidence in the persistence of the novel as a relevant cultural form in the future. Franzen recalls having written to DeLillo 'in distress', to be thus reassured by the latter in his response: 'Writing is a form of personal freedom. It frees us from the mass identity we see in the making all around us. In the end, writers will write not to be outlaw heroes of some underculture but mainly *to save themselves, to survive as individuals*' (HA 96, my italics).

From a narratological point of view, it is not difficult to notice that Heath and DeLillo perform an essential role in Franzen's own salvational metanarrative: they become *helpers*, to use the term coined by the semiologist A. J. Greimas (1966). Through their mediation, Franzen regains his faith in the novel and starts writing fiction that emanates from his *true self*, achieving therefore literary and personal salvation. From an external point of view, the less becoming aspect of this transformation is that it implies getting rid of previously avowed literary and ideological professions. This renunciation could be very generally synthesized as a dismissal of literary and ideological radicalism and the forsaking of a public sphere perceived as beyond repair. And though prior persuasions are duly denigrated and publicly abjured in the *Harper's* essay and 'Mr. Difficult', these moves seem not to be enough for Franzen, possibly because of his awareness of deeply entrenched cultural prejudice against this sort of disavowals. As a result, these salvational narratives, whose power Franzen had discovered at the end of *Strong Motion*, gain prominence in his subsequent novels. Franzen's protagonists are debased by different types of selfishness, dishonesty or self-delusion until an epiphany-like moment in which they humbly come to terms with themselves. It is therefore an epiphany related to self-recognition. Franzen's heroes are redeemed by rejection of their previous pretension as well as by ethical commitment to the closest community of family or lovers. This is a fairly obvious pattern in *Strong Motion*, *The Corrections* and *Freedom*, though not in *Purity* (2015), Franzen's latest novel. Regardless of this pattern, however, *Purity* shares with the other three its orientation towards romance, a *pre-realist* narrative genre characterized, according to Fredric Jameson, by the presence of a 'salvational or redemptive perspective of some secure future' (Jameson, 2002: 90).

Franzen's latest novel notwithstanding, his narratives of salvation are so similar from a structural point of view that they lend themselves easily to classic formalist and structuralist analysis. The fundamental biographical events that articulate the plots in Franzen's novels (degeneration, humiliation, self-improvement, reconciliation, social integration) appear as clearly drawn in their structural role as the narrative *functions* described by Vladimir Propp in his time-honoured study of the morphology of the Russian folk tale.[2] Indeed, the recurrent presence of fixed plot elements might allow us to talk, as Tzvetan Todorov did in his structuralist examination of Bocaccio's *Decameron* (Todorov 1969a), of a kind of narrative *grammar* in Franzen's fiction. In this sense, it is conspicuous that, at a certain level of abstraction, the main narrative patterns that Todorov discerns in the *Decameron* are remarkably close to those we identify in Franzen's novels, which suggests that the novelist is drawing on an ancient and probably universal repository of narrative resources. The critic argues that all stories in Boccacio's compilation are informed by the same broad schema: 'two moments of equilibrium, similar and different, are separated by a period of imbalance, which is composed by a process of degeneration and a process of improvement' (Todorov, 1969b: 75). But for Todorov it is possible to make a distinction between two kinds of stories in the *Decameron*: what he labels narratives of 'avoided punishment'; and those of 'conversion', which are essentially descriptions of an improvement process through which a character gets rid of a certain flaw (1969b: 75). Readers of Franzen's novels will surely recognize that his protagonists (Louis Holland, Chip Lambert, Walter, Patty and Joey Berglund) are invariably beset by a moral blemish, be it selfishness, hypocrisy, self-delusion or a daimonic determination (such as, for instance, Walter's environmental engagement) which is obviously perceived as misguided. All of them get close to receiving irreversible punishment in the form of any of the following: utter dejection and loneliness, clinical depression, definitive estrangement from the loved ones, or even material poverty. And all of them achieve redemption through humiliation, enhanced sympathy and ethical and amorous commitment. They are in this way freed from their flaws or at least – in typically novelistic fashion, as we will see – they learn to live with them.

Crucially, these structural models can also be applied to the narrative through which Franzen presents his literary career in the *Harper's* essay. For example, the times of dejection suffered by Franzen in the early nineties would correspond to Propp's twelfth function, or *first function of the donor*, whereby the hero is tested, preparing the ground for his receiving a magical agent or helper – the *donor*, a role which would in this case be

---

[2] As is known, in his study originally published in Russian in 1928, Propp managed to reduce the variety of plots that can be found in Russian folk narrative to a total number of just thirty-one structural elements involving a change of state (all of them appearing in the same sequence), which he called *functions* (Propp 1968).

performed by the encouragement received from Heath and DeLillo. If we choose to apply the less empirical and more synthetic *actantial* model of narrative devised by Greimas, we see that the basic scheme also holds. In his *Sémantique Structurale*, Greimas is able to further refine Propp's analysis of narrative structure by subsuming the Russian critic's thirty-one functions into three pairs of more abstract dimensions of narrative or *actants*, a category which includes characters and situations. According to Greimas, these six actants are articulated along two axes: Sender-Subject-Receiver and Helper-Object-Opponent. For Greimas, one actant can be realized by one or more agents and vice versa. In this model Franzen is obviously the *subject*. The role of the *object* is split between Franzen's personal happiness and a valid form of the novel that is suited to our times. The *sender* that sets the narrative in motion is embodied by contemporary cultural decay, admittedly the cause of Franzen's depression. The *receiver* is formed by the members of the community of readers, whose supply of spiritual nourishment is further secured thanks to Franzen. But the novelist himself can be also seen as a *receiver*, inasmuch as he is the first beneficiary of a newly acquired vision which gets him out of his despondency. The *helper* is represented, as we have seen, by Heath and DeLillo. Finally, the *opponent* is realized by the hegemonic techno-consumerism inimical to literature which Franzen deplores in his essays and novels. It may be added, in this sense, that in the subsequent instalment of this narrative constituted by 'Mr. Difficult', the role of the *opponent* is also performed by postmodernist experimental fiction and specifically, as we know, by Gaddis, who becomes a veritable *villain* in this story.

But it is not my intention to conduct a formalist or structuralist narratological study of Franzen's fiction, even though advantage is taken of categories and insight from such disciplines. To be sure, narratology has traditionally been more oriented towards the logic of formal structure than to the actual content of stories. Obviously, the objective of this book is different. My aim is to transcend the study of form to grasp its *content*: its social, historical, ideological and even psychological import, always bearing in mind that there is not a clear separation between form and content, as the former is always meaningful, historical and ideologically charged. This will require a constant awareness of the diachronic aspects of the novelistic form throughout this book. From this critical perspective, I shall look into the political implication of Franzen's narratives of self-amelioration, which quite obviously boils down to the belief that salvation can only be individual. Similarly, we will observe that these narratives consistently end with acts of reconciliation which in the light of the theories of Fredric Jameson and Franco Moretti I will interpret as symbolic resolutions of social and individual contradictions.

It should be clear that this arrangement of the narrative materials in Franzen's fiction does not reveal a kind of master plan, but rather constitutes a piecemeal series of legitimizing responses to literary and ideological moves. Certainly, the novelist did not have in mind the closing of *Freedom* while he was at work with The *Twenty-Seventh City* or *Strong Motion*. It is far from my intention to forge any type of organic reading of Franzen's fiction. I am not proposing the array of salvational narratives as a *meaning* of Franzen's work which I have arrived at through some hermeneutic process. Instead, these narratives are analysed as recurrent rhetorical instruments of persuasion and ideological and political self-legitimation which are informed by a pattern that gets ever clearer after each novel. This caveat will not prevent us from noticing an obvious evolution in the way these narratives of salvation are presented, especially as regards the increasing assertiveness of their closings. This suggests that each one of Franzen's novels includes an implicit evaluation of the previous one, a circumstance which by means of accretion rather than planning gives substance to a metanarrative. The fact that *Purity* (even though sharing the same ideological stand as Franzen's previous novels) does not conform to this metanarrative corroborates that the latter achieves its closure with *Freedom*. The chronology of the deployment of these salvational narratives could be roughly drawn as follows: the first one appears at the end of *Strong Motion* (1992) as an escape from the dismal perspectives that characterize the ending of The *Twenty-Seventh City* (1988). Personal salvations, ethical commitment, melodramatic elements, reconciliations and neat dramatic closure surface in the last chapters of *Strong Motion* to rescue Franzen's second novel from ending with the same disheartening literary, social and political grimness of the first one. And just as there is no master plan, there is no manifesto either: four years after the release of *Strong Motion*, the *Harper's* essay does not document a novelist that has resolved his stylistic and ideological contradictions, but rather one that is still wrestling with them, as Stephen J. Burn rightly claims. Burn has argued that the *Harper's* essay does not represent a successful resolution of the creative problems that plagued Franzen after the release of his second novel. He has even characterized its conclusion as a 'simulated epiphany'. In his words, 'Perchance to Dream' 'charts the resolution of an aesthetic problem that Franzen had not really resolved and did not resolve for several more years' (Burn, 2008: 50). Burn is quite right here. My disagreement with him lies in his resistance to considering the ideological dimension of Franzen's 'aesthetic problem'. At any rate, the hybrid and contradictory quality of *The Corrections*, released in 2001, would be proof enough of these uncertainties. But in that novel the shift of focus with respect to the previous ones is so pronounced that, as a result, the salvational and reconciliatory elements must acquire centrality and the legitimating effect over Franzen's move must be more intense, as the biographical narrative of Chip Lambert sharply illustrates. The success of *The Corrections* prompts critics to turn their attention to the *Harper's* essay and to interpret it as a literary declaration of principles which came to be realized with Franzen's third novel. However, it is actually with the publication of 'Mr. Difficult' in 2002 that Franzen's strategy of legitimation becomes clear, in an essay which even includes an explicit justification of narrative choices. Finally, again after nearly a decade, Franzen's metanarrative reaches its culmination with *Freedom*. As we shall see, this novel, which at times reads as a vehement apology of liberalism, constitutes Franzen's ultimate element of legitimation of his abandonment of radicalism and of his relinquishment of initiatives aimed towards social transformation. Fittingly enough, the rotund, melodramatic way in which the novel's characters finally attain salvation through reconciliation represents the real closure of Franzen's (meta)narrative of conversion.

In this introduction to Franzen's rhetorical devices of self-justification, I cannot leave unmentioned another, secondary but conspicuous, self-legitimating strategy that recurs in his non-fiction essays and even in his novels since *The Corrections*, namely a strikingly aggressive denigration of critical and literary theory. The rejection of a critical theory seen as essentially phony in favour of the ethical commitment to the close, substantial community of the family is of course enacted by Chip Lambert, a disgraced ex-professor of Cultural Studies, in *The Corrections*. In a more subtle way, it can also be perceived in the failure of Walter Berglund's radical and theory-driven environmentalist views in *Freedom*. More recently, Franzen has dwelt on the subject in different essays. For example, in his 2011 address at Kenyon College entitled 'Pain Won't Kill You':

> The first thing we jettisoned was theory. As my soon-to-be wife once memorably remarked, after an unhappy scene in bed, 'You can't deconstruct and undress at the same time.' ... But what really killed theory for me – and began to cure me, more generally, of my obsession with how I appeared to other people – was my love of fiction. ... If you really love fiction, you'll find that the only pages worth keeping are the ones that reflect you *as you really are*. (FA 10, my emphasis)

Similarly, in his essay 'On Autobiographical Fiction', compiled in the same volume, Franzen directs mordant remarks to Harold Bloom and his theory of poetic influence (FA 121). In fact, the execration of theory has come to be so frequent in Franzen's work that its motives seem to go beyond the obvious wariness of criticism on the part of a novelist who invariably seeks to be interpreted in his own terms.[3] Several reasons of consequence may be

---

[3]We may remember, as an instance of Franzen's attempts to shape the public image of his work, that in the *Harper's* essay he proposes his own critical term to define it: *tragic realism* (HA 91). More recently, in *The Kraus Project*, the novelist has referred to 'the "disease" of French theory that became epidemic in American English departments after 1980 and engendered several decades of jargon-choked American criticism' (KP 21). In the same work, the novelist acknowledges his interest in critical theory during his formative years. Bloom was especially influential in Franzen's understanding of his relation to Pynchon (KP 173).

discerned behind this animosity. The most evident one is that postmodernist fiction, especially at its most experimental, seems indissolubly linked to theory: it is usually written by novelists of remarkable theoretical awareness and tends to be the object of study of academic critics who apply to it their abstruse theoretical apparatuses. More often than not, experimental postmodernist novels are difficult readings that are highly regarded at elitist academic circles. They constitute then the embodiment of the 'Status' type of fiction which Franzen fiercely attacks in 'Mr. Difficult'. We should remember that Franzen is also a novelist with a high degree of theoretical training and that this fact was very evident in his first two novels. Critical theory is therefore part of the object of Franzen's disavowal. In his religious analogy, Rebein likens Franzen to a reformer, but he could just as well have chosen the figure of the convert, usually characterized by heightened hostility towards the old faith. But there are other, perhaps subtler, motivations for his open rejection of theory. For one, critical theory stands for radicalness. To be sure, much critical theory, especially the different kinds of negative criticism developed in the wake of post-structuralist thought, is characterized by a kind of abstract rigour and a relentless quality that, as Franzen no doubt suspects, cannot but pose a threat for the political liberalism he has embraced and its traditional tendency towards compromise. Franzen's antipathy towards theory then would amount to a sort of pre-emptive strike. However, Franzen's proposed substitute for out-and-out theory, a sort of common-sense, natural, or, to use his own term, 'Contract' approach to literature, clearly amounts to just another kind of theory – an implicit theory which, like hegemonic ideologies, seeks to come through as the natural, non-ideological way to see things. In this, Franzen's attitude recalls that of those literary critics who present their work as non-ideological. As Terry Eagleton puts it, 'The power of ideology over them is nowhere more marked than in their honest belief that their readings are "innocent"' (Eagleton, 1996: 173). There is no literary theory that is not ideological or political, as all of them involve a series of explicit and implicit assumptions about what is meaningful or valuable or desirable in the real world. And so is the case with Franzen's tacit one. Indeed, Franzen's *theory* is inseparable from his own narrative of conversion and the salvational narratives of his novels. It can be then viewed as one more instrument of self-legitimation.

3 Theoretical coordinates: Socially symbolic narratives

For this study, of course, theory has a very different meaning. If Franzen is adept at presenting theory as ineffective speculation that gets in the way between the subject and the world, in this book theory is seen as precisely the instrument that allows us to trace the complex relationships between the literary work and the world of which it forms part. Jonathan Franzen is avowedly a writer of social concerns who conceives of the novel as having a performative power worthy of what used to be known as social engagement. Indeed, much of the discussion of Franzen's work – including his own contribution to it in his essays – turns around the old concept of the social novel: the degree to which Franzen's production corresponds to that concept, the viability of a socially engaged novel in our time, or the (de) merits of this type of fiction as opposed to other genres of supposedly more private preoccupations (see for example Wood 2001a). This means that I will be concerned, to put it very briefly, with issues regarding the way in which novels reflect society and the way in which society receives novels. In this approach to Franzen's work, the Marxist critical tradition has proved to be the best equipped to highlight the social and political dimensions of the novelistic genre. As Jameson has put it, 'there is nothing that is not social and historical ... everything is, "in the last analysis" political' (Jameson, 2002: 5). Certainly, not all the authors on whose theoretical work I have relied can be inscribed in that tradition, but the awareness of the social character of literature is common to all of them. As will be evident, in this study the work of Fredric Jameson has been central in its three most significant aspects: I have been inspired by Jameson as the leading analyst of the reflection of our mode of production in contemporary culture, as an investigator of realism, and as a fundamental theorist of narrative.

Jameson (in 2009: 44 and 2002: 60–1) has proposed a model of critical interpretation conducted within three concentric frameworks of analysis which are intended to restore the full historical and political significance of a literary work. The objective is to produce a semantic enrichment and enlargement of the apparently inert givens and materials that form the social and historical ground of a particular text. These three levels of analysis can be briefly described as follows:

1 The examination of punctual historical events belonging to the realm of political history.
2 The evocation of larger class and ideological conflicts and traditions.
3 Finally, our attention should be directed to impersonal socio-economic patterning systems brought about by the evolution of the mode of production (e.g. reification and commodification) as they are reflected in the text.

Additionally, for Jameson the treatment of agency in the literary work should be mapped across these three levels. In many respects, my reading of Franzen's novels abides by these principles:

1 Regarding the first level of Jameson's approach, this study traces in the novels world-historical episodes such as the decay of American

cities, the Cold War, the fall of the socialist bloc, the Iraq War, the latest financial crisis, the advance of globalization, and other which together constitute the immediate external historical context of the novels and as such contribute to their meaning in an important way.

2 With respect of Jameson's second level, different aspects of Franzen's social perspective are examined, such as his vindication of (his particular vision of) the middle class; his views on gentrification; his use of distinction as a social marker; the class antagonism behind his support of environmentalism, which is also perceptible in his take on the so-called culture wars; or his yearning for class reconciliation in his own terms.

3 As for larger issues related to the mode of production, for example, an account is provided for Franzen's views on the decline of communities and the advance of individualism and social fragmentation; the contemporary weakening of historical thought is addressed; the component of Utopian thought perceivable in Franzen's work is analysed, including Utopian aspects of his environmentalism; Franzen's tackle of globalization (which entails a new awareness of the mode of production that can be observed in *The Corrections*) is also examined.

As far as agency is concerned, I look into Franzen's vision of an apathetic society in his first and second novels; I probe his pessimistic vision of activism in *Strong Motion* and *Freedom* – a gloom that is somewhat relativized in *Purity*. Finally, I consider his general tendency towards ideological conformism.

Arguably no other contemporary critic has been more penetrating than Jameson in tracing the relation between form and ideology, as well as that between the latter and the mode of production. One perceptible consequence of his influence on my approach to Franzen's work is the attention paid to the way in which the mode of production manifests itself in it. The following will illustrate my procedure. The current stage of capitalism corresponds to its purest and most homogeneous expression to date, as previously extant 'enclaves of socio-economic difference' (Jameson, 2009: 43) have been already colonized or commodified. One consequence of this is the universalization of what the critic has famously called the cultural logic of late capitalism. For Jameson, this situation has entailed an enfeebled sense of history and a resistance to totalizing thought. This circumstance has a crucial importance in my assessment of Franzen's use of realism, which is of course a central issue in this study. As Erich Auerbach (2003) and Mikhail Bakhtin (1981) realized, realism is a trans-historical category with historical materializations to be studied in social and ideological, rather than merely stylistic terms. In Ian Duncan's words, 'realism is not a revelation of nature but a rhetoric and an ideology' (Duncan, 1992: 6). To Auerbach and György

Lukács, I owe the notion that no true realism is possible without a sense of history and a dynamic vision of society as formed by different groups with transformative potential. This conception has crucial implications when we bring it to the analysis of much contemporary fiction, including Franzen's, which is implicitly informed by typically contemporary ideas about the end of history. For Auerbach, as for Lukács, the ability to think the present in historical terms, that is, as the product of past history and the ground for future historical development, is a precondition of the realist novel. However, Jameson has identified the decline of historical thought as one of the traits of the culture of late capitalism (Jameson, 1991: ix). This entails a painful situation for novelists of a progressive persuasion such as Franzen: a closed horizon of events that precludes the possibility of imagining a different future for society; a total immersion in the ideology of late capitalism which, as all dominant ideologies do, presents what is the product of historical contingency as the natural state of affairs for good. Indeed, Jameson has often pointed out, it has become far easier to imagine the end of the world than the end of capitalism or bourgeois society, as innumerable products of contemporary mass culture prove.

With this we have come to a central point in my analysis of Franzen's fiction, which is the examination of its Utopian content. I believe, with Ernst Bloch and Fredric Jameson, that even in the cultural artefacts more rigidly constrained by dominant ideology there can be found Utopian content which is the expression of latent emancipatory impulses. This is perceptible in Franzen's novels, especially in his first two: *The Twenty-Seventh City* and *Strong Motion*. Franzen's first and second novels are dominated by the weight of a blocked future that shows in their collapsing endings. In both novels, the conclusion seems to disavow perspectives of social and political hope previously opened by their plotlines. In them we can find two evoked possibilities of political rupture, two potential Events, in the sense given to the term by Alain Badiou: in the first one, a conspiracy of Indian origin seems to be intent in taking over a hopelessly decaying St Louis for the benefit of the common good. In the second, a small group of young activists reveals that the malfeasance of a chemical giant has caused a series of destructive earthquakes in Boston, opening thus the eyes of its citizens to the reality of corporate greed. Eventually, these potentialities turn out to be pseudo-events that do not change the basic status quo. But independently of their actual outcome, their simple presence in the novels is a symptom of what Jameson has called a 'hunger for the sheer event' (Jameson, 1991: 309), a disposition which undoubtedly has a strong Utopian charge.

Although ongoing political issues (e.g. globalization, neocon hegemony, the Iraq War) also occupy an important place in Franzen's subsequent novels, in them the novelist refrains from evoking acts of systemic rupture and concentrates instead on narratives of personal salvation within the realm of the family. This kind of substitution of private for public salvation, a pattern which starts at the end of *Strong Motion*, can be interpreted as a consequence of the frustration of the implied political potentialities of the first and second novels – a frustration which the hegemonic ideology of late capitalism compels to appear as well-nigh obligatory. This is, however, a dissatisfaction also invested with Utopian significance and, following the conceptualization by Bloch and Jameson of the ideological and the Utopian as dialectically related, we can identify a sublimated Utopian drive in Franzen's advocated retreat to the small communities of family and lovers. Similarly, we can also trace Utopian implications in Franzen's treatment of nature in his early novels: his fondness for the drawing of deserted natural spaces reflects the yearning for an outside to the all-encompassing system of late capitalism.

At this point, it seems fitting that a theoretical tenet that has been crucial in my approach to Franzen's fiction is specified, namely Jameson's notion of a political unconscious of literature. In his seminal *The Political Unconscious* (1981), the American theorist argues that 'all literature, no matter how weakly, must be informed by what we have called a political unconscious, that all literature must be read as a symbolic meditation on the destiny of community' (Jameson, 2002: 56). Jameson proceeds to apply his argument to the study of narrative and predicates of the latter the character of a symbolic act aimed at the resolution of unsolvable social – or ideological, we may add – contradictions. The idea brings its own hermeneutics with it. In the critic's own words, 'the will to read literary or cultural acts as symbolic acts must necessarily grasp them as resolutions of determinate contradictions' (2002: 66). This kind of criticism is necessarily ideological, as it concentrates on the ideological dimension of artistic production: 'ideology is not something which informs or invests symbolic production; rather the aesthetic act is itself ideological, and the production of aesthetic narrative form is to be seen as an ideological act in its own right, with the function of inventing imaginary or formal "solutions" to unresolvable social contradictions' (Jameson, 2002: 64).

Following this principle, we will observe that Franzen's novels stage a retreat from a public sphere perceived as intractable into the small community of the family. The latter is to be sure a realm turbulent enough but, as his novels reflect, in contrast with what seems to be the norm in the public sphere, reconciliation and peace can be finally attained within the family. With this move, Franzen opens a symbolic space in which deplored historical facts are not quite irreparable or definitive and ideological contradictions not so unsurmountable. Of course, this symbolic strategy is an ideological act that implies that there is no room for collective emancipation and then salvation can only be individual. This is the path signalled by the reconciliatory ending of *Strong Motion* and is then unfalteringly followed and developed in Franzen's subsequent novels.

Given that ideology is a central concern of this study, it is probably necessary to stop to specify here that my conception of it derives mainly from the work of Louis Althusser, the thinker who in the 1960s brought to Marxism the new views and procedures of French post-structuralist thought. Althusser incorporated a new dimension taken mostly from Jacques Lacan's psychoanalytical theory to the classic Marxist concept of ideology as 'false consciousness', or the misrepresentation of the real workings of the capitalist system. The particularities of Althusser's notion of ideology may be succinctly illustrated by his famous (re)definition of it as 'the imaginary relationship of individuals to their real conditions of existence' (Althusser, 2008: 36). In contrast with previous accounts of ideology, Althusser places a double remove between the subject and the *real* conditions of existence, which are not only imagined but, following Lacan, can never be really grasped since our access to them is mediated by language and the *symbolic order* we inhabit. This notion of ideology can also be traced, with logical individual differences, in the work of some of the theorists who have influenced this study, such as Jameson, Eagleton, Žižek or Laclau and Mouffe.

The other theoretical source of my conception of the novel as a symbolic form can be found in *The Way of the World* (1987), Franco Moretti's essential study of the classical *Bildungsroman* or novel of formation, where its author proposes a view of the novel as a symbolic device comparable to Jameson's. For Moretti, the novel is also a symbolic artefact which tends to the assuagement of social and psychological conflicts, particularly those arising from the individual's need for self-determination and the commanding demands of socialization. But if for Jameson the novel enacts symbolic resolutions of social contradictions, for Moretti it rather teaches us how to live with them, and holds social reconciliation and the protection of the Ego as ultimate ends. For Moretti, the history of the *Bildungsroman* constitutes:

> a constant elusion of historical turning points and breaks: an elusion of tragedy and hence, as Lukács wrote in *Soul and Forms*, of the very idea that societies and individuals acquire their full meaning in 'a moment of truth'.
>
> An elusion, we may conclude, of whatever may endanger the Ego's equilibrium, making its compromises impossible – and a gravitation, in contrast, to those modes of existence that allow the Ego to manifest itself fully. (Moretti, 2000: 12)

As in liberal politics, mitigation, rather than radical or transforming measures, is the key for the novel's symbolic function – and accordingly compromise is its recurring theme. Moretti's theory will then help us understand Franzen's incorporation of elements from the *Bildungsroman* in his novels, his penchant for acts of reconciliation and, especially in *Freedom*, his clear rejection of radicalism, his praise of liberalism and his general embrace of compromise. This is the sense, for example, of Walter Berglund's abandonment of his most radical environmentalist views regarding population control and his final acceptance of the conflicts of his family life.

The problem with this kind of rhetorical or thematic operations conducive to the defusing of conflicts is that they tend to go accompanied by ideological implications that will not be acknowledged by the novelist or, to be more precise, by the novel itself. This fact was analysed by the French critic Pierre Macherey. Even if his work is not as openly present in this book as that of Jameson, his pioneering *Pour une théorie de la production littéraire* (1966) has provided it with a distinctive perspective into Franzen's fiction which has also proved crucial. In fact, the critical approaches of both Macherey and Jameson are easily complementary. In some respects, certain insights of the former look like a precedent of key issues later expanded by the latter. This is the case of their views on the ideological value of inherited forms, discussed below, or their notion of an 'unconscious of the work' (Macherey, 1989: 92). I have tried to follow the French critic's injunction to tackle and bring to light that which the work cannot say because it would threaten the ideological tenets that brought it into existence in the first place, but which is nevertheless inevitably implied by it. Macherey clarifies that this analysis should not be equated to a deconstruction or demystification of the work, but to 'the production of a new knowledge; the enunciation of its silent significance' (1989: 150).

As we shall see, a great part of the silences and denials in Franzen's work are related to class issues. Some examples of what Franzen's novels resist recognizing or showing are the following: the persistence of class struggle and the novelist's own partaking in it; the reality of class domination that underlies his liberal stance; the failure of the latter to cope with pressing social contradictions, the obviously class-ridden character of his environmentalism; the inherent contradiction between his scientism and his Utopian visions of nature; the limits of sympathy and reconciliation, whose healing properties, both in the individual and social domains, are vested with rather unrealistic powers in Franzen's novels. These ideological contradictions coexist more or less easily in Franzen's first novel, unabashedly radical and open-ended. But they become more acute, and paradoxically more readily perceptible within this critical approach, as he tries ever more forcibly to conceal them by means of the closing powers of narrative and the soothing elements brought from *Bildungsroman*, romance and melodrama. We could say that in *Freedom* they finally become glaring, they just will not let themselves be smoothed out. Therefore, my critical task has not been to gloss any kind of unity or organic quality in Franzen's work, but rather to recognize its transformations and contradictions. As Roland Barthes argues in *S/Z*, we should assume 'the multivalence of the text, its partial reversibility' (Barthes, 1974: 20).[4] Therefore my discovery of a linear rhetorical strategy of legitimation across Franzen's novels should not be taken as a sort of unitary reading which reconciles contradictions. Instead, what I have called the narrative of conversion actually amounts to Franzen's attempt to hold together his multifarious and contradictory formal and ideological materials by virtue of the meaning-conferring powers of narrative.

4 Questions of mode: The end of postmodernism?

So far it will be clear that a key aspect of the critical discussion of Franzen's work is concerned with the contrast between postmodernist and realist narrative. There is a general consensus on his transition from a typically postmodernist fiction, heavily influenced by writers such as Thomas Pynchon or Don DeLillo, to what is commonly regarded as a distinctively realist narrative. Critics such as James Wood (2001b) or Michiko Kakutani (2001) have specifically pointed to classic nineteenth and early-twentieth-century realist novels as Franzen's new reference in this evolution, a process which is seen as beginning in *The Corrections* and achieving completion in *Freedom*.[5] Rebein, on his part, has argued that Franzen was always been a realist at heart, whose natural inclinations, traceable in his early novels, had been suffocated by his commitment to postmodernist ways: 'And yet even in this early work [*The Twenty-Seventh City*] Franzen was already showing a sign of the realist writer hidden beneath all the Po-Mo machinery. ... *Strong motion* continues this drift toward realism, particularly in the second half, where Franzen's more rounded characters seem poised to escape the squirrel cage of his plot' (Rebein, 2008: 204).

Discussion of Franzen's work as illustrating a general exhaustion or phasing-out of postmodernism is also a critical commonplace. It is noticeable in Rebein's essay, included in a volume significantly entitled *The Mourning After: Attending the Wake of Postmodernism,* or in the no less explicit Burn's monograph *Jonathan Franzen at the End of Postmodernism.* Such analyses usually suggest a slow but widespread comeback of realism over the last decades, as in Rebein: 'Literary postmodernism has been losing

---

[4]As the French critic argues, 'if the text is subject to some form, this form is not unitary, architectonic, finite: it is the fragment, the shards, the broken or obliterated network – all the movements and inflections of a vast 'dissolve', which permits both overlapping and loss of messages' (Barthes, 1974: 20).

[5]See, for example, Kakutani 2001, where *The Corrections* is compared to Thomas Mann's *Buddenbrooks,* or James Wood 2001b, a review of *The Corrections* under the significant title 'What the Dickens'.

ground to a revitalized realism since at least 1980, if not before' (2008: 220); or at least propose new hybrid modes where realism has become a major component again, as in the *post-postmodernism* proposed among other by Christophe Ribbat (2002) and Burn (2008). Ribbat (2002), one of the very earliest academic critics to devote a paper to Franzen's work, observes that the novelist tries to unite the textual games of the postmodern, 'Pynchonesque' novel and the 'direct simplicity of neorealism'. Ribbat comments on the somewhat artificial distinction between realism and postmodernism, categories which should be referred to as 'coexisting strategies of representation', rather than styles or period labels, since the differences between them are gradual (Ribbat, 2002: 560). He sees one reason for Franzen's commercial and critical success in the fact that 'his fiction finds an especially comfortable middle position between these two camps' (2002: 561).

Ribbat quotes an interview with Sven Birkerts in *Esquire* where Franzen mentions the emotional content of his novels as setting them apart from the work of writers such as DeLillo or Gaddis – 'For better or worse, I'm … an emotions guy' (Ribbat, 2002: 562) – to support his claim that Franzen's straightforward treatment of emotions (as opposed, in his view, to the elusive, paradoxical, and problematized way in which they are typically handled by postmodernist writers) might be a sign of a turn toward 'post-postmodernism' (2002: 562). For the critic, such emotional import is also present in the work of generational peers such as David Foster Wallace and Jeffrey Eugenides. Although it is not discussed in his essay, the new focus on the emotional charge of literature postulated by Ribbat cannot but bring to mind the plausibility of a way out of the 'waning of affect' which Jameson theorized as characteristic of postmodernism (Jameson, 1991: 10).

Ribbat was not the only one to relate Franzen to a new 'post-postmodernist' current. For Robert McLaughlin (2004), a reaction against the perceived dead end reached by postmodernism has been crystallizing since the late 1980s; a reaction caused by 'postmodernism's detachment from the social world and immersion in a world of non-referential language' (McLaughlin, 2004: 55). McLaughlin, one of the critics who analyse the *Harper's* essay as Franzen's programmatic manifesto, identifies an 'aesthetic sea change' motivated by 'a desire to reconnect language to the social sphere or, to put it another way, to reenergize literature's social mission, its ability to intervene in the social world' (2004: 55). For the critic, this post-postmodernist backlash is led by two novelists: Jonathan Franzen and (especially) David Foster Wallace, accompanied by other young writers such as Rick Moody, Lydia Davies, Bradford Morrow, Richard Powers or Cris Mazza. McLaughlin turns to Franzen and Wallace because they have been 'the most articulate in expressing the post-postmodern discontent and in speculating on directions for the future of fiction' (2004: 59). McLaughlin even posits as 'the agenda of post-postmodernism' the production of a socially engaged fiction that is theoretically aware enough to lay bare the language-based nature of many oppressive constructions, thus opening our eyes to the fact that other realities are possible. It could be argued, however, that the problem with this post-postmodernist agenda is that it would make a rather unreliable criterion to tell a post-postmodernist novel apart from many classic postmodernist texts.

Susanne Rohr (2004) is one of the critics who have discussed more perceptibly the modal and stylistic complexity of Franzen's narrative. She sees *The Corrections* as a hybrid novel, sharing in both modernist and postmodernist features, and yet making use of narrative realism: 'This novel neither gives primacy to wild modernist aesthetic experiment nor does it delight in anarchic post-modernist playfulness. ... Yet although the novel is moved by epistemological concerns related to those of modernism and post-modernism, it chooses a different narrative strategy for staging them. It follows the conventions of literary realism' (Rohr, 2004: 98). The critic claims that the novel's realist construction is an example of a 'new conventionalism' that is making its way into contemporary fiction. For Rohr, this trend, which allows for extended study of character, manners and social relations, is easily understood as a reaction to 'decades of laborious efforts in both literature and literary criticism to undermine subjects and subject positions in every imaginable way' (2004: 102). Rohr also interprets the increasingly common withdrawal into the boundaries of family matters as a reaction to the threats of globalization, and proposes *The Corrections* as an example of 'a new form to the genre of the novel: the novel of globalization', a new kind of 'post-urban city novel', concerned with 'the undermining forces of insecurity, disintegration, and loss of familiar structures of experience – all of which are related to the threats of globalization' (2004: 103).

In 2008, Burn publishes what was the only monograph on Jonathan Franzen for several years and as such an unavoidable reference for scholars of Franzen's work. Burn studies Franzen as the most significant figure of a new mode in fiction, namely post-postmodernism, and discusses his work in relation to the other two most prominent representatives of the movement according to him: David Foster Wallace and Richard Powers. Burn traces the development of the current along the 1990s, pausing at landmarks such as Wallace's essay *E Unibus Pluram* (1997) or the fiction compilation *Avant Pop: Fiction for a Daydream Nation*, edited by Larry McCaffery in 1993. Burn then makes an attempt at defining the differentiating features of the movement as opposed to those commonly attributed to postmodernism, a rather tricky task if we bear in mind the enormous flexibility and inclusiveness of that concept. As the most important traits he identifies a greater importance given to plot as opposed to form in post-postmodern works; a less frequent use of metafictional techniques, usually employed to different ends; a deeper concern with character development; or the influence of neuroscientific research. Burn has a point in criticizing Rebein's (2007) account of Franzen's stylistic evolution as unsubtle: 'Rebein has attempted to glibly smooth the finer distinctions of Franzen's relationship with postmodernism with a reductive formula that asserts that Franzen said "no" to Po-Mo' (Burn, 2008: 130). However, the extent to which Burn's criteria suffice to differentiate post-postmodernism from different forms and nuances of what is usually called postmodernism is certainly debatable and has been refuted by Parrish (2010), who claims that Burn does not articulate a valid way to tell an alleged post-postmodernism apart from postmodernism. For Parrish, Burn's attempt 'only underscores the degree to which these writers remain postmodernist and arguably belated in relation to Gaddis, Pynchon and DeLillo' (2010: 652), since in his opinion 'nearly all of the qualities he identifies as post-postmodernist are exactly what Hutcheon and Jameson describe as postmodernist' (2010: 651). In any case, Burn is especially pertinent in drawing a clear distinction between Franzen's novels and his essays, which are usually taken by critics as the keys to his fiction. For Burn, 'In his essays, Franzen frequently expresses his divided feelings about a subject, or presents an opposition, but he nearly always reaches some kind of resolution by the end of the essay' (Burn, 2008: 48). However, as Burn rightly claims, in his fiction Franzen does not resolve these oppositions, but maintains a 'double vision', which creates 'an unsettling tension at the heart of his works that is absent from his essays' (2008: 48). This tension, for Burn, is a reflection of the unresolved opposition between postmodernism and more traditional modes of fiction to be found in Franzen's novels. If for many critics the *Harper's* essay expresses Franzen's resolution of an aesthetic problem, Burn shows persuasively that such a problem would remain unsolved for several years, as is proved by Franzen's own accounts of the process of writing *The Corrections*. Burn's conclusion that Franzen's comments on his own work are misleading is an important one, given the extent to which such comments have informed the critics' response.

Of course, attempts to escape the usual, neat binary opposition between realism and postmodernism are not exclusive of critics of Franzen and can be traced back in time. In her exploration of the concept of postmodernism, Paula Martín Salván (2006) refers to some of these theoretical efforts, such as Paul Maltby's distinction between 'introverted postmodernism' and 'dissident postmodernism'. Likewise, Salván studies Alan Wilde's proposal of the term 'midfictional' (Wilde 1987) to identify a kind of narrative which escapes the conventions of realism yet keeps the ability to refer to a reality outside itself. A similar position is defended by Amy J. Elias, who proposes the term 'postmodern Realism' to describe this kind of fictional 'middle ground' (Salván, 2006: 32). In any case, it would seem that, when discussing Franzen's relation with postmodernism, critics such as Green, Rebein, Burn or McLaughlin have tended to use rather restrictive notions of the concept. Indeed, by postmodernism they have mostly meant – possibly following Franzen's own account of it – the work of a small group of American writers such as William Gaddis, Thomas Pynchon, John Barth, Robert Coover or Don DeLillo. A similar assumption seems to underlie certain journalistic reviews of Franzen's novels. It is perceptible, for example, in Richard Lacayo (2001). For the reviewer, with *The Corrections* Franzen improved on its postmodernist predecessors: 'when you correct certain problems in the postmodern novel – its cartoonish characters, its repetitive paranoia and absorption in Big Patterns – you get a better book' (Lacayo, 2001: n.pg.). In his review of *Freedom*, on his part, Sam Tanenhaus reminds us that with *The Corrections*, 'Franzen cracked open the opaque shell of postmodernism, tweezed out its tangled circuitry and inserted in its place the warm, beating heart of an authentic humanism' (Tanenhaus, 2010: n.pg.). The most significant representative of this view of Franzen's stylistic evolution is surely Wood, who also posited Franzen's third novel as a sort of *correction* of typical postmodernist drawbacks. He compares *The Corrections* to DeLillo's *Underworld*, 'the most influential American novel of the last 15 years', and one that 'seeks to represent the interconnectedness of American Society by picturing it as a web threaded on strings of paranoia and power – a kind of *Bleak House* of the digital age' (Wood 2001b: n.pg.). For Wood, there is a problem with DeLillo's novel that Franzen sets out to correct, and we can notice that the quasi-religious notion of *fulfilment of a promise* is already present here:

> His novel was a Dickensian novel without any humans in it. ... There are no human beings in the novel, no one who really matters and whose consciousness matters to himself. ... Franzen realised something like this when he read *Underworld* and pledged to put the matter right by producing, in his novel *The Corrections*, a book of DeLillo-like breath and intellectual critique which was centred on human beings. He proposed, in effect, a softened DeLilloism. (Wood 2001b: n.pg.)

But if we go beyond these limited views of postmodernist fiction it is easy to realize that Franzen's postmodernist affiliation as shown in his early novels becomes problematic. It is out of my scope, certainly, to offer here a comprehensive account of the virtually unmanageable concept of postmodernism. Let us simply remind ourselves that in her influential treaty on postmodernism, Linda Hutcheon (1988) advanced the notion of *historiographic metafiction* as the quintessential form of postmodernist narrative. According to Hutcheon, this novelistic form is characterized among other traits by the way it foregrounds its own process of signifying, deliberately pointing towards the problems of reference and our knowledge of the world, inviting the reader, in short, to contemplate the work both from within and from the outside, both as a result and as a process. Some of these procedures can be identified in Franzen's first two novels, but a close examination of them also shows very different purposes and concerns, which reveals an ambivalent and limited commitment to postmodernist ways.

Similarly, it could be argued that Franzen's critics have taken for granted the not unproblematic distinction between being a postmodernist and a chronicler of postmodernity – or, to put it other way, can a novelist offer a picture of our times without being herself a postmodernist in some way or other? Salván summarizes the critical positions regarding this dichotomy as splitting into those who think, like Linda Hutcheon, that to bear witness to postmodernity 'implies being a postmodernist writer'; and those who, as Amy J. Elias does, differentiate between 'postmodernist experimentalism and the realistic representation of a postmodern world' (Salván, 2006: 31). Furthermore, critical accounts of Franzen's work have tended to obviate the historical dimension of postmodernism as a cultural dominant derived from our mode of production in the sense advanced by Jameson, that is, as 'the reflex and the concomitant of yet another systemic modification of capitalism itself' (Jameson, 1991: xii). Certainly, if we posit postmodernism as the cultural manifestation of late capitalism, the viability of post-postmodernism as a mode is rendered unlikely, unless as a mere nuance of the former. Even the more limited sense of artistic dominant mentioned by Brian McHale (1987) has usually been overlooked as well. This circumstance precludes the possibility, for example, of asking oneself about the likelihood of stepping out of postmodernism in a postmodern age. As an example of the complexity of this issue we may note that *Freedom,* apparently a straightforwardly realist novel, stages a symbolic discarding of radical and totalizing theory – embodied in Walter's abandonment of his large-scale environmental scheme in favour of limited local action – that could be taken as a sign of what Jean-François Lyotard (1979) saw as the distinctively postmodern abandonment of grand narratives or metanarratives. Likewise, the way Franzen freely uses the literary past as a repository of generic and narrative resources (be it romance, melodrama, *Bildungsroman* or the Gothic), which most of his public seems to accept as unproblematic, attests to his adaptation to a postmodern cultural context where the past has come to be ahistorically contemporary.

5 What we talk about when we talk of realism

Naturally enough, the issue of realism has also had a prominent place in the discussion of Franzen's fiction. Certainly, in this book the true extent of his commitment to either postmodernism or realism, the contour of Franzen's evolution towards realism or the political implications of each narrative mode are central concerns. However, as in the case of postmodernism, the concept of realism has generally been used in unsystematic and partial ways by media reviewers and even academics. For example, in their otherwise valuable contributions, influential critics such as James Wood (2001a) or Robert Rebein have identified realism solely with a greater emphasis on the description of character and locale (in opposition to postmodernism's alleged lack of interest on these aspects of narrative), ignoring thus its innate and inseparable social dimension. In general, most critics have handled this highly complex concept as if it were self-explanatory. This unfortunate circumstance is revealing of the general disregard that realism has suffered as a subject of critical enquiry along the last decades, especially when compared with the academic attention received by other broad literary movements such as modernism or postmodernism itself. It seemed to me that if the concept of realism was going to be a pivotal one in the analysis of Franzen's novels I should try to restore to it at least part of its complexity, historicity and its social and political implications. For this book, this purpose has entailed a return to a group of inescapable but sadly neglected group of critics: Erich Auerbach, György Lukács, Peter Brooks and Fredric Jameson, among others. As we shall see, an enriched notion of realism yields a picture of Franzen's stylistic evolution which is more complex than the simplistic outline – to a great extent based on Franzen's own account of it – which his critics usually operate with. Franzen's chronicle of his own career holds that the period of personal crisis he underwent in the early nineties concluded in a sort of revelation which involved discarding postmodernism, the narrative mode he had used in his early novels – and which, according to the novelist, had turned into sterile literary pyrotechnics, to adopt a much more congenial and reader-oriented realism. Some critics, as we have seen, assumed that this change was announced in the *Harper's* essay and fulfilled five years later by his third novel, *The Corrections*. But I have found it hard to concur with the opinion that Franzen wrote two wholeheartedly postmodernist novels followed by two realist ones. Admittedly, *The Twenty-Seventh City* and *Strong Motion* are obviously influenced by certain American postmodernist novelists, especially Thomas Pynchon and Don DeLillo. In emulation of these masters, Franzen adopts the typically postmodernist subgenre of the Systems novel (LeClair 1987) and the also characteristically postmodernist conspiratorial theme. Yet he uses these elements in very particular ways that suggest an affinity with the classic realist novel. In other words, from the very beginning, Franzen's fiction shows certain concerns and aspirations typically associated to the realist novel embedded in a more or less postmodernist format.

Partly due to unsolvable ideological contradictions, in his third novel Franzen intensifies his focus on family-oriented matters (which were already a significant concern in his fiction). He also drops typically postmodernist traits such as the use of conspiracies, the structural irony which was so conspicuous in *The Twenty-Seventh City* or the low emotional temperature that corresponds to a characterization technique less based on sympathy.

However, in a similar way to Rohr, rather than as a realist novel I see *The Corrections* as a hybrid text, a complex amalgam where we can find numerous typically postmodernist motifs and linguistic practices together with an exercise in sociocultural analysis which is truly remarkable in the width of its focus and evinces an undeniably realist lineage. In turn, these two orientations, the postmodernist and the realist, coexist within a narrative structure that can be seen as that of a contemporary family romance, as *The Corrections* is marked by the adoption of elements from romance, novel of formation and melodrama which, although not historically uncommon in the realist novel, are not properly realist. As we shall see, Franzen's reliance on these *para-realist* formal components only deepens after *The Corrections*. The approach to Franzen's work through the lens of a fuller concept of realism generates then a more complicated account of the former, one which does not lend itself easily to the application of generalizing labels. But this is, from my point of view, the most productive move.

6 Realism, contingency and the weight of inherited forms

One of the key aspects of the realist novel brought to bear in my analysis of Franzen's fiction is the attitude towards contingency. From the young Lukács I have taken the historical vision of the novel as a response to a de-sacralised world marked by contingency (Lukács, 2006b: 70). In fact, contingency can be taken to be a mark of true realism – what Moretti has referred to as a sort of *compulsory meaninglessness* (Moretti, 2000: 120). This notion has important bearings in the study of Franzen's fiction, as it comes to complicate – once again – the common conception of Franzen's first novel. In this sense, *The Twenty-Seventh City* is usually considered as the most clearly postmodernist, and hence the least realist, of Franzen's novels. Granted, the novel shows a conscious attempt to adopt some of the trappings of the classic American postmodernist novel: metalinguistic awareness, conspiratorial plot, concern with *the System*, unrelenting irony. Yet, following Moretti, this study underscores its worldview characterized precisely by contingency, its deliberate avoiding of not only a happy end but any kind of reassuring closure, and other characteristics such as its aspiration to the rendering of social totality, discussed below, to claim for this novel a nucleus of realism which is diluted in Franzen's subsequent work. In any case, we should not forget that, as J. P. Stern put it quoting G. G. Hough, unalloyed realism is rare since realism itself is 'an unstable compound'. In Stern's words, 'only among the realists of the nineteenth century and their heirs do we find a complete commitment to the mode, though even in their writings its instability is obvious' (Stern, 1973: 122). In fact, for Stern, realism is characterized by a singular kind of balance among writing modes: 'neither the heightened meaning of symbols nor the sentient self nor language-consciousness in its several forms is a stranger to it' (1973: 164). That is, there is no realism that does not incorporate to some extent or other that which is most distinctive about symbolism, modernism or postmodernism. In this Stern is certainly right, though he could have also included in his statement those novelistic modes that were long ago superseded by the realist novel but which nevertheless tend to reappear as more or less significant ingredients of it: romance, melodrama, *Bildungsroman*, the Gothic novel. As far as Franzen's fiction is concerned, just as the realist novel incorporated parts of the non-realist genres which it had destroyed in the course of its historical development as the hegemonic narrative form, such as romance, melodrama or *Bildungsroman*, in his subsequent novels Franzen includes non-realistic ingredients from those same genres so as to escape the truly depressing conclusion of *The Twenty-Seventh City*. In this way, from *Strong Motion* on we find in Franzen's novels recognizable melodramatic plot sequences such as the one formed by the structural elements *courting/falling in love/adultery/estrangement/ reconciliation of lovers* in *Strong Motion* and *Freedom*. There are picaresque episodes such as those which can be found in many novels of formation, as is exemplified by the participation of Chip Lambert and Joey Berglund in different swindles and deceives in *The Corrections* and *Freedom*, respectively. We can also observe the traditional romance-novelistic motif of the rise or fall of social class in all of Franzen's novels. In turn, the dark allure of the Gothic novel is invoked in *Purity*. Of course, pride of place is reserved for the biographical pattern that takes characters from selfishness, self-deception and illusions of grandeur, through the humbling illumination produced by the clash with reality, to a kind of moral coming of age which, like in a classical *Bildungsroman*, involves an equilibrium between individual needs and social integration – an integration whose only valid starting point for Franzen seems to be the family. It is the case of Louis Holland, Chip Lambert, and Walter, Patty and Joey Berglund. Here we may remember Eagleton's remark apropos of the persistence of disguised elements of romance in the nineteenth-century English novel, as it seems to fit Franzen's fiction just as well: 'In fact, nothing less than the magical devices of romance will do if, like the Victorian novelist, you are going to conjure a happy ending from the refractory problems of the modern world' (Eagleton, 2005: 2–3).

But these structural components are not ideologically neutral. On the contrary, in this regard they have, so to speak, an autonomous life of their own. Macherey showed that these formal elements, like the linguistic sign for Bakhtin, carry an ideological weight that is independent of the author's intention and is not completely dissolved in that of the new work: 'they are not neutral transparent components which have the grace to vanish, to disappear into the totality they contribute to, giving it substance and adopting its forms' (Macherey, 1989: 41–2). Jameson has argued in a similar way when discussing the ideological import of inherited structural elements: 'inherited narrative paradigms, conventional actantial or proairetic schemata' (Jameson, 2002: 137), which constitute 'narrative unities of a socially symbolic type' or *ideologemes* (2002: 172). One of the keys of this study rests on the interpretation of these ideologically charged formal and generic components.[6]

Of course, these structural components do not only comprise plot elements. Rather they can be found at all levels of the literary work. Especially important is the construction of characters, which usually has significant implications of class discourse. It is the case, for example, of Franzen's frequent presentation of working-class characters as hostile, anti-intellectual and politically reactionary. In any case, the presence of these forms, which Macherey (1989: 91) designates as *themes*, is not necessarily obvious or easy to trace, as they are subject to a sort of historical transformation that modifies their formal properties and ideological value. In this sense, for example, we do not find in Franzen's fiction the most evident recurring structural elements that Northrop Frye identifies as constitutive of the genre of secular romance in Hellenistic adventure narratives: 'stories of mysterious birth, oracular prophecies about the future contortions of the plot, foster parents, adventures which involve capture by pirates, narrow escapes from death, recognition of the true identity of the hero and his eventual marriage with the heroine' (Frye, 1976: 4). We do find, however, some of its modern-day equivalents in the actantial elements of Franzen's novels. In them we can observe recurrent narrow escapes from punishment, as we have seen, and there is also a clear narrative pattern formed by a sequence of recognitions: the epiphany-like recognition (or *anagnorisis* in its classical formulation) by the hero of his true self in the first place is followed by – or presented as simultaneous to – his recognition of his closest other(s), a development heretofore prevented by the hero's egocentric self-delusion, and finally by the recognition of the hero by the members of a small community which

---

[6]The term *proairetic* was introduced by Barthes in *S/Z* (1970), his structuralist analysis of Balzac's novella *Sarrasine*. In this study, Barthes proposes five structural and semantic dimensions or *codes* whereby texts are constituted. Two of them are especially relevant for the study of narrative: the hermeneutic code, a set of practices that drive the narrative forward by creating an enigma which generates suspense until it is disclosed; and the simplest code of all, the proairetic, which makes reference to the sequences of actions and events that occur in the text (Barthes, 1974: 18–19).

is usually that of his family.[7] Of course, In *Purity*, the most romance-like of Franzen's narratives, the heroine's anagnorisis is not metaphoric but literal. As in traditional romance, reconciliation is a fundamental ingredient in Franzen's novels, where we can find acts of reconciliation of lovers and spouses, parents and their offspring, estranged friends, etc. In fact, such reconciliation is presented as *salvation* for the hero and as such is the culmination of the narrative, as it is obvious in the endings of *Strong Motion*, *The Corrections* and *Freedom*. It is this salvational element in Franzen's narratives that is the most distinctively related to romance. I have already advanced that a defining characteristic of romance narratives is their orientation towards salvation or redemption. As Jameson has synthetically put it in his examination of Frye's theory of romance: 'Romance is for Frye a wish-fulfillment or utopian fantasy which aims at the transfiguration of the world of everyday life in such a way as to restore the conditions of some lost Eden, or to anticipate a future realm from which the old mortality and imperfections will have been effaced' (Jameson, 2002: 96–7).

This is certainly a definition of romance which is consistent with the interpretation of Franzen's salvational narratives proposed in this book. But once the form is identified, as Macherey suggests, the adscription of its ideological import should not be an automatic, straightforward affair. On the contrary, it is to be carefully and individually examined. As regards the case under consideration here, there is no such thing as a single, historically invariable ideological value of romance. As both Frye (1971: 304–5) and Jameson (2002: 91) have recognized, the fact that romance is a form driven by wish-fulfilment implies a measure of unstable political ambiguity, which opens the possibility for it to become a vehicle for the expression of the desire for social change. Moreover, since romance is typically unconcerned with the creation of true-to-life and historically dimensioned characters and settings, unlike the realist novel, it is free from the inherent ontological

---

[7] I am using masculine reference here because in Franzen's novels the hero of this narrative pattern is typically a male protagonist: Louis Holland, Chip Lambert, Walter and Joey Berglund. What is then the role in this scheme of two superbly etched female characters such as Renée Seitchek and Patty Berglund? If we draw again on Greimas' actantial model, from the point of view of the male hero we may regard both female protagonists as *helpers* that are necessary for the attainment of the hero's *object*, which is redemption and happiness. It should be noticed that here being *necessary* does not imply becoming a mere *instrument*, as in this case the *object* is inseparable of the *helper*. Renée and Patty are the heroines of their own narratives, which are virtually identical to those of their masculine counterparts in terms of their actantial structure. However, the *focalization* of Franzen's narrative accompanies for longer the point of view of their male heroes in the story-telling or *récit*, to use Genette's terms, and thus the stories of Renée, Patty, and also Denise Lambert, are on the whole less developed than those of Louis, Chip and Walter. That being said, we should remember that the point of view of Patty Berglund is given centrality during a considerable stretch of the text by means of a curious and somewhat archaizing plot device: an inserted biographical narrative presented as written by the character at the suggestion of her therapist. Of course, the pattern explained above does not apply to *Purity*, whose young heroine follows a different trajectory.

conservatism of the latter. In the case of Franzen's fiction, however, the function performed by romance is more soothing and closer to what Frye called 'sentimental romance'. For Franzen, romance is the instrument that allows him to transcend social and ideological contradictions that he is unable or unwilling to confront and thus attain the bliss of social and personal reconciliation. It is the means by which he seeks to impose the comforting and meaningful closure of narrative upon a world, the fallen, contingent world evoked by Lukács in *The Theory of the Novel* (1920), which stubbornly resists any closure. It is, in short, the means whereby he manages to shun Sartrean *viscosities*. In any case, no one should be shocked by the realization of Franzen's leaning towards romance, or by the way he blends it with the analytical procedures of realism. After all, as Moretti (2000) and Duncan (1992) have noted (albeit each one with his own different valuation of the fact), romance is at the spine of the great tradition of the English nineteenth-century novel, which not only includes the more openly sentimental fiction by Dickens but also the ambitious, comprehensive social analyses of Eliot. In fact, Duncan goes as far as to claim that the best achievement of British prose fiction should be credited to romance, rather than to the novel as such (Duncan, 1992: 3).

7 Realism, totality and late capitalism

As was advanced above, contingency is not the only realist attribute exhibited by Franzen's first novel. As Peter Brooks (2005) has shown, the realist novel is typically characterized by an explanatory vocation which is the result of its rise in the middle of a frantically changing world and the need for its readers to make sense of it. The typically urban worlds (re)created by the realist novel can be regarded, according to Brooks, as small-scale models built with the aim of gaining better knowledge of their real-size referent. This function is evident at first sight in the clear topographic quality of *The Twenty-Seventh City* and *Strong Motion*, realized in the abundance of visual renditions (including maps and aerial views) of actually existing places. But, perhaps more importantly, we may find the analytico-pedagogical calling of realism in the investigation into the workings of the system, synthetically reflected in one city, which *The Twenty-Seventh City* constitutes. Similarly, at the heart of *Strong Motion* lies a true quest for understanding of the systemic processes that shape our world and influence people's lives – an endeavour symbolized by the scientifically driven activism of its indefatigable heroine Renée Seitchek. And, we should also notice, this analytical impulse is characterized by a globalizing scope which is unabashedly influenced by Marxist theory, as can be perceived with special clarity in *Strong Motion*. Certainly the belief that the world can be analysed and made intelligible, possibly related to his declared interest in science, is a distinctive mark of Franzen's fiction which is consistent with the traditional demystifying impulse of realism (see Jameson, 2002: 138). We cannot think otherwise in sight of the way he renders the economic dynamics of late capitalism in *The Corrections*. Shunning the allegories of elusive conspiratorial networks of mysterious undergrounds, unaccountable transnational corporations and obscure government agencies that writers such as Pynchon and DeLillo have turned into a mainstay of the American postmodernist novel, Franzen describes the economic processes of globalization in down-to-earth terms of governmental de-regulation, privatization, outsourcing, speculation, and corporate greed, which are far from unknowable or undecidable. In the chapter dedicated to *The Corrections,* I argue that globalization (as later the global financial crisis that broke out in 2008) has brought about a sort of *de-familiarization* of capitalism that has stimulated its systematic, totalizing study in ways which have rendered conspiratorial views of totality outdated. Although Franzen's flare for a globalizing focus was present in his novels from the beginning, it seems clear that it is *The Corrections* that benefits the most from the new awareness of global interconnection.

Franzen's globalizing approach to social reality and his obvious interest in demystification can be regarded as part of what for Lukács was an indispensable feature of the realist novel: its vocation for the description of *totality*. For the Hungarian critic, the aspiration for totality, for the portrayal of the synchronous interrelation of social events across social groups, and for the account of the mediating social circumstances on individual acts, should be the guiding principle of the realist artist, the one which will invest her work with depth. There can be few other notions more discredited by postmodern thought than that of totality. Yet abstract totalizing thought is necessary to see through the confusion of immediacy, that is, the overwhelming variety of social epiphenomena we are incessantly confronted with and eventually achieve some sort of effective agency. This brings us again to Jameson and his analysis of the cultural manifestations of the mode of production. For the critic our time is characterized by a resistance to totalizing thought not only at a broadly cultural level, but also at the more specific of critical theory. In Jameson's view, this distrust of totality characteristic of a postmodernism usually focused on difference and margins is due to a misconception. For him, totality can be basically made of differences and still constitute a system: 'the notion that there is something misguided and contradictory about a unified theory of differentiation also rests on a confusion between levels of abstraction: a system that constitutively produces differences remains a system' (Jameson, 2009: 37). In accordance with his belief in the social determination of thought, Jameson interrogates the conditions of possibility of totalizing thought ('Why is it that the "concepts of totality" have seemed necessary and unavoidable at certain historical moments, and on the contrary noxious and unthinkable at others' [2009: 39]), and concludes that the latter is, like the realist novel, the product of a historical alignment of socio-economic factors. In this way, for the theorist, writers such as Walter Scott or William Faulkner inherited a 'historical raw material', namely the memory of civil wars and revolutions, which entailed an awareness of the coexistence of different modes of production that is inscribed in their work. For Jameson then, the ability to think a new reality and articulate a new paradigm presupposes a certain 'conjuncture' of (historical) circumstances: 'a certain strategic distance from that reality, which tends to overwhelm those immersed in it' (2009: 43). That is, the observer must be in some way an 'outsider'. This helps explain contemporary difficulties to think our system (which sometimes, according to Jameson, amount to a veritable repression of that concept) and the waning of our sense of history: 'Where everything is henceforth systemic the very notion of a system seems to lose its reason for being, returning only by way of a "return of the repressed"' (2009: 43). And the logical consequence of the weakening of our ability to systematically think of the complexities of our mode of production is, in the final analysis, our inability to ascertain our true place and function within it.

A recurrent point in Jameson's analysis of contemporary culture is the pressing need to regain the awareness of our place within the system through a kind of orientational practice which the theorist has called *cognitive mapping*. In this sense, with their analytic intention and their theory-fuelled systemic approach, *The Twenty-Seventh City* and *Strong Motion* can be regarded as orientational efforts with a totalizing slant which is truly outstanding among contemporary novelists. We just have to consider how the motif of conspiracy, a kind of consoling substitute for adequate cognitive mapping in Jameson's view, is put at the service of an analytical vision of the capitalist system. The problem for Franzen lies in the inevitable frustration arising from the awareness of the seemingly unshakeable reality of ideologically legitimized oppression and exploitation which characterizes the system, and the perception of the impossibility of effective transforming action. Then, in keeping with the contemporary *Zeitgeist* discussed above, the analytical and demystifying impulse that characterizes Franzen's fiction does not lead to the assertion of effective agency in his novels. *The Twenty-Seventh City* is characterized by a destruction of evoked hopes and ends with a triumph of apathy; *in Strong Motion* and *Freedom* activism brings no solid results. In fact, *The Corrections* and *Freedom* stage a retreat from public arenas into the realm of the family. Ultimately, this impotence can be viewed as the consequence of a conception of system which implies a network of ideology and power of such perfection that precludes any real possibility of change, which is to say an unassailable system like the one described in Franzen's two Systems novels: *The Twenty-Seventh-City* and *Strong Motion*. In this sense, Jameson has criticized as one such concept of system the one theorized by Michel Foucault. This is one of the reasons behind Jameson's preference of the concept of mode of production as a category of analysis over that of system (a view which is consistent with Laclau and Mouffe's rejection of the determinist notion of a 'sutured' society).

8 The problem of perspective

Franzen's inability to imagine a valid form of transformative political action or *agency* does not invalidate in itself the critical power of his two first novels, as some of his critics would have it. Critics like Annesley (2006) or Hawkins (2010) have decried Franzen's lack in this respect in terms that recall Lukács's disparaging opinion of modernist writers such as Kafka, expressed in *The Meaning of Contemporary Realism* (1955). For Lukács, the modernist worldview ultimately involves the unintelligibility of outward reality, which in turn implies reinforcing a sense of inalterability. Under what he calls the ideology of modernism, human activity is rendered impotent and meaningless and all that is left is a 'vision of a world dominated by angst' (Lukács, 2006a: 36). This is a view I find hard to agree with. As I argue in the chapter dedicated to *The Twenty-Seventh City*, there *is* a critical potential in expressions, for example, of anxiety and frustration. But there are other factors explored by the Hungarian theorist that do set a limit to the critical leverage of Franzen's novels. Indeed, there is an important want related to Lukács's concept of the realist novel which undermines Franzen's totalizing impulse in spite of the orientational value of his fiction, namely the narrowness of his social *perspective*. For Lukács, perspective is the novelist's principle of selection of the materials for her novel, and as such it includes a 'hierarchy of significance' (Lukács, 2006a: 34): 'in any work of art, perspective is of overriding importance. It determines the course and content; it draws together the threads of the narration; it enables the artist to choose between the important and the superficial, the crucial and the episodic' (Lukács, 2006a: 33).

If we bear in mind that the basic working mechanism of the realist novel is *synthesis*, a metonymical process whereby characters, situations and events in a novel acquire a symbolical quality and became representative of larger social realities, the crucial importance of the novelist's perspective becomes obvious. Perspective, according to Lukács, depends on the novelist's ability to grasp what is *typical*, in terms of characters and situations, in a given society at a specific historical time. It must be noticed that Lukács does not mean typical as average but rather as representative or essential. The more penetrating the writer's perspective, the truer to social totality will be her work. In fact, as Lukács observes, subsequent historical development tends to confirm the social perspective of great novelists, with which the term acquires a diachronic dimension as well as a synchronic one. In the critic's words: 'a typology can only be of lasting significance if the writer has depicted the central or peripheral significance, the comic or tragic characteristic of his types, in such a way that subsequent developments confirm his portrait of the age' (Lukács, 2006a: 57). As might be expected, for Lukács the depth of a novelist's perspective is related to her social class, as a writer will naturally concentrate on the class she knows from within. Logically, a perspective restricted to one social group is bound to be lacking as regards its account of totality. This is, to be sure, Franzen's case: the focus of his novels is unfailingly directed to middle or higher-class white families. In this norm, Franzen's first novel constitutes an exception once again. There is of course the conspicuous fact that the conspirators are Indian. But it is perhaps more important that only in *The Twenty-Seventh City* can we find a black, working-class character of some (small) significance. The ensuing reduction of perspective seems quite an impoverishment for a novelist of realist aspirations. It also has important ideological implications. Since its inception as a genre, the novel has powerfully contributed to mark the limits of what is significant, of what is to count as real. Substantial limitations in perspective then tend to transmit a specific class discourse and favours particular relations of power within society. This circumstance has been analysed by Raymond Williams:

> In modern class societies the selection of characters almost always indicates an assumed or conscious class position. The conventions of selection are more intricate when hierarchy is less formal. Without formal ramification, all other persons may be conventionally presented as instrumental (servants, drivers, waiters), as merely environmental (other people in the street) or indeed as essentially absent (not seen, not relevant). ... The social hierarchy or social norms that are assumed or invoked are substantial terms of relationship which the conventions are intended (often, in the confidence of a form, not consciously) to carry. They are no less terms of social relationship when the hierarchy or selection is not manifestly social but based on the assignment of significant being to the selected few and the irrelevant many. (Williams, 1977: 175)

In fact, it is not only that in Franzen's novels lower and working-class characters are obviously underrepresented. It is that when they appear as sideshows they tend to be drawn in rather deprecatory ways. This is evident in *Freedom,* where working-class characters invariably assume the role of antagonists of the novel's protagonists.

The concept of social class as a category for social interpretation is not one that elicits enthusiasm in the contemporary ideological climate dominated by interested notions of the end of history and ideology in a technocratic society. However, with the caveat that it is prone to fall into the perfunctory and shallow, the analysis of class discourse remains indispensable in any serious ideological analysis. In Jameson's words: 'Nothing has, of course, more effectively discredited Marxism than the practice of affixing instant class labels (generally "petty bourgeois") to textual and intellectual objects. ... But abuse of class adscription should not lead to over-reaction and mere abandonment of it. In fact, ideological analysis is inconceivable without a conception of the "ultimately determining instance" of social class' (Jameson, 2007: 201).

We will find that Franzen's novels abound in expressions of social antagonism and class/group vindication and legitimation that coexist with an urge towards (conditional) reconciliation. I would like to emphasize that my interpretation of class discourse in Franzen's novels will not be limited to the mere identification of class motifs and values, as in traditional sociological interpretation. Rather, I will try to reveal its relational character, that is, the fact that class values are, in Jameson's words, 'always actively in situation with respect to the opposing class, and defined against the latter' (Jameson, 2002: 69). All this will be particularly evident in the analysis of *Freedom*, where the class background of ongoing cultural or ideological struggles in the United States is examined. For example, I will analyse the class antagonism inherent in Walter Berglund's environmentalism in the light of Slavoj Žižek's contribution to the theory of ideology. In the same chapter it is also shown how, in his search for the legitimation of his political stance, Franzen tries to transcend conventional social positioning in terms of class and supports instead less objective social markers based on his particular conceptions of dignity, distinction and enlightenment.

In any case, a contemporary analysis of social division should be consistent with contemporary social and epistemological theory. Therefore, following Laclau and Mouffe (2001), the account of class discourse in Franzen's fiction provided in this book reflects the plural and often contradictory character of social groups, avoiding essentialist views of classes as stable, homogeneous agents. This study also intends to avoid the kind of moralistic judgement that to an extent mars some of the left-wing criticism of Franzen so far. Indeed, traces of disappointed political hopes are perceptible in the critical analyses of Annesley (2006), Hawkins (2010), or Hutchinson (2009). It should be borne in mind that in spite of the avowed influence of Marxism in Franzen's intellectual formation, so visible in his first and second novels, Franzen has made explicit his distance from that political stance (see, for example, Connery and Franzen 2009), and has repeated time and again his conception of the novel as a politically liberal form (e.g. Franzen 2012b). Relatedly, as regards political import, my analysis of Franzen's fiction takes into account an important aspect of the realist novel which is usually overlooked by critics, namely the inherent conservatism of the genre, often pointed out by authors such as Jameson or Terry Eagleton. For the former,

The literature of realism has the ideological function of adapting its readers to bourgeois society as it currently exists, with its premium on comfort and inwardness, on individualism, on the acceptance of money as the ultimate reality (we might speak today of the acceptance of the market, of competition, of a certain image of human nature, and so forth). ... The realistic novelist has a vested interest, an ontological stake, in the solidity of social reality, on the resistance of bourgeois society to history and to change. (Jameson, 2013: 5)

These circumstances are behind the traditional ill disposition of the realist novel towards acts of political rupture: they threaten a premise on which its rhetorical power lies – the stability of what is. In consequence, it would seem that the realist novel is much more suited to the support of reform than revolution. Even more, it could be argued with Eagleton that the realist novel is reformist in spirit, yet realism itself tends to undermine that reformism:

You cannot, as a novelist, argue that the world should be changed in certain respects unless you dramatize what is wrong with it as compellingly as possible. But the more effectively you do this, the less changeable the world may come to seem. Dickens's later novels portray a society so false, warped and stiflingly oppressive that it is hard to see how it could be repaired. (Eagleton, 2005: 12–13)

This means that there are certain possibilities of radical criticism that are available to certain kinds of symbolic or experimental narrative – be it of postmodernist lineage or not – which are by definition out of reach of realism. This is something that can be observed in Franzen's fiction too: the same realist logic towards which the first and second novels gravitate, and which makes for sharp and comprehensive sociocultural analysis, demands the failure of the evoked possibilities of rupture. On its part, the reformist impulse sported by the main characters of *Freedom* eventually leads to a rejection of radicalism and a celebration of compromise and reconciliation.

9 Community issues

Another major concern of this study is the relation between Franzen's fiction and recent theoretical approaches to community. Certainly, communitarian longings are at the heart of the Utopian dimension of Franzen's novels, possibly because the desire for true community is the Utopian impulse *par excellence*. The current problems of community in the United States are an overt preoccupation for Franzen, present in both his novels and essays. As countless other contemporary commentators, Franzen denounces and laments what he perceives as an ongoing loss of community in America. Here we may acknowledge the pertinence of Jean-Luc Nancy's remarks in his *La communauté désoeuvreée* (1986). For Nancy we should be wary of lamentations for the decay of community, as this feeling of loss has been a constant feature of Western thought from its very beginning. As the French thinker argues, our idea of community is a metaphysical concept developed as the archaic worldview based on immanence receded. In Nancy's words:

> Thus, the thought of community or the desire for it might well be nothing other than a belated invention, that tried to respond to the harsh reality of modern experience: namely, that divinity was withdrawing infinitely from immanence, that the god-brother was at bottom *himself* the *deus absconditus* (this was Hölderlin's insight), and that the divine essence of community – or community as the existence of a divine essence – was the impossible itself. (Nancy, 1991: 10)

In my opinion, Nancy's interrogation of the metaphysical notion of community is compatible with Jameson's accounts of the reification and fragmentation of human bonds brought about by capitalism, which form part of the theoretical grounding of this study. It may well be that, as Nancy has put it, 'community has not taken place' (Nancy, 1991: 11), but this does not prevent actual communitarian bonds from being eroded on a daily basis by what Ulrich Beck (1992) describes as the individuating processes of modernization. Indeed, it seems safe to affirm that late capitalism has brought about an increased momentum to the destruction of older communitarian formations. For Franzen, the current dissolution of community is parallel to the eclipse of what Habermas (1991) described as the public sphere, and both are embodied in his fiction in the ongoing decay of the American city. Just as the public sphere, the agora-like symbolic space of public intervention in the matters of the polis, is corrupted by privatizing forces, the classic American city is drained by white flight in favour of wealthy homogenized suburbs. The poorer inhabitants of the city are abandoned to their fate or expelled by gentrification and the face of the city literally vanishes. This phenomenon is explicitly thematized in The *Twenty-Seventh City*, but the concern is also present in the rest of the novels. Franzen's first and second novels are remarkable, nevertheless, for the way in which the process is clearly presented as a dynamic inherent to capitalism.

In my examination of the way in which Franzen's novels reflect the fragmentation and individualization of contemporary society I have relied on the sociological analyses of Zygmunt Bauman and Ulrich Beck. The former is the author of already classic descriptions of the instability and insecurity that the economic logic of capitalism has entailed for great parts of the population in advanced countries over the last decades, and has also been concerned with the communitarian yearnings that this situation has produced. The latter was one of the leading investigators of the relentless process of individuation that modernization has brought with it, and of the multiple ways in which the effects and conflicts entailed by this individuating dynamic are staged in people's everyday life. Like Jameson in his own way, both Bauman and Beck coincide in identifying a new stage in the process of modernization which advanced countries have already entered. Bauman then differentiates between classic or heavy modernity and liquid modernity; while Beck on his part refers to industrial society as opposed to advanced modernity or risk society. For the purposes of this study, Bauman's and Beck's dichotomies are perfectly complementary, and their descriptive categories have guided my exploration of the distinctive nostalgia for American industrial society that can be detected in Franzen's novels. The reason for such longing is evidently the perception of industrial society as a more favourable soil for community than the exacerbated anomie of liquid modernity. This lament for a disappearing age already occupies a central place in *The Twenty-Seventh City*, where, like the ruined city itself, the protagonist Martin Probst stands for the decline of American classic modernity. The theme can also be found in *Strong Motion*, with its eulogy for infrastructure based on its communitarian value, pertinently recognized by Bruce Robbins (2007), and retakes a pivotal place again in *The Corrections*. In this sense, Franzen's third novel is partly organized around a Midwest/East opposition which roughly corresponds to the contrast between American modernity and postmodernity. Here the elder Lamberts represent traditional Midwestern communitarian values which are opposed to the fierce individualism of the postmodernity inhabited by their offspring. Similarly, the type of security which used to characterize industrial societies – the stability that dominated the realms of labour, family and close community – is contrasted with the maddening evanescence of liquid modernity. However, Franzen does not idealize American industrial society or its fundamental institution the classic nuclear family. On the contrary, his novels also dramatize the manifold social, ideological and environmental contradictions that used to characterize it and which are at the root of our present-day disorientation. His nostalgia is then a conflicted one.

As I discuss in the chapter dedicated to *The Corrections*, in Franzen's stance regarding the rampant individualism of contemporary society we can observe a notable coincidence with Daniel Bell's views on the 'cultural contradictions of capitalism' (Bell 1973). In consequence, Franzen's critical position suffers from the same problems as that of Bell and other more recent intellectuals that have deplored the decay of American communities, such as Amitai Etzioni (1994) or Robert D. Putnam (2000). Both Bell and Franzen conceive of the realms of economy and culture as essentially separate. This entails that for them the causes of the cultural disorders they lament, such as unchecked individualism, exaggerated consumerism, lack of moral values, etc. remain within the sphere of culture, rather than in the economic base of the system. As Robbins (1999) has accurately argued, this position leads to the current vulnerability of liberals before the political Right in the ongoing ideological struggles known in the United States as culture wars, as it implies that only the realm of culture is to blame for the perceived moral disorder. Culture then becomes the scapegoat of the ills wrought by a productive system that once again remains out of sight. The ensuing impotence of liberals before the conservatives, all the more frustrating for not being well understood, produces the exasperation and despair that is so apparent in *Freedom*, especially as embodied by the character of Walter Berglund. And when despair of larger communities dominates, it is the small communities of family and lovers that appear as a meaningful refuge. In fact, it can be argued that liberalism is a factor in Franzen's anxieties about community: with its intrinsic individualism and its distinctive distrust of supra-individual political and ideological constructions, liberalism seems destined to forsake larger social communities and drive all communitarian concerns into the private realm of the family.

Another aspect of Franzen's thought in which his despair of larger communities transpires is his often-quoted proposal of a community of readers which he advanced for the first time in the *Harper's* essay. Its symptomatic value is evident: the solution to the disorders of the realm of culture (social fragmentation, techno-consumerism, social irrelevance of literature, etc.) is to be found within the same realm of culture, avoiding thus coming to terms with the economic base of society. Only this time it is not a solution – which is deemed impossible – but mere consolation. In 'Mr. Difficult', Franzen tries to draw populist credit from the notion of such community through his idea of a 'contract' between writer and readers. However, it is hard not to see his proposed virtual community of isolated readers as an acknowledgement of impotence. There is indeed a feeling of precariousness in Franzen's proposal, which is perceptible in the very imagery of exile he uses to describe it. Franzen's literary community recalls a 'community of those who do not have a community', to use the Bataillean phrase quoted by Maurice Blanchot as a frontispiece of *La communauté inavouable* (1988 [1984]). His community of 'matching diasporas', devoid of collective or political agency, is only left with the possibility of individual self-amelioration. This should not be taken as a condemnation of Franzen's political stance: not only because it is not my purpose in this study to pass this kind of judgement on Franzen, but because I actually consider that his novels constitute imperfect but valuable exercises of cognitive mapping. Indeed, in spite of all the class bias, limitations of perspective and ideological blind spots that can be found in Franzen's social vision, the analytico-pedagogical impulse that characterizes his fiction, his vocation for the rendering of synthetic visions of totality, his keenness on demystification are truly remarkable in contemporary American fiction. Not to mention that *Purity*, in keeping with Franzen's increased reliance on the symbolic power of romance, presents an undeniable change of scenario regarding social hope. Franzen's latest novel is characterized by a curious mixture of a dismal view of contemporary digital culture and a tentative optimism for society embodied by the younger generation. What is more, Franzen's advocacy of investigative journalism suggests a measure of hope for the social sphere.

All in all, a fundamental premise of my analysis of Franzen's fiction is the claim that the novel has historically been a fundamental means (never ideologically neutral) for societies to interpret themselves. Part of the communitarian import of the genre is to be found in this capacity to help communities understand themselves. In this the novel performs a symbolic function in the maintenance of communities akin to that accomplished by infrastructure, a recurrent motif in Franzen's novels, as we will see. But this function clearly requires a novel that is interested in the social dimension of human beings, a novel which for a variety of historical reasons has come to be ever rarer. It is in this cultural context that Franzen's effort is best understood.

2

Knowable conspiracies:
The Twenty-Seventh City

First we take Manhattan, then we take Berlin.

LEONARD COHEN

1 Introduction: Striking up a conversation

Jonathan Franzen's first novel, *The Twenty-Seventh City*, published in 1988 when he was twenty-nine, was a remarkably ambitious debut, with its bold story line, which makes use of multiple, relaying points of view; its wide-ranging social and political critique; a concentrated narrative voice that is not afraid of linguistic experiment; and the obvious determination to take the stand in a literary room – the American postmodernist novel – already full of towering figures. In many ways, *The Twenty-Seventh City*, a novel which would probably alienate a considerable part of Franzen's current readership, remains a strange, grim piece of fiction with an undeniable compelling power.

The Twenty-Seventh City is commonly taken as the most markedly postmodernist of Franzen's novels. This view is supported not only by fundamental generic and thematic choices which I will be discussing shortly, but also by the obvious influence of certain theoretical currents closely associated to postmodernist fiction. The following excerpt, for example, clearly shows an awareness of the problematic nature of language, of its materiality, that is central to post-structuralist theory and by the same token to much postmodernist literature: '*Words crowd together single file, individuals passing singly through a single gate. The pressure is constant, the flight interminable. There is plenty of time. Born in motion, borne by syntax, stranger marrying stranger, they stream into the void*' (TS 152, italics in the original).

The whole picture, however, as well as the complete story of Franzen's stylistic transition, is a more complex matter than what critical accounts tend to imply, as this study aims to demonstrate. In this sense, I will be examining how Franzen's first novel presents certain distinctively realist attributes, namely an obvious topographic quality, a calling – even if not fully realized – for the representation of different social groups as inextricably connected, the description of the integration of the fate of small groups such as families into the wider social totality as a central aim, a worldview relentlessly based on contingency, and, not least of all, an aversion to showing radical social change, all of which may be regarded as nothing but realist. This makes for a remarkable, unresolved tension between two different approaches to the novelistic form that coexist within *The Twenty-Seventh City*. These are characteristics that this novel shares to one extent or other with Franzen's second, *Strong Motion*. However, as I will be arguing in this chapter, there is an important circumstance that sets *The Twenty-Seventh City* apart from the rest of Franzen's fiction, namely the absence of the (individual) salvational perspectives that we find in the other novels. *The Twenty-Seventh City* therefore does not contribute in itself to that metanarrative devised by the novelist on his own fiction that we have called the narrative of conversion and which will be the object of discussion in the following chapters. However, with its distinctive radicalness and gloomy conclusion, the novel sets the departing ground for the mentioned narrative, which will be presented as a way out of such dismal dead end.

From another point of view, the novel already shows some of the most significant concerns that will characterize all of Franzen's work: his interest in personal relationships at the domestic level – where according to critics such as James Wood (2001a, b), he is at his deepest and best – goes accompanied by a preoccupation with larger sociopolitical issues. In this sense, however, *The Twenty-Seventh City* also stands out from the rest of Franzen's fiction as the only novel which is concerned with showing the inner workings of the political activity as it unfolds in the quarters where the significant decisions are made. Even more, the possibility for an alternative political vision taking hold of these centres of power is evoked. In contrast, as if in an implicit acknowledgement of impotence, in the subsequent novels political activity adopts the somewhat disguised form of activism (especially environmentalist), and takes place at a hopelessly remote distance from the decision-making circles.[1] In any case, at the heart of these two parallel concerns – the sociopolitical and the domestic – lies a deep yearning for a lost sense of community, and ultimately a wish for truer, closer personal

---

[1] Franzen's subsequent avoidance of the exercise of politics as an overt novelistic subject may reflect what Badiou sees as the current disappearance of politics. The French philosopher regards politics as 'all the processes by means of which human collectivity becomes active or proves capable of new possibilities as regards its own destiny' (Badiou, 2013: 5). For Badiou, politics as such has virtually vanished from our age, as it was also absent in other historical periods such as the reign of Louis XIV or the end of the Roman Empire (2013: 4).

relationships down to the most intimate circle of family, the realm that Habermas (1991) has called 'the intimate sphere'. Thus, in *The Twenty-Seventh City* the conflicts and disorientation of a upper-class white Midwestern family – a recurrent motif in Franzen's novels – are embedded in an extravagant plot which affords Franzen his extensive sociopolitical critique.

Franzen has referred to his use of 'large, externalized plots' (Antrim, 2001: n.pg.) in his first two novels as motivated by the influence of postmodernist novelists. Most notably, *The Twenty-Seventh City* and *Strong Motion* present conspiracy, paranoia, and the dread at the seeming connection of things in an elusive and overwhelmingly complex system as constitutive features of contemporary life. This is, famously, a distinctive characteristic of much of the fiction by Thomas Pynchon and Don DeLillo, two novelists whose influence on Franzen is evident. For a long time, Franzen described his relation with the classic American postmodernists at the beginning of his literary career as a rather easy, unproblematic affair; far from the agonic sense of belatedness and Oedipal rivalry described by Bloom in *The Anxiety of Influence* (1973). In his interview with Donald Antrim, Franzen referred to his attempt in characteristically domestic terms which were an implicit denial of anxiety: just as he was a late kid with much older parents and was therefore often engaged in interaction with 'serious grown-ups', his first novel amounted to 'a conversation with the literary figures of my parents' generation. The great sixties and seventies Postmoderns. I wanted to feel like I belonged to them, much as I'd spent my childhood trying to be friends with my parents and their friends. A darker way of looking at it is that I was trying to impress them' (Antrim, 2001: n.pg.). In keeping with this homeliness and lack of drama in the discussion of influence, Franzen's first novel acknowledges its indebtedness with nonchalance:

'What are you, paranoid or something?'

'Yeah. Paranoid.' He leaned back in the seat, reached out the open window, and adjusted the extra mirror. 'My life's gotten kind of weird lately'. He pushed the mirror every which way. 'Do you know Thomas Pynchon?'

'No.' Luisa said. 'Do you know Stacy Montefusco?' (TS 55)

The wider cultural context probably lent a hand here. This form of unembarrassed appropriation-as-a-tribute has become of course a common practice in all arts. Indeed, it is arguably part of the 'relief' brought about by postmodernism (Jameson, 1991: 317): a lightness that contrasts with the oppressive weight that used to invest the work of the great modernist figures. However, in the more recent *The Kraus Project* (2013) we learn of a darker story. With remarkable outspokenness, Franzen admits that getting out of Pynchon's engulfing shadow was an excruciating process. Specifically,

Pynchon's *Gravity's Rainbow*, with its all-encompassing hugeness, felt disabling for Franzen. There were Oedipal fears and struggle after all:

> Pynchon's Gravity's Rainbow seemed to me a novel of dizzying capability. Its melding of the gonzo and the literary was so effortless and brilliant it felt inevitable, and it dealt squarely with the two contemporary issues that weighed on me the most: the nuclear peril and the impenetrably complex modern System that rendered individuals powerless. Pynchon's narrative voice was scarily authoritative the way my father was. (KP 178)

In any case, Franzen eventually put together a novel obviously in tune with typically postmodernist themes: 'I adopted a lot of that generation of writers' concerns – the great postwar freak-out, the Strangelovian inconceivabilities, the sick society in need of radical critique. I was attracted to crazy scenarios' (Antrim, 2001: n.pg.). To be sure, in *The Twenty-Seventh City* the scenario is indeed crazy: a cabal from India infiltrates the St Louis police force to gradually take control of the city's politics and economy. On its part, the social critique is certainly wide, ranging from the appropriation of institutions by groups of interest, the baneful effects of real estate speculation or the manipulative power of the media. This critique, however, focuses on a single city which is taken as a representative sample of countless other cities, and by dint of this synthetic operation is both real and symbolic.

2 Mapping 'the inner city of fiction'

The city and its problems are a constant preoccupation in Franzen's work, present not only in all his novels but also in several of his essays. In this way, for example, in 'First City' (1995), the novelist articulates his concerns with urban issues. He discusses the differences between European and American cities in the light of their respective historical, cultural and economic origins and different development patterns. With the acknowledged addition of some idealized nostalgia, Franzen laments the erosion of the open public space the city affords and the subsequent loss of the civic values it harbours: 'The first decades of this century were the heyday of urban life in America. I generally resist wishing I'd live in an earlier era ... but I make an exception for those years when the country's heart was in its cities, the years of Lou Gehrig and Harold Ross, Automats and skyscrapers, trolley cars, fedoras and crowded train stations' (HA 184). Similarly, in 'Lost in the Mail' (1994, also included in HA) the writer carries on a factual journalistic essay on the decay of the Chicago postal service and its subsequent replacement by private courier companies. This decadence is presented as a correlate of the downfall of American cities, abandoned by the wealthy in favour of suburban or exurban locations. Interestingly, Franzen has occasionally drawn a parallelism between urban decline and the waning importance of the novel in contemporary American culture. Thus, in 'Why Bother?' he argues:

> The literary America in which I found myself after I published *The Twenty-Seventh City* bore a strange resemblance to the St. Louis I'd grown up in: a once-great city that had been gutted and drained by white flight and superhighways. Ringing the depressed urban core of serious fiction were prosperous new suburbs of mass entertainments. Much of the inner city's remaining vitality was concentrated in the black, Hispanic, Asian, gay and women's communities that had taken over the structures vacated by fleeing straight white males. (HA 62)

The parallelism is appropriate insofar as the development of the novel and the attainment of its classic form in the nineteenth century were so closely associated to the growth of European cities. For Fredric Jameson, the novel performed a fundamental part in the insertion of individual experience into the larger social realm. In his words, 'In the already more distant horizon of the industrial metropolis and the nation-state, the realist novel has often been taken (e.g. by Lukács) as the classical moment of balance, in which the narrative of individual experience can still adequately map larger social boundaries and institutions' (Jameson, 1984: 116). Moreover, if we assume with Jameson the formative role the novel played in what he calls the great 'bourgeois cultural revolution' (Jameson, 2002: 138), as realized, for example, in the constitution of ideological structures such as the *centred subject*, it seems logical to suggest for it, as Julián Jiménez Heffernan does (2007: 28–9), a shaping function in the consolidation of essentially urban concepts such as the civil society.

At this point, we should also remember, with Peter Brooks (2005: 132), the novel's role in the working out of the 'semiotic crisis' that the new urban experience of the eighteenth and nineteenth centuries represented. For Peter Brooks (2005), one fundamental function performed by the realist novel, as it attained its classical form in the nineteenth century, was that of making sense for its readers of a bewilderingly new environment, that of industrial capitalism, characterized by the secularization of older transcendental narratives, by the contingency introduced by the laws of the market, and, in short, by the all but complete commodification of human activity and relations. Significantly for the purposes of this study, communitarian issues seem central to the novel from its very outset. More specifically, community appears as both an essential preoccupation and an indispensable prerequisite of the realist novel. As the processes of urbanization and industrialization that were taking place in England and other European countries entailed the uprooting of communities at an hitherto unknown scale, writers such as George Eliot set out to reproduce those disappearing communities as if to better understand what was being lost, while in parallel they examined the new forming urban milieus to test their communitarian potential. The thought of Tory politician and novelist Benjamin Disraeli, marked by acute nostalgia for a lost *organic* society, was a prominent example of the sense of loss of community that had come to be frequent in contemporary England. In this way, the protagonist of his *Sybil* (1845) claims:

> As for community ... with the monasteries expired the only type we ever had in England of such an intercourse. There is no community in England; there is only aggregation, but aggregation under circumstances which make it rather a dissociating than a uniting principle. ... It is a community of purpose that constitutes society ... without that men may be joined into contiguity, but they still continue virtually isolated. ... It is their condition everywhere; but in cities that condition is aggravated. A density of population implies a severer struggle for existence, and a consequent repulsion of elements brought into too close contact. In great cities men are brought together by the desire of gain. They are not in a state of cooperation but of isolation, as to the making of fortunes; and for all the rest they are careless of neighbours. Christianity teaches us to love our neighbour as ourself; modern society acknowledges no neighbour. (qtd. Jiménez Heffernan, 2013: 9)

As the passage suggests, at the heart of the investigations of the realist novel in the nineteenth century is, to be sure, the city. Certainly, the novels of writers such as Balzac or Dickens seem devised to get to grips with that disconcerting 'new total context of modern life' (Brooks, 2005: 131) formed by the city. Then, if the encounter with the city and its perplexing, stimulating mixture of perils and possibilities involved a crisis for the disoriented newcomer and the baffled reader, the classic realist novel provided both a physical chart and a handy guide to the city's new sign-systems and social codes. However, it is easy to feel with Franzen that the novel seems of much less value today for the dwellers of a place deserted by its potential – middle-class – readers. In the same way, the increasing fragmentation of the 'knowable communities' which Raymond Williams[2] identified as essential to the realist novel cannot but limit the novel's scope, drawing it towards the exploration of the isolated individual's consciousness characteristic of the high modernist novel and the postmodern experimentalists; or alternatively to the confined, sheltered environments that form the setting of much contemporary fiction such as the *campus novel*. As Franzen puts it: 'I miss the days when more novelists lived and worked in big cities. I mourn the retreat into the self and the decline of the broad-canvas novel for the same reason I mourn the rise of the

---

[2]'Knowable communities' is the title of Williams' fundamental essay on George Eliot included in *The Country and the City* (1973).

suburbs: I like maximum diversity and contrast packed into a single exciting experience' (HA 80).

While there is a microcosmic quality to the reflection above, the extent to which Franzen has attained this kind of realist synthesis in his novels of white middle-class dysfunctional families is of course a different question. In any case, *The Twenty-Seventh City* is certainly the novel that dramatizes most clearly Franzen's concern with the city. For example, the included map of St Louis and its vicinity reinforces the actuality of the subject and points at a clear referential intention on the writer's part. For Rebein, who defends that there was always a realist writer in Franzen, 'hidden beneath all the Po-Mo machinery' (Rebein, 2007: 204), *The Twenty-Seventh City* 'offers up as earnest a depiction of place and regional mannerisms as anything we may find in Chopin, Joyce, or Faulkner', evincing Franzen's 'abiding interest in place' (Rebein, 2007: 213), which for the critic already tells him apart from the postmodernist writers he was trying to join at the time. Franzen's attempt in the novel, Rebein argues, is 'not to *create* a fictional world but rather to *document* one that already exists – to demonstrate a mastery or ownership of place' (2007: 214). Certainly, the novel abounds in geographical references and visual accounts of the city and its suburbs, such as: 'One fifteen in the afternoon. Jammu stood at the window of a twenty-second floor in the Clarion hotel and directed a yawn at the Peabody Coal and Continental Grain installations across the Mississippi. On the near side of the river, conventioning Jaycees in paper boaters straggled along the footpaths to the Arch' (TS 74).

This kind of topographic referentiality, or, to use Even-Zohar's term, this kind of *réalème* is of course a classic resource by means of which the realist novel attains what Barthes called *l'effet de réel*. Probably to a greater extent than in the rest of Franzen's work, in *The Twenty-Seventh City* the city's topography is integrated in the *texture* of the novel, including its political and emotional import and even the construction of its characters, as the symbolic identification of Martin Probst and the city clearly exemplifies. As J. Hillis Miller explains:

A novel is a figurative mapping. ... This [novelistic] space is based on the real landscape, charged now with the subjective meaning of the story that has been enacted within it. The houses, roads, paths and walls stand not so much for the individual characters as for the dynamic fields of relations among them. This is a complex form of metonymy whereby environment may be a figure for what it environs, in this case the gents who move, act, and interact within the scene. (Miller, 1995: 19–20)

In fact, the way in which Franzen manages to invest with symbolism his realistic rendition of St Louis is truly remarkable, as we will be showing in this chapter. For a contrast, we may remember Michael Chabon's *The Mysteries of Pittsburgh*, another outstanding debut novel published as well in 1988. In the latter, the city is also a shaping total environment made tangible by precise topographic descriptions, but there is not an overt symbolic intention comparable to Franzen's.

In any case, the most significant aspect of Franzen's rendition of St Louis is certainly its decadence. In the novel, St Louis is presented as an example of the seemingly unstoppable decay of formerly thriving American cities. The figure in the novel's title refers to the position, in terms of population, of St Louis among American cities in 1980 (450,000, half the 1930 figure), in sharp contrast to its position as the nation's fourth city after New York, Philadelphia and Brooklyn in 1870.

If, as Jameson has famously claimed, our age 'has forgotten how to think historically' (Jameson, 1991: ix), Franzen seems to be consciously striving to attain 'historicity', understood as 'the perception of the present as history' (Jameson, 1991: 284). This perception, which was mainly the product of late eighteenth-century sociopolitical and philosophical developments in Europe, was one of the constitutive features of the realist novel. City, novel and historical consciousness went hand in hand, attesting to the fact that, as Guy Debord puts it, 'the city is *the focal point of history*, because it embodies both a concentration of social power, which is what makes historical enterprises possible, and a consciousness of the past' (Debord, 2009: 118). It must be added, however, that while Franzen's novel certainly shows a consciousness of the past, it also testifies to the tremendous difficulty for our age to perceive the present as part of *future* history, as its collapsing ending shows. Be it as it may, *The Twenty-Seventh City* goes to some length in the second chapter (TS 24–26) to trace the causes of St Louis's decadence. Following the administrative segregation of the city of St Louis and the surrounding St Louis County, a number of historical, economic and legal circumstances going back to the nineteenth century converged to start the process whereby the white upper- and middle-class population and the businesses they ran, gradually left the city to set in the different municipalities that form the St Louis County along the central part of the twentieth century. Therefore the inner city was deprived of its tax base and was increasingly unable to provide services for its inhabitants. The process was not a large-scale deliberate scheme but the result of dynamics inherent to a capitalist economy: 'Everyone worried about the city's schools, but it was an exercise in hand wringing' (TS 25). The novel emphasizes though that class and race prejudice were also determinant: the arrival of poor black families from the South hastened the migration of the white population to the suburbs, as white middle-class is characterized by a desire to avoid contact and share resources with the black community. As a member of the ruling elite of St Louis cynically recognizes in the novel: 'A big reason the white middle class moved out to the county is, as we all know, their desire for good schools and, more specifically, their fear of black areas. If the city comes back into the county, there won't be any place to run' (TS 290).

There were different initiatives to counter this process, nevertheless. St Louis was the location of two important architectural attempts at urban regeneration of a marked modernist character. The first one, passingly mentioned in the second chapter (TS 25), was the Pruit-Igoe project, a gigantic social housing scheme completed in 1956 which soon became notorious for its concentration of abject poverty and crime. The last buildings of the project, designed by Japanese architect Minoru Yamasaki, were demolished in 1976, an event which is sometimes held to mark the end of High Modernism in architecture. The second was more successful, even if it did not achieve its ultimate goal as catalyst for the reverse of the city's decline by means of its iconic power: it was the Gateway Arch, so prominent in the novel, designed by Finnish-American architect Eero Saarinen in 1947 and erected between 1963 and 1965. However, since these and other initiatives did not address the underlying structural economic problems of the city, no efforts at urban renewal seemed to succeed. Even the Arch, built to celebrate the prosperity of commerce and Westward expansion, being deprived of its reference, becomes an enigmatic, ambiguous sign in the novel. By the 1970s, the process was complete: 'The seventies became the Era of the Parking Lot, as acres of asphalt replaced half-vacant office buildings downtown' (TS 26). The splendour of St Louis, like that of Detroit, Cleveland, Philadelphia and a host of other now-declining American (and European) cities, was the product of modernity, the historical process which dissolved the structures of feudal society and in the nineteenth century brought about what Ulrich Beck (1992) has analysed as *industrial society*. However, as the German sociologist argues, this socio-economic configuration, which has been predominant in much of the Western world during the greater part of the twentieth century, is in the process of transformation – or dissolution – as the logic of its own immanent premises is carried through. As Beck puts it, 'modernization today is dissolving industrial society and another modernity is coming into being … modernization within the horizon of the experience of pre-modernity is being displaced by *reflexive* modernization' (Beck, 1992: 10). For Beck then, we are immersed in the beginning of a new modernity 'beyond its classical industrial design' (1992: 10). Under this new paradigm, the destiny of St Louis seems inescapable: its ruins represent the fate of industrial society, while the vacant space left by depopulation at the heart of the city stands for the void left by the eclipse of the unfinished project of modernity.

3 Vanishing city: The wasteland of vacant lots

The disappearance of the city's face is a central motif in Franzen's picture of St Louis, which thus inscribes itself in an old tradition of sombre urban portraits.[3] If in Defoe's *The Journal of the Plague Year* (1722) the face of London is strangely altered by the houses closed and abandoned as a consequence of the disease, in St Louis's 'cratered streets' (TS 389), gloomy vacant lots and tracts of empty asphalt quickly disfigure the physiognomy of the districts infected by the 'blight', a common, fearful metaphor for urban deterioration. On the other hand, whereas in Smollet's *The Expedition of Humphrey Clinker* (1771) London becomes an 'overgrown monster' (Smollett, 1983: 82) on account of its unrestrained, cankerous growth, St Louis's monstrosity is a deformity caused by amputation and absence. A scary deformity which, like a leper's, only speeds up the hurried flight of those who can. The sprawl becomes then also an escape from the monster. The result is a literally *fantôme* city:

> The question, if it arose at all, arose in silence, in the silence of the empty city's streets, and more insistently, in the silence of the century separating a young St. Louis from a dead one. What becomes of a city no living person can remember, of an age whose passing no one survives to regret? Only St. Louis knew. Its fate was sealed within it. Its special tragedy special nowhere else. (TS 26)

In *The Invisible City* (1972), Italo Calvino imagined the city as a pattern of threads marking relationships. The image points to the *textual* (i.e. *knitted* in its etymological sense) character of any city, a quality also suggested by Brooks, for whom, as we have seen, the city can be regarded as a system of signs (Brooks, 2005: 132).[4] But as the fabric of St Louis is undone by multiplying holes there is no longer any sense to be made of it. The disintegration of St Louis due to the multiplication of empty spaces destroys what in his classic study on urbanism Kevin Lynch called the 'legibility' of its cityscape: 'the ease with which its parts can be recognized and can be organized into a coherent pattern' (Lynch, 1960: 3). The city then becomes unintelligible beyond the aid of any map, or any novel for that matter. And just as a city needs some kind of linear pattern to come into being, so does the novel, or at least the (nineteenth-century-influenced) kind of novel that Franzen seems to favour. This is afforded by a *plot*, a term which, as Brooks has observed (Brooks, 1992: 11), has the primary sense of a bounded piece

---

[3]The texts by Defoe and Smollett mentioned below are discussed by Jiménez Heffernan in his essay 'Campos de Londres: Tópica del monstruo de Defoe a Amis', included in Jiménez Heffernan (2007).
[4]In 'The Right to the City', Henry Lefebvre uses textual metaphors in a similar way to discuss the problems of the city in terms of intelligibility: 'The object, the city, as consummate reality, is falling apart. ... As social text, this historical city no longer has a coherent set of prescriptions, of use of time linked to symbols and to a style. This text is moving away. It takes the form of a document, or an exhibition, or a museum. The city historically constructed is no longer lived and is no longer understood practically. ... Yet the *urban* remains in a state of dispersed and alienated actuality' (Lefebvre, 1996: 148).

of ground; and also the senses of a ground plan, as for a building; a sequence of events forming the outline of a narrative; and a plan made in secret by a group of people: a conspiracy. Brooks remarks that 'common to the original sense of the word is the idea of boundedness, demarcation, the drawing of lines to mark off and order' (1992: 12). We know that the development of the urban experience helped shape the novelistic form in the nineteenth century. According to Brooks (2005) and Moretti (2005), the sheer spatial and social density of the city made for 'a particularly concentrated form of existence, an exacerbation, and exhilaration, of human forces' which afforded the novelist with 'the primary stuff of the novelistic' (Brooks, 2005: 147). It is not hard to see then what the decay of the inner city and its abandonment for low-density and homogeneous suburban settings entails for the novel: a most un-novelistic state of *eventlessness*. Therefore, if Franzen's plea for the city is also an entreaty for the novel, he introduces his plot of conspiring Indians to buttress both – as if seeking to resolve, to use Moretti's phrase, 'the spatial in terms of the sequential' (Moretti, 2005: 112).

However, not all the emptiness in Franzen's St Louis is the consequence of the blight. The inner city is also affected by a massive clearance process engineered by the newly appointed police chief S. Jammu, which is part of a real estate speculative operation involving the gentrification of downtown areas. Clarence Davis, whose own sister will also be expelled from home by gentrifying pressure (TS 456), her rented house sold to a white family, drives down the now deserted poor districts of the downtown at night: 'But Clarence is scared, scared in a mental way nothing like the gut fear of murder he once might have felt down here. It's the scope of the transformation; square *miles* fenced and boarded. Not *one* man visible, not *one* family left' (TS 256). This dispossession is the last step of a process that has configured a truly *absent* city which no longer belongs to its inhabitants, any trace of community already erased. As Singh, one of the conspirators puts it: 'I like St. Louis. ... Buildings sit well here. Almost too well, if you know what I mean. The city is such a physical ramification – the brick, the hill, the open spaces – that the architecture and the landscape completely dominate. I don't say there aren't people, but for some reason they seem to get lost in the larger visuals' (TS 241).

The whereabouts of the inhabitants of the cleared areas do not seem to be the concern of the wealthy citizens who form the majority of the novel's cast, although everybody appreciates the sharp fall in crime rates achieved by the new police chief. It is only at the end of the novel that we learn that the poorest inhabitants of the city have been secretly – and forcibly – driven across the river by the police to the forsaken ghetto of East Saint Louis. The novel thus reflects several phenomena which according to Zygmunt Bauman (2001) accompany the process of 'ghettoization'. These include the institutionalization of urban fear and the criminalization of poverty. This in turn leads to a reshaping of public spaces according to the safety concerns of the wealthy. Ghettos then become prison-like places from which their insiders cannot get out: as Loïc Wacquant defines them, they combine spatial confinement with social closure (Bauman 2001: 116). David Harvey, following Engels, argues that this process of dispossession and ghettoization is inherent to the general dynamics of capitalism in the city: 'A process of displacement and dispossession, in short, also lies at the core of the urban process under capitalism. This is the mirror image of capital absorption through urban redevelopment' (Harvey, 2012: 18). It is to be noted, besides, that, as Bauman points out, 'ghetto life does not sediment community', but rather 'dissolves solidarity and mutual trust', turning into 'a laboratory of social disintegration, atomization and anomie' (Bauman, 2001: 122). This kind of anomie is a crucial circumstance that prevents the inhabitants of the ghetto from being a cohesive social group that might eventually become what Laclau and Mouffe (2001) term a *subject position* in the general picture of social antagonism. Rather, these people are closer to what classic Marxism viewed as lumpenproletariat.

From another point of view, St Louis's ghetto, whose destitution and rampant crime – urban crime is often a figure for class struggle, according to Jameson (1991: 273) – embodies the necessary underside of capitalism, also becomes a sort of Lacanian Real for the city: East St Louis is the terrifying site of what cannot even be thought, if its respectable, well-to-do citizens are to keep placidly pursuing their own affairs. It is precisely the ruthless chaos of the ghetto that will bring about Barbara Probst's absurd death, in what Žižek might explain as 'an irruption of total contingency' characteristic of the Real (Žižek, 1989: 191). With the shock of encounter enhanced by unexpectedness, Franzen depicts East St Louis as a murky hell where one can only dimly discern the menacing figures that mill around, all the more horrible because of a featurelessness that prevents orientation: 'She was lost in the place of her nightmares, of the nightmares of every citizen of Webster Groves' (TS 497). If any city, as we have seen, may be regarded as a text, then the speculative 'renewal' process taking place in St Louis's inner city can be taken as an attempt at its re-textualization or, in other words, a re-symbolization. It is not surprising therefore that East St Louis acquires some of the qualities Žižek predicates of the Real: 'the product, remainder, leftover, scraps of this process of symbolization, the remnants, the excess which escapes symbolization and is as such produced by the symbolization itself' (1989: 191). The ghetto is both the necessary result of the dynamics of capitalist development prevailing in the city, and an intractable entity that resists any attempts at rational management.

Against this dark urban vortex, the novel contrasts the peacefully dull suburban security of Webster Groves, home to the Probsts and the very place where Franzen grew up:

Although the streets of Webster Groves connect with those of its neighbours, and aside from Derek Creek in the north the town has no natural boundaries, its residents experience it as an enclosure, an area where Christmas can occur in safety. It's a state of mind. ... There are no open fields, no high-rises or trailer parks or even shopping malls, no zones of negative potential into which spirit can drain. ... Born lucky, residents guess. This is a home that feels like home. (TS 264)

This psychological as well as topographic rendition of Webster Groves as a protective, homely environment recalls Gaston Bachelard's exploration of the literary reflections of the typical bourgeois house which has traditionally protected and nurtured the childhood of its infant dwellers (Bachelard, 1994). In the following chapters – especially in the one dedicated to *The Corrections* – I shall have the opportunity to use Bachelard's theoretical framework to analyse Franzen's emotionally charged allusions to suburban family houses. But moments of relative (and guilty?) fondness such as this notwithstanding, the overall tone of Franzen's depiction of both city and suburbs in *The Twenty-Seventh City* is one of spiritual dryness and meaningless repetitions in the absence of real events. Appropriately then, in his rendering of a disjointed, fallen city, Franzen often invokes – in another act of appropriation as tribute – the famous poem by St Louis's native T. S. Eliot, *The Waste Land* (1922). Franzen especially resorts to the elements Eliot took from Jessie L. Weston's book on the Grail legend, *From Ritual to Romance* (1920), with its theme of death and regeneration. In his monograph, Burn (2008) traces the numerous allusions to the poem in the novel. These range from mere textual playfulness to more substantial, if also ironic, parallelisms. This way the city, whose 'air smells like tar' (TS 254), becomes a parched wasteland: 'a city gone dead', a 'dry river' (TS 201, 203). In short, 'the land needed rain' (TS 160). Martin Probst, the self-made businessman whose company built the Arch, and a model of *probity* as his name suggests, becomes a Fisher King of sorts whose inner turmoil mirrors the agitation in the city's body politic: 'What if he was the city? ... He was sick and the city was sick on the inside too' (TS 216–217). However, although his sexual intercourse with Jammu brings the long-awaited rain to the city (TS 453) in April ('the cruelest month' according to the poem and also the time of Barbara Probst's death in the novel), in the end he is unable to cure its ills.

4 City of boredom: Highways, malls and the hunger for the Event

If the novel's rendering of St Louis is ironically consistent with *The Waste Land*, it is also attuned to Debord's remarks on urban life in what he called 'society of the spectacle'. Debord's observations seem particularly relevant to a novel whose characters spend significant time driving in solitude down the highways that have emptied a formerly lively public urban space, only to arrive home to consume the images that reinforce their alienation:

> The general trend toward isolation, which is the underlying essence of urbanism, must also include a controlled reintegration of the workers based on the planned needs of production and consumption. This reintegration into the system means bringing isolated individuals together as isolated individuals. Factories, cultural centers, tourist resorts and housing developments are specifically designed to foster this type of pseudocommunity. The same collective isolation prevails even within the family cell, where the omnipresent receivers of spectacular messages fill the isolation with the ruling images – images that derive their full power precisely from that isolation. (Debord, 2009: 116)

There is certainly a feeling of drabness to images such as: 'Stopped at the Sappington Road intersection, by a Crestwood Plaza just lately closed for the night and tomorrow, drivers in neckties smile at other drivers in neckties, or do not, depending' (TS 264). Similarly, the expression of Barbara Probst's weekly routine as an enumeration enhances the sense of vapidity:

> In an average week she made five breakfasts, packed five lunches and cooked six dinners. She put a hundred miles on the car. She stared out windows for forty-five minutes. She ate lunch at restaurants three times. ... She spent six hours at retail stores, one hour in the shower. She slept fifty-one hours. She watched nine hours of television. (TS 89–90)

And Franzen leaves no doubt about the tedium that dominates the life of Luisa, the Probsts' teenage daughter: 'She [Luisa] had been bored in August, bored in September, and bored in October now, too' (TS 49). Even more, 'Depression is the challenge of the eighties,' proclaims a pop psychologist interviewed on St Louis radio station KSLX (TS 88). Actually, *ennui* seems to be the fate of the suburbs, according to Debord. For the French thinker, the destruction of urban environment and its replacement by a formless spread of semi-urban tissue 'governed by the imperatives of consumption' (Debord, 2009: 116) entails the creation of an artificial, ahistorical 'neopeasantry' which is totally alien to the traditional relations between country and city, and is characterized by a 'historically manufactured apathy'. For Debord, these pseudo-cities' motto could be: '*Nothing has ever happened here and nothing ever will.* The forces of *historical absence* have been able to create their own landscape because historical liberation, which must take place in the cities, has not yet occurred' (2009: 118).

Theodor Adorno has been concerned with boredom as a distinctive sign of bourgeois society. For him, 'unfreedom is gradually annexing "free time" and the majority of unfree people are as unaware of this process as they are of the unfreedom itself' (Adorno, 2001: 188). This is so because the pervading reification that is characteristic of the world of labour under capitalism has colonized the realm of 'free time', which has become just a continuation of other profit-oriented forms of social life (2001: 189). This circumstance has political implications, as Adorno relates boredom and apathy. Ultimately, what this kind of generalized dullness reveals is an induced and generalized impoverishment of the imagination which logically tends to prevent any socially transformative actions, as these are rendered not only unfeasible but even unthinkable. As we will see, Adorno's remarks seem particularly pertinent to *The Twenty-Seventh City*. As the theorist argues:

> Boredom is the reflection of objective dullness. As such it is in a similar position to political apathy. The most compelling reason for apathy is the by no means unjustified feeling of the masses that political participation within the sphere society grants them ... can alter their actual existence only minimally. Failing to discern the relevance of politics to their own interests, they retreat from all political activity. The well-founded or indeed neurotic feeling of powerlessness is intimately bound up with boredom: boredom is objective desperation. (Adorno, 2001: 192)

Indeed, the dreariness that pervades both city and suburbs, which is most clearly embodied in the characters of Barbara and Luisa Probst, has become so unbearable that it would seem that anything happening, even a nightmare, would come as a welcome relief. There is in the novel a perceptible 'hunger for the sheer event' (Jameson, 1991: 309) which recalls the mood identified by Jameson in Kafka's portrait of life under the bureaucracy of the Austro-Hungarian Empire.[5] A tacit longing for something to happen that goes beyond its characters and setting to stand for a deeper yearning in the culture – a vague, not well understood but generalized discontent that certainly carries a Utopian potential.[6] In the same way, there is also a parallelism between the novel's determined march into an increasingly darker territory, and what Jameson discerns in Kafka's embrace of the 'pleasures of the nightmare': an 'appropriation of the negative by a positive, indeed Utopian force that wraps itself in its wolf's clothing' (1991: 309). This Utopian longing for an event to come may be interpreted from the point of view of Badiou's philosophy. For the French thinker an Event is 'something that brings to light a possibility that was invisible or even unthinkable. ... It

---

[5] This correspondence is consistent with the parallel between the protagonist of Kafka's *The Trial* (1925), Joseph K., and Martin Probst who, suddenly and for no visible reason, is the victim of a conspiracy that seeks to ruin his life; an affinity acknowledged by Franzen in his interview with Burn (Burn, 2010: 53).

[6] As Žižek has remarked, 'In the developed West, frantic social activity conceals the basic sameness of global capitalism, the absence of an Event' (Žižek, 2002: 7).

indicates to us that a possibility exists that has been ignored' (Badiou and Tarby, 2013: 9). In this sense, the possibility of an organized political group taking control of the power structures of St Louis and its county, determined to radically modify them with the final aim of the common good would be such an Event, and it is precisely this possibility that is evoked by Franzen and left hovering for a considerable part of the novel. Of course, as we read on we learn that in fact such possibility never existed, which constitutes a conspicuous denial of the very Event that the novel had suggested, and a gesture whose ideological implications I discuss below.

Meanwhile, in the tedious wait for something to happen, money – its circulation – makes the novel's world go round. In this consumption-geared, automobile-based suburban environment, the substitute for the downtown is the mall. In *The Twenty-Seventh City*, an ailing, anxious Martin Probst visits Plaza Frontenac mall and is gradually soothed by his purchases: 'Buying, he was calming down' (TS 218).[7] This scene has a close precedent in DeLillo's *White Noise* (1985), where Professor Jack Gladney indulges in furious shopping after a dispiriting encounter at the mall with a colleague whose remarks undermine his self-esteem (DeLillo, 1986: 83–4). In both novels the fact of being recognized as the subject of an act of consumption is presented as the ultimate buttress for an individual's identity. It is capitalism itself which grants Jack Gladney and Martin Probst such identity. This way, in *White Noise*: 'I inserted my card, entered my secret code, tapped out my request. ... Waves of relief and gratitude flowed over me. The system had blessed my life. I felt its support and approval. ... I sensed that something of deep personal value, but not of money, not that at all, had been authenticated and confirmed' (DeLillo, 1986: 46).

In a similar way, *The Twenty-Seventh City* shows us Probst's signature, a token of his identity (in an insertion of actual handwriting amid the novel's printed text), as he signs his American Express purchase (TS 218). As Chip Lambert discerns in *The Corrections*, the only subject certified as valid by the system is the subject of consumption. The act of purchase (or that of electronically checking one's account as Gladney does for that matter) becomes then a ritual of ideological recognition of the kind described by Althusser (2008: 46), whereby we are granted our status as (*always already*) subjects. In this way, capitalism takes the place of the 'Unique and Absolute Subject' which *interpellates* individuals and thus constitutes them as

---

[7]In 'First City' there is a similar account of the soothing effect of consumption. In this article Franzen characterizes the mall as an opium den of sorts: 'For my part, I'm willing to admit to an almost physical craving for the comforts of the suburban mall. Natural opiates flood my neural receptors when I step from the parking lot into the airlock. Inside, the lightning is subdued, and every voice sounds far away ... I have cash in my wallet, my skin is white, and I feel utterly, utterly welcome. Is this a community? Is the reality artificial, or am I part of a genuine promenade? I don't know ... I'm too busy enjoying the rush of purchase to pay much attention' (HA: 190).

subjects. This Subject (with capital *S*) secures mutual recognition by means of a double mirror connection in which the subjects (with small *s*) *subject* themselves to the Subject where in turn they contemplate their own image (Althusser, 2008: 54). In obvious reference to post-structuralist views of the subject, Franzen goes one step further to suggest the precarious nature of such an identity, which for Probst seems to be destabilized, right as he stares at his signature, by the effects of a bad cold and increasing paranoia. It is also significant that, by means of the momentary presence of the excluded from society, both writers insert in the mentioned scenes a glimpse of the necessary obverse of the apparently smooth functioning of the system. In this way, Jack Gladney contemplates how 'a deranged person was escorted from the bank by two armed guards. The system was invisible, which made it all the more impressive, all the more disquieting to deal with' (DeLillo, 1986: 46). Similarly, Martin Probst shares a bench at the mall for a while with a disturbing old woman who seems to be mentally ill (TS 217). Two examples of what Althusser characterizes as those '*bad subjects* who on occasion provoke the intervention of one of the detachments of the (repressive) State apparatus' (Althusser, 2008: 55).

5 Visions of (second) nature: Songbirds and concrete

An inevitable side effect of consumption, and a lasting concern for Franzen, as shown not only in his novels but also in essays such as 'Scavenging' (1996, included in HA), is garbage. Paula Martín Salván (2009) has studied the prominent place occupied by rubbish in DeLillo's narrative, as one of the main tropes used by the novelist to explore our contemporary condition, much as a detective finds out about a family's habits by looking at their trash can. In Franzen's novels, garbage has a conspicuous presence mainly in two ways: as the industrial by-product of an economic activity which degrades the environment and endangers life (e.g. chemical waste in Boston in *Strong Motion*, radioactive cinderblocks in Lithuania in *The Corrections*); and, at a more domestic level, as the suffocating accumulation of useless junk that becomes a symbol of the enslavement entailed by consumption. Significantly, both Martin Probst (in *The Twenty-Seventh City*) and Alfred Lambert (in *The Corrections*) are relentless accumulators of trash, much to their wives' vexation: 'She [Barbara Probst] envisioned a life untyrannized by objects, a life in which she and Martin would be free to leave at any time and so by staying prove the choice was freely made' (TS 280).

Consumerism, suburban development and environmental damage are closely related in Franzen's novels. It is noticeable how the emptying of the inner city contrasts with the seemingly endless expansion of its suburbs, an ever farther-reaching pouring of concrete over former woodland that inevitably recalls the 'eclipse of nature' that, in Jameson's words (1991: 35), attends the expansion of late capitalism. *The Twenty-Seventh City* and also *Strong Motion* are novels where the characters may notice from time to time a metallic taste in the tongue; novels impregnated by 'the smell of infrastructure' (SM 191) which is a distinctive mark of the kind of environment that has become our actual nature. As Burn has noted (Burn 2008: 65), even Mohnwirbel, the Probsts' gardener, seems to spend most of his time raking concrete, instead of tending to nature (TS 87). To be sure, this bleak vision is consistent with *The Waste Land*'s theme. However, contrary to the Grail legend, in *The Twenty-Seventh City* no regeneration of nature can be discerned, and the 'Era of the Parking Lot' seems to be here for good. It is possible, nevertheless, to perceive a non-explicit Utopian element inscribed in the novel in the prospective, inevitable even if distant in time, regain by nature of the abandoned concrete foundations of the Westhaven development, just as large areas of cities such as Detroit or St Louis itself have been left to revert to nature as 'urban prairie' over the last decades. The possibility of nature taking over what was once its own is already suggested by the birds that colonize the empty downtown:

> No part of the city was deader than downtown. Here in the heart of St. Louis, in the lee of the whining all-night traffic on four expressways, was a wealth of parking spaces. Here sparrows bickered and pigeons ate. Here City Hall ... rose in two-dimensional splendor from a flat, vacant lot. The air on Market Street, the central thoroughfare, was wholesome. On either side of it you could hear the birds both singly and in chorus – it was like a meadow. It was like a backyard. (TS 7–8)

In fact, the novel does include an actual instance of land regained by nature in the former cornfields where Buzz Wismer built his atomic bomb refuge, a vast enclosure left untouched for many years over which nature holds sway again: 'The land was beautiful. Secondary growth, the scrub oak and cottonwood, sycamore and sassafras, hawthorn and sumac had crept from the safety of the ravines and vaulted, annually, ever farther into the old cornfields, converging and rising' (TS 155).[8]

Nature and its degradation will become major concerns in Franzen's subsequent novels, especially in *Strong Motion* and *Freedom*, gradually replacing the more specifically sociopolitical preoccupations of *The Twenty-Seventh City*. However, the dirge for a ravaged nature is already present here. There are references to the former inhabitants of the territory, the disappeared Cahokia people (TS 154), whose way of life in presumed

---

[8]A vast enclosure of land left solely to nature, untouched by human hands, is the objective of Walter Berglund's environmental project in *Freedom*.

harmony with nature contrasts with the current advance of asphalt. In Probst's dream, a fleeting bird overflies the expanse of concrete: 'A skin of rainwater covered the concrete, mirroring the blue sky, but the sky wasn't blue; it was the color of concrete. A purple bird flew across it, heckling and jeckling in its spiny tongue' (TS 143).

6 Suburban sprawl and the quest for orientation

The replacement of urban tissue by an amorphous suburban spread, no less monstrous in its own way than Smollet's city, has also entailed a high degree of homogenization, putting an end to the former autonomy of the provincial town. In Jameson's words, 'What was once a separate point in the map has become an imperceptible thickening in a continuum of identical products and standardized spaces from coast to coast' (Jameson, 1991: 281). This is a territory devoid of what Lynch termed 'imageability': the ability to evoke a strong mental image in an observer (Lynch, 1960: 9). This uniformity partly explains the constant need for cities to market themselves, emphasizing their difference from competitor cities by means of recognizable, iconic structures frequently assigned to celebrity architects, or generating (usually ephemeral) enthusiasm and media hype by means of contrived public celebrations – or pseudo-events – such as the St Louis Night promoted by Jammu in the novel. Real image is thus replaced by a spectacle of commodified images.[9] Even the very appointment of the young female police chief of Indian background is presented as a fresh form of attracting valuable attention to the city: 'Jammu became the star of a hitherto glamourless city' (TS 326). The bemoaning of reductive cultural homogenization has a longer tradition than what is usually acknowledged, as the case of Henry James exemplifies, but it has certainly become a distinctive contemporary complaint. In the *Boundary 2* interview, Franzen refers to this contemporary standardization: 'Things are neither Midwestern nor American anymore. It's all sort of mush. Things are neither urban nor rural, it's all exurban mush' (Connery and Franzen, 2009: 45). Hence the playful allusion to *Anna Karenina*: when Jammu's plan is apparently succeeding and the city seems on the path of prosperity again, 'St Louis was just another success story, happy in the one-dimensional way that all thriving cities are'.[10] For the novel, a genre which, as Henry James observed, feeds on 'manners, customs, usages, habits, forms',[11] cultural

---

[9]In Lefebvre's words, the city becomes 'an object of cultural consumption for tourists, for an estheticism, avid for spectacles and the picturesque' (Lefebvre, 1996: 148).

[10]See the famous beginning of Tolstoy's novel: 'All happy families resemble one another, but each unhappy family is unhappy in its own way'.

[11]See Ruland and Bradbury (1991: 213).

homogenization certainly means an impoverished soil. In the *Harper's* essay, Franzen famously laments this loss of diversity, which together with the widespread substitution of mere consumer complaints for true dramatic conflict he takes as signs of doom for the novel. It is remarkable nevertheless how Franzen manages to portrait that kind of conflict as arising out of sheer drabness and boredom, as exemplified by Barbara and Luisa Probst.

If cultural uniformity involves a loss of vitality for the novel, for the inhabitants of the city, on the other hand, the aftermath of the formlessness and lack of distinct and significant features of contemporary urban areas – environments which can no longer be made sense of – is of course a heightening of their alienation. Jameson, following Lynch, argues the necessity of regaining a sense of place in the city:

> Kevin Lynch taught us that the alienated city is above all a space in which people are unable to map (in their minds) either their own positions or the urban totality in which they find themselves. ... Disalienation in the traditional city, then, involves a practical reconquest of a sense of place and the construction or reconstruction of an articulated ensemble which can be retained in memory and which the individual subject can map and remap along the movements of mobile, alternative trajectories. (Jameson, 1991: 51)

As Jameson explains, Lynch's notion of a mental representation of the city may be taken as a spatial analogue of Althusser's famous redefinition of ideology as the imaginary representation of the subject's relationship to his or her real conditions of existence. As is known, Jameson has elaborated on Lynch's concept, extrapolating it to 'that mental plan of the social and global reality we all carry around in our heads in variously garbled forms' (Hardt and Weeks, 2000: 282): an aid to orientation in a multi-dimensional and constantly changing totality, the product of a set of aesthetic, theoretical and political practices known as cognitive mapping. Franzen seems intent on such a task in the novel. Not just because he provides us with an actual map of the city and its surroundings – which the reader is bound to often resort to along the novel – but also because he does try to map St Louis's power relations. Relations which he depicts as an obscure, unstable network of clientelism linking local businessmen and city officials, with the latter generally serving the interest of the former, to the extent that even respected leaders of the black community such as alderman Struthers are revealed as mere collectors of votes to feed the power schemes of the elite.

7 Conspiracy or the end of the public sphere

The notion, present throughout the novel, of power being in the hands of a clique is vividly dramatized, for example, in the meeting where the members of Municipal Growth discuss the financial and political consequences of a possible merger of the city and the county (TS 283–97). Franzen shows clearly how such association of local notables, together with its new competitor, Urban Hope, both supposedly devoted to promote the city's common good, are nothing but business lobbies intent on pursuing their own interest, which is more often than not the opposite of the city's. Franzen also takes advantage of the somewhat bizarre character of actually existing institutions, namely the Veiled Prophet of Khorassan,[12] to highlight the occultist configuration of power in the city: a shadowy, coterie-like circle whose power depends on the handling of privileged information. This kind of information is of course the constituent stuff of a conspiracy, and therefore the concern with information is constant throughout the novel: it is gathered by espionage, it is deciphered and interpreted by analysts, it is broadcast, conveniently manipulated, by the media, or ultimately, it is kept secret. And when secrecy is the means of access to power, the logical outcome is paranoia. Paranoia becomes the natural state of those excluded from the circle of information: 'Probst trusted no one. He had no knowledge of anyone's motives. How could he be central when he was so abysmally ill-informed? Was he uninformed *because* he was central? If so, then the conspiracy was working both ways, excluding him from the news and the news from him' (TS 216).

In the novel, St Louis is obviously a real city, presented with all the trappings of realistic referentiality, but it also becomes an ideal: the correlate of that realm of rational public intervention aimed at influencing executive decisions in matters of public consequence which was defined by Habermas in his classic study as *the public sphere* [*Öffentlichkeit*]: 'The bourgeois public sphere may be conceived above all as the sphere of private people come together as a public ... [a sphere] regulated from above against the public authorities themselves, to engage them in a debate over the general rules governing relations in the basically privatized but publicly relevant sphere of commodity exchange and social labor' (Habermas, 1991: 27).

For Habermas, this ambit of unmistakably bourgeois origin coalesced in the eighteenth century – approximately at the same time as the novel, another invention closely associated to the urban bourgeoisie. In fact, Habermas suggests that the appearance at that time of a relatively numerous reading public was a necessary condition for the development of what is now known as public opinion and the public sphere. As *The Twenty-Seventh City* shows, for Franzen this public realm has fallen prey to small, closed and unaccountable groups of interest which secretly manage public

---

[12]The Veiled Prophet Ball is an annual celebration established in St Louis in 1878 by the local elite in which a masked prominent citizen, elected by the secret society of the Veiled Prophet, presides over in such capacity, dressed in a sheikh-like garb. The ceremony has long been criticized on account of its secrecy and as a classist expression of social exclusion.

affairs for their own private benefit, while they manipulate public opinion and conceal information in order to obtain the public's passivity or support. If we follow Habermas' analysis of the disintegration of the public sphere in contemporary mass culture, we may observe that the public sphere is the concept where Franzen's concerns with politics, social fragmentation, the benumbing effect of consumerism and mass media and, not least of all, with the growing cultural irrelevance of the novel as famously expressed in the *Harper's* essay, all converge. The German philosopher attributes the undergoing dissolution of the public sphere to its commercialization, which brings about a mutual infiltration of the public and private spheres that distorts both, together with a widespread decrease in people's critical capacities which is the result of the loss of contact – also due to its dilution through commercialization – with the realm of literary experience which helped produce critical conscience in the first place. The decline of the public sphere and the decrease in numbers of the reading public are then two sides of the same process. In this sense, the closeness of Habermas' and Franzen's stances is remarkable. Similarly, in his 1998 essay 'Imperial Bedroom', cued by the way in which president Clinton's Lewinski affair became an all-important political issue in the United States, Franzen argues for the necessity of keeping the public and private spheres separated (included in HA).

The Twenty-Seventh City shows how the public debate concerning the administrative merging of the city and its county becomes a personalized choice between the charismatic images of chief Jammu and Martin Probst. We could argue then, using Debord's concept, that the public sphere has been replaced by an empty spectacle which conceals the fact that all the important decisions concerning public matters are taken outside the heed of the public, which is occasionally summoned to provide assent – in the novel's case, by means of a referendum – after pertinent informative and ideological manipulation. The real factors that are involved in the decision, such as the current transfer of capital and resources from the city to the county, or the intended speculative real state operation in inner St Louis never become apparent. As Habermas argues: 'The process of politically relevant exercise and equilibration of power now takes place directly between the private bureaucracies, special-interest associations, parties and public administration. The public as such is included only sporadically in this circuit of power, and even then is only brought in to contribute its acclamation' (Habermas, 1991: 176).

When the exercise of power takes place outside the public sphere, because the latter has become blurred and is in the process of disappearing, power itself turns into something arcane. In characteristically postmodernist fashion, Franzen's mapping of power gets fuzzy in a curious allegory coached in esoterically scientific language. Franzen proposes a Middle Ages – inspired, hierarchical division formed by three spheres in which power gets increasingly rarefied and enigmatic, going from the lower realm of basic regulations, such as traffic laws, and the second sphere ('mezzanine') of common politics and public opinion to the highest, celestial sphere where power is an elusive, incomprehensible entity akin to quantum particles: 'Call it power, call it plasma, call it cryogenic circuitry. Agencies, in any event, no longer obeyed constitutional dictates or the inertial tuggings of the policy dynamics, but flowed without resistance, the energy of reason but a corollary of the deep quantum mechanical numen and free to run backwards in time' (TS 328).

There is a certain inconsistence between this account of power as an elusive force which is characteristic of the Systems novel, and Franzen's previous, demystifying depiction of it in terms of ruthless pursuit of interest by an oligarchy which has taken control of public institutions for its own profit; an inconsistence which can be seen as part of the tension between the different novelistic paradigms that are represented in *The Twenty-Seventh City*. Of course, the choice of one or other concept of power would be crucial for the political import of the novel, but in this respect Franzen seems undecided. Different conceptualizations of the nature of power determine different requirements for viable agency and resistance. As Jameson has argued, certain apparently unassailable theoretical conceptions of power, such as Foucault's inescapable grid, actually work to fence off any attempt to come to grips with such power (Jameson, 1991: 5–6). In a similar way, although for opposite reasons, Franzen's vision of an intangible, indescribable power, which is seemingly subject to a sort of Heisenberg principle and defies the known laws of causality, also renders any kind of political agency very unlikely. Franzen's latter depiction of power could be described in Derridean terms as 'disseminated', and may be understood as a typically postmodernist extrapolation of the *undecidability* of the sign in post-structuralist linguistics – or of the intangibility of capital in modern financial products for that matter – but it could also be regarded as faulty cognitive mapping: an allegorical representation of an otherwise ungraspable reality, much in the same way as Medieval theology made use of allegory to represent a properly non-representable divinity. It would be a similar case to the popular postmodern motif of conspiracy, which forms the skeleton – the plot – that sustains the novel.

Conspiracy has been defined by Jameson as a substitute for an adequate mapping of an all too complex totality; a soothing imaginary tracing of the mysteries of an often incomprehensible reality to a single source of power, which explains its success in contemporary popular culture. *The Twenty-Seventh City* acknowledges this *pop* character of conspiracy theories with an often parodic enacting of the notion. The novel satirizes American fears of infiltration dating back to the post-war period, evinced by McCarthyism and thinly disguised in countless B-series science-fiction films of the era. For example, there is a deliberate inconsistence in the way the conspiratorial head, S. Jammu, is sometimes characterized as an uncannily omniscient female Fu Manchu, sometimes as a latter-day *femme fatale* intent on seducing the naïve Martin Probst, and some others as the typical overworked police officer with a messed-up private life of a Hollywood action thriller. Similarly, some of her methods reproduce those which are popularly attributed to certain governmental agencies, and are generally regarded as proper to what, especially since the inception of 1960s counter-culture, has been derogatorily called 'the system':

> Duane took it from her. 'Looks like a bug'.
> 'What?'
> 'A bug, don't you think? The FBI or somebody. This was always a student place. Maybe there used to be some radicals here.' (TS 276)

As the novel reflects, these fears evince generalized, deep anxieties of vulnerability which certainly read somewhat different in the post-9/11 era. It would seem that America's (mostly) triumphant history and global pre-eminence breed a particular propensity towards this kind of apprehension. In the 1980s, a decade which began with an intensification of Cold War on account of the setting up of atomic weapons in Europe by both superpowers, the defining dread is certainly nuclear annihilation. As Duane Thompson reflects in his diary: 'The whole world could die like a single person used to. That's what the nuclear age is: the objectification of the terror of total subjectivity. You know you can die any day. You know the world can die' (TS 272). Similarly, Buzz Wismer imagines nuclear warheads falling on St Louis (TS 360). Fear is indeed a constant presence in the city: from the fear of a nuclear war to the fright of the bombings by mysterious Native-American terrorists, fear of urban crime and 'fear of black areas' (TS 290). This fear of death or physical harm fuses in the novel with the secret dread of the wealthy for the security of their position. Therefore, Buzz Wismer's fear of nuclear destruction is not so distant from Luisa and Duane's fear of a flamboyant black youth at the Laundromat (TS 234); or from that of the KSLX's employees harassed by 'street people' (TS 483). Fear, and especially the propagation of a sense of emergency, has long been known to be an invaluable factor in the manipulation of public opinion by those in power. In this sense, with a vision strikingly anticipatory of the post-9/11 years, the novel presents how the panic created by alleged Native-American terrorists is used by chief Jammu to compel public assent for her heavy-hand policies. It also shows how our culture has long assumed the possibility of being killed in a terrorist attack as one more hazard in the contemporary *risk society* (Beck 1992) we inhabit. As the scene of the bombing of St Louis Arena during a baseball match vividly evinces, this is a concern that Franzen shares with Don DeLillo: a preoccupation with 'the iconic fears of the moment – trampling crowds, psychic unravelling, organized terror ... isolation and death', as Vince Passaro (1991, n.pg.) compellingly puts it in his discussion of DeLillo's *Mao II* (1991).

From a different point of view, in postmodernist novels, such as the ones by Pynchon and DeLillo which were so influential upon Franzen's work, conspiracy is also an instrument of metanarrative investigation. Salván has argued that conspiracy is a trope for all narrative activity (Salván, 2009: 55). The use of a plot/conspiracy always involves a reflection on the construction and organization of a narrative. Similarly, all interpretation of a narrative is in a sense a conspiracy theory which attempts to attain meaning through a reconstruction of events. In this way, the reader of *The Twenty-Seventh City* makes sense of the novel as she accompanies Colonel Norris trying to make sense of the conspiracy (TS 328–30). After all, narrative and conspiracy share a reassuring quality for the reader: both imply a fundamental assertion of the principle of causality and its capacity for bestowing meaning on events. In fact, as Brooks recognizes, clandestine schemes and machinations for the accomplishment of an objective understood as hostile to the establishment have certainly become a frequent organizing principle in modern narrative. They provide a driving force for the narrative and direct it to a closing. Since 'plots are not simply organizing structures, they are also intentional structures, goal-oriented and forward moving' (Brooks, 1992: 12), this kind of plot tends to require a certain closing, which is usually death. Thus, in DeLillo's *White Noise*, Jack Gladney reflects: 'All plots tend to move deathward. This is the nature of plots. Political plots, terrorist plots, lovers' plots, narrative plots' (DeLillo 1984: 26). In *The Twenty-Seventh City*, Barbara Probst is the clearest victim of this fatal tendency of plots, although her death does not actually close the novel, which is followed by an anticlimactic finale. Jammu, the plot's mastermind, does kill herself, attesting to its failure.

It is easy, however, to observe certain particularities in Franzen's use of conspiracy which differentiate it from classic postmodernist references. As was advanced above, rather than as an allegorical rendering of totality of the kind studied by Jameson, the novel's Indian cabal can be taken as a mere narrative device. It may be noticed that the mysterious workings of the system evoked by the classic use of conspiracy in postmodern cultural artefacts are mostly absent from the cabal's machinations: there is not much room for mystery since we are shown both sides of the conspiracy, that of the schemers and that of their victims, while in turn the curtain on its true motives and objectives is gradually lifted along the novel. For Franzen, conspiracy is here rather an instrument for his critical intentions. His 'large, externalized' plot (taking the term in two of its senses: a sequence of events and a hidden scheme), offers him the opportunity to cast his satiric look upon the widest possible spectrum of social, cultural and political spheres, addressing thus 'the sick society in need of total critique' (Antrim, 2001: n.pg.). The panopticon-like surveillance network set up by Jammu is a narrative means used by Franzen to pry into different quarters of St Louis – from bedrooms to power hubs – and in this way widen the scope of his vision in the novel. As such, the novel's conspiracy performs an analytic function, which is one of the main attributes of classic realism. If in much postmodernist fiction the conspiracy is a manifestation of *undecidability*, in *The Twenty-Seventh City* Franzen uses it to make us *listen* and *see*. This is confirmed by Franzen in his interview with Burn, where he recognizes his debt to Pynchon's *Gravity's Rainbow* (1973) but also recounts his intention, at the time of writing his first novel, to offer his own version of the conspiracy theme: 'I saw that I might be able to go beyond the unseen conspiracy to a *seen* conspiracy, inhabited by complicated characters with whom we might, moreover, sympathize' (Burn, 2010: 62). In a way, then, we could speak, paraphrasing Raymond Williams, of a *knowable* conspiracy, and one that is intended to increase the reader's social and political awareness.

8 The (non-)politics of irony: Agency and apathy

There are some interesting peculiarities as well in the conspiracy shown in the novel. Its sheer unlikeliness and the suspension of disbelief it requires are revealing of the difficulty of conceiving radical change in a contemporary American society which (as most Western societies) not only has lost trace of the relations of production but also the memories (or knowledge) of any other modes of production. Hawkins argues that choosing a foreign origin for the conspirators enables Franzen to 'render literal the xenophobia that is the byproduct of the exceptionalist nature of American nationalism' (Hawkins, 2010: 65). It seems more likely though that what the Indian origin of the plot really affords Franzen is the possibility of bringing forth a group of people who, following an old Mao's motto sometimes cited by Badiou, 'Dare to fight, dare to win', seem genuinely capable of transformative action, subversion, potentially revolution. It is significant that such people must come from the Third World, a locus which for a long time has evoked in the Western imagination, to use Jameson's term, a still unassimilated 'outside'. It seems hard indeed to conceive of any such capacity for agency as originating in an American soil that appears to be completely refractory to effective radical political movements. The (dubious) revolution will have to be imported then, smuggled in under suspicious certificates of verisimilitude, from what Žižek has called 'the mythical Other Place where the authentic happens ... and for which Western intellectuals have an inexhaustible need' (Žižek, 2008: 108). The system, however, will prove unassailable. The conspiracy fails mainly due to generalized, endemic apathy. In the novel, the only foreseeable event of consequence would be nuclear war, a possibility which does not seem to change the widespread torpor either, perhaps because after all an impending apocalypse renders any prospective change pointless. The novel ends with a suffocating atmosphere of stagnation which has earned Franzen hard-hitting criticism from otherwise perhaps not so distant ideological quarters (see Annesley 2006 or Hawkins 2010). In order to fully grasp the nature of this critical animosity, we need to briefly examine the novel's plot.

The Twenty-Seventh City is a novel in which a group of people, the Indian conspirators led by chief S. Jammu, are intent on carrying out a large-scale political and financial operation aimed at the reversion of the flow of capital from the increasingly derelict inner St Louis to the affluent municipalities of the surrounding St Louis County. This operation, involving the administrative merger of the city and the county and the subsequent redistribution of wealth via taxes and business relocation, is presented as reasonable and fair, a last chance for a city in a shambles. However, Franzen soon proceeds to undermine this apparently desirable move. We learn that the conspirators, former Marxists whose methods are rather iniquitous, are actually after spurious objectives: moneymaking by means of a large speculative operation involving real estate in the inner city. To make things worse, we are shown that the process is causing great social damage through gentrification and forced relocation to East St Louis. Finally, after a considerable build-up of expectation, the whole enterprise fails because people just cannot be bothered to vote on the referendum on the merger. The plot self-deconstructs, and the novel seems to collapse in what Hawkins has called 'an act of novelistic bath faith' (Hawkins, 2010: 67). Apathy reigns triumphant and any chances of intervention to change the status quo are rendered futile:

> America was outgrowing the age of action. ... With a maturity gained by bitter experience, the new America knew that certain struggles would not have the happy endings once dreamed of, but were doomed to perpetuate themselves, metaphorically foiling all attempts to resolve them. No matter how a region was structured, well-to-do white people were never going to permit their children to attend schools with dangerous black children. ... Taxes were bound to hit the unprivileged harder than the privileged. ... The world would either end in nuclear holocaust or else not end in a nuclear holocaust. ... All political platforms were identical in their inadequacy, their inability to alter the cosmic order. (TS 503–4)

This and the accompanying paragraphs, whose bitter pessimism as to the possibility of true progressive reform in an advanced industrial society seems inspired by Marcuse's classic *One-Dimensional Man* (1964), have caused dismay in Franzen's critics.[13] Hawkins deplores that the novel, instead of offering a prospect for change, 'extends an olive branch of irony to the reader,

---

[13]In *The Kraus Project*, Franzen recalls his interest, during his formative years, in the thinkers of the Frankfurt School (KP 226).

who is encouraged to join Franzen in shaking his or her head in mutual understanding of the nation's intractable awfulness' (Hawkins, 2010: 70). From a similar point of view, Hutchinson summarizes the novel's ending: 'Historical forces grind on, crushing all agency and resistance' (Hutchinson, 2009: 194), although it rather looks like it is the *end* of history what actually makes agency futile, as we argue below. At any rate, for Hutchinson the novel invokes 'a tired sense of defeatism' (Hutchinson, 2009: 192) and already shows the dominant political tone in Franzen's novels: 'one that both accepts and regrets the apparent draining of all possible resistance, conflict or meaningful difference. "Unideological" in this sense is not the true absence of ideology, but rather a complete surrender to the power of the prevailing ideology' (Hutchinson, 2009: 193). And he finally summarizes: 'although the novel's categorical and ethical reversals make it aesthetically pleasing, they compromise Franzen's professed project of writing a social novel that combines aesthetic achievement with progressive engagement, in that the work's subversive intent falls victim to a content that emphasizes capitulation and quietism' (Hutchinson, 2009: 194).

Hawkins and Hutchinson are representative of a current of academic criticism of Franzen informed by an ambivalent mixture of hopeful excitement at the possibility of a successful socially engaged novel, raised precisely by Franzen's work (more precisely by the success of *The Corrections* in 2001) and disappointment at what they regard as a failure in satisfactorily producing such a novel. It is then a judgement drawn upon Franzen by his own declared social preoccupations. At any rate, it is a criticism informed by a tacit Lukácsean view of what a socially critical novel should be like, to the point that its reproaches to Franzen's shortcomings powerfully recall the Hungarian critic's decry of Modernism in the 1950s. We have seen that for Lukács the ideology of Modernism 'asserts the unalterability of outward reality', while 'human activity is, a priori, rendered impotent and robbed of meaning' (Lukács, 2006a: 36). The result for Lukács is *angst*, the basic disposition informing Modernism. As an example, Lukács brings forth the mood of impotence and paralysis before unintelligible circumstances reflected in Kafka's *The Trial*. Hutchinson and Hawkins' demand of effective agency in the novel may be seen then as an unacknowledged Lukácsean requirement that the (realist) writer should select his materials so as to illustrate what's most *typical* of a certain historical time. And by 'typical', Lukács means, in Terry Eagleton's summarizing, 'those latent forces in any society which are from a Marxist viewpoint most historically significant and progressive, which lay bare the society's inner structure and dynamic' (Eagleton, 2002: 26). This view of course implies an at least questionable denial of any critical power to dystopian social pictures that do not offer effective instances of opposition to the state of affairs, and involves an equally contentious dismissal of any subversive or critical thrust that might lie in the expression of disgust, anxiety or angst.

At this point, it seems best to avoid moralizing judgements and try instead to ascertain whatever factors drive Franzen to undermine and ultimately deny the possibility of a change that he obviously regards as desirable, in an admittedly political novel written with the intention of 'bringing news to the mainstream' (HA 95). As Hawkins has noticed, the way in which the novel abruptly denies the possibilities of sociopolitical change that it has previously evoked is essentially ironic. This reversal may be seen in turn as determined by the pervading irony that permeates our postmodern culture and which has become a distinctive feature of much postmodernist fiction. In *A Poetics of Postmodernism* (1988), Linda Hutcheon celebrated the critical power of irony in postmodern art (including the distinctively postmodern form of fiction which she describes as historiographic metafiction), mostly deployed through what she identified as one of the most distinctive postmodernist modes: parody. For Hutcheon, parody involved an ironic rethinking of history which critically illuminated both past and present (Hutcheon, 1988: 39). From a different point of view, however, irony may be regarded in the first place as a symptom of the impossibility of achieving what Jameson has called 'critical distance' in current postmodern culture, of articulating a position of one's own outside 'the massive Being of capital' (Jameson, 1991: 48) from which to criticize it, in a system which furthermore seems to instantly reabsorb and disarm any radically critical intervention. Irony is then an acknowledgement of the inevitable, ineradicable ideological infection that one shares with everyone else.[14]

It is to be noticed that Hutcheon has later engaged in a much more nuanced exploration of the implications and potentialities of irony, one that acknowledges the inescapable pitfalls of its essential ambivalence. In *Irony's Edge: The Theory and Politics of Irony*, Hutcheon points at a 'transideological' nature of irony (Hutcheon, 1994: 10) which inevitably works to undercut the ironist's stance. Indeed, it seems clear that if irony does have an obvious subversive potential, it can also work as a powerful deterrent of engagement. As Moretti has put it,

A culture that pays tribute to multiple viewpoints, doubt and irony is also, by necessity, a culture of *indecision*. Irony's most typical feature is its ability to stop time, to question what has already been decided, or to re-examine already finished events in a different light. But it will never suggest what should be done: it can restraint action, but not encourage it. (Moretti, 2000: 121)

---

[14]Franzen's remarks in his *Boundary 2* interview seem to endorse this last view: 'I think irony is the cultural flip side of American supremacy. ... It's a fundamentally moral response to being a citizen of the crushing, hegemonic U.S. Like, how can you look in the mirror with all the privilege you have and all the power that is wielded around the world to sustain that privilege? Everyone's laughing about stuff here. Everything is real flip, real ironic' (Connery and Franzen, 2009: 40).

In his discussion of Franzen's fiction, Robert L. McLaughlin (2004) has brought to bear David Foster Wallace's essay 'E Unibus Pluram: Television and U.S. Fiction' (1997). In this piece, the novelist traces the origins of postmodernism in the United States back to a rebellion, by means of irony, against the hypocritical myth of America spread by television and advertising. However, Wallace explains, postmodern tools such as irony and self-referentiality were gradually co-opted by TV and have since become agents of despair and political paralysis, in a culture characterized by a weary cynicism:

> I want to convince you that irony, poker face silence, and fear of ridicule are distinctive of those features of contemporary U.S. culture (of which cutting-edge fiction is a part) that enjoy any significant relation to the television whose pretty hand has my generation by the throat. I'm going to argue that irony and ridicule are entertaining and effective, and that at the same time they are agents of great despair and stasis in U.S. culture, and that for the aspiring fictionist they pose terrifically vexing problems. (Wallace, 1997: 171)

As Wallace observes, not only is irony 'singularly unuseful when it comes to constructing anything to replace the hypocrisies it debunks' (1997: 183), but it also 'tyrannizes us' (1997: 183) posing the threat of ridicule over any proposition that presents itself as meaningful. Certainly, in a cynical environment, shedding one's shield of irony renders oneself vulnerable. In this sense, it is easy to relate the novel's general low emotional temperature with that pre-emptive power of irony. However, Wallace's suggested way beyond postmodernist sterile irony points in that way: a return to a plain, convinced treatment of human troubles and emotions, in defiance of the hip ironist's scorn. It is tempting to suggest that Franzen pre-emptively deconstructs the novel himself before he can be charged with naivety. In the same way, it may be argued that an important part of Franzen's narrative evolution after *The Twenty-Seventh City* has consisted of an ever more determined adoption of Wallace's injunction. In his 2002 essay for *The New Yorker*, 'Mr. Difficult', where he disavows the most self-referential trends in postmodernism, Franzen seems to acknowledge postmodern irony as a sort of defence mechanism: 'Indeed the essence of postmodernism is an adolescent fear of getting taken in, an adolescent conviction that all systems are phony. The theory is compelling, but as a way of life it's a recipe for hate. The child grows enormous but never grows up' (Franzen, 2002b: 111).

9 Systemic paralysis and Utopian drives

Together with the political ineffectiveness of irony, there's a quality in the lineage of postmodernist fiction in which *The Twenty-Seventh City* seeks to inscribe itself that works as well against the assertion of agency. In other words, there seems to be a problem with the chosen form. Jameson has shown how 'an already constituted "narrative paradigm" emits an ideological message of its own right without the mediation of authorial intervention' (Jameson, 2002: 73). In 'Mr. Difficult', Franzen refers to *The Twenty-Seventh City* as his 'own Systems novel of conspiracy and apocalypse'. Such a distinctively postmodernist genre was defined by Tom LeClair in his study of DeLillo's narrative *In the Loop* (1987) as a scientifically informed variety of fiction, strongly influenced by systems theory, distinctively concerned with the workings of 'the System', which is conceived as an intricate network of systems of all kind: economic, ideological, etc. As it is to be expected in an age obsessed with language, the ultimate model for any system is language itself, which in our post-structuralist era means of course a bottomless play of free-floating signifiers in which the referent is forever out of reach and subject positions always precarious. This implies the representation of an ultimately incomprehensible society which certainly, like Foucault's theorizing in its own way, makes little room for assertions of agency. In Hawkins' words:

> *The Twenty-Seventh City* is a Systems novel, a text that attempts to expose the workings of the System that is consumer capitalism, even as it reinforces the System's power by replicating many of its structures without submitting an alternative vision of human relations. In this way, the System looks all-consuming and inescapable except for those, such as the author himself, who have armed themselves with the theoretical tools capable of naming it and thereby withdrawing from it. (Hawkins, 2010: 65)

That theoretical knowledge may allow anyone to 'withdraw from the system' is a questionable proposition indeed. However, Hawkins' remarks on the Systems novel are pertinent inasmuch as they point to the fact that, as Jameson has frequently observed, successive advances in the systematization of totality may paradoxically lead to a feeling of impotence before the immense 'global system of domination and exploitation' (Hardt and Weeks, 2000: 24) formed by late capitalism. More specifically, he has called attention on 'the dangers of an emergent "synchronic" thought in which change and development are relegated to the marginalized category of the merely "diachronic"' (Jameson, 2002: 76). Jameson exemplifies the political implications of such a view with Baudrillard's suggestion of a 'total-system' concept of society which reduces all possibility of resistance to 'anarchist gestures, to the sole remaining protests of the wildcat strike, terrorism and death' (2002: 76). From a different point of view, Beck has examined the ethical implications of overplaying the concept of system, which ultimately amount to the dissolution of responsibility and agency. For the German sociologist, in a highly systemized environment, 'corresponding to the highly differentiated division of labor, there is a general complicity, and the complicity is matched by a general lack of responsibility. Everyone is cause *and* effect, and thus *non*-cause' (Beck, 1992: 33). As a consequence, 'one acts physically, without acting morally or politically. The generalized other – the system – acts within and through oneself' (1992: 33). Žižek, on his part, has related these circumstances with an abandonment of the Hegelian notion of *determinate negation* and the generalization of the 'wholly Other' as the Utopian prospect of overcoming the global techno-capitalist system. In his words:

> The idea is that, with the 'dialectic of Enlightenment' which tends towards the zero-point of the totally 'administered' society, one can no longer conceptualize breaking out of the deadly spiral of this dialectic by means of the classical Marxist notion according to which the New will emerge from the very contradictions of the present society, through its immanent self-overcoming: the impetus for such an overcoming can only come from an unmediated Outside. (Žižek, 2008: 337)

Such perceived deadlock may easily involve a certain feeling of despair which was surely not uncommon in a decade marked for its greater part by an escalation of Cold War (whose approaching end apparently no one seemed able to foresee), while conservative governments in different countries seemed intent on removing all previous legal restrains on capitalism. The collapse of the Soviet Union and its satellites, the great historical turn beginning in 1989, paradoxically only added to the generalized feeling of history coming to a halt which would be sang triumphantly by Fukuyama (1992) and others. An age characterized, in Jameson's words, by an 'inverted millenarism' (1991: 1) that predicates the end of politics, art or history itself. In 1988, some twenty years after his *Society of the Spectacle*, Debord sees the process of spectacular transformation of society as having achieved completion in the state of 'integrated spectacle', characterized by a complete destruction of history which suggests a closed future: 'The society whose modernization has reached the state of the integrated spectacle is characterized by the combined effect of five principal features: incessant technological renewal; integration of state and economy; generalized secrecy, unanswerable lies; an eternal present' (Debord, 1998: 11–12).

It seems likely that Debord would have received criticism similar than the one levelled at Franzen by critics such as Hawkins, Hutchinson or Annesley, as *The Twenty-Seventh City* obviously chimes in with such depressing pictures. Perhaps, however, it is time now to complicate the picture of the novel's disavowal of its own investment in the perspective of radical political change, by recalling the fact that it is not only the postmodernist genre of the Systems novel that is characterized by conceiving of the status quo as basically unchangeable. On the contrary, as critics such as Jameson and Eagleton have argued, realism is characterized by a distinctive kind of inherent conservatism which Jameson has described as an 'ontological commitment to the status quo as such' (Jameson, 2013: 145). For Jameson,

> realism requires a conviction as to the massive weight and persistence of the present as such, and an aesthetic need to avoid recognition of deep structural social change as such and of the deeper currents and contradictory tendencies within the social order. To posit the imminence of some thoroughgoing revolution in the social order itself is at once to disqualify those materials of the present which are the building blocks of narrative realism. (Jameson, 2013: 145)

From this point of view, the novel's final vision of social stasis would be in keeping with Franzen's realist leaning, and yet one cannot discount a postmodernist drive to provide a mimetic account of a postmodern society. Another important aspect that the critics mentioned above seem to overlook in their account of Franzen's fiction is that, as Jameson has consistently argued following Ernst Bloch, although our impoverished sense of history may atrophy our Utopian imagination, that is, our ability to envision future alternatives to the present, Utopian drives will inevitably find their way in every future-oriented elaboration, whether consciously or not, and most likely in disguise.[15] For Jameson, Utopian text is usually non-narrative and 'somehow without a subject position' (Hardt and Weeks, 2000: 384). Even more, there is always something to be learnt from the failure of Utopian thought, from the flaws and elusions of Utopian vision, since they may negatively define the limits of our imagination and representation abilities – which is to say our capacity to map the totality – as they are inevitably shaped by the present state of affairs. In Jameson's words, 'the best Utopias are those who fail the most comprehensively' making us then more aware of our mental and ideological imprisonment' (Jameson, 2007: xiii).

A great deal of Utopian impulse involves a desire for community and *truer* human relationships, which means an escape from the ruthless anomie and contingency imposed by capitalism, freedom from the tantalizing psychological dynamics of consumerism, and ultimately a liberation from the prison-house of ideology and the constraining slots into which it makes us fit. Such liberation is often symbolized by a different relation to a nature that used to be our other, but also a nurturing, mother. Such harmonic relationship with nature is inscribed in the novel by the allusions to the old Cahokia people. Likewise, in *The Twenty-Seventh City* we can find visions of nature reigning again over old cornfields and expanses of concrete. In the

---

[15]Marcuse (1964: 6) argues in the same way. For him, 'The more rational, productive, technical, and total the repressive administration of society becomes, the more *unimaginable* the ways by which the administered individuals might break their servitude and seize their own liberation' (my italics).

same way, nature is heralded by songbirds, which migrate of their own accord following natural rhythms and represent a realm still uncolonized by capitalism. This is also the case with certain spheres of the Third World evoked by the novel, such as the Indian Marxist circles of Jammu's youth. But if these longings for an outside are obviously palpable in the The Twenty-Seventh City, so are the anxieties that can also accompany the envisioning, even if disguised, of change: a fear of Utopia defined by Jameson as 'a thoroughgoing anxiety in the face of everything we stand to lose in the course of so momentous a transformation that – even in imagination – it can be thought to leave little intact of current passions, habits, practices and values' (Hardt and Weeks, 2000: 388). The fact that the possibility of nuclear warfare looms in the novel is also revealing, for what is apocalypse itself (be it nuclear or environmental), but the ultimate, global expression of the resistance to change of a system which will follow its set path to the end, rather than engaging in any effective self-questioning and rethinking? As Jameson has put it, 'It seems to be easier for us today to imagine the thoroughgoing deterioration of the earth and of nature than the breakdown of late capitalism; perhaps that is due to some weakness in our imagination' (Jameson, 1994: xii).

But the mechanisms of ideological resistance at work in the novel cannot conceal the fact that the corrupt, failed conspiracy of Jammu and her followers furnishes a flickering blueprint of the possibility of public officials acting as revolutionary leaders determinedly taking effective action in favour of the needy, deftly reversing the generally regarded as irresistible forces of capitalism, successfully fighting them with their own (financial) weapons. This is a prospect which would have hardly been acceptable in the novel, but rather would have been dismissed as wish-fulfilment, had it been textually dramatized in good faith. As Jameson argues apropos of Olaf Stapledon's novel The Last and the First Man (1968), 'At this point the expression of the Utopian impulse has come as close to reality as it can without turning into a conscious Utopian project' (Jameson, 2007: 8). To this Utopian charge, furthermore, we may add the implicit communitarian element that can be found in the topos of conspiracy, since even a criminal circle entails the creation of interpersonal bonds. After all, conspiracy etymologically means 'to breathe together'. To conspire is then to create a community: the community of those who share a whispered secret.

At this point, readers of the novel are likely to be wondering why a novel so ostensibly concerned with the workings of the system can dedicate so many of its most brilliant pages to a splendid dramatization of the problems of communication and disenchantment of an upper-class white family who live in Webster Groves. In The Political Unconscious (1981), Jameson declares that all narrative acts are symbolic acts which address an unsolvable social contradiction. It would be logical to add that they also seek to symbolically mend their author's ideological and psychological contradictions. Then it would make sense to ask what the novel is trying to do for its author with its 'swashbuckling, Pynchon-sized megaplot' (Antrim, 2001: n.pg.). To which question it could be answered that what the novel is trying to compensate for is the fact that it is a novel about an upper-class white family that lives in Webster Groves (and written to boot by a middle-class white writer who happened to grow up in Webster Groves). Previously we alluded to the difficulties inherent to the form chosen by Franzen for his novel, when it comes to articulating positions of resistance and effective agency. It is interesting, however, to inquire as to the available choices for Franzen to choose from, or, to put it other way, what is that which makes the postmodernist Systems novel the genre of choice for so many American white straight male novelists with social concerns. The answer is likely to be found in the current compartmentalization of an identity-based literary scene which turns around the margins, especially as regards sociopolitical criticism – those same margins, by the way, which according to Franzen form the last vestiges of vitality in 'the inner city of fiction'. It is plausible then that the difficulties involved in articulating a critical position of one's own in the middle of *mainstream America* are a factor that contributes to drive these writers' focus towards the system at large, a circumstance to which we shall return in the chapter dedicated to *The Corrections*.

10 Nostalgias of the industrial age

In any case, there is in *The Twenty-Seventh City* an undeniable vindication of the middle class that transpires in its characterization of the Probsts. Any objections as to Martin Probst's class affiliation in sight of his (self-assigned) hearty income of $190,000 a year should be dismissed in the face of his congenially drawn middle-class funny little ways. Probst is after all a self-made man, only one generational step removed from actual poverty, a firm believer in hands-on work with a built-in abhorrence of speculative operations possibly inherited from parental experiences previous to the Depression. But, as Jameson reminds us following Bakhtin, class discourse is essentially dialogical in structure and mostly antagonistic, so that 'the individual utterance or text is grasped as a symbolic move in an essentially polemic and strategic confrontation between the classes' (Jameson, 2002: 70–1). The antagonistic class in *The Twenty-Seventh City* is certainly an oligarchic upper class represented by actually rich, conspiring or contra-conspiring elements whose aristocratic debauchery – as in the case of Probst's brother-in-law Rolf Ripley – or whose politically reactionary stand – as in the case of Colonel Norris – contrast vividly with Probst's integrity and paternalist entrepreneurship.

Probst, the builder of the Arch, stands, like Alfred Lambert in *The Corrections*, or Walt Kowalski, Clint Eastwood's character in *Grand Torino*

(2008), for a classic tradition of American productiveness, of proud, solid, hands-on work which has all but vanished before the intangibility of modern financial industry.[16] In this sense, his symbolical identification with the city is apt enough, as both seem destined to irrelevance and decay in the elusive, speculative times of what Bauman (2000) has described as liquid modernity or light capitalism. It is surely not hard to perceive a certain authorial identification with Probst, which can also be interpreted as an expression of nostalgia for American industrial society, in Beck's sense of the term. Franzen seems to feel that the latter, in a way the golden age of the American middle class, was more promising community-wise than the ongoing phase of late capitalism in spite of the inescapable ideological and environmental contradictions it entailed and which the novel also shows. Indeed, in this respect there seems to be an irremediable ambivalence in Franzen's stance. There is a nostalgic yearning for a time in which American inner cities thrived and harboured vibrant communities, together with an idealized vision of the city as the agora-like actual site of the public sphere. In the following chapters we will observe how public utilities and infrastructure itself become a symbol of a planned, collective vision with obvious communitarian implications. However, Franzen is also aware that industrial society, the classic urban model, was no less dependent on social inequality than the present times are: the ghetto of East St Louis was not created by Jammu – it was already there for her to fill it with the human refuse of gentrification. In the same way, the novelist reflects that it is that same industrial society, or heavy modernity, in Bauman's expression, that initiated the unending expansion that has led to what Jameson describes as the abolition of Nature and the disappearance of the Outside: it is Probst himself, after all, who has covered in concrete enormous expanses of former woodland as part of the suburban expansion of St Louis County. Bauman has referred to the era Franzen seems to long for in the following oppressive terms:

> That part of history, now coming to its close, could be dubbed, for the lack of a better term, the era of *hardware*, or heavy modernity ... the epoch of weighty and ever more cumbersome machines, of the ever longer factory walls enclosing ever wider factory floors and ingesting ever more populous factory crews. ... To conquer space was the supreme goal – to grasp as much of it as one could hold, and to hold to it, marking it all over with the tangible tokens of possession and 'No trespassing' boards. (Bauman, 2000: 113–14)

---

[16]From a different point of view, it is significant that the three mentioned characters share a paternalist attitude towards women, as if attesting to the patriarchal quality of industrial society.

It turns out then that the seeds of what is lamented today lay within the past that one idealizes. We may notice a similar circumstance in *The Corrections*: when Franzen sets the solid, productive world of Alfred and Enid Lambert's youth against the evanescence of life under contemporary late capitalism as experienced by their offspring, it becomes apparent that the latter world is nothing but the product of the former. Franzen's nostalgias are then irremediably conflicted. Ultimately, what is highlighted is just the obvious point that postmodernity was contained in modernity. Last but not least, there is the unavoidable fact that Probst's paternalism is inseparable from the patriarchal character of industrial society. As Beck argues, industrial society is based upon a specific distribution of gender roles which, insofar as they are ascribed to the individual by birth, confers upon it a certain feudal character. For Beck, this distribution of roles between the sexes is 'both the *product* and the *foundation* of the industrial system, in the sense that wage labour *presupposes* housework, and that the spheres and forms of production and the family are separated and *created* in the nineteenth century' (Beck, 1992: 106). Needless to say, this separation of the spheres of production and family involves male ascendancy. This configuration of roles and its distinctive kind of antagonism between the sexes is visible in the Probst family. For Martin, home is the haven of well-earned tranquillity where to daily retire, always in command, after the exertions of an exhausting but comfortingly structured, reassuring world of work where a man can find 'the consolations of pure activity, pure work, the advancement of physical and organizational order' (TS 461). Not incidentally, if for Bauman classic modernity – a concept comparable to Beck's industrial society – was the era of hardware, here we see how Probst embodies such modernity by his own visualization as machinery:

> Of course, he could also see that for thirty years he'd worked too hard, could see himself in hindsight as a monstrosity with arms and hands the size of Volkswagens, legs folded like the treads of a bulldozer. ... He'd failed as a father and a husband. But if anyone had ever tried to tell him this he would have shouted them down, since the love he felt for Barbara and Luisa at the office had never waned. (TS 461)

In his longings, however, Probst seems again as outdated as the city itself. As Beck explains, reflexive (advanced) modernity and its dynamic of individuation do not stop 'at the gates of the family, marriage, parenthood and housework' (Beck, 1992: 106). Individuals are liberated from traditional forms as well as from ascribed roles 'in the search of "a life of their own"' (1992: 105). Thus, he ends up in baffled estrangement from his wife and daughter, who flee from the suffocating positions allocated to them in the realm of the family.

11 History, form and ideology

In Jameson's theory the conditions of possibility for realist or modernist praxis are historically determined, and are therefore not equally accessible for writers inhabiting different socio-historical circumstances. In the same way, certain forms of political and ideological resistance seem not to be readily available for Franzen, as resistance against the mainstream is always best deployed from the margins, which is especially true in a postmodern theoretical environment that tends to focus on the 'ex-centric' (see Hutcheon, 1988: 59). Realism, that long-standing way of investigating reality and using it to back up one form or agency or other, is another not easily accessible (not to mention disreputable) tool for a postmodern novelist. It is not just a question of 'Po-Mo machinery', it is that realism is certainly incompatible with a worldview informed by the notion that history has come to an end. Indeed, within that paradigm a Systems novel would be more *mimetic*. Without a sense of history there can be no 'perspective', a notion which for Lukács implied not only a social point of view but also a diachronic vision of evolutionary unfolding in history. Obviously, certain key elements of classic realism are absent here: Lukács' class consciousness has succumbed to social entropy; and Auerbach's 'social forces' pale in the face of the overriding, hegemonic force of capital. And what Balzac, for example, was bound to perceive as a merely contingent arrangement of the status quo, a temporary state in the flow of history, seems quite naturally to Franzen an intractable, elusive and consequently unassailable 'system'; not the least because, if 'our imaginations are hostages to our own mode of production' (Jameson, 2007: xiii), Balzac's contemporaneity with more than one of such modes is very different from our own total immersion in liquid modernity, to use Bauman's term. Jameson, always preoccupied with the ways in which specific socio-historical configurations determine the conditions of possibility for specific literary forms, provides us with valuable insight into two issues that are central to this study: the reasons – common to some of his contemporaries – behind Franzen's use of weird plot arrangements in *The Twenty-Seventh City* and *Strong Motion*; and the narrative way out which he finds in the latter novel to escape the ideological and literary deadlock of the former, namely the narrative structures of romance and melodrama. Already in 1971, the American critic argued in a way that is particularly relevant to the discussion of Franzen's narrative:

For the realistic mode of representation, the possibility of narration itself, is present only in those moments of history in which human life can be apprehended in terms of concrete, individual confrontations and dramas, in which some basic general truth of life can be told through the vehicle of the individual story, the individual plot. Yet such moments have become relatively rare in modern times: and there are others in which nothing real ever seems to happen, in which life is felt as waiting without end, perpetual frustration of the ideal (Flaubert); in which the only reality of human existence seems to be blind routine and the drudgery of daily work, forever the same day after day (Zola); in which, finally, the very possibility of events seems to have disappeared, and the writer seems relatively reconciled to a framework in which the truth of the single day can stand as the microcosm of life itself (Joyce). In these historical situations, even when the literary work itself seems violent and agitated, such explosions will turn out on closer inspection to be mere imitations of events, pseudoevents, imposed from above by the novelist, who despairs of evolving any genuine events from the colorless stream of experience itself. Indeed, melodrama (as in Zola) is one of the principal devices by which modern literature has sought to conceal its contradictions. (Jameson, 1974: 200–1)

These difficulties notwithstanding, it is evident that Franzen strives for historicity: he investigates the city's past; traces Martin Probst's background to Dust Bowl Oklahoma; and he even provides a substantial account of the personal background of the Indian plotters. There actually is a clear microcosmic quality to *The Twenty-Seventh City*, in that the sociopolitical and economic workings of St Louis are intended to be representative of those of the nation and indeed the wider world of Western capitalism, much in the same way as Baltimore is presented in David Simon's series *The Wire* (2002–8), another fictional artefact which relies on wiretapping both as a framing narrative device and as a way to show a certain perspective on social totality. Nevertheless, Franzen's attempt falls short of a Lukácsean synthesis in which characters are both individual and representative of the most significant features of a historical period. Furthermore, although we are shown the overall dynamics of St Louis's economy and we are informed of the unfairness of its social consequences, the actual narrative focus is as unevenly distributed as the city's wealth. It is not necessary, for example, to compare *The Twenty-Seventh City* to Eliot's *Middlemarch* to notice that, apart from the police chief, only one of the characters actually lives in the city that is the concern of the novel, namely RC White, the only significant black character in a novel about a mostly black city. He forms the only counterpoint to the wealthy suburbanites and conspirators who form the *dramatis personae* of the novel. Albeit in somewhat tepid scenes, we follow White through the novel, from his employment in menial jobs to his appointment as a police officer, and eventually witness his ouster from his house due to triumphant gentrification. This is something that tells *The Twenty-Seventh City* apart from the rest of Franzen's novels: we will not find a similar case of sustained concern with the fate of a lower or working-class character in Franzen's subsequent fiction, in which the perspective is exclusively upper middle class.

But there is yet another important circumstance related to realism that is exclusive to *The Twenty-Seventh City* within the whole of Franzen's novelistic production, namely the virtual absence of rhetorical strategies and proairetic schemata derived from genres such as romance, *Bildungsroman* or melodrama to *soften* the hard edge of realism or symbolically make up for unsolvable social contradictions, as is increasingly the case in Franzen's subsequent novels. Unlike in those novels, in *The Twenty-Seventh City* there are no individual perspectives of salvation, and no comforting retreat to the more manageable, small communities of family and lovers to compensate for the intractability of the system and the decomposition of the public sphere. On the contrary, the novel's central family, the Probsts, is as beset by disintegration as the city itself and their house ends up burnt to the ground. The end of the novel is marked not only by the failure of Jammu's plan to merge the county and the city due to generalized apathy and reluctance to change, but also by Barbara Probst's absurd death, Jammu's suicide, and Martin Probst's bewilderment at such a relentless display of pure contingency. These grim circumstances, which powerfully contrast with the Austen-like kind of epilogue that the rest of Franzen's novels end with, suggest a kind of hard core of realism in *The Twenty-Seventh City* which is diluted in Franzen's subsequent work. According to Eagleton, 'realism is calculated contingency' (Eagleton, 2005: 10). And, as the critic has put it elsewhere, 'you cannot marry everyone happily off in the last ten pages and claim that this is how life is' (Eagleton, 2003: n.pg.). Moretti has also identified unhappy endings as a distinctive feature of realism, which he discusses in terms especially relevant to our analysis of Franzen's novels:

> The identification of real and rational, of legality and legitimacy, so characteristic of the classical *Bildungsroman* and of Hegel philosophy of history, has fallen apart. Reality's essence lies not in embodying a society's professed values, but in its violent rejection and open derision of anyone who tries to realize them.
>
> This is why realistic narrative does not tolerate happy endings: these portray the harmony of values and events, while the new image of reality is based on their division. There must be no justice in this world: a realistic story must be *meaningless*, 'signifying nothing'. Even though it comes at the end, the unhappy ending proves here to be the rhetorico-ideological *foundation* of nineteenth-century realism: narrative verisimilitude itself is initially sacrificed by the compelling *need* of these novels to finish unhappily. (Moretti, 2000: 120)

In a way, this takes us to where we started, to that striking tension between two novelistic paradigms, the postmodernist and the realist, coinciding within the same novel. The first one is embodied in the chosen topic and form: the workings of late capitalism are explored through the typically postmodernist subgenre of the Systems novel. To the influence of that paradigm we can also ascribe the use of a conspiracy as a fundamental narrative resource. This is also the case of the pervading irony, an irony which we can describe as *structural*, since it may be perceived across different dimensions of the novel, such as the detached narrative voice, the tricky plot itself and its perplexing conclusion. At times, we can perceive as well a certain affinity with the linguistic experimentalism of the likes of William Gaddis and John Barth. Not least of all, there is an acute metalinguistic awareness and in general an evident influence of post-structuralist theory – a cornerstone for much postmodernist fiction, probably the narrative mode most clearly informed by critical theory – such as that of Derrida or Althusser. Not incidentally, a rejection of critical theory played an important part in Franzen's subsequent politico-literary disavowal. But set against this stance of postmodernist influence we find a decidedly referential impulse and – crucially – an explanatory vocation which is a sure mark of the realist novel. This is apparent in Franzen's interest in showing the mechanisms of different spheres of political and economic power in a St Louis which is representative of many other American and Western cities. But perhaps Franzen's referential intention is nowhere more evident than in the topographic quality of the novel, realized in abundant locale description and reinforced by the inclusion of an actual map. In this sense, the novelist honours a central aspect of the realist tradition which is the attempt to recreate a typically urban world perceived as actually existing in a synthetic, small-scale model-like way, in order to analyse it and thus make better sense of it. This takes Franzen's first novel close to what McLaughlin posits as 'the agenda of post-postmodernism' (McLaughlin, 2004: 67): the production of a socially engaged fiction that is theoretically aware enough to lay bare the language-based nature of many oppressive constructions, thus opening our eyes to the fact that other realities are possible. Be it as it may, the aforementioned strain between two different approaches to narrative that characterizes *The Twenty-Seventh City* will decrease visibly in Franzen's following novels. Certainly, it is still noticeable enough in *Strong Motion*, but I will have the opportunity to discuss how at the end of that novel Franzen introduces the crucial salvational elements around which he articulates his metanarrative. None of this is present here, but this does not mean that the novel is unrelated to Franzen's *conversion*. As Franzen argues in the *Harper's* essay, precisely writing this kind of fiction was a factor in the depression he underwent in the early 1990s, which in Franzen's metanarrative constitutes a fundamental source of justification for his act of political and literary recantation.

3

Strong Motion: Activism of the private sphere

Se querían de noche, cuando los perros hondos
laten bajo la tierra y los valles se estiran
como lomos arcaicos que se sienten repasados
VICENTE ALEIXANDRE

1 Introduction: Reassessing Franzen's disavowal

As it has already been advanced in this book, Franzen's career up to *The Corrections* is often viewed in the light of a well-established narrative mediated by Franzen's own account of his work in the *Harper's* essay and other pieces, and subsequently accepted by most critics after the attention-calling success of that novel. Such narrative is a sort of confessional story with obvious religious overtones redolent of the conversion to a new faith: that of character-focused realism. Within that critical framework, Franzen's second novel *Strong Motion* is seen as still a product of Franzen's old beliefs – a novel which is mainly intent on a postmodernist-influenced, 'systemic' sociopolitical critique on a grand scale. According to Franzen, in *Strong Motion* such critique was more radical and straightforward than in his first novel: 'this time, instead of sending my bombs in a Jiffy-Pak mailer of irony and understatement, as I had with The *Twenty-Seventh City*, I'd come out throwing rhetorical Molotov cocktails' (HA 62–3). This attempt, following common critical opinion, was carried out once again relying on one of those Pynchonesque 'externalized plots', at the expense of the deeper sphere of character and dramatic conflict. Such was the contention, for example, of Rebein (2007), one of the main promoters of 'the conversion view'. For Rebein, even though *Strong Motion*'s characters were 'more rounded' than those in Franzen's first novel, they were still trapped in 'the squirrel cage of his plot' (Rebein, 2007: 204). The critic goes as far as to claim that 'these characters exist for the sole purpose of turning the wheel of the plot' (2007: 214). A similar assumption seems to lie in James Wood's influential review of *The Corrections*, where he welcomes Franzen's third novel as 'a correction of DeLillo in favor of the human' (Wood, 2001a: n.pg.).

However, that view of Franzen's narrative is an oversimplification with important inconsistencies, which is perhaps not surprising since in most of the critical literature on Franzen to date *Strong Motion* has deserved but a passing account before turning to the study of *The Corrections*, the commonly agreed-upon landmark in Franzen's evolution towards realism. This neglect is certainly unfortunate, as the study of Franzen's work as a whole shows that virtually all the identifiable concerns that may be found in *The Corrections* and *Freedom*, together with some of the central themes of *Purity*, are already contained in *Strong Motion*. Indeed, in Franzen's second novel we can find the most significant political issues that will mark his subsequent fiction: the preoccupation with the environment, the exploration of the possibilities of activism, the despair of the public sphere and the globalizing scope. Similarly, the more *individual* issues that will be central in *The Corrections*, *Freedom* and *Purity* are also here: *Strong Motion* deals with themes that will be elaborated on in the subsequent novels, namely unhappiness and depression, the economy of family bonds (which is rather bleakly presented with *competition* as its fundamental driving force), and the pitfalls and promises of the relationships between the sexes. But perhaps the most relevant token of the significance of *Strong Motion* within Franzen's work is the fact that in it we are presented with the blueprint of an authorial rhetorical device of self-legitimation which, after the necessary cornerstone of the *Harper's* essay, will be re-enacted in *The Corrections* and, having then developed into a metanarrative, will achieve closure in *Freedom* – a metanarrative that I have called, drawing on Rebein's analysis, the narrative of conversion. This rhetorical strategy involves the escape from the insoluble ideological contradictions and political dead end arrived at in *The Twenty-Seventh City* by displacing them to what Habermas calls the intimate sphere, where, transformed into personal problems, they are susceptible of being worked out as individual perspectives of salvation are opened. This way, the end of *Strong Motion* suggests that all attempts to change an essentially unfair status quo are destined to fail before the intractability of the system, but the individual may be saved through self-amelioration, always after being taught humility by painful, sobering blows. In all subsequent novels, the salvation of the main characters from impending abysses of depression, loneliness, self-deception, entanglement in webs of corruption or sheer stupidity involves a sort of epiphanic recognition which is followed by a variety of acts of renunciation – to different kinds of pretension, pride, greed, sexual fantasy or intellectual radicalness – and the acceptance of what the individual finally perceives as his true self and the true nature of his relation to his closest others. The salvation process culminates with the individual's ethical and/or amorous commitment within the ambit of the intimate sphere, which opens the way to the possibility of happiness. This pattern is inaugurated in *Strong Motion* with the personal trajectory of Louis Holland and is confirmed by the vicissitudes of Chip Lambert in *The Corrections*, as well as those of the Berglunds – including their son Joey – in *Freedom*. In these novels, it becomes clear that these characters' individual stories strikingly resemble the confessional account provided by Franzen in the *Harper's* essay. In fact, in combination with the latter, these biographical narratives can be interpreted as so many acts of self-justification of Franzen's politico-literary decisions, in a trajectory which is inevitably marked by a publicly staged act of renunciation.

There is also an obvious problem with the common critical opinion that classifies *Strong Motion* together with *The Twenty-Seventh City* as Franzen's second postmodernist novel on account of the alleged weak making of its characters – constructions that are seen as all but a lame excuse for Franzen to launch his systemic critique. It is hard indeed to reconcile these views with the evidence of the novel devoting the greater part of its extension to develop and explore the personal conflicts of a small group of characters, and even harder in sight of the remarkable affinity of concerns that *Strong Motion* shares with prototypical realism.[1] What is true, nevertheless, is that Franzen's sociopolitical critique is here conveyed in a more external, arguably more obtrusive way than in his first novel. In *The Twenty-Seventh City*, the critical content was more evenly distributed and integrated in the plotline, paradoxically through the deployment of an unlikely conspiracy – a *plot* – which aimed to take control of the city's power hubs. This enabled Franzen to pry into a variety of domestic, political and economic quarters in a way that was incorporated in the structure of the novel. In contrast, *Strong Motion* relies on more obvious digressions which are in charge of the narrating voice or are assigned to the character of Bob Holland, a Marxist history professor, a political explicitness that earned Franzen harsh accusations of lecturing and sermonizing readers.[2] As regards the scope of Franzen's sociopolitical critique, we may succinctly advance here that the target is again on the economic, social and ideological workings of capitalism. It is worth noting nevertheless that if in his first novel Franzen focused on economics, politics and their interrelationship, here he diversifies

---

[1] In his interview with Burn, Franzen argues for the substantiality of the main characters in his first two novels. For him, it is only the minor ones that have a merely instrumental role: 'Going into my first two books, I did have several characters firmly stuck in my head, but many of the smaller characters were invented to serve the systems. Whereas, in my last two novels, the systems are there to serve the characters. There are lingering elements of the old method in *The Corrections*' (Burn, 2010: 63).

[2] See, for example, *The Entertainment Weekly*'s review: 'Franzen, however, finally succumbs to the American novelist's most irresistible temptation and mounts a pulpit' (Klepp, 1992: n.pg.). In similar terms, for *The Washington Post Book World*, Franzen 'indulge[s] himself in a small orgy of sermonizing' (Yardley, 1992: 3).

his critical strategies by openly addressing the environmental effects of our mode of production while bringing in as well the critical power of feminism and even postcolonial theory, if we may regard as such the novel's explicit discussion of the European colonization of North America.

The novel's plot itself, which revolves around the wrongdoing of a rogue corporation, is sure to have drawn upon it the charge of political crudeness, summarized with both irony and oversimplification by Josh Rubins in the title of his review for *The New York Times*: 'How Capitalism Causes Earthquakes' (Rubins 1992). This plot is worth summarizing here: Louis Holland, a twenty-three-year-old radio technician from Evanston, Illinois, relocates to Somerville, near Boston, to work at a financially troubled radio station. There he finds out that his mother has inherited 22 million dollars' worth of stock from Sweeting-Aldren, a large chemical concern. However, his mother mysteriously refuses to offer him any financial support. Subsequently, Louis meets and then moves in with Renée Seitchek, a thirty-year-old Harvard seismologist. Renée finds evidence suggesting that Sweeting-Aldren may be responsible for the chain of small earthquakes that have been taking place lately in the Greater Boston's area, since apparently the corporation has been getting rid of dangerous chemical waste by secretly pumping it down an injection well in Boston's vicinity. Louis leaves Renée after he is found by Lauren Bowles, a psychologically unstable girl from Houston, who had previously rejected him but now offers him her love. Renée, who is pregnant – a circumstance unknown to Louis – and in emotional turmoil, has her pregnancy terminated and is subsequently shot by either Sweeting-Aldren employees or anti-abortion militants (the novel is ambiguous about this circumstance). Learning of that, Louis comes back to Renée (being accepted by her) and devotes himself to assist her in her painful recovery. At the end of the novel, a stronger earthquake caused by Sweeting-Aldren practices produces dozens of casualties and important damage, although no executive from the company can be brought to justice.

It should be noticed that the first of the critical asides more obviously external to the plot only arrives after three hundred pages (an extravagant *excerpt* from a computer programme which claims to simulate the average American intelligence by means of 11,000 lines of software, a passage of obvious postmodernist, Systems novel-like filiation). It can be argued then that if *Strong Motion*'s 'Molotov cocktails' may appear as more intrusive than in Franzen's first novel it is precisely because they become readily noticeable next to what the reader perceives as the novel's main interest: the story of Louis Holland, Renée Seitchek and their troubled relationship to each other and their families. Against Rebein's opinion then, the novel's extensive social critique is rendered to some extent ancillary because of the very centrality achieved by its two troubled main characters. If *The Twenty-Seventh City* already pointed at Franzen's concern with the conflicts of Midwestern middle-class families, *Strong Motion* confirms this preoccupation as a fundamental theme in Franzen's work. Actually, Franzen's study of family and love relationships in his second novel prefigures the further examination that he carries out in his subsequent novels, and especially in *Freedom*, the novel with which *Strong Motion* shares perhaps the most concerns, as I discuss below.

2 Family affairs

The family that Franzen studies in his novels is, needless to say, a flawed, conflicted one. In *The Twenty-Seventh City*, the Probsts are afflicted by the (system-induced) apathy of a routine that leads to lack of communication and mutual understanding, but their troubles pale before the bitter estrangement between the next novel's young protagonists and their families. In the case of Louis and Renée, both families respond to a frequent pattern in Franzen's novels: the presence of a self-absorbed, non-nurturing mother and a withdrawn, ineffectual father. The motif of selfish parenthood was already present in *The Twenty-Seventh City* in the parents of Duane Thompson and it will return more clearly in *Freedom* for most of its main characters. In *Strong Motion,* it is evident in the case of Peter Stoorhuys, permanently angry at his dishonest father, an executive of Sweeting-Aldren, and at his acquiescent mother. The extreme case, however, of the damage that such parenting may inflict on children is represented in the novel by the emotionally disturbed Lauren Bowles, an adopted though paradoxically unwanted child.[3] For Louis and Renée, the result of their lack of adequate parental support is a perceptibly low self-esteem. This is evident in Louis going nowhere through menial jobs (always asking for 'minimum wage and no benefits' [SM 507]); while in the case of Renée it is disguised by her fierce competitiveness at her Harvard's department (Renée is in this respect a forerunner of Patty Berglund, competition being a central issue as well in *Freedom*). Low self-assurance also generates other lateral effects in the form of mechanisms of defence, such as Louis's obduracy, or Renée's self-righteousness and exaggerated pride. Both are angry people, prone to irate ranting. The feeling of worthlessness, in any case, is certainly a hindrance for the attainment of any form of happiness, and a crippling obstacle for the establishment of satisfactory human relationships, as the novel illustrates. Ultimately, it is the very doorway for depression, which is, as we know, another basic preoccupation in Franzen's narrative, again especially prominent in *Freedom*. In 'Why Bother?' Franzen acknowledges having been depressed during the early nineties, which suggests an autobiographical component in

---

[3]In *Freedom*, we can find several examples of characters psychologically damaged by bad parenting: Patty's best friend at college Eliza, Patty's aspiring actress sister Abigail and, of course, Patty herself. In *Purity*, this is obviously the case of Andreas Wolf.

Strong Motion. His remarks on the nature of depression are consistent with the rendering of Louis's ailing through the novel. From another point of view, he interestingly relates realism with anger and depression:

> Depression presents itself as a realism regarding the rottenness of the world in general and the rottenness of your life in particular. But realism is merely a mask from depression's actual essence, which is an overwhelming estrangement from humanity. The more persuaded you are of your unique access to the rottenness, the more afraid you become of engaging with the world; and the less you engage with the world, the more perfidiously happy-faced the rest of humanity seems for continuing to engage with it. (HA 87)[4]

Franzen draws a convenient analogy between realism and depression, both of them leading to a literary and vital dead end which he will transcend by means of the exhilaration of melodrama and the salvational perspectives of romance, as we will see. Be it as it may, *Strong Motion*'s emotional landscape seems overcast with lingering sadness, a sadness which has a reflection in the rather wearying urban environment that constitutes the main setting of the novel. For example, in Chapter 3, Louis argues with his mother over what he feels as a protracted unfairness and lack of support on her part and then he feels depressed, depression being, according to the narrating voice, 'an isotope of anger: slower and less fierce in its decay but chemically identical' (SM 58). It is noticeable how many of Franzen's adult characters are haunted by similarly unresolved conflicts with their parents, in such a way that they seem to get 'stuck' in childlike situations in all matters concerning their relationship with them, and then live a sort of perennial adolescence. Franzen implies a background of neglected infantile needs for these psychological problems involving low self-esteem and the compulsion to repeat unpleasant experiences, which is consistent with Freud's explanation in *Beyond the Pleasure Principle* (1920). This way, Franzen is starting a pattern of characterization that will be confirmed in his subsequent novels and will achieve central thematization in *Purity*. Significantly, there is a time for all of Franzen's important characters when, for a variety of reasons, they temporarily go back to their parents' house

---

[4]Depression reappears as a central issue in *Freedom* and, again, the relation between anger and depression deserves special attention. Thus, a Walter Berglund who seems to be modelled to a certain extent on the Franzen protagonist of the *Harper's* essay reflects on the apparently inextricable relation between anger and depression: 'He was aware of the intimate connection between anger and depression, aware that it was mentally unhealthy to be obsessed with apocalyptic scenarios, aware of how, in his case, the obsession was feeding on frustration with his wife and disappointment with his son' (*Freedom*, 315).

and sleep on their childhood's bed. For all of them, this coincides with a time of soul-searching and personal crisis.[5]

For Franzen there seems to be no escaping from family heritage in any way, and this way the novel introduces another of the themes that will remain constant in Franzen's subsequent fiction. Even though Franzen's embittered fictional children try to lead lives that are very different from their parents' lives, mostly by leaving the Midwest for the East Coast, the particular determinism of family never fails to track them down: 'A man hates in his wife those traits that he hates in her family; he hates the proof of how deeply the traits are rooted, how ineluctable heredity' (SM 388). Indeed, the weight of one's upbringing can become unbearable, as Renée realizes going through the memorabilia kept in her room at her parent's home: 'Even if I throw it away, it's like this tremendous weight of implication, which I can ever, ever, *ever* escape?' (SM 241). Family's imprint may be truly indelible, and Franzen's characters are often horrified to realize how they come to replicate those very traits and dispositions that they sourly resent in their parents. It is the case of Gary Lambert, Patty Berglund and, of course, Renée Seitchek: 'Meanwhile she was too selfconscious to fail to see the ironies: That even as she was being vigilant about not turning into a superficial person like her mother, she was spending huge amounts of time worrying about décor, clothes and cooking' (SM 269).

But the family is not the only source of pain for Franzen's young characters. The torments of peer pressure can also become acute, especially for such *uncool* characters as Louis and Renée. Teenage traumas account as well for the feeling of lingering adolescence over many of Franzen' characters. Accordingly, for example, the novel opens with the image of Louis being viciously beaten by another kid at his high school's gym, in contrast with the *popularity* enjoyed by his sister Eileen, much better-adjusted to meet familial and social demands. Louis is characterized by the distinctive kind of stoical endurance developed by neglected and socially unsuccessful children. Few images can evoke neglect and non-belonging as clearly as the sight of teenage Louis walking alone down endless suburban streets and roads which are obviously not meant to be walked: 'Even in the middle of a jammed and laughing back-seat she [Eileen] would glance out a window just in time to see her brother striding along the trashy shoulder of some six-lane suburban thoroughfare' (SM 4). Even his rather *uncool* interest in amateur radio, which is presented as an uncertain search across the radio waves for the resonance of a distant intelligible voice among the labyrinth of languages, suggests a lonely person seeking companionship in an incomprehensible world. In this sense, Louis's dubious search for companionship through radio

---

[5]In 'House for Sale', the opening piece for *The Discomfort Zone* (2006), Franzen shows himself in the same situation. Special poignancy is added by the reason of his visit to his parents' house: he is in charge of the sale of the now empty family residence after his mother's death.

frequency inevitably recalls Franzen's predication of a community of readers and writers – described as 'matching diasporas' (HA 89) in 'Why Bother'.

Both Louis and Renée show an obvious lack of social skills which is apparent, for example, in their clumsy ways at Eileen's party in Chapter 6. However, for all the pain their marginal position may entail, it also affords them a certain potential for critique and action that the more socially fortunate Luisa Probst and Duane Thompson do not even contemplate in Franzen's first novel. It could even be argued that, within such an acutely capitalist worldview as the American, Louis and Renée are truly subversive in their literally and notoriously not caring about money: Renée first destroys an advantageous contract with Louis's mother and later burns a check worth $600,000, while Louis is characterized by unfaltering austerity and lack of ambition. This circumstance recalls Franzen's praise of marginal literary characters in the *Harper's* essay: 'Since the making of money has always been of absolute centrality to the culture, and since the people who make a lot of it are seldom very interesting, the most memorable characters in U.S. fiction have tended to be socially marginal: Huck Finn and Janie Crawford, Hazel Motes and Tyron Slothrop' (HA 89–90).

It is difficult not to sense some nostalgia or yearning in Franzen's fondness for troubled adolescence as a novelistic subject. Not only are we informed of the characters' problematic teenage years, but we can see that unresolved problems of adolescence – concerning filial complaints, conflict among siblings or unsatisfactory social integration – still plague many of Franzen's adult characters: Louis and Renée, the younger Lamberts, Walter and Patty Berglund. It is possible to relate this fixation with Franzen's calling for romance. In this sense, Ian Duncan has identified in Dickens's vision of childhood in *Dombey and Son* (1848) a kind of manifesto for romance. For Duncan, the latter would be 'a mode of imagining in which desire is disconnected from "reason," that is, from an economy of definite objects endlessly attainable and exchangeable, for a pure receptivity of pleasure that seems to consist in the contemplation of an image of one's own simplicity and vulnerability in childhood' (Duncan, 1992: 250).

We have seen that, for Frye, romance is a kind of wish-fulfilment that aspires to transform the world of everyday life in an attempt to restore a lost Edenic state. If we accept this notion, we may wonder as to the specific characteristics of the Eden wished for by Franzen. The novelist has often referred to his current literary views as a sort of maturity or adulthood, but the cast of teenagers afflicted by the agonies of misfit adolescence, or else adults still stuck in the mesh of adolescent relationships which populate his novels suggest that, as Duncan predicates of Dickens's novel, that longed-for realm could be the uncomplicated world of childhood, a world yet untroubled by unsolvable social problems and vexing ideological contradictions. That would be a world lacking conflicts that refuse to be solved by means of well-meaning, scientifically enlightened thought and where one is free from the suspicion of occupying a place in a chain of oppression. A world where the young can attain the bliss of belonging to a small community right behind the back of the adult world. This is the world, in sum, from which Louisa Probst and Duane Thompson, Louis Holland and Renée Seitchek, or Huck Finn and Holden Caulfield for that matter, resist being expelled, unknowing that they have already been.

3 Geophysics of the Other

So far, it should be obvious that the relationship between Louis and Renée is one of the main concerns of the novel. Through their story Franzen conducts a rather unsentimental exploration of love relations. As in his subsequent novels, especially in *Freedom*, Franzen portraits love as a tectonic-like slow and painful process of accommodation of two radically different subjectivities, until they are finally driven together to an always unstable match by the forces of mutual need. In *Subjects of Desire*, Judith Butler discusses this necessity of the Other in the light of Hegel's *Phenomenology of the Spirit* and Lacan's thought in terms consistent with Franzen's view:

> The reflection of the subject in and through the Other is achieved through the process of reciprocal recognition, and this recognition proves to be – in the terms of that section – a satisfaction of desire. Our task is to understand the project of desire – the negation and assimilation of otherness and the concomitant expansion of the proper domain of the subject – in the encounter with another subject with a structurally identical set of aims. (Butler and Salih, 2004: 73)

According to Butler, the subject embarks in a narcissistic seek of recognition in the Other, as it discovers that implicit in its own identity as a desiring being is the necessity of being claimed by another. However, the project is full of traps and perils, since the Other is always a potential site of enslavement and engulfment for the subject. As if attesting to Lacan's famous (and scandalous) dictum *il n'y a pas de rapport sexuel* (Lacan, 1991: 134), at the beginning of their affair Louis suffers from the pangs of non-recognition:

> He wondered why he had to feel so alone when they made love, so alone with her pleasure as he propelled the long wave train that led to her satisfaction (on the green plotting screen in the computer room she'd shown him what a large and distant earthquake looked like as it registered on the department's digital seismograph. ...) It wasn't that they didn't fit together or come enough; it just seemed as if at no point, not even in this most typical of acts between sexes, did she ever present herself or give herself or even let him see her as a woman. (SM 209)

In order to escape this kind of trap, the subject proceeds to adopt what Hegel views as the role of the Lord, while the Other must in turn be reified to become a Bondman if the Lord is to prevail. The urge of the subject is actually to annihilate the Other that threatens the subject's identity but, since as we have seen this identity is already compromised in the Other, its destruction would wreck the subject's project. Domination then appears as a substitute for the death of the Other. This entails the obscuring of the sameness of the Other and of the mutual dependency that holds them together. This game certainly requires a dose of cruelty which the subject disguises both to the other and itself:

> He was perplexed by her stubbornness. He honestly believed that she'd be a happier person if she could loosen up a little; but all he got for his pains was the feeling that he was an odious Male. Of course, maybe he *was* an odious Male. The odious Male seeking control over a virtuous and difficult woman won't scruple to exploit whatever weakness he can find in her – her age, her mannerisms, her insecurity, and her loneliness above all. He can be as cowardly and cruel as he wants to as long as logic is on his side. And the woman, yielding to his logic, can do no more to save her pride than demand his fidelity. She says: 'You've humiliated me and won me now, so you'd better not hurt me.' But hurting her is precisely what the man is tempted to do, because now that she has yielded he feels contempt for her, and he also knows that if he hurts her she'll become virtuous and difficult again. ... These archetypes forced entry to the apartment on Pleasant Avenue like vulgar relatives. Louis wanted to turn them away, but it's not so easy to slam the door in your relatives' faces. (SM 194)

Of course, Louis does hurt Renée, leaving her for a younger, prettier girl. When Lauren finds him, Louis joins her as if compelled by an irresistible urge. It is partly the overwhelming impulse, shared by other Franzen's characters, to have an old debt from adolescence repaid. But there is also the titillating intoxication of domination and cruelty: 'He was aware of making a mistake, but he had no control. He was fascinated by the pain in Renée's face. He was finally seeing her. She was finally naked' (SM 215).

However, as Louis painfully discovers, maddening Lauren, troubled by psychic – also family-rooted – problems of her own, is not available for recognition; and when he learns that Renée has been shot almost to death he finds himself literally undone. These circumstances lead him to what Butler describes as an understanding of the Other as co-author of the self (Butler and Salih, 2004: 77), and even to abjectly reclaim a Bondman's role for himself. Louis then begins a process of atonement as Renée's caregiver during the recovery of her wounds, discovering a sense of purpose in being needed, finding the solace and strength provided by self-denial and sacrifice: [Three months ago] 'He would have sneered at a person who said that love could teach him ... patience and grace, and certainly at the person who said that love was a gold ring which if grasped carried you upward with a force comparable in strength to the forces of nature. But this is exactly what he felt now' (SM 486).

It is remarkable how often in Franzen's novels the yearned-for recognition of the self by the Other, the relentless need it seeks to satisfy in the encounter, ultimately boils down to the modest, but nonetheless indispensable reassurance of being needed. When confidence and self-esteem falter, we absolutely need to feel needed. However, the consolation obtained in such circumstances will always feel precarious. Indeed, the fear of otherness is still there for Louis, now literally at Renée's mercy: 'She wasn't someone he knew, this underweight woman with the hectic face and overgrown hair and wire-frame glasses. A deft change had been effected, and no fraud was involved – the woman was clearly who she seemed to be. She just wasn't the ghost made of memories and expectations that he had seen at breakfast' (SM 494).

Albeit reluctantly, Louis is finally accepted back by Renée, since after all her own need for recognition is also still there, even more demanding than before after the insecurity brought about by Louis's defection and the sequels of her wounds. As at the end of *Freedom*, there is room for a disenchanted kind of hope in the state arrived at by Louis and Renée at the end of the novel. It has taken painful upheavals, but finally Renée and especially Louis have reconciled with both the radical alterity of the Other and the power of that Other over the self. In such a state, as Butler argues, 'desire here loses its character as a purely consumptive activity and becomes characterized by the ambiguity of an exchange in which two self-consciousnesses affirm their respective autonomy (independence) and alienation (otherness)' (Butler and Salih, 2004: 77).

Strong Motion is perceptibly constructed upon a set of analogies relating the self and the earth. In this way, the ultimately non-cognizable character of the Other is invoked in the novel by the repeated allusions to seismic activity as a process 'not well understood' (e.g. SM 476). 'The science of earthquakes is a science of uncertainties', Renée acknowledges (SM 211). And just as scientists can never be wholeheartedly sure of what goes on under the surface of the earth (which, by the way, constitutes Sweeting-Aldren's line of defence to deny responsibility for the tremors), we can never be certain as to whatever processes are taking place in the other or, perhaps even more disquieting, under our own outer crust. Even our memory may be affected by seismic-like alterations in its configuration: 'Similar upheavals and subsidences were occurring in the landscape of his memory, familiar landmarks dropping out of sight, replaced by remembered scenes of a nature so radically different that he was almost surprised to realize that these things, too, had had a place in his life' (SM 180).

In this analogical system, a central symbolic part is played by the well drilled by Sweeting-Aldren. The well transcends the more obvious allusion to the environmental damage caused by industrial capitalism that may have made reviewers frown, to become a symbol of the self's relation to the other. The well was at first an oil exploration prospect, just as most initiatives upon the other seek to satisfy a subject's need. Subsequently, it comes to represent the channel for the destabilizing, unpredictable intrusion of the other into the self. An encroachment which cannot but cause inner commotions and rearrangements. Sweeting-Aldren's injection well becomes then a particular instance of what J. Hillis Miller has described as the *anastomosis* of human relations: the pervading linear imagery in the depiction of interpersonal connection which, according to Miller, is always implicitly sexual since, indeed, 'in one way or another it refers, however obscurely, to the act of coupling copulation' (Miller, 1992: 147). In the same way, linearity is also characteristic of the seismic waves produced by the inner tremors that accompany the confrontation with the other – tremors which for Louis, as we have seen, reach a peak during sexual interaction (SM 209). However, ultimately there seems to be little to be learnt from such personal upheavals, since the other must remain fundamentally unknown: 'You can make recordings of strong motion, though unfortunately everything's so complicated by the local geological context that it's hard to extract much information about the earthquake itself' (SM 184). And since the novel tends to adopt Louis's perspective in the presentation of his relation to Renée (a position of 'default gender' acknowledged in the title of its first section), in *Strong Motion* that unknown other is fundamentally female: the enigmatic target for male analytical discourse engaged in a debate in which women are denied a stake. 'Women, Science's Unknown,' as Luce Irigaray (1985) famously points out at the beginning of *Speculum of the Other Woman*.

Telluric analogies are also evident in the novel's depiction of sexual intercourse, that most evident site of encounter with the other. Sex, another battlefield for the subjugation and self-satisfaction struggles described above, is granted a central part in *Strong Motion*:

> Always it seemed to suit some obscure purpose of hers to have the two of them be the same sex, excitable through matching nerves and satiable through matching stimulation. Some principle of seduction, some acknowledging of difference was missing. And it seemed as if whenever she sensed that he felt an absence she started talking, in a voice orgasm-drunk and lulling – pro him, pro them, pro-sex. (SM 210)

Franzen also draws a parallelism between earthquakes and the personal upheavals that sexual intercourse may unleash: 'It was still dark when he woke up DR. RENÉE SEITCHEK, whose internal anatomy he imagined had been rearranged in the escalating violence of their union' (SM 133).

Similarly, as if in response to the conspicuous hunger for actual events that transpires in *The Twenty-Seventh City*, in *Strong Motion* the exhilaration produced by the experience of a tremor is more than once attributed orgasmic qualities. In this way, Renée recounts a seismic episode in terms that recall the 'cosmic libido' attributed to women by Hélène Cixous (Cixous, 1976: 889): 'That's exactly what this event was like. It was this *thing* coming across the mountains, this visible rolling wave, and then suddenly we were in it' (SM 133); or, in Bob Holland's explicit words, 'And just when I thought it was over, it all *intensified*, wonderful, wonderful, this final climax – Like she was coming! Like the whole earth was coming!' (SM 83)

4 Natural history and historical nature

In accordance with the novel's analogy between the earth and the self, its environmental concerns are matched by an obvious interest in the human body. Indeed, Franzen seems to revel unabashedly in corporeality. This interest is not only apparent in the novel's sex scenes, which are characterized by a matter-of-fact, ironic tone that is the result of the abrupt juxtaposition of the abstract and the explicit. Franzen's concern is also evident in his focus on Renée's physical pain and her wounded body that eventually comes to stand for the ravaged body of the earth. A body which, like Renée's, has been forced to barrenness by (male) iniquity. In this way, in the course of his process of atonement for the wound inflicted on her, Louis kisses Renée's geological, fault-like scars like a saintly penitent (SM 497). Physicality is also conspicuous in the presentation of Renée's abortion, also characterized by a grim, disturbing mixture of matter-of-factness and dark irony:

> The speculum was inserted; it said: 'This may pinch a little.' The tenaculum was applied, chloroprocaine hydrochloride administered by needle. With her slender, nimble fingers Dr. Wang tore the sterile paper wrapping from a 6-millimiter cannula.
> K-Y jelly applied. Vacuum cleaner activated, hose attached. In and out the cannula went. In and out, up and down. A revelation was the scraping sound it made. It wasn't a sound you expected from a body; it was the sound of an inanimate object, a trowel scraping the side of a plastic bucket, the last drops of milkshake being sucked from a waxed-paper cup. In and out the cannula went. Ruff, ruff, said the uterus. (SM 345–6)

The abortion is really the last straw for Renée, who during the last frantic weeks has had to endure the shock of Louis leaving her, the relentless harassment of anti-abortionists and the threats of Sweeting-Aldren employees. Outside the clinic after the operation, a shaken Renée addresses a crowd of protesters with a loudspeaker and acknowledges her abortion. Just as Cixous exhorts women to do, she defies discourse restrictions on women's speech in the male-dominated public space and makes an impassionate defence of women under such circumstances. Soon afterwards, she has a moment of mystic-like communion with nature on occasion of a thunderstorm:

> She thought she'd never breathed more beautiful air. She felt badness draining out of her. The weather, which was nature's, had taken over the green spaces and paved spaces between buildings. The air smelled of midsummer and late afternoon and love, and the temperature was so exactly the temperature of her skin that being in it was like being in nothing, or meeting no boundary between herself and the world. (SM 350)

Mysticism in women has been the concern of feminist theory, where it has sometimes been regarded as a sign of resistance to hegemonic male-oriented ideology. For critics such as Luce Irigaray (1985), the mystic experience amounts to an escape from the constraints imposed by male-dominated discourse; an expression of the yearning for an access to the self, the body and hence nature – of which the body is seen as a part – that is not mediated by the limiting, repressive structures of what Cixous has referred to as *phallogocentrism*.[6] This is not the place to examine the feasibility of such unmediated experience but, in any case, Renée's rationalist mind is not suited to mystic élan. Inevitably then, the episode must be short-lived, although apparently the longing for wholeness is bound to linger on: 'She wanted to embrace it all by breathing it, but she felt that she could never breathe deeply enough, just as sometimes she thought she could never be close enough physically to a person she loved' (SM 350).

In the identification of Renée's body with the earth, and her predicament with environmental damage, the novel seems to specifically address the concerns of ecofeminism, a heterogeneous intellectual movement which underscores the connections between women's subjection and environmental destruction. For ecofeminism, a trend which has been acquiring visible academic presence since the 1990s, both women and the environment suffer from oppression by Western patriarchal society. This movement also argues a special relation between women and nature which is founded on traditional interactions and holistic modes of thought that are considered typically feminine. For ecofeminists, this relation is repressed by a patriarchal ideology which relies on male-oriented concepts of logic and reason supporting a whole system of domination and exploitation. Allusions to this oppressive

---

[6]Renée Seitchek's experience has a strikingly similar precedent in the unnamed narrator of Margaret Atwood's *Surfacing* (1972). In this novel, after an accumulation of painful and stressing circumstances that also include a traumatic abortion, the narrator undertakes a process of withdrawal from social and ideological conventions which are seen as fundamentally repressive and sexist to gradually approach a state envisioned as of communion with nature.

form of discourse are explicit in an already discussed excerpt (SM 194). However, to limit Franzen's environmental views to this consonance with ecofeminist tenets, as Burn (2008) implies, is to offer an incomplete picture.[7] Indeed, from the analogy drawn in the novel between the earth and the female body we should not infer an actual endorsement of any essentialist or mystic-like positions such as those present in the ecofeminist movement, or more conspicuously in the Gaia theories advanced by James Lovelock. Rather, Franzen's use of these symbols is fundamentally aimed at the creation of an aesthetic resonance, a hermeneutic richness, as is the case with the play of parallelisms between *The Twenty-Seventh City* and T. S. Eliot's *The Waste Land*. Then, just as in his first novel, Franzen strived for historicity in his account of the decay of St Louis, in spite of the numerous allusions to the legend of the Grail; in *Strong Motion* he is also decidedly historical in his view of ecological transformation. In fact, it is easy to see the novel's mockery of New Age esoteric visions of nature, represented by the character of Rita Kernaghan and her followers, as a way of dismissing ahistorical approaches. In marked contrast, Franzen's approach to nature is consistent with Raymond Williams' views on the subject: 'A considerable part of what we call natural landscape ... is the product of human design and human labour, and in admiring it as natural it matters very much whether we suppress that fact of labour or acknowledge it' (Williams, 2005: 78). Franzen even seems to follow the British thinker in conceiving of economics and ecology as one single discipline, as Williams proposed (2005: 84). In any case, as Franzen declares in the acknowledgements to the novel, the environmental views expressed in *Strong Motion*, most explicitly in Chapter 13 through the speech of Bob Holland, are basically informed by the work of the environmental historian William Cronon. In his classic *Changes in the Land* (1983), Cronon analyses the way in which New England's environment and subsequently the rest of what was to become the United States were dramatically transformed by the new (capitalist) patterns of economic activity brought by European colonists. Cronon contrasts the different conceptions of property held by Native American and colonists, and their respective environmental effects. Contrary to what is usually believed, Cronon shows

---

[7] In his monograph, Burn pertinently identifies the affinities between ecofeminist positions and the novel's concerns. He is also right in noticing that the essentialism of ecofeminism – what he describes as 'the very neatness of the dualities outlined by ecofeminism' (Burn, 2008: 74) – matches very uneasily Franzen's more complex vision. For Burn, Franzen complicates the linearity of ecofeminism with his 'use of chaos theory and the systemic form of *Strong Motion*' (2008: 74). What Burn seems to overlook here is the key element of the *historicity* of Franzen's environmental approach and its political bearings. Probably more telling of Franzen's relation to feminism is his denunciation of the shallow portraits of women and disregard of women's concerns to be found in novels he otherwise admires, such as Joseph Heller's *Catch 22* (see 'Why Bother') or Pynchon's *Gravity's Rainbow*. In fact, as he explains in *The Kraus Project* (with perceptible antagonism), it was the realization of Pynchon's sexism that allowed Franzen to move out of his suffocating influence (see KP 178).

how before the arrival of the Europeans, Native Americans took an active part in changing and shaping New England's ecosystems to their benefit. However, being alien to the concept of property over the land, their use of it was characterized by communality and sustainability, in contrast with the system of ownership followed by exploitation until exhaustion practised by Europeans. As Raymond Williams puts it, 'Once we begin to speak of men mixing their labour with the earth, we are in a whole world of new relations between man and nature, and to separate natural history from social history becomes extremely problematic' (Williams, 2005: 76). Accordingly, Bob Holland's free indirect speech rendering of the story has an unsurprising Marxist character: it is the story of the transformation of New England's natural resources into private wealth by exploited labour. A tale, in short, of reification:

> If you'd look very closely, though, you would have seen that the wealth had merely been transformed and concentrated. All the beavers that had ever drawn breath in Franklin County, Massachusetts, had been transmuted into one solid-silver tea service in a parlor on Myrtle street in Boston. ... And when New England had been fully drained ... then the poor English farmers who had become poor American farmers flocked to the cities and became poor workers in the foundries and cotton mills that the holders of concentrated wealth were building to increase their income. (SM 381)

The character of Professor Holland also affords Franzen the opportunity to make a few points on the current condition of the political Left and certain ideological trends in American university quarters. Holland is part of what the rest of the faculty and students call 'the Old Drones', a rather unimportant group of Marxist professors forever nostalgic of the 1960s and wholly displaced from all academic decision making now. It is significant that the childishly rebellious Old Drones are an exclusively male bunch, and their marginalization is a telling sign of the current balance of power in American colleges. Be it as it may, Bob Holland's historic-environmental reflections are determinedly endorsed by the narrating voice. In this way, for example, Samuel Dennis' office in Boston is thus described: 'It was the terminus of various income streams rising in the mill towns ... and was the depot of old, old dollars: dollars with beaver blood on them (and mink blood and cod blood). ... Certainly a democratic nation's stock market made no distinction between old wealth and new' (SM 383).

Through chapter 13, similar disquisitions by the narrating voice are subtly juxtaposed and intertwined with Bob Holland's concurring explanations. This practice produces a conflation of narratorial and character speech which is noticeable through Franzen's novels. Bob Holland – a man for whom 'driving a car was an act of personal immorality' (SM 33), and a clear forerunner in his environmentalism of Walter Berglund in *Freedom* – extrapolates New England's unsustainable development to a world-wide scale economics. In this move, we notice Franzen's interest in global processes, which was already hinted at in *The Twenty-Seventh City* and was to be the object of much critical commentary upon publication of *The Corrections*. This interest may be best understood in the light of Franzen's formal evolution: if a fully-fledged realism must aspire to render a (however necessarily partial) view of totality in its Lukácsean sense, a global perspective is a logical objective: 'Look around. Look at our house, our car, our bank accounts, our clothes, our eating habits, our appliances. ... Even if you're not rich you're living in the red. Indebted to Malaysian textile workers and Korean circuit assemblers and Haitian sugarcane cutters who live six to a room ... indebted by proxy to Japanese and German bond investors' (SM 382).

As it may be readily observed, in this chapter the novel's critical arguments acquire a markedly discursive, 'external' character which contrasts with the more integrated – even if not strictly *verisimilar* – quality of *The Twenty-Seventh City*'s sociopolitical critique. Probably to make up for this discursiveness, Franzen opens the chapter, in true postmodern pastiche fashion, with a humorous passage in mock seventeenth-century English in which he parodies the classic description of New England offered by the English traveller William Wood in his *New England's Prospect* (1634). In this work, Wood laid the foundations for that enduring vision of New England as a fallen Eden that would haunt later writers such as Thoreau: 'The Countrey, according to the first Englishmen to see it, more resembled a boundless green *Parke* than a Wildernesse. From the rocky shores inland as farre as a man could journey in a week, there stretched a Forrest suche as teemed with Dere and Elke and Beares and Foxes' (SM 375).

It would seem that in *Strong Motion* Franzen's intention is to take full advantage of the standpoint provided by a decidedly historical kind of environmentalism in his indictment of capitalism, which is depicted as a system based on ruthless, unsustainable exploitation of both people and nature. Then, both environmentalism and feminism reveal themselves as usable critical tools to forge a way out of the apparent political deadlock arrived at by certain contemporary left-wing positions, a dead end which was so visibly invoked in *The Twenty-Seventh City*. In addition, it is interesting to notice how Franzen seems to strive for an *inclusive* depiction of nature, one that seeks to trace and reveal those areas of nature which our culture tends to obscure. Raymond Williams argued that the dominant vision of nature in our age is one of a realm that is separate from the human sphere. A perceived separation which is paradoxically the product of the endless, inextricable interaction with nature which characterizes the industrialized modern world (see Williams, 2005: 83).

As if to counter this pattern of estrangement and commodification of nature, Franzen not only draws parallelisms between the earth and the body, but is always ready to remind us of our adscription to the physical world. He also shows that what we usually conceive as 'natural' is actually the product of human activity, as his discussion of the transformation of New England's landscape clearly exemplifies. In the same way, Franzen is keen on showing that the thoroughly transformed environment we inhabit is governed by natural laws: springtime comes to Somerville and brings forth green sprouts in forgotten urban patches of lawn scattered over its surface of concrete and litter (SM 87). This hard face of the town, which by now has become its 'more indigenous ground cover' (SM 87), is described in a long, typically postmodernist enumeration of random pieces of rubbish uncovered by the thaw of winter snow (SM 88). This inventory of junk is – like the detailed account of the contents of the Gladneys' trash can in DeLillo's *White Noise* discussed above – ultimately a kind of medical sample, an analysis of social workings. And if this artificial environment has long become our true nature, it may logically lend itself to the use of the pathetic fallacy:

> There's a specific damp and melancholy ancient smell that comes out in Boston after sunset, when the weather is cool and windless. Convection skims it off the ecologically disrupted water of the Mystic and the Charles and the lakes. The shuttered mills and mothballed plants in Waltham leak it. It's the breath from the mouths of old tunnels, the spirit rising from piles of soot-dulled glass and the ballast of old railbeds, ... In a city where there is no land that has not been changed, this is the smell that has come to be primordial, the smell of the nature that has taken nature's place. Flowers still bloom, mown grass and falling snow still alter the air periodically. But their smells are superimposed; sentimental; younger than those patiently outlasting emanations from the undersides of bridges and the rubble of a thousand embankments ... the smell of infrastructure. (SM 191)

Money may not smell then, as the Latin saying attributed to Vespasian goes, but the accoutrements required for the accumulation of capital certainly do. However, under the filth of the images, it is possible to sense a note of sympathy for the decaying and abandoned pieces of infrastructure. Infrastructure is, after all, an expression of planned, collective vision perdurable in time and, as such, as Robbins (2007) has pointed out, it may stand for values of stability and community building that are currently being dissolved in advanced modernity, paradoxically under the anomie and the disintegrating forces that are inherent to the same capitalism that produced this same infrastructure in the first place. Here we find, again, Franzen's conflicted nostalgia for the industrial age: a tension between the sympathetic evocation of a communitarian dimension which was present in traditional industrial society and is perceived as lost in the world of late capitalism, and on the other hand the uneasy awareness of the environmental, social and ideological contradictions that used to characterize the previous phase of our mode of production.

5 The quest for truth in *Risikogesellschaft*

A frequent trait of Franzen's human habitats is their potential toxicity, which is made all the more disquieting because of the diffuse, uncertain quality of the threat. In his depiction of toxic menace, Franzen follows closely again the example of DeLillo's *White Noise* and its 'airborne toxic event'. DeLillo's novel contains one of the sharpest novelistic illustrations of Ulrich Beck's notion of contemporary society as *risk society*, as the following excerpt shows. Its influence on Franzen is apparent:

> They had to evacuate the grade school on Tuesday. Kids were getting headaches and eye irritations, tasting metal in their mouths. A teacher rolled on the floor and spoke foreign languages. No one knew what was wrong. Investigators said it could be the ventilating system, the paint or varnish, the foam insulation, the electrical insulation, the cafeteria food, the rays emitted by microcomputers, the asbestos fireproofing, the adhesive on shipping containers, the fumes from the chlorinated pool, or perhaps something deeper, finer-grained, more closely woven into the basic state of things. (DeLillo, 1986: 35)

Similarly, in *Strong Motion* we at first find mysterious spills of 'greenish effluent' (SM 91) and finally, like in DeLillo's novel, we discover a whole 'plume' escaping from the damaged facilities of Sweeting-Aldren, spreading chemical waste all over the surrounding residential areas, where it is also feared that the earthquake has caused a radioactive spill from the nearby nuclear plant (SM 465). All these events are answered by authorities with the deployment of fearful officials dressed in Mylar suits and a lack of information which naturally contributes to public alarm (SM 472). Significant of the prominence acquired in contemporary culture by the ever-present threat of toxic emergencies is the presence at Eileen's fancy-dress party of a guest clad in a Mylar suit.

The affinities between Franzen's social portrait and Beck's analysis are remarkable. For Beck, advanced modernity is defined by the pervading presence of risks which are the result of productive processes. Beck draws a fundamental distinction between contemporary risks and the different types of danger that have threatened human life in previous historical stages. As he argues, contemporary risks are *'hazards and insecurities introduced by modernization itself*. Risks, as opposed to older dangers, are consequences which relate to the threatening force of modernization and to its globalization of doubt. They are *politically reflexive'* (Beck, 1992: 21, italics in the original). One of the defining characteristics of the risks produced by modernization is that their identification, the assessment of their consequences and ultimately the political decisions concerning their legal definition and limitation are always dependent on scientific knowledge. This fact, far from warranting rationality in the management of risks, opens the door for unsolvable problems which are the product in the first place of the intractable difficulty of scientifically assessing the risks, which involves the impossibility of arriving at an indisputable scientific truth about them; secondly, of the opposite interests of the producers of risks and those affected by them; and finally of the crucial fact that science has ceased to be (if ever was) a universally accepted epistemological foundation for any political decision concerning risks. As Beck has argued, contemporary society is characterized by complete *scientization*, and in its unprecedented expansion science inevitably becomes *reflexive*, bringing about its own critique and eventually undermining itself as a foundational discourse. This is apparent in the novel when the accusative claims put forth against Sweeting-Aldren by Renée, drawn by means of science and presented in scientific discourse, are denied by other scientific quarters using the same type of language: 'Almost no one in seismology would absolutely guarantee that Boston had seen the last of strong motion. The sole exception was Mass Geostudy, a private research venture sponsored by the Army Corps of Engineers and the nuclear power industry' (SM 247). As Beck argues, science proves capable of being used to defend opposite views on the same issue, leading to what the German sociologist calls a *feudalization* of its cognitive practice (Beck, 1992: 168). The ensuing inconclusiveness produces a type of impasse that is all too familiar in advanced modernity and cannot but be in the benefit of the producers of risks. According to Beck (1992: 45–6), in the conflict between the producers of risks and those affected by them, the logic of wealth production tends to win, supported by an interested use of scientific discourse which denies or downplays the hazards.

Interestingly, in the novel Franzen draws a parallelism between toxic hazard and another great contemporary source of social risk and uncertainty: the job market, characterized by an ongoing decline of the value of labour and increasing insecurity. According to Beck, two fundamental axes of living of the industrial age, standardized wage labour and the nuclear family, are being dissolved in advanced modernity, losing thus their former protective functions. Beck defines this process as the transition from a system of standardized full employment to a system of flexible and pluralized unemployment (Beck, 1992: 140), a new, hazardous environment of 'employment by-products' (SM 146) which Louis is well acquainted with: 'To Louis, all the thousands of jobs listed in the paper seemed like noxious effluents that the companies were trying to pay people to get off their hands. ... He could feel their anger at the expense of disposing of all this garbage' (SM 146).

Significantly, set against these artificial, hazardous and for the most part decaying urban milieus, in Franzen's novels there is a recurrence of images, generally fleeting, of secluded landscapes unspoiled by human presence. This is clearly the case of the birdlife reserve planned by Walter Berglund in *Freedom*. In some cases, nature slowly regains the land that was conquered by humans. It is the case of Buzz Wismer's hunting enclosure in *The Twenty-Seventh City*, and it is also an implied potential destiny in that novel for much of what is occupied and built by humans, as I discuss in the previous chapter. Bob Holland himself, putative spokesman for Franzen's views in *Strong Motion*, has allowed his front and backyard to revert to original prairie state. Even if it is easy to charge Franzen with a measure of misanthropy here, such as the one displayed by Walter Berglund, it is also possible to identify a Utopian yearning. If, according to Jameson, late capitalism has been defined by an enormous expansion of capital and a colonization of previously un-commodified areas such as nature, the Third World or even the unconscious (Jameson, 1991: 36), if then there is no longer an outside from the being of capital, Franzen's penchant for intact, unpopulated or just plainly deserted spaces is an expression of the wish for such an outside. This comes to remind us once again of the *artificial* – that is, articulated by human beings – character of the concept of nature.

As in Franzen's first novel, but now much more explicitly, in *Strong Motion* Native Americans provide a model for a non-capitalist – and by the same token supposedly community-focused – way of relating to nature. These allusions can be inscribed in a central literary myth in American literature, whereby the first inhabitants of the continent have often been depicted as forming pastoral communities.[8] On his part, with his approach to nature, Franzen joins the literary lineage of Thoreau, whose *Walden* (1854) constituted a rejection of capitalistic exploitation of natural resources that has become central in subsequent critiques of capitalism in the American context. Franzen seems to be positing nature as a symbolic realm of transcendence where to escape from the pervading reification brought about by our mode of production. This, of course, takes us to Ralph Waldo Emerson and his Transcendentalist manifesto *Nature* (1836), where the natural world is sacralized as a manifestation of the divine. It is ultimately a Romantic affinity on Franzen's part which is evinced in the following passage by the faint echo of Wordsworth's *A Slumber Did My Spirit Seal*. This is Franzen's account of the consolation that Louis sometimes finds in nature for his persistent grief: 'He saw that as a material thing himself he was akin to rocks. The waves in the ocean, the rain that eroded mountains, and the sand that would form the next epoch's rocks would all survive

---

[8] A prominent early version of this view can be found in John Fenimore Cooper's series of novels known as the *Leatherstoking Tales* (1823–41).

him. ... He felt that, if nothing else, he could always anchor himself on the rocks in the world' (SM 504).

6 Urban novel and novelistic city

Like all of Franzen's novels, *Strong Motion* is concerned with the city and its problems. In the previous chapter I argued, following Jameson, that the configuration of contemporary culture is such that severely restricts the possibility of realism as an available form for the writer of fiction. The transformation of closely knit urban tissue into low-density, formless suburban environments that has characterized the advent of advanced modernity is certainly not unrelated to this difficulty. It is revealing of the intimate connection between the city and the realist novel that, once again, Franzen's dealing with urban issues brings about the crystallization of key aspects of his search for a contemporary realist vision. While the preoccupation with the city is not as centrally thematized as in *The Twenty-Seventh City*, it is significant that the opening of his second novel shows the same structure as that of the first one: the presentation of one of the central characters is followed by an account of the main, troubled urban setting: in this case the working-class, drab dormitory town of Somerville, near Boston. In consistence with the themes of barrenness and natural decay – mostly taken from Eliot's *The Waste Land* – that punctuate *The Twenty-Seventh City*, Somerville is referred to as a place which earlier in the century had been 'the most densely populated city in the country, a demographic feat achieved by spacing the street narrowly and dispensing with parks and front lawns' (SM 22). Indeed, the city's physical and spiritual estrangement from nature is underscored from the very outset: 'trees tended to be hidden behind houses or confined to square holes in the sidewalks where children tore their limbs off' (SM 22).

As nature disappears from the city, its dehumanizing quality becomes more apparent. Federico García Lorca once described his newcomer's impression of New York as 'geometry and anguish' (Lorca, 2002: 185). Similarly, almost in the way of Lorca's *Aurora de Nueva York*, Franzen's image of Boston's Commercial Street is that of the blind, reifying forces of capitalism: 'On Commercial Street there were a thousand windows, bleak and square unornamented windows reaching up as high as the eye cared to wander. ... It seemed as if the only glue that kept these walls and streets from collapsing, the only force preserving these clean and impenetrable and uninspired surfaces, was deeds and rents' (SM 19). And when the only force that binds society together is that of the 'cash nexus', the concept advanced by Carlyle and subsequently appropriated by Marx and Engels for *The Communist Manifesto*, unbearable isolation and loneliness in the city is the logical consequence: 'The walking and the cold air had numbed him to the point where the entire darkening city seemed like nothing but a hard projection of an individual's loneliness, a loneliness so deep it muted sounds – secretarial explanations, truck engines, even the straining woofers outside appliance stores – till he could hardly hear them' (SM 19).

Like Franzen's first novel, *Strong Motion* is also concerned with suburban life and, once again, his view of the suburbs is deeply ambivalent. On the one hand, we find the depressive picture of vapid, eventless tedium that was so present in *The Twenty-Seventh City*. Louis walks around the suburban Wesley Avenue at dusk looking for Renée's family house: 'Now the wind and the light had died, and Wesley Avenue was so deserted – the whole neighborhood so obviously empty of watchful human beings – that it seemed the day might as well had never happened, or at best should have gone in record books with an asterisk' (SM 365). But in *Strong Motion* there is also the distinct fondness of one for whom the suburb has also been a home and a playground. Again we find in Franzen's topographic renditions of the suburb a quality akin to Bachelard's notion of the bourgeois house as protective and nurturing of childhood. This certainly transpires in the nostalgic, affectionate depiction of the suburban houses as mothers who must helplessly see their now grown-up children leave. We can also notice, from another point of view, the inconsistency of the attribution to the suburb of a closer, almost Arcadian relation to nature – in marked contrast to the novel's depiction of Somerville – in spite of Franzen's usual decrying of the suburb's environmental unsustainability:

> Nature's appearance was inexpressibly benign here in the suburbs. She lay down and whispered like the warm surf between black-bottomed sea and parched land: between the scarred mourning woods, and the city where a new nature had taken nature's place. Lawns freely gave away their smell of grass and earth, lay comfortably naked beneath a sky that could be trusted. Each house was like a mother, silent, set back from the roads with windows lit, as an object always welcoming and sheltering, but as an object always betraying consciousness of the truth that children stop being children, that they'll leave and that an enclosure that welcomes and shelters will ache with their absence, will have ached all along because it's an object. (SM 450)

With this ambivalence in the rendering of the suburban life, which was already present in Franzen's first novel and will reappear in his subsequent fiction, Franzen dodges joining the populous ranks of (mostly male) white American novelists who have depicted the suburban experience in terms of alienation and abasement. In *White Diaspora*, Catherine Jurca has described this phenomenon – whose inaugurating landmark she identifies in Sinclair Lewis' *Babbitt* (1922) – as dishonestly presenting a 'model of middle-classness based counterintuitively, and indeed incredibly on the experience of victimization'

(Jurca, 2001: 6). For Jurca, this stance involves a fraudulent attempt to capitalize on the 'empowering rhetorics of victimization' (2001: 19), while it 'reinvents white flight as the persecution of those who flee, turns material advantages into artifacts of spiritual and cultural oppression, and sympathetically treats affluent house owners as the emotionally disposed' (2001: 9). According to Jurca's analysis then, such kind of novel performs a distinctive ideological function in sustaining the position of prominence of the American white middle class over other social groups. From another point of view, Franzen's ambivalence in his rendition of the suburbs may be understood in the light of Robert Beuka's study of the portrayal of the suburban landscape in American fiction and film. According to Beuka (2004), the depiction of suburban life in American culture has been characterized by a polarization between dystopian and utopian visions. Thus, we can find the familiar view of the suburbs as alienating strongholds of conformity and homogenization, but also visions of social perfectibility and utopian ideas of community and neighbourliness. For Beuka, such disparity of views is a consequence of the suburbs having acquired the status of what Foucault defined as 'heterotopias', that is, conceptual sites which every society produces and that act as mirrors of the culture. In Foucault's words, quoted by Beuka, heteropia is a 'kind of effectively enacted utopia in which the real sites, all the other sites that can be found within the culture, are simultaneously represented, contested and inverted' (Beuka, 2004: 7). For Beuka, in American culture the suburb 'emerges as a place that reflects both an idealized image of middle-class life and specific cultural anxieties about the very elements of society that threaten this image' (2004: 7). In this sense, while Franzen's vision of the suburban experience may not be wholly consistent, it does illuminate contemporary communitarian longings and concerns about social fragmentation, urban deterioration and environmental sustainability.

In any case, Franzen's undeniably inclusive approach to the urban is revealing of an analytical, explanatory intention applied to an amorphous contemporary reality of sprawl, decentring and disorientation. As Jameson has observed,

> Where the world system today tends toward one enormous urban system ... the very conception of the city itself and the classically urban loses its significance and no longer seems to offer any precisely limited objects of study, any specifically differentiated realities. Rather the urban becomes the social in general, and both constitute and lose themselves in a global that is not really their opposite either (as it was in the older dispensation) but something like their outer reach, their prolongation into a new kind of infinity. (Jameson, 1994: 28–9)

The novel provides us with a wide perspective of the varied urban settings existing in Greater Boston with a look especially alert to social contrast. If in *The Twenty-Seventh City*, the novelist's rendering of St Louis is mostly a picture of disintegration, in *Strong Motion* Franzen's vision of Boston and its vicinity is one of social inequality and pervading dirt which reflects the human and environmental effects of industrial capitalism. In this sense, in her comings and goings around Boston's area as she tries to uncover Sweeting-Aldren's conspiracy, Renée becomes a Balzacean *flâneureuse* of sorts, registering the different urban environments. For example, she walks down decaying areas in Peabody: 'She cruised the working people's neighborhood behind the bank building, past white bungalows nearing condemnation, through varying concentrations of acetone fumes, up and down all the streets that dead-ended against the high corporate fence with its sign saying ABSOLUTELY NO TRESPASSING' (SM 306).

As we have seen, Jameson has argued the contemporary necessity of regaining a sense of orientation in a multidimensional and constantly changing social totality which seems more overwhelming than ever, a procedure that he has termed 'cognitive mapping'. The American theorist built his contention as an extrapolation of Kevin Lynch's study of the psychological effect of urban organization and cityscapes, to which he incorporated Althusser's insight on ideology (Jameson, 1991: 51–4). In this orientational task, the novel has a crucial role. And even if the objectives of the mapping are ultimately global, the endeavour must be locally rooted or, even more precisely, urban focused: totality begins at home, and a global scope is inane without an understanding of local power configurations, as Franzen's first novel shows. Quite fittingly, then, in *The Twenty-Seventh City* Franzen includes a map of St Louis and its surrounding counties while in *Strong Motion*, Renée provides us with an actual bird's-eye view from a small plane in the course of her investigations of Sweeting-Aldren malfeasance: 'Proud mansions spread their green velvet skirts on land wedged between the old brick phalluses of industry and the newer plants. ... The most permeable of membranes separated a country club from acres of bone-colored slag. ... Everywhere wealth and filth were cheek by jowl' (SM 287).

Crucially, Renée's view highlights not only the contiguity but also the interconnectedness of the different spheres of production and consumption, of wealth and impoverishment. This attests to an aspiration to the rendering of social totality which is a distinctive mark of realism. Then, just as in Franzen's first novel the expansion of capital by means of real estate speculation in inner St Louis required the confinement in the ghetto of the city's poorest population, in *Strong Motion* the accumulation of wealth in some areas is shown to command the accretion of dirt and hardship elsewhere. In *The Twenty-Seventh City* St Louis County's prosperity was shown to require the ruin of the city. Similarly, in Franzen's second novel the gloss of the privileged seems to entail the tarnish of the less distinguished areas. Glitter and litter are thus seen as interdependent. From a related point of view, the rhetoric of emptiness which is so central in *The Twenty-Seventh*

City is also present here, accompanied again by a sympathetic lament for decaying industrial areas: 'Renée ... considered how the glassy wealth of downtown Boston required a counterweight in these industrial square miles, where vacant lots collected decaying windblown newsprint, and the side streets were cratered, and the workers had faces the nitrite red of Fenway Franks' (SM 316).

Therefore, what sets Franzen's rendering of the urban milieu apart from other contemporary urban visions which tend to focus on fragmentation and disjunction is his determination to trace connections between what otherwise would seem intractable myriad free-floating social and environmental circumstances. Without denying the reality of alienation, Franzen's vision is engaged in an attempt at making sense of the (urban) world which is heir to the interpretative efforts that Peter Brooks regards as characteristic of the nineteenth-century realist (urban) novel (Brooks, 2005: 132). Here it becomes apparent that Franzen's engagement with the Systems novel departs substantially from the postmodernist landmarks that defined the genre. In *Strong Motion* the rendering of the different systems informing contemporary society is not an overwhelming vision of *undecidability*, but rather an explanatory attempt with a political intention. In his interview with Burn, Franzen reflects on the particularity of his interpretation of the Systems novel: 'I had an idea of the social model that I didn't realize was already outmoded. I rather naively believed that, if I could capture the way large systems work, readers would understand their place in those systems better and make better political decisions' (Burn, 2010: 63). In this statement, Franzen seems to be addressing Jameson's concept of cognitive mapping, a notion which as we know involves the ascertaining of our own place in the mode of production and the demystification, to use Althusser's terms, of our imaginary representation of our relation to our real conditions of existence. It is significant that in a 2010 interview, Franzen considers such a goal for the novel 'outmoded'. In contrast, for Jameson the development of an aesthetic of cognitive mapping is a pressing necessity in the shifting world of late capitalism. We need 'a pedagogical political culture which seeks to endow the individual subject with some new heightened sense of its place in the global system' (Jameson, 1991: 54). For the critic, we are in need of new modes of representation which enable us 'to begin to grasp our positioning as individual and collective subjects and regain a capacity to act and struggle which is at present neutralized by our spatial as well as our social confusion' (1991: 54).

In contemporary attempts to interpret social totality, the element of the conspiracy occupies a central place, and this is also the case of Franzen's second novel. However, as in *The Twenty-Seventh City*, his use of it differs noticeably from that of the postmodernist writers who had influenced him. We have seen that in English the word 'plot' may refer to a conspiracy, a sequence of events and to a small, delimited piece of ground. It is then consistent that in Franzen's hands Sweeting-Aldren's plot becomes an essential framing device which demarcates the novel's materials and concerns, preventing thus the inherent risk of meaningless, amorphous spillage which always afflicts the genre (as well as, significantly, its historical partner: the city). At the same time, Renée's endeavour to unravel Sweeting-Aldren's conspiracy is symbolic of the novelist's – and the reader's, for that matter – undertaking in making sense of a seemingly incomprehensible social reality. In this sense, as if ironically endorsing Jameson's view of conspiracy theories as the poor man's substitute for an adequate cognitive mapping of totality, a jaded, Pynchonesque official at a rather grotesque Environmental Protection Agency's bureau lectures Renée on the exaggerated credibility generally granted to conspiracies, making for a metaliterary joke very much in postmodernist fashion: 'Malfeasance and conspiracy. I guess I used to think that way myself, a long, long time ago. It's very satisfying, very romantic. But 99.9 per cent of the time it's not the way the world really works. You might keep that in mind' (SM 256). The irony is complete when we learn that there *was* a conspiracy after all, but one whose rather mediocre originating motives were the incompetence of Sweeting-Aldren's geologist Anna Krasner and her sexual appeal for one of the company's executives.

In any case, as I argued in the previous chapter, any conspiracy theory is ultimately a theory of fiction, and Renée's quest for truth, her attempt to apply some principle of order to an apparently chaotic reality which is also 'not well understood', mirrors what used to be considered the essential task of the writer of fiction. An all but relinquished function which, according to Zygmunt Bauman, the disoriented inhabitants of postmodernity are in desperate need of:

> Postmodern discontents are born of freedom rather than of oppression. It is the other qualities of artistic fiction, those spelled out by Umberto Eco – the ability to simplify the baffling complexity, to select a finite set of acts and characters out of the endless multitude, to cut the infinite chaos of reality down to an intellectually manageable, comprehensible and apparently logical size, to present the discordant flow of happenings as a story with a readable plot – that seem cut to the measure of postmodern discontents: of the pains and sufferings of postmodern men and women, bewildered by the paucity of sense, porousness of borders, inconsistency of sequences, capriciousness of logic and frailty of authorities. (Bauman, 1997: 124)

It is easy to see that these remarks on fiction tacitly address a particular type of fiction known for its sense-making and order-imposing capacities which we call realist fiction. However, a close examination of these same arguments also reveals that realism is truly a *fiction* in the etymological sense of the word: an artifice based on ultimately arbitrary procedures of interpretation, selection and montage. There is no escaping the fact that, as Jameson argues, realism is both the most complex epistemological tool for the analysis of society and a very elaborate lie, the literary incarnation of false consciousness and the artistic expression of bourgeois ideology (see Hardt and Weeks, 2000: 179).

7 Agency and community: Liberals and radicals

In their denunciation of the weak vision of agency offered by Franzen, critics such as Hutchinson (2009) and Hawkins (2010) have focused on the final failure of the conspiracy's master plan in *The Twenty-Seventh City*, and in the apparently hopeless social apathy and resistance to change that the novel's ending asserts. But, as Jameson has claimed, failed Utopian thought provides valuable information as to the limits of our political imagination. Arguably then, in that novel the most interesting authorial statements on agency lies in the uncanny road set for it: a bizarre conspiracy of infiltrated Indian agents who try to take control of St Louis. In contrast, in *Strong Motion* the possibility of agency is more clearly affirmed, with a small group of relatively average young people decidedly opposing a powerful chemical corporation, constituting themselves in the process into a small political community whose motives are, unlike those of the Indian conspirators of Franzen's first novel, nothing but commendable.

On the other hand, as critics have not failed to remark, at the end of the novel the status quo remains basically untouched. Hutchinson, for one, has rightly noted: 'The status quo once more reasserts itself, not least because of widespread apathy. As in *The Twenty-Seventh City*, there is neither apocalypse nor revolution' (Hutchinson, 2009: 194). Indeed, there is a striking ambivalence as regards Renée's fighting of corporate wrongdoing: her attempt is genuinely brave, and Sweeting-Aldren is finally exposed, but the effort turns out to be all but useless in front of powerful socio-economic and ideological inertias. It has already been argued here that it is Louis and Renée's relatively marginal positions that allow them the possibility of a critical social perspective which was unavailable for the young characters in Franzen's first novel. However, their middle-class activism may hardly be described as really hard-hitting, and it is sometimes reminiscent of the harmless investigations undertaken by the characters of traditional children's fiction. It would seem as if middle-class rebellion against the state of affairs is likened to Peter Stoorhuys's revolt against his father: an always incomplete, impossible event. It is revealing that after denouncing the connivance of Peter's father with Sweeting-Aldren's malfeasance, Louis, Renée and Peter spend the day by the latter's swimming pool (SM 455).

It would be short-sighted, however, to limit the cause of the ineffectuality of the characters' activism to a lack of wholehearted commitment or their ineptitude in gathering significant social support to their cause. The problem is to be found in the unavoidable difficulty for the groups affected by risks in contemporary society – what Beck (1992: 48) calls 'commonalities of danger' – to articulate themselves into actual political subjects. Beck acknowledges that there is a political potential in socially recognized risks, especially in great disasters (1992: 24). However, these newly formed communities, which face the overwhelmingly pluralistic structure of interest groups, are often incomprehensible communities as a result of the incomprehensibility of the problem they arise in response to (1992: 48). According to the sociologist, in lieu of the strong political subjectivities of class society, such as the proletariat, in risk society there is only 'the victimization of all by more or less tangible massive dangers ... But can intangible, universal afflictions be organized politically at all?' (1992: 48–9). This entails an obvious impoverishment for emancipatory politics, even in the case that the opposing community achieves successful political articulation, to use Laclau and Mouffe's (2001) terminology. As Beck argues, 'in the transition from class to risk society, the *quality* of community begins to change' (1992: 49). While in class society the utopian motive force, the base of its value system, is *equality* in its different formulations (be it equal opportunities, socialism, welfare state, etc.), in risk society the basic aspiration and driving motive is *safety*. In this way, 'whereas the utopia of equality contains a wealth of substantial and *positive* goals of social change, the utopia of safety remains peculiarly *negative* and *defensive*. Basically, one is no longer concerned with attaining something "good," but rather with preventing the worst' (1992: 49).

This vision of a radical curtailment of emancipatory value in contemporary risk-related activism, which is also perceptible in Walter and Lalitha's environmental projects in *Freedom*, has a correspondence in the current predominance of what Badiou (2001) sees as a cult of negatively defined human rights. In the same way as in risk society people's ultimate goal becomes, in Beck's graphic expression, 'being spared from poisoning' (1992: 49), according to Badiou, in the contemporary climate dominated by the ethics of human rights the latter become just 'rights to non-evil: rights not to be offended or mistreated with respect to one's life, body or cultural identity' (Badiou, 2001: 9). In spite of its apparent self-evidence, the problem with this ethical vision of Kantian lineage is that its negative definition and its exclusive concern with victimization (in order to avoid or mitigate it) render it blind to any perspective of positive social transformation. As the French thinker puts it, this kind of ethics 'confirms the absence of any project, of any emancipatory politics, or any genuinely collective cause. By blocking, in the name of evil and of human rights, the way towards the positive prescription of possibilities ... it accepts the play of necessity as the objective basis for all judgements of value' (Badiou, 2001: 31–2). For Badiou, at the core, this ethics is actually nihilistic because it assumes that 'the only thing that can really happen to someone is death' (Badiou, 2001: 35).

But the group formed by Renée and her friends is not the only example of activism in *Strong Motion* – there is another instance which confirms the suspicion of collective, organized forms of political intervention that can be observed throughout Franzen's work. In this sense, the anti-abortionist sect led by Reverend Stites, which is clearly a political community, illustrates such distrust. In fact, Franzen's depiction of the congregation can be regarded as one more act of legitimation of his own politico-literary disavowal: as a disparaging portrait of a radical community it plays a part in the narrative of conversion.

The reverend's group grants its members the longed-for blessings of community, especially those concerning a sense of purpose and self-esteem. Noticeably, those categories appear in association to, or as a consequence of, wholehearted commitment to a cause. A member of the church tells Renée that 'the last five months had been the most meaningful and light-filled time she'd ever known' (SM 317). As Simon Critchley argues, Christian fundamentalism is one of the main ideologies that currently make up for what he sees as 'a motivational deficit at the heart of liberal democratic life' which afflicts contemporary societies where secular liberal democracy fails to motivate subjects sufficiently (Critchley, 2012: 7). It is significant that the members of the congregation, who live in a sort of commune in an abandoned building damaged by the earthquakes, relate to the risks that affect them – mostly that their dwelling should collapse – in a very different way than that of society in general: they sublimate fear into faith. As the reverend tells Renée: 'I can live without fear because I can feel how I'm hanging right over death, in the hands of God. If you get your life in balance with your death, you stop panicking. Life stops being just the status quo that you hope won't end for a long time' (SM 324).

At first sight, the encounter of Renée and the reverend seems a simple staging of the conflict, rather familiar in American contemporary culture, between the discourses of science and religion. But then it is striking to notice that Stites's critique of consumerist society is remarkably similar to the opinions expressed by the narrator in the final part of the novel, or to Franzen's own views as expressed in pieces such as the *Harper's* essay. Particularly noticeable is the resemblance with the bitter, misanthropic social view of Walter Berglund in *Freedom*, especially as regards a perceived fetishizing of the notions of happiness and liberty in the United States. For example, Stites argues:

'The human race has never been without suffering in its history, but Mr. Boston Globe and Mr. Massachusetts Senator are suddenly smarter than everybody else in human history. They're certain they've got the answer, and the answer is statutory this and statutory that and university studies of human behavior and the U.S. Constitution. But I tell you Renée, I tell you, the only reason anyone could possibly think the Constitution is the greatest invention in human history is that God gave America so many fantastic riches that even total idiocy could make a showing in the short run, if you don't count thirty million poor people and the systematic waste of all the riches God gave us and the fact that to most of the downtrodden people of the world the word America is synonymous with greed, weapons, and immorality'.

'And Freedom'.

'A code word for wealth and decadence. Believe me. What the majority of Russians think is great about America is McDonalds and VCRs. Only politicians and anchormen are stupid enough to act otherwise.' (SM 328)

We may also notice that the reverend criticizes the American conservatives in very much the same terms as Walter does in *Freedom*. It is interesting to note that so far Franzen still keeps, by means of the interposed figure of Stites, a critical distance with liberalism – a caution which is all but absent in his fourth novel, much more biased towards that political stance: 'Listen, liberalism's so dishonest it won't even admit that everything good about it, the supposed compassion at the center of it – which is irrational, mind you, just like all religion is – comes straight from the two-thousand-year tradition of Christianity. But at least it's got that compassion. ... The conservative side is just pure cynical economic self-interest' (SM 329). The passage is also interesting as it brings to the fore, probably against Franzen's conscious purpose, the complex and usually unacknowledged relation between liberalism and fundamentalism. According to Slavoj Žižek, fundamentalism is a product or, to be more precise, a *supplement* of liberalism. In his words:

Liberalism and fundamentalism form a 'totality', for their opposition is structured so that liberalism itself generates its opposite ... Liberalism is, in its very notion, 'parasitic', relying as it does on a presupposed network of communal values that it undermines in the course of its own development. Fundamentalism is a reaction – a false, mystificatory reaction of course – against a real flaw inherent within liberalism, and this is why fundamentalism is, over and again, generated by liberalism. (Žižek, 2009: 76–7)

But in spite of the obvious points of agreement between Stites and its author, the fact remains that the reverend's group is characterized by oppressive ideological indoctrination, dishonest propaganda, aggressive, intolerant methods and a narcissistic leader. And in the end, of course, the last earthquake reveals that the strength of its bonds was illusory and the congregation is disbanded. Again, as in *The Twenty-Seventh City*, the possibility of radical political action is evoked to be subsequently discarded as corrupt or otherwise inadequate and ultimately unviable. It is easy to feel that Stites's religious congregation stands for a radical political community, and that its inevitable failure prepares the ground for the disavowals to come in Franzen's succeeding work. This perception is supported by the evident points of coincidence between the reverend's and Franzen's own views. The implication would be that in organized radical politics good motives are inevitably superseded by a series of side effects such as the ones listed above which eventually end up ruining everything. Political communities are thus to be replaced by the smaller, core communities of family or lovers, where truth, to use Badiou's terminology, can still be generated. Ultimately, individual self-amelioration as that undertaken by Louis at the end of the novel is the only way. Salvation will be individual or not be at all. A related instance of this rejection of radical political action may be found in the somewhat embarrassed distance with which Franzen recounts a day spent with a group of young socialists protesting in Washington, on occasion of George W. Bush's re-election, in his journalistic essay 'Inauguration Day' (included in HA).

Undeniably, these rhetorical strategies imply some degree of retreat from the political and the social, as has been pointed out by Green (2005) and subsequently deplored by left-leaning critics. We should consider here the ideological limitations imposed by Franzen's available range of formal choices. On the one hand, there is the inherently static Systems novel which, as we have seen, tends to produce undecidable or inescapable networks of power. On the other hand, there is Franzen's evident inclination to realism. But we have seen that the realist novel has ideological bearings of its own. As critics such as Eagleton or Jameson have claimed, realism has a stake in the solidity of what exists which has obvious political implications. In particular, being the social form it is, realism has a vested interest in the stability of the society it seeks to reflect. This is the inherent ontological conservativism of the realist novel I have discussed in my analysis of *The Twenty-Seventh City*. It turns out then that Franzen is being nothing but *realist* in his pessimistic examination of the possibilities for transformative action in the uneventful times attending the alleged end of history. In any case, what makes Franzen's narrative vision in *The Twenty-Seventh City* and *Strong Motion* unique in contemporary American fiction is precisely this tension between intention and form. We know, however, that at the end of his second novel the tension will be resolved by means of the salvational perspectives of romance. The ending of *Strong Motion* stages a renunciation to the insights of radical critical theory and an embracement of the powers of the novel as a symbolic problem-solving device – both in the social and psychological realms – with a favouring of sympathy as the all-important foundation of the novelistic genre.

What is then the actual political significance of *Strong Motion* and to what extent does it deviate from that of Franzen's first novel? We may notice that the failure of the small group of activists to make any significant impact in the status quo, especially after bringing to light the outrageous workings of Sweeting-Aldren, inevitably arises a feeling of frustration, not unlike the despair of society which is the ending note of *The Twenty-Seventh City*. As the bitter last chapter of the novel seems to ask, what are the real chances of subverting a system that reaches farther than ever, is characterized by endless powers of co-optation and is constantly fed by ever-bigger ideological machinery? It is difficult not to attribute a symbolic compensational character, in Jameson's sense of the term, to the novel's great event, the final earthquake that brings destruction and considerable distress to Boston's metropolitan area. The final tremor is the obvious symbol of Franzen's intention: shake people out of their ideological torpor and open their eyes to the oppressive reality of corporate capitalism. It is significant that both of Franzen's early novels rely on rather far-fetched events to set their narratives in motion and direct them towards a closing. It tells us in the first place that social novels seem to require substantial events to organize their materials and their perspective while providing a source of narrative interest. It is also revealing of the difficulty of imagining such events in contemporary bourgeois society. Rachel Bowlby reminds us that in the nineteenth-century English industrial novel of writers such as Dickens and Gaskell 'the necessary "event" within an otherwise repetitive routine is typically provided by a strike that has the effect of exacerbating and personalizing the underlying class tensions' (Bowlby, 2010: xvi–xvii). Franzen's earthquake is his way of both getting the narrative going and pointing to the ideological, economic and environmental contradictions of his time – an attempt which is constrained on the one hand by the generalized *post-industrial* worldview (in Daniel Bell's sense of the term) in which Franzen in his own way also partakes, and by the novelist's rather limited social perspective on the other.

The aftermath of the earthquake, in its sheer altering of the normal order of things, imbues Louis with an acute sense of unreality: the tremor has performed what in formalist terms we may call a *defamiliarization* of a reality which we usually take for granted uncritically, questioning and challenging common assumptions. For one, it has brought death, which is usually hidden in our society, to the foreground. Now, for Louis, the sight of a dead man by the road makes for 'an image as unreal as everything else about this earthquake, as unreal as war reportage or assassination footage on television, except that unreality wasn't quite the word either for what he'd felt there ... surrounded by aftermath and wondering why he lived and what a world that encompassed death was really made of. The word was mystery' (SM 468–9).[9]

---

[9] The allusion to 'mystery' recalls Franzen's mention in 'Why Bother' of Flannery O'Connor's remarks on the purpose of fiction: 'Flannery O'Connor ... insisted that the "business of Fiction" is "to embody mystery with manners."' Franzen then defines this 'mystery' as 'how human beings avoid or confront the meaning of existence' (HA 68).

However, Franzen seems to acknowledge, the estranging capacity of the earthquake is bound to be short-lived as it is quickly assimilated and neutralized by the ideological output of the omnipresent media: 'All Monday, all Tuesday, the earthquake held the country hostage. Giant headlines marching in lockstep like fascist troops booted everything else off the face of the front pages' (SM 470). Instead of questioning of assumptions, the disaster brings about 'this endless, endless televised repetition of clichés' (SM 471). Soon enough, the destabilizing effects of the earthquake and the findings as to its cause are subsumed and ideological conformity reigns again. Indeed, as the novel shows, media treatment of images of violence and disaster seems to have an important place in contemporary culture and significant ideological effects. In this regard it is possible to observe, once again, DeLillo's influence on Franzen. In *White Noise*, the Gladneys are shown spending a Friday evening watching disaster footage on TV with disquieting fascination. As a perplexed Jack Gladney recognizes, 'Every disaster made us wish for more, for something bigger, grander, more sweeping' (DeLillo, 1986: 64). Elsewhere, DeLillo has analysed the effect of the constant exposition to images of violence and disaster that characterizes our culture and identifies a kind of sickly addiction which nevertheless constitutes a distinctive collective bond: 'These things represent moments of binding power. They draw people together in ways that only the most disastrous contemporary events can match. We depend on disaster to consolidate our vision' (DeLillo, 1997: n.pg.). But the fact that a part of our collective identity is based on the contemplation of violence and disaster has disabling political consequences, not least in the form of a weakening of the possibilities for agency. In this sense, as Green has pointed out, 'Disaster footage presents the image of a passive, victimized (collective) subject' (Green, 2005: 167).

Indeed, it is difficult not to feel that the ideological effect of disaster images has never been more intense as in the period after the 9/11 attacks, when, as Žižek argues in *Welcome to the Dessert of the Real!*, the endless repetition of the 'libidinally invested' (Žižek, 2002: 15) images of the destruction of the World Trade Center was deployed as a fundamental element in a massive act of interpellation at the service of hegemonic American ideology (2002: 46–7). Žižek has also observed the way in which ideology tends to prevent social change by obscuring the historicity of the present: 'The predominant notion of ideology is that it fixates on or "naturalizes" what is in fact the contingent result of a historical process; the antidote is thus to see things as dynamic, as part of a historical process' (Žižek, 2009: 404).

At any rate, from Franzen's point of view the fact seems to be that in our allegedly post-historical times, any potentially difference-making event is bound to become a pseudo-event:

And now the disaster which had been promising to make you feel that you lived in a special time, a real time, a time of the kind you read about in history books, a time of suffering and death and heroism, a time that you'd remember as easily as you'd forget all those years in which you'd done little but futilely pursue sex and romance through your purchases: now a disaster of these proportions had come, and now you knew it wasn't what you wanted either. (SM 470)

The passage clearly evokes, as transparently as the plot proposal of *The Twenty-Seventh City*, a strong yearning for an Event in the sense developed by Badiou. Particularly, the narrator evinces a longing for the epic of revolution and its capacity to invest events and actions with meaning, which is consistent with Jameson's view – following Badiou – of revolution as 'the one supreme salvational or providential Event' (Jameson, 2013: 201). Of course, nothing of the sort occurs and disappointment is the main aftermath of the earthquake for the narrator. Again, as in Franzen's first novel, we are witnesses to a futile act of what the Marxist tradition has called 'voluntarism', in this case embodied in the activism of Renée and her friends. As in *The Twenty-Seventh City*, the failure of voluntarism is a token of social non-ripeness. As Jameson has put it, drawing a parallelism between Marxist and Protestant teleology, 'an infantile leftism or anarchist voluntarism now becomes that "external sign" that revolution is not yet in the agenda and that the situation has not yet politically "matured"' (Jameson, 2013: 201). The pattern will be confirmed, as we know, in *Freedom* with the failure of Walter and Lalitha's initiative. It is easy to see, however, that one likely consequence of this recognition of society's immaturity for substantial change is a certain kind of ideological conformism. In this sense, it may be argued that the disappointing voluntarism observable in *Strong Motion* and later in *Freedom* consolidates the ground for Franzen's overall politico-literary renunciation. This is not the case of Franzen's first novel, where, in truly realist fashion, in the end the reader is not offered anything in compensation for her frustrated expectations. However, in the other two we are granted important symbolical compensations for all that sociopolitical bitterness – compensations which are marked by a distinctive salvational character: the consolations of ethical commitment in the community of lovers and, in *Freedom*, also a powerful evocation of social reconciliation. *Purity*, in its own way, fulfils the same basic strategy.

8 Perspectives of salvation

In a sense, *Strong Motion* ends with as sour a conclusion as that of *The Twenty-Seventh City*, one that despairs of the possibility of change, as the system is so pervading and well established, so well founded and fed by its ideological apparatuses that not even an earthquake caused by corporate greed will shake people out of their conformity. The novel's end surely cues the most caustic authorial remarks on society, as Franzen openly addresses the *Unbehagen* of a schizophrenic culture, drawn by commerce into a yearning for (sexual) violence, only to subsequently 'feel sick with contrition, because all these sexy images and hints have long since become bridges to span the emptiness of their days' (SM 471). As in Franzen's first novel, in those remarks there is a perceptible resonance with Marcuse's bitter ideological critique of advanced industrial society in *One-Dimensional Man*. However, there are important differences in this respect that tell *Strong Motion* apart from Franzen's first novel and which critics have tended to overlook. Certainly a measure of agency has been asserted and, even if modest, results have been achieved. The defining characteristic of this frail prospect of emancipation, however, is that it is strictly individual. In Franzen's world there seems to be no room for collective action, but there does exist the possibility of a relative kind of ideological opting out, once the concealing cloths on reality have been withdrawn. It is certainly not a radical plunge into an outside of the system but a sort of increased awareness of the makings of social totality and of our place in it. In Jameson's terms, we can call it a step into a higher quality cognitive mapping, which is represented by Louis's heightened sympathy at the end of the novel, both towards his community (after the tremor, he offers his gas mask to an unknown man [TS 467] and even becomes a blood donor [TS 483]) and his closest others: Renée, his family. In this sense, Louis becomes a forerunner of later Franzen's characters, namely Walter Berglund or Chip Lambert, that find that the only possible answer to broad social questions is in the first place individual, an answer which is presented as implying an ethical commitment to the closest other. This commitment is basically what Critchley (2012: 11) describes as a yielding to or approval of the (ultimately unfulfillable) demand placed on the self by the other. Franzen's implicit point is that in the subject's perception of the demand placed by the other, a fundamental part is played by sympathy, the capacity to feel with the other. In this belief, Franzen is following a philosophical tradition whose most prominent representative is probably Rousseau, for whom the ethical experience always began with the demand of the suffering human other. Bearing in mind Franzen's conception of the novel as a genre defined by its reliance on sympathy, it is only logical that at the end of *Strong Motion* Louis takes to reading novels (SM 499), thus becoming a member of Franzen's advocated 'community of readers'.[10] The problem with Franzen's ethical proposal, however, is that it is not wholly consistent with the previous dynamics of the relationship between Louis and Renée in terms of Hegel's Lord and Bondman and its conclusion with the

---

[10]Louis's choice of Thomas Hardy and Henry James for his readings seems apt: the former's tragic vision and characteristic sadness suits his condition. James was temporarily based in Boston and attended Harvard University. The allusion is also appropriate as a tribute to that spirit of reform reflected in *The Bostonians*, to which Renée could be considered an heir.

subject's (Louis) desperate need for recognition, which ultimately takes the form of an overwhelming need to be needed.

Not unrelated, in *Strong Motion* we may also observe the coming to the fore of one of the main concerns through Franzen's fiction: the question of happiness (and sadness), a problem that at times seems to become Franzen's fundamental preoccupation, and which is succinctly summarized in *Freedom* as 'how to live'. Significantly, in *Strong Motion* sadness and depression are presented as a socially induced ache, while the escape from that condition is portrayed, in somewhat Protestant fashion, as a personal task. It is known that the Declaration of Independence of the United States consecrates the right to pursue happiness, a legacy from the Enlightenment that has undoubtedly contributed to shaping a distinctive American ethos. However, as Bauman has argued (see 2001: 83), in modern societies the pursuit of happiness has rather become a duty and a supreme ethical principle. This impossible demand, reinforced more recently by consumerist culture, as Franzen has repeatedly denounced, is obviously bound to cause endless suffering and psychological trouble. Then, under certain circumstances, one could even regard one's depression as an oppositional stance, in consistence with the previously stated relatedness of depression and anger. Thus, Louis clings to 'the lump of sorrow' inside him, since 'for the moment, this sorrow was the only thing he had that indicated there might be more to the world than the piggishness and stupidity and injustice which every day were extending their hegemony' (SM 503). It is difficult not to see Franzen's picture of grief in *Strong Motion* in the light of his biographical account in 'Why Bother?'

> However truly you believe there's a sickness to existence that can never be cured, if you're depressed you will sooner or later surrender and say: I just don't want to feel so bad anymore. The shift from depressive realism to tragic realism – from being immobilized by darkness to being sustained by it – thus strangely seems to require believing in the possibility of a cure. But this 'cure' is anything but straightforward.
>
> I spent the early nineties trapped in a double singularity. Not only did I feel that I was different from everyone around me, but I felt that the age I lived in was utterly different from any age that had come before. For me the work of regaining a tragic perspective has therefore involved a dual kind of reaching out: both the reconnection to a community of readers and writers, and the reclamation of a sense of history. (HA: 92–3)

There is a way, then to deal with disappointment and pain that leads not to crippling anguish but sees them as an illuminating, constitutive part of the world from which to somehow existentially profit, as Franzen has kept telling (others and himself) to this day in his essays.[11] And in this way, serious

---

[11]See, for example, 'Pain Won't Kill You' in the collection *Farther Away* (2012).

(realist) fiction plays a fundamental explanatory role. There *is* an escape from sorrow and as the novel shows it seems to lie in love, or, according to Franzen's unsentimental view of it already discussed, in an acknowledged mutual need that transcends mere selfishness. Very much like *Freedom*, the novel ends with an epilogue which clarifies family situations, in this case enumerating three weddings and one divorce in the novel's cast of characters, and a note of tentative hope that is individual rather than social. It has taken pain and convulsions untold but finally a tectonic-like match has been completed and Louis finally envisages happiness with Renée:

> He walked away from her, over the crest of the bridge and down the other side. He was reaching into the familiar place inside him, but what he found there didn't feel like a sorrow anymore. He wondered if it had really been a sorrow to begin with.
> 'Oh, what's wrong, what's wrong?'
> 'Nothing's wrong. I swear to you. I just have to walk now. Walk with me, come on. We have to keep walking.' (SM 508)

This is what tells *The Twenty-Seventh City* and *Strong Motion* apart, the most important difference between the two novels and a capital landmark in the evolution of Franzen's fiction: a proairetic schema which certainly alleviates the feeling of frustration caused by the intractability of the system. Here the possibility of radical, progressive social change seems as unlikely as in the first novel, but while the latter ended with the absurd deaths of Barbara Probst and Chief Jammu, and Martin Probst was left overwhelmed and bewildered by his meaningless loss, in *Strong Motion* Louis and Renée are saved by their commitment to each other, by becoming a community of lovers, a world of two where, in spite of all the suffering experienced, truth can always be generated. With this, *Strong Motion* inaugurates a pattern as this will be the type of ending that Franzen will deploy in all his subsequent novels to date. Of course, this circumstance comes to complicate the commonly accepted view of Franzen's literary evolution, as this kind of narrative closure including a happy end is nothing but a dilution of true realism with a borrowed measure of romance.

9 The novel and the problem of alterity

One of the concerns of this chapter has been Franzen's treatment of alterity, an examination which raises a question that is central to the novel as an art form, and to Franzen's concept of it, namely the question of the access to otherness. As I have argued, for Franzen our knowledge of the other is bound to be problematic, incomplete. To use J. Hillis Miller's simile, our neighbour is a text that we always misread because our reading is mediated by our own desires and needs (Miller, 2001: 69). However, in this study I have also posited sense making as the novel's historic main purpose: the comprehension of a world seen as complex, changing and essentially contingent, as well as the ascertaining of our position in it, on the basis of the assumption, with obvious ethical implications, that, even if full knowledge of the social totality will always elude us, the ultimate vocation of the form is to always contribute to the perfection of an intelligible picture of it. The novel was developed to make sense of a new world and in the process has contributed to creating it. How can this historical function be reconciled then with the view of the other as never to be completely understood? A view, furthermore, which Miller shows as shared by novelists such as Austen or Eliot, whose novels' plots are often based on the characters' misinterpretation of the other. The answer lies in the novel's capacity for the creation of sympathy. By means of narrative devices such as first-person narration, free indirect speech or an omniscient narrator that can enter the mind of characters, the reader can experience what Miller describes as 'a total knowledge of another person, from the inside' (Miller, 2001: 66). Then even if a certain misreading of our neighbour is ultimately inevitable, a fundamental core of sameness may be asserted. Miller has claimed that one of the main social functions of the novel is 'to demonstrate and reinforce, perhaps to generate, the assumption that the other is another person like me' (Miller. 2001: 66). A kind of sameness, Miller points out, that is 'the indispensable basis of any viable and just community' (2001: 66). For the American critic, 'Reading novels breaks down egoism and develops sympathy. It does this because novels present a virtual or imaginary community made of fictive persons with whom the reader is invited to sympathize' (2005: 66). Nancy Armstrong has discussed the way in which Darwin's theory of evolution (especially his proposition regarding the survival of the fittest) was incorporated by the ideology of bourgeois capitalism to *naturalize* its distinctive acquisitive individualism. Significantly, the critic sets the community-solvent effect of a world view based on competition against the collectivizing drive of sympathy: 'In setting man against man in territorial competition, Darwin's theory set the competitive drive on a collision course with the very notion of sympathy that had performed the cultural work of transforming individuals into a collective body' (Armstrong, 2005: 99). This tension between the competitive impulse and the necessity of sympathy finds an echo in *Strong Motion*, where competition within the family (especially in its version of sibling rivalry) is one of the main motives for the characters' acts, a circumstance that is further amplified and extended to love and friendship relationships in *Freedom*.

From the considerations above follows that the novel, or at least a certain kind of it, *creates* community by itself and thus may be deployed against what many people, obviously including Franzen himself, perceive as an ongoing decay of communitarianism. Raymond Williams (1973) showed that the realist novel requires the existence of communities of truly interlinked individuals on the basis of which to perform its characteristic synthesis. This is a kind of community, Williams argues, whose increasing scarcity apparently signalled the fate of the classic realist novel along the twentieth century. It would seem, however, that the realist novel incorporates instruments of its own with which to generate (at least part of) its own native soil, the most important of which being sympathy.

Community and its problems have long been a concern of Franzen, who has famously regretted the social fragmentation and individual isolation that for him define a paradoxically massed contemporary culture. In 'Why Bother?' he contended that such culture, homogenized and benumbed by consumerism offered little nourishment for an art form that thrives on the analysis of manners and human conflict, and by the same token could derive little interest from it. In that essay, Franzen also advocated the power of literature to create a community of readers and writers to escape the generalized alienation produced by our cultural climate, a position which was criticized by critics such as Annesley as despairing of social change and promoting withdrawal. Franzen's discussion of the novelistic genre has more recently shifted its focus to openly address the question of sympathy, posing it as a key element for the form. In the *Boundary 2* interview he refers to the novel as 'the venue for sympathy' (Connery and Franzen, 2009: 37), the latter being a 'by-product' to good fiction (2009: 46). For Franzen, sympathy involves an open-mindedness that reaches towards the understanding of the other and contemplates people and situations in complex terms, which he summarizes as 'seeing both sides' (2009: 49).

However, the political implications of sympathy, and its effects in the critical depth of Franzen's fiction, are more complex than what might seem at first sight. On the one hand, sympathy constitutes a necessary foundation for community, as well as a requisite for political commitment, and as such seems a much-needed capacity in what are widely perceived as times of fragmentation and decline of politics. From another point of view, it would seem that, from *Strong Motion* on, Franzen is positing ever more clearly a dichotomy between ideology (especially understood as a set of *radical* political professions) and sympathy in which he favours the latter without acknowledging it as an ideology in itself. After all, sympathy and the capacity to see both sides advocated by Franzen may deactivate our capacity to perceive what Moretti has called the abstract one-sidedness that lies at the foundation of each culture (see Moretti, 2000: 54), which cannot but have a politically disabling effect. Such is the uncertain ground traversed by Franzen in *Strong Motion*, but as I will be discussing in the following chapters, his ideological position in this respect becomes clearer in his subsequent novels as he enacts his salvational narratives again.

4

The Corrections: A family romance for the global age

General Motors is bigger than Holland
GARY SNYDER

1 Introduction: *The Corrections* as a hybrid novel

The Corrections was the novel that in 2001 gave rise to a lively critical debate about the putative phasing-out of postmodernism and accompanying comeback of realism. It is perhaps striking then to realize that it can hardly be regarded as a properly realist novel as there is so much more than realism in it. This is not to deny the profound changes with respect to Franzen's previous fiction that can be observed in his third novel but to avoid widespread reductionist views. A simple examination of the novel's intricate structure – the most complex of Franzen's novels to date – with its five intertwined plotlines, relaying points of view and multiple chronological leaps back and forth in time points more to experimental fiction – be it of modernist or postmodernist filiation – than to usually more straightforward realism. In the introduction to this book I referred to *The Corrections* as a complex amalgam formed by three basic textual and narrative ingredients: typically postmodernist motifs and concerns, a large-scale attempt at sociocultural analysis of a distinctively realist lineage and a strategic use of narrative elements taken from genres such as romance, *Bildungsroman* and melodrama. With the latter, the novel confirms a narrative pattern that, inaugurated in *Strong Motion*, culminates in *Freedom*. This rhetorical strategy, supported by important pieces of non-fiction, involves a symbolical resolution of apparently unsolvable social contradictions by means of the opening of individual salvational perspectives for the protagonists of the novels. In this way, Franzen's novels offer self-amelioration in lieu of effective sociopolitical reform, and the intractable antagonisms of society at large are replaced by the conflicts of the intimate sphere – a realm where, although not without painful processes of struggle that eventually lead to increased sympathy and ethical commitment to the closest other, reconciliation is shown as possible.

The origin of this mixed quality in *The Corrections* – a kind of formal complexity which is substantially reduced in Franzen's subsequent novels *Freedom* and *Purity* – is to be found in its protracted, excruciating evolution as a work in progress for almost a decade. As Franzen recounts in a 2001 interview, the earliest version of the novel had 'an incredibly elaborate plot, involving prisons and insider trading and racial street warfare in Philadelphia and orphans and the Catholic Worker' (Franzen and Smith Rakoff, 2001: 31). The writing of the novel involved radical reworking and the discarding of hundreds of pages. In 1996 Franzen had published 'How He Came to Be Nowhere' (Franzen, 1996a: 111–23) which was intended to be the first chapter of *The Corrections*. Significantly, in this text the Lamberts are absent, while the projected main character, the bizarrely named Andy Aberant, was left out of the final version. Franzen had obviously envisioned his third novel to develop after the model of the Systems novel that had influenced his previous work. Apparently, he was intent on a postmodernist-influenced *tour de force*, a massive 'encyclopedia of the information Age', as Burn has put it (Burn, 2008: 96), in the style of contemporary novelists such as Richard Powers and David Foster Wallace. The impact of several personal crises is generally held to be accountable for Franzen's change of literary direction. In the *Harper's* essay he had famously dealt with his depression and his despair at the seemingly unavoidable fate of cultural irrelevance for the novel and the novelist in contemporary society. In his 2001 interview with Donald Antrim, Franzen brings to bear more biographical circumstances: 'Well, my father died in 1995. Up until then I'd been trying, sporadically and unsuccessfully, to write a book that was similar to the first two, with an elaborate, externalized, and exceedingly complicated plot. Within a few months of his death, I began writing stuff that came from a very different place'. (Antrim, 2001: n.pg.)

It is easy to concur with Burn (2008: 96) and see *The Corrections* as a sort of palimpsest in which the final product still bears the mark of the writer's first intention. Burn is one of the critics who have shunned the most conventional views on Franzen's literary evolution. He has pertinently highlighted the persistence of postmodernist motifs and references in *The Corrections*: 'the apparently conservative retreat in *The Corrections* is balanced by a corresponding move toward more extended language games and toward a more extended intertextual dialogue with Franzen's postmodern predecessors' (Burn, 2008: 92). Indeed, along with certain abstract passages of linguistic experimentation, we can notice the presence of a whole catalogue of typically postmodernist themes – or, in Christopher Nash's (1993) terminology, anti-realist *thematic topoi* – that I proceed to analyse now.

2 Postmodernist essentials: Conspiracies, representation, visions of the self

For Lukács, the characteristic analytic impulse of realism is reflected in the ambition to portray a social whole. He finds this drive, which he describes as the aspiration to totality, in the great classic realists such as Balzac. Although a complete account of totality is by definition out of our reach, as the critic recognizes, he defends the ideal of totality as the 'guiding principle' for the truly realist artist. For Lukács, it is this approach that will invest the novelist's work with real depth. Such task, however, has proven increasingly difficult in the evanescent times of liquid modernity, characterized by a profound aversion to totalizing thought (when not sheer repression of it). For Jameson, the emergence of abstract conceptions such as totality or mode of production was historically determined: to be thought at all, these notions presuppose a strategic critical distance that is mainly given by the awareness (or memories) of the coexistence of different modes of production, a set of circumstances that has all but vanished in the late form of capitalism we are immersed in (Jameson, 1998: 41–3). There can be little doubt that the current – and also historically determined – abandonment of totalizing thought which has been broadly coincident with the consolidation of a truly global world system of ever-increasing complexity has had a decisive effect on the novel of our time. Already in 1984, Jameson noticed a pressing 'spatial dilemma confronted by contemporary fiction in the "world system"', which he saw as 'the increasing incompatibility – or incommensurability – between individual experience, existential experience, as we go on looking for it in our individual bodies, and structural meaning, which can now ultimately derive only from the world system of multinational capitalism' (Jameson, 1984: 116).

This surely accounts for the contemporary success of conspiracy theory, a distinctive and recurring resource for postmodernist fiction which in Jameson's words represents 'a degraded attempt – through the figuration of advanced technology – to think the impossible totality of the contemporary world system' (Jameson, 1991: 38). Conspiracy has become a substitute for adequate cognitive mapping and has replaced totalization as an explanatory device in much postmodernist fiction. Particularly, conspiracy theory is used to provide an explanation, perforce inconclusive, to what is perceived as a mysterious, disturbing network of connections underlying all sorts of states of affairs at national or even worldwide level. The multinational corporation and the obscure government agency (famously conflated in what Eisenhower termed in his 1961 farewell speech 'the military-industrial complex', which has since assumed the role of the villain in so many fictional products), with their secretive pursuit of money and power in the underside of the public sphere are of course the most obvious conspiratorial agents, not only in postmodernist fiction but in contemporary popular culture. Probably to a hitherto unparalleled extent, many citizens in America and the rest of Western countries have come to feel that their conditions of living are at the mercy of powers above the governments they nominally elect – powers not only beyond accountability but also past common cognoscibility. This is widely perceived as a loss of community, as is apparent in novels such as Pynchon's *The Crying of Lot 49* (1966), Coover's *The Public Burning* (1976), Gaddis' *Carpenter's Gothic* (1985) or DeLillo's *The Names* (1982), *White Noise* (1985) and *Underworld* (1997). The list of works could certainly be much longer, which, together with the sheer length of the time span involved in it, shows the depth and persistence of that concern. As Jerry Varsava has put it:

> American life today is controlled by governmental and corporate organizations to a degree unprecedented in peacetime, and this circumstance does indeed militate against the formation of those communities that might be inclined to oppose given governmental and corporate agendas ... The complexity and operational secrecy of these systems, not to mention their sheer number, have made it very difficult for citizens of the late-twentieth-century liberal state to establish links between events and phenomena, to conceptualize any sort of integrated notion of their own historicity. (Varsava, 2003: n.pg.)

Peter Knight has pointed out that the recurrence of conspiracy in contemporary culture theory is also symptomatic of a deep dread at the heart of our societies, signalling to 'a far more general anxiety about the loss of individuality and autonomy in the face of the increasingly vast and anonymous bureaucratic forces that seem to control our lives, and even our most intimate thoughts and body processes' (Knight, 2002: 10). The theme of conspiracy also has an important presence in Franzen's novels, as we have seen. It is certainly a structural element in *The Twenty-Seventh City* and *Strong Motion* although, as we have seen, in both novels conspiracy takes on a distinctive character that sets it away from the more typical conspiratorial displays in contemporary fiction There are no conspiracies in *The Corrections*, but its typically postmodern preoccupation with connectedness has obvious conspiratorial overtones, which have moved critics to relate it to DeLillo's *Underworld* (1997), a novel intent, according to James Wood, on showing 'the interconnectedness of American society by picturing it as a web threaded on strings of paranoia and power' (Wood, 2001b: n.pg.). In his novel, DeLillo manages to draw uncanny connections between the Agent Orange used in the Vietnam War, Minute Maid orange juice and Prokofiev's opera *Love for Three Oranges*. In *The Corrections*, similar paranoia-tinged suggestions of interconnectedness abound, as the one which relates C. S. Lewis' *The Chronicles of Narnia* with the design drug that a bogus doctor provides Enid with during her sea cruise (previously we have seen Chip Lambert taking a caplet of 'Mexican A' with the logo of Midland Pacific railroads in it). Certainly, the most obvious vehicle for such disturbing images of connection in the novel is provided by tentacular multinational corporations like Orfic Midland, Alfred Lambert's last employer, responsible for the dismantling of Midland Pacific and the liquidation of public assets in Lithuania. Similarly, a company called Axon Corporation has developed a revolutionary brain therapy which is at the same time promising and potentially dystopian, using, in another eerie coincidence, one of Alfred's metallurgic findings. In this way, the so-called Corecktall process purports both to provide a cure for Parkinson's disease and to solve the problem of crime by reprogramming the brain of criminals. Franzen, finally, even makes a point of showing one of his detested SUVs, the imaginary Ford Stomper, as the automobile of choice of both American wealthy suburbanites and Lithuanian criminal warlords (TC 452).

There is a parallelism between the representation of power in *The Twenty-Seventh City* as hierarchically stratified in increasingly evanescent and incomprehensible spheres (TS 328), and the depiction of multinational corporations as vastly powerful and semi-secretly operated organizations which are apparently unaccountable for their deeds. In both cases power is presented as in the hands of a restricted circle of *illuminati*. Interestingly, just as in the case of Franzen's first novel power was shown as affected by a sort of uncertainty principle, or, according to another analogy, disseminated in the way meaning is conceived to be in post-structuralist linguistics, so is – perhaps too explicitly – corporate responsibility in *The Corrections*:

> Orfic Midland had joined the ranks of the indistinguishable bland megafirms whose headquarters dotted the American exurbs; its executives had been replaced like the cells of a living organism or like letters in a game of substitution in which SHIT turned to SHOT and SOOT and FOOT and FOOD, so that, by the time Gary had okayed the latest bulk purchase of **OrficM** for CenTrust's portfolio, no blamable human trace remained of the company that had shut down St. Jude's third largest employer and eliminated train service to much of rural Kansas. (TC 177)

In the novel, we can also find the familiar concern with the problematic processes of representation and meaning – a distinctive outcome of post-structuralist thought – which has become a fixation in postmodernist fiction. Indeed, a defining characteristic of such genre is a high degree of theoretical awareness, to the extent that a postmodernist work of art that does not bring to the fore its consciousness of the conventional character of its own process of representation seems scarcely possible. Consequently, in *The Corrections* we attend Alfred Lambert reflecting on the impasse between reality and our mental representations of it:

> The floor's nature was to some extent unarguable, of course; the wood definitely existed and had measurable properties. But there was a *second* floor, the floor as mirrored in his head, and he worried that the beleaguered 'reality' that he championed was not the reality of an actual floor in an actual bedroom but the reality of a floor in his head which was idealized and no more worthy, therefore, than one of Enid's silly fantasies. (TC 315)

In fact, the exploration of Alfred's consciousness becomes at times an overt formulation of typically postmodernist concerns with the constructed character of reality: 'The suspicion that everything was relative: That the "real" and "authentic" might not be simply doomed but fictive to begin with. That his feeling of righteousness, of uniquely championing the real was just a feeling' (TC 315). From this point of view, the enigmatic narratorial sentence 'the betrayal had begun in Signals' (TC 78) takes on a distinctive post-structuralist flavour.[1] Similarly, Sylvia Roth also ponders on the quandary of the mind's access to reality and realizes the irresistible power of spectacular image, not only as mediation between the world and consciousness but as a shaper of consciousness itself: 'She wondered: How could people respond to these images if images didn't secretly enjoy the same status as real things? Not that images were so powerful, but that the world was so weak ... the world was *fungible* only as images. Nothing got inside the head without becoming pictures' (TC 352).

To complete the picture, the novel is also deeply concerned with neurochemistry and mind-altering drugs – a preoccupation which, in its insistence on the material base of mental processes, chimes in with post-structuralist denunciations of traditional humanist conceptions of identity and consciousness as transcendent metaphysical entities. Ultimately, this preoccupation is another expression of the contemporary anxiety described by Knight about a perceived loss of individuality and autonomy of the individual, since such technological advances are seen not only as facilitating mental manipulation but also as paving the way for the total reification of the self and the ensuing commodification of a realm which is generally seen as that of the innermost sources of identity. This preoccupation, also noticeable in the work of Franzen's fellow novelists such as in David Foster Wallace's

---

[1] It is easy to take the sentence as pointing to the disintegrating effect produced by the ascendancy of liquid modernity in both the ill-fated railway which employs Alfred Lambert and in the latter's mind, quite symbolically affected by Parkinson's disease. However, testifying to the hybrid nature of the novel, later on we learn that the remark was more referential than we might have thought. There was an actual betrayal in Alfred's life: that of the subordinate employee of the Signals department who seduced his teenage daughter Denise.

Infinite Jest (1996), has been explored perhaps most notably by DeLillo in novels such as *Great Jones Street* or *White Noise*. For example, in the latter Jack Gladney and his wife surreptitiously rely on a new pharmaceutical called Dylar to get rid of their fear of death. Franzen's interest in highlighting the organic, biochemical basis of thought and consciousness and their new susceptibility to commodification produced by technological development is evident in *The Corrections*. We are acquainted with Gary's envisioning of his own state of mind as a sort of stock exchange market where key neurochemicals in his brain rise and fall like the value of shares, which is certainly consistent with his materialistic worldview (TC 159–60). We are also shown how Enid Lambert's sense of shame and failure is held at bay by Aslan, the illegal drug she is provided with during her cruise holidays (and which is named, in another knot in the novel's network of interconnections, after one of the characters in *The Narnia Chronicles* saga read by Gary Lambert's children). By means of that prescription, Enid is able to buy out of that tragic sense of life that Franzen in the *Harper's* essay calls 'the Ache' and which, it should be remembered, the novelist sees as a prerequisite for the appreciation of serious fiction: 'Death, Enid thought. He was talking about death. And all the people clapping were so *old* … But where was the sting of this realization? Aslan had taken it away' (TC 388). Finally, of course, there is Alfred Lambert, whose mental disintegration is told in modernist fashion with profusion of abstract detail, but whose illness might be cured, we are told, by changing the chemical composition of his brain. It is interesting to notice how for Franzen this particular scientific advance seems to entail spiritual impoverishment and ultimately a detriment to the novel, continuing then the fundamentally humanist point he had made in the *Harper's* essay. As he puts it in his interview with Donald Antrim:

> There's a vulgar intellectual materialism that is encapsulated, for instance, in the currency of the term 'clinical depression'. If I say, 'At that time in my life I was clinically depressed', in a way this ends the conversation. It replaces a potentially interesting story with a very simple, material story. 'I was clinically depressed. The chemicals in my brain were bad. And I took this material thing into my body, and then the chemicals in my brain were better, and I was better'. Obviously I'm not trying to minimize the seriousness of actual profound depression. But what we gain as science learns how to correlate the organic with the psychological, we lose in terms of the larger conversation. The poetic, the subjective, and particularly the *narrative* account of what a person is and what a life means – I feel like the novelist's vision is engaged in a turf war with the scientific, biological, medical account. (Antrim, 2001: n.pg.)

In a way, in the above-mentioned choice of themes and motifs, Franzen is being the proverbial postmodernist. However, the contrast with the deeper realist and romance-like elements that sustain the novel renders them in a way secondary and suggests that such display of postmodernist *topoi* would be part of an attempt to meet the requirements of postmodernist credibility or to sheer imitativeness.

3 The realism of *The Corrections*

Franzen's approach to social reality can be inscribed within the parameters of the classic realist novel. The genre developed as an explanatory device which enabled changing societies to explain themselves to themselves (Denith, 2010: 41), and it is necessarily based on the assumption that reality (especially *social* reality) is there to be understood. Thus, while in DeLillo's *Underworld* the world system is awe-inspiring and well-nigh preternatural in its being beyond any possible conscious knowledge, in Franzen's world conspiracies may be unravelled, knowledge can be gained, and truth may be attained, even if for no great practical effects from a political point of view, as is shown in *Strong Motion*, where Renée Seitchek, its determined *seeker-heroine*, finally attains the truth of the conspiracy she investigates. The kind of narrative and epistemological closure achieved by Renée contrasts sharply, for example, with the *undecidability* that Oedipa Maas finds herself in at the end of Pynchon's *The Crying of Lot 49* (1966). As Ihab Hassan has put it: 'The mystery that Oedipa Maas pursues through the labyrinths of signs remains a mystery; for self and society in America have dissolved into these same esoteric signs – hieroglyphs of concealed meaning or meaningless (we never know which)' (Hassan, 1981: 101).

Franzen also keeps away from typically postmodernist views of the system as inscrutable in *The Corrections*. As befits a novel published in 2001, *The Corrections* is concerned with the process of globalization. Anthony Giddens defined that phenomenon as 'the intensification of worldwide social relations which link distant localities in such a way that local happenings are shaped by events occurring many miles away and vice versa' (Giddens, 1991: 64). Franzen, however, tightens this neutral definition to emphasize the way in which actions taken by unaccountable, a-national corporations in search of short-term benefit influence the innermost daily life of people living in some cases across the world from where the decision was made. The instability and insecurity that this situation brings upon the lives of millions of people is a defining feature of what Bauman has termed liquid modernity and Ulrich Beck has defined as *Risikogesellschaft*. Of course, Franzen's visions of structural social and economic mutability inscribe themselves in a long-standing tradition. Cultural and artistic representations of life under capitalism had often fallen into two different types: the vision of capitalism as tedium and stagnation typical of a certain bourgeois art (e.g. Flaubert's);

and the view of capitalism as continuous, turbulent change which found one of its most perdurable expressions in *The Communist Manifesto*:

> Constant revolutionizing of production, uninterrupted disturbance of all social conditions, everlasting uncertainty and agitation distinguish the bourgeois epoch from all earlier ones. All fixed, fast-frozen relations, with their train of ancient and venerable prejudices and opinions, are swept away, all new-formed ones become antiquated before they can ossify. All that is solid melts into air, all that is holy is profaned, and man is at last compelled to face with sober senses his real conditions of life, and his relations with his kind. (Marx and Engels, 2010: 25)

Franzen's view of the social effects of late, globalized capitalism in *The Corrections* implicitly shares this approach, which contrasts with the general immobility portrayed in its previous novels. It can be argued then that with globalization a certain sense of moving history enters Franzen's fiction. This fact may be understood in terms of Jameson's account of the conditions of possibility for totalizing thought as dependent on the awareness of the coexistence of different modes of production, which I have discussed above. In this sense, it is safe to affirm that the phenomenon of globalization has been widely perceived as involving a degree of transformation of the system of late capitalism. The factuality of such transformation is of course the subject of a debate which is out of my scope here, but the fact is that such sense of change – which has allowed a measure of critical distance to think the global system again in the kind of abstract, totalizing terms that Jameson has found missing in much postmodern thought – seems to be making new room for the perception of world-historical events. This is reflected in Franzen's fiction too. Indeed, the sociopolitical transformation of the Eastern bloc is the background of a substantial part of *The Corrections*. It must be added that for Franzen this historical motion takes mostly the form of an unstoppable increase of the power of finance capital, now free to devour formerly public assets around the world or bankroll the transmutation of former Soviet republics into veritable mafia states. Thus, as Annesley (2006), Hutchinson (2009) and Hawkins (2010) have rightly pointed out, in the novel there is not much for the individual to do about this overpowering hegemony of capital, except to be carried away by it or retreat to the (relatively) safer sphere of family – a stance on Franzen's part to which I shall come back below.

It is true that in his novel Franzen does not articulate any effective forms of resistance against a state of affairs that he evidently laments. However, his critics overlook the way in which Franzen casts a demystifying look at a world system which contemporary American fiction has so often portrayed as an essentially unknowable entity – a sort of impenetrable, all-encompassing conspiracy.[2] There is nothing actually unfathomable in the way an American-based corporation may buy previously privatized public assets in post-Soviet Lithuania to liquidate them subsequently for a marginal profit. Similarly, the apparent omnipresence of Orfic Midland in the novel may be disquieting, but behind it there is actually nothing more than the relentless, speculative pursuit of benefit of two Southern investors, the Wroth brothers, whose actions, in synthetic fashion, are representative of the usual ways of *hedge funds*.[3] What these cases reveal is not a paranoid vision of undecidable interconnections within a spectral world system, but rather the utter lack of regulation of an economic activity which governments around the world have renounced to control for the common benefit of their citizens:

> Chip was struck by the broad similarities between black-market Lithuania and free-market America. In both countries wealth was concentrated in the hands of a few; any meaningful distinction between private and public sectors have disappeared; captains of commerce lived in a ceaseless anxiety that drove them to expand their empires ruthlessly; ordinary citizens lived in ceaseless fear of being fired and ceaseless confusion about which powerful private interest owned which formerly public institution on any given day. (TC 511)

As in his previous novel, Franzen is keen on revealing the ways in which ideology works to uphold the socio-economic state of affairs. If in *Strong Motion* the incessant ideological production of the media manages to quickly neutralize the consciousness-shaking effect that an earthquake caused by corporate greed ought to have, here Franzen specifically mentions the same ideological vectors he deals with in the *Harper's* essay, namely techno-consumerism and benumbing forms of entertainment. The true nature of this ideological pressure is highlighted by means of a memorable comparison with its starkly undisguised Lithuanian equivalent: 'The main difference between America and Lithuania, as far as Chip could see, was that in America the wealthy few subdued the unwealthy many by means of mind-numbing and soul-killing entertainments and gadgetry and pharmaceuticals, whereas in Lithuania the powerful few subdued the unpowerful many by threatening violence' (TC 511).

---

[2] As Jameson has put it, 'Realism as a form (or mode) is historically associated ... with the function of demystification' (Jameson, 2013: 4).

[3] It is significant that instead of the more probable board of anonymous executives, Orfic Midland is presented as directly run by two specific individuals, the Wroth brothers, for whom Franzen even provides some personal background. This kind of personalization, of obvious pedagogical qualities, is of course a distinctively novelistic device which may be regarded as more *realist* than *realistic*.

In any case, it is conceivable that typically postmodernist social visions based on conspiracy and paranoia have been made obsolete by the enormous amount of research and discussion generated by globalization over the last decades, together with the new, sharpened awareness of socio-economic processes that the ongoing global financial crisis has inevitably brought about. Indeed, it may be argued that both the transformation of late capitalism produced by globalization (be it qualitative or merely quantitative), as well as the magnitude of the financial crisis that became suddenly visible in 2008 have led to the generalization of a new focus on the capitalist system as a whole and by this token to a revival of totalizing thought which naturally avoids substitutive worldviews based on conspiracy. As Lukács reminds us, for the Marxist tradition the relations of production form a whole. However, during the periods of smoother functioning of the capitalist system, and as a result of its structural logic, 'the surface of capitalism appears to "disintegrate" into a series of elements all driven towards independence' (Lukács, 2007: 32). As can be noticed in postmodern conspiracy fiction, this perception is reflected in the artistic production of the age in question. However, as Lukács observes, following Marx's *Capital*, 'The underlying unity, the totality, all of whose parts are objectively interrelated, manifests itself most strikingly in the fact of crisis' (2007: 32).

4 Suburban ambiguities

Unsurprisingly, the potential of the novel for social analysis has always been one the focuses of Marxist criticism. Most notably, Lukács emphasized the novel's role in fighting alienation by disclosing the generally hidden workings of capitalist society and by revealing the social forces in action within it. But ever since the publishing of *La Comédie humaine*, the credibility of the realist novel as an interpretational device of reality has certainly been eroded. In fact, the adequacy of the realist novel for social analysis has been questioned not only on epistemological and linguistic grounds by post-structuralist thought, but also by socio-economic changes and the overall development of our mode of production. Even realism's inveterate commitment to the description of urban environments seems outdated. 'Realism is nothing if not urban', Brooks has asserted (Brooks, 2005: 131), but a mere glimpse at the configuration of most developed countries reveals that our urban world is remarkably different from that of the writers who gave canonical form to the realist novel. Paradoxically, when the percentage of the world's population living in urban areas is larger than ever before, the traditional, well-delimited city is becoming increasingly void, blurred and meaningless, lost amid the irresistible spread of an amorphous and featureless suburban environment. It is significant that while in The *Twenty-Seventh City* Franzen's urban analysis could metonymically function to an extent as an examination of the system at large, this proves more difficult in *Strong Motion* without resorting to Marxist-influenced external digressions on global economic flows. In *The Corrections* and *Freedom* Franzen no longer uses the city as the central grounding of his systemic analysis. The prevailing interest has shifted towards family affairs and the recreation of a specific urban location is not as central as in his two previous novels. Indeed, in *The Corrections* there is an evident transfer of interest from the city to the house, which is to some extent made up for by its more extended global preoccupations. This is not to say, however, that urban issues are absent from *The Corrections*: there are succinct though pregnant visions of St Jude (standing for St Louis, and ultimately, in a more general way, for the Midwestern city), New York City and Philadelphia. The latter's decay ('the whole inner city is going back to farmland' [TC 465]) is described in terms that are reminiscent of the rhetoric of emptiness and urban *de-textualization* characteristic of the portrait of inner St Louis in *The Twenty-Seventh City*:

> Cinderblock was the material of choice over here for blinding windows. There were fire-gutted LUNC ONETTES and P ZER AS. Friable houses with bedsheet curtains. Expanses of fresh asphalt that seemed to seal the neighborhood's fate more than promise renewal. (TC 461)

Similarly, from his office block, an indifferent Gary Lambert discerns the decadence of older industrial areas: 'Gary could see out across the river to the floodplain landscape of Camden, New Jersey, whose deep ruination, from this height and distance, gave the impression of a kitchen floor with the linoleum scraped off' (TC 259).

In contrast with the blight-afflicted inner Philadelphia and decaying industrial New Jersey, we are shown Gary's wealthy suburb, the actually existing Chestnut Hill, whose streets, as ironically Franzen reminds us, are named after 'decimated' Native-American tribes. Chestnut Hill, an almost exclusively white district in a mostly black city, with its houses protected against intruders by means of sophisticated and expensive security systems ('floodlight and retinal scanners, emergency batteries, buried hotlines, and remotely securable doors' [TC 259]), is still not one of those *gated communities* which have proliferated in the United States and elsewhere, but it seems in the process of becoming one. Such fortified communities, Zygmunt Bauman has argued, powerfully symbolize what he has called 'the secession of the successful' (Bauman, 2001: 51–2), which actually means, first and foremost, 'an escape from community' (Bauman, 2001: 57). In *The Corrections* there is a telling incident where Gary's wife, Caroline, anxiously phones her husband as there is a stranger in a car across the street (TC 256). Significantly, Caroline tells Gary that she has already phoned the police, but has been replied that there is nothing that they can do, since it is 'a city street', that is, not a private one. The incident illustrates the isolating, exacerbating effect of these 'voluntary ghettoes', as the Polish thinker has called these areas (2001: 117). The mentioned passage is revealing of the ongoing process described by Bauman whereby public spaces are reshaped as fortresses of the rich (2001: 114). This is accompanied by the institutionalization of urban fear, constantly reinforced by the media, which keeps people out of public spaces. For Bauman, the notion that urban life is fraught with dangers leads to a communitarian dream based on the exclusion of difference, a communal unity based on division and segregation. Unrestrained consumption then appears as the necessarily unsatisfactory compensation for what is essentially an experiential loss. This is apparent, for example, in the piles of technological gadgetry that accumulate, abandoned after merely anecdotic use, in Gary's house (especially in the children's rooms). Ultimately, according to Bauman, such dynamics leads people to forget the necessary skills to share in public life. Similar concerns are expressed by Franzen also in his essay 'First City', where he adds that, unlike in most suburbs, 'there's something in the very nature of cities which enforces adult responsibility.' According to Franzen, it is not that city dwellers are indifferent to the drives of consumerist culture, but that 'it's far easier on the streets of New York to have experiences that have nothing to do with the spending of money than it is in the typical galleria' (Franzen, 2002: 191).

Perhaps it must be pointed out that in the contemporary American literary scene, characterized by a perceived fragmentation and emphasis on marginal identities, Franzen's claiming of suburban life as a substantial enough subject matter for serious novelistic use is not to be taken for granted. After the stylistic turn brought by The Corrections, this aim has earned Franzen comparisons with other novelists who have made suburban family life the main subject of their writing, such as John Updike and Sinclair Lewis (see, for example, Kakutani 2001). It is not difficult, however, to realize that Franzen's social concerns are still evident, and they transcend the placid surface of the suburb to look for the economic and ideological processes that sustain its existence, as well as the social and environmental consequences that an essentially unfair distribution of wealth entails. This is an endeavour that was central in Franzen's two first novels and which is all but absent from the work of the mentioned novelists. A similar comparison may be drawn between Franzen and other contemporary novelists that share his suburban concerns. In this sense, for example, Rick Moody's The Ice Storm (1994) shows a similar, penetrating involvement with the dysfunctions of wealthy suburbanite families, and he also shares Franzen's attentive eye to the painful circumstances of troubled adolescence. As in The Corrections in its own way, in Moody's novel the characters are completely immersed in the dynamics of consumerism of early 1970s' American society, but there is little in the way of testing the workings – economic, political, ideological – of such system. With the exception of a short visit to a New York City apartment, the scope of the novel never leaves, either physically or imaginatively, the affluent surroundings of New Canaan. Similarly, the recreation of historical details remains within the superficially satisfying realm of what Jameson has described as nostalgic pop images. A different case is that of Jeffrey Eugenides' *The Virgin Suicides* (1993), also concerned with suburban life in the early 1970s. Although the action is entirely set in the flat, featureless Midwestern suburb of Grosse Pointe, Michigan, a larger social picture is suggested. The novel shows how an orientational shift of perspective may be attained simply by climbing a rooftop, revealing what lies beyond the boundaries of the peaceful suburb forming both its reverse and existential prerequisite – the labour of factories, the squalor of slums, the din and chaos of city life:

> From the roof of Chase Buell's house where we congregated after getting out of our dress-up clothes to watch what would happen next, we could see, over the heaps of trees throwing themselves into the air, the abrupt demarcation where the trees ended and the city began. The sun was falling in the haze of distant factories, and in the adjoining slums the scatter of glass picked up the raw glow of the smoggy sunset. Sounds we usually couldn't hear reached us now that we were up high, and crouching on the tarred shingles, resting chins in hands, we made out faintly, an undecipherable backward-playing tape of city life, cries and shouts, the barking of a chained dog, car horns, the voices of girls calling out numbers in an obscure tenacious game – sounds of the impoverished city we never visited. (Eugenides, 1994: 34)

Similarly, the troubled relations of production which underlie suburban affluence are recurrently suggested in *The Virgin Suicides* by means of a protracted, symbolic strike of cemetery workers, a protest which complicates the funerals of the deceased in the suburb and brings to light the normally hidden labour implications of even such an intimate, apparently private event as dying.

In the previous chapters of this study, we have observed that Franzen's portrait of the suburbs is characterized by profound ambiguity and the complex symbolic import that is characteristic of heterotopias. We have seen, especially in *The Twenty-Seventh City*, that in Franzen's narrative the suburban spread is sometimes seen as the first cause of the decline of the city, mainly through the process of tax base drainage entailed by white flight. The result, according to Franzen, is not only to be deplored in terms of social justice, but also because the city constitutes the quintessential site of public space, the symbol of an open realm of political and intellectual intervention whose eclipse Franzen has repeatedly lamented in his essays. Besides, as I have already discussed, in their perceived uneventful, ahistorical existence, the suburbs represent in Franzen's novels the most perfected incarnation of a contemporary view, profoundly inimical to literary realism, which presumes that the course of history has come to its end. Characteristically, nevertheless, each of Franzen's novels includes some passage in which the drabness of suburban life may be read in the less symbolic, more personal terms of the Midwest-bred youth who has fled his hometown for a more stimulant coastal life:

> The midmorning light of a late-winter thaw, the stillness of a weekly nonhour in St. Jude, Gary wondered how his parents stood it. The oak trees were the same oily black as the crows perching in them ... a mailman whistling something Celtic and slamming mailboxes harder than he had to, because the deadness of these streets, at such a nonhour, in such a nonseason, could honestly kill you. (TC 201)

And a similar kind of ennui characterizes Gary Lambert's Chestnut Hill: 'The Land that Time Forgot, Gary called it. Most of the houses here, including his own, were made of a schist that resembled raw tin and was exactly the color of his hair' (TC 164).

Indeed, an urge to flee the drabness of suburban life may be perceived in all of Franzen's novels, as if he had interiorized Edith Wharton's injunction against suburban fiction in her 1925 review essay 'The Great American Novel', discussed by Jurca (2001). In that piece Wharton deplored what she perceived as the reductionist materialism that had taken over American culture and accused novelists who focused on the reality of dull bourgeois life of reproducing the very spiritual barrenness they aimed to criticize. Wharton was thus contributing to lay the foundations of one of the most powerful and enduring American literary myths, that of the large, inclusive novel which provides a wide, historical portrait of the culture. Franzen is surely among the believers in the power of such narrative concept, yet he is also a suburb-bred novelist, which creates noticeable tensions and ambiguities in his suburban pictures. Certainly, there is more than mere dullness to Franzen's suburbs. Fondness for the remembered scenery of childhood is often present too, and we have seen how in Franzen's previous novels the suburb is also affectionately portrayed as a cosy haven of neighbourliness and family bonds. This view is consistent with the experiences of childish pranks and adolescent bonding which Franzen recounts in autobiographical essays such as 'Then Joy Breaks Through' and 'Centrally Located', included in his memoir The Discomfort Zone (2006). We may remember here that in the first of these essays he rejects the image of Wester Groves spread by a 1966 CBS prime-time television documentary as a 'suffocatingly wealthy, insular, conformist town with a punitive social hierarchy' (DZ 60). Without denying its 'prevailing conservatism', Franzen refers to the suburban town where he grew up rather as 'an unusually congenial community' (DZ 61). After all, in his monograph on the cultural representation of

American suburbs, Robert Beuka (2004) observes that most surveys reveal a considerable degree of satisfaction among their inhabitants as concerns community values. Generalized Philistinism and prying neighbours may be felt as suffocating by a young aspiring lover of literature, but Franzen is keen to characterize the Lamberts' suburban St Jude – a fictional version of the Webster Groves he grew up in – with a certain egalitarianism that seems to be rooted in the pioneering origins of Midwestern culture. This contrasts not only with the snobbish Eastern world of Lambert's offspring, but also with the unabashed classism of Klaus Müller-Karltreu, a wealthy Austrian doctor with St. Judean connections:

> 'Do you know what I rilly [sic] hate of St. Jude?'
> 'No,' Denise said. 'What do you really hate about St. Jude?'
> 'I rilly [sic] hate the phony democracy. The people in St. Jude pretend they're all alike. It's all very nice. Nice, nice, nice. But the people are not all alike. Not at all. There are class differences, there are race differences, there are enormous and decisive economic differences, and yet nobody's honest in this case. Everybody pretends! Have you noticed this?' (TC 454)

Later, Franzen makes Denise Lambert elaborate on Müller-Karltreu's remarks apropos of her soon-to-be new lover, Robin Passafaro: 'maybe because some sentimental part of her was taken in by the egalitarian ideal that Klaus Müller-Karltreu found so phony in St. Jude, but the word she wanted to apply to Robin Passafaro, who had lived in urban Philly all her life, was "Midwestern." By which she meant *hopeful* or *enthusiastic* or *community-spirited*' (TC 465, italics in the original).

Nevertheless, Franzen makes sure that this rather unlikable doctor has a point in what he says: after all, St Judean equality extends to a rather closed circle, as its communitarian membership seems reserved to affluent white families. This character is then reminiscent of the anti-abortionist Reverend Stites, who in *Strong Motion* makes a critique of consumerist society which at times sounds remarkably close to Franzen's own views, albeit from very distant ideological positions.

A marked cultural contrast may be noticed when Gary, imbued in Eastern elitism and irony, visits his former hometown. Accustomed to Eastern fierce individualism, he resents Midwestern old-fashioned rituals of civility as invasions of privacy and lavishes sarcasm over a shop assistant at a medical supply store in St Jude, whom he sees as overly friendly (TC 558–9). What the incident suggests, of course, is that such ardent defence of privacy is ultimately an extension – or a justification – of the disengagement from community on the part of the wealthy I have discussed above.

The difference in outlook between the East and the Midwest, nevertheless, does not prevent Gary from noticing the increasing tendency towards cultural homogeneity worked by consumerist society, which he presents as the Midwest being intent on adopting Eastern ways and, more specifically, Eastern *distinction*, to use Bourdieu's term (or *cool*, in Gary's parlance). This category, as the French sociologist demonstrates (see Bourdieu 1984), is essentially realized by consumption habits that act as markers of social status. By this token, the generalization of those habits corrupts their meaning as social signifiers, in the same way as the proliferation of stolen alarm signs in Gary's suburbs undermines their deterrent function. This explains Gary's displeasured look on the new St Judean cool: 'At the same time, all the restaurants in St. Jude were suddenly coming up to European speed ... and shoppers at the mall near his parents' house had an air of entitlement offputtingly similar to his own, and the electronic goods for sale in St. Jude were every bit as powerful and cool as those in Chestnut Hill' (TC 226).

Actually, it is the eagerness and haste with which *uncool* sections of the country adopt features of distinction from the cool ones – thus devaluating them – which keeps the (mostly Eastern-based) sociocultural system for the production of distinction-bestowing tokens in continuous functioning. In this sense, significant purchasing power is of course a prerequisite of distinction but, in being too transversal, does not constitute a valid criteria on its own (in fact, true distinction tends to conceal its own dependence on wealth and considers vulgar any ostentation of means). True distinction, as the novel shows, is a matter of educated taste. Franzen is particularly adroit at characterizing his creatures by means of more or less *distinguished* consumption choices. Especially significant is the division between the sophisticated taste of the younger Lamberts as regards food, decoration or entertainment choice, and (what they perceive as) the old-fashioned, suburban tackiness of their parents.

5 *On the House*: Domestic symbolism in *The Corrections*

Franzen's ambiguous mix of embarrassment and affection in his approach to suburban life is further developed in his exploration of the private sphere of family matters in *The Corrections*. In this task, the Lamberts' family house is granted a prominent position, one that is both real and symbolic. There is an obvious identification in the novel between the family and the Lamberts' house in *The Corrections*. This house matches Gaston Bachelard's critical version of the classic bourgeois three-story house whose walls, corners and nooks have nurtured and protected childhood. However, now it is only inhabited by the ailing elder Lamberts. In a way, the container stands for the contained: at the beginning of *The Corrections* we learn that the Lamberts' residence, like that of the Lisbons in *The Suicide Virgins*, has fallen into disrepair, reflecting in somewhat Gothic fashion the fragmentation of the family – the falling apart that had set for the Lamberts a vague but distressing 'alarm bell of anxiety' (TC 2), or perhaps, in Bachelard's words, 'the cosmic anguish [that] precedes the storm' (Bachelard, 1994: 44). Indeed, at the very opening of the novel we see the Lamberts' house threatened by 'the madness of an autumn prairie cold front coming through' (TC 3), in obvious anticipation – wind being traditionally associated to madness – of Alfred's mental illness. A deranged patriarch and a fragmented family: the evocation of *King Lear* is evident. But the layers of symbolism in the setting go deeper. Alfred spends most of his time in his chaotic cellar, a part of the house which Bachelard identifies, following Jung, as the *irrational* part of the building: 'the dark entity of the house, the one that partakes of subterranean forces' (Bachelard, 1994: 18). Subterranean forces, by the way, which can also be symbolically related to the metallurgic experiments he conducts there. In any case, in Bachelard's words, Alfred's cellar becomes 'buried madness, walled-in tragedy' (1994: 20). More than in any other of Franzen's novels, the house is given centrality at key moments of *The Corrections*. In the superb scene of *the dinner of revenge*, where infant Chip is punished for refusing to eat his meal of liver, there is a moment when we can visualize the house as a whole, with Alfred working in his laboratory in the cellar, Chip still sitting alone at the kitchen table on the ground floor, and Enid and Gary at the latter's bedroom upstairs. As the night falls and the scene advances, the story is permeated by a certain air of un-reality and Franzen's symbolic intentions become evident:

> Whether anybody was home meant everything to a house. It was more than a major fact. It was the only fact. The family was the house's soul. The waking mind was like the light in a house. The soul was like the gopher in his hole. Consciousness was to the brain as family was to house. (TC 309–10)

We can relate this un-real quality of the scene to *daydreaming*, the activity which for Bachelard is most emblematic of the childhood sheltered by the house, and which will inevitably tinge later recollections of it: 'The house shelters daydreaming, the house protects the dreamer, the house allows one to dream in peace … Therefore, the places in which we have *experienced daydreaming* reconstitute themselves in a new daydream, and it is because our memories of former dwelling-places of the past remain with us for all time' (1994: 6).

Another key moment in which the Lamberts' house gains prominence in the novel is during the incomplete family meeting that Enid has been desperately trying to organize for Christmas. The novel emphasizes that the house protects the family from the biting cold outside: 'Cold drafts were finding ways through the windows, faintly stirring the open curtains. The furnace was running almost constantly' (TC 631). Indeed, as Bachelard puts it, 'The house derives reserves and refinements of intimacy from winter' (1994: 40). And the colder it gets outside, the warmer it feels inside, which is to say the clearer it becomes the mutual need of the members of the small community formed by the Lambert family. As we shall see, in the climactic reconciliation scene in *Freedom* a freezing-cold outside is also used to symbolically emphasize the need for communion, in this case within the small community of lovers formed by Walter and Patty.

Besides, as the French philosopher explains, the house's 'virtues of protection and resistance can be transposed into human virtues. The house acquires the physical and moral energy of a human body' (1994: 46). In this way, as in *Strong Motion*, in *The Corrections* we can find the occasional identification of the house and the anxious, neglected mother which, in its emphasis on her protective role, seems to pose the latter as the real heart of the family:

> To Enid at this moment came a vision of rain. She saw herself in a house with no walls; to keep the weather out, all she had was tissue. And here came the rain from the east, and she tacked up a tissue version of Chip and his exciting new job as a reporter. Here it came from the west, and the tissue was how handsome and intelligent Gary's boys were and how much she loved them ... and it rained harder and harder and she was so tired and all she had was tissue. (TC 357)

In 'A House for Sale', the opening essay in *The Discomfort Zone*, Franzen sets a mother again (his own) as the true spirit of the family house: 'The house had been my mother's novel, the concrete story she told about herself' (DZ 24). This piece, in which Franzen recounts the proceedings of the sale of his parents' house in Webster Groves, St Louis, after the death of his mother, makes for a moving sort of epilogue to *The Corrections*.

6 Family pictures and social elegies: Franzen's *sympathetic* types

In the traditional analytico-pedagogical vocation of the realist novel, characterization has a fundamental role to play. For Lukács, the value of a novel ultimately lies in its capacity for resisting the alienating forces of capitalist society by creating an explanatory microcosmic model of social totality, revealing its inner dynamics and contradictions. For this, the novelist must be able to reconcile individuality and typicality. The 'type' is then the central concept in realist literature according to the critic, a particular synthetic construction (be it a character or a situation) which binds together the general and the particular (see Lukács 2006b: 383–4). This requires that the novelist portrays individuals as essentially social beings, showing, in Lukács words, the 'inner dialectic of their social and individual existence' (2006b: 387). It is evident that Franzen's third novel relies on that dialectic relationship between the individual and social dimensions of its characters to a greater extent than his previous work. Franzen manages to provide us with a substantial social vision by means of the interaction of a group of characters that in synthetic way are both individual and representative. It is interesting to notice that critics have tended to ignore or even deplore the social content of the novel, and found the claim to realism in *The Corrections* instead in its in-depth exploration of highly individualized characters, to the detriment of the aspirations to social criticism that prevailed in his previous novels. One of these critics was Wood, who dismissed Franzen's attempt at social analysis: 'The novel of intimacy, of motive, of relation, creates a heat that burns away feebler energies such as the social novel' (Wood, 2001a: n.pg.). We can notice that Wood's opinion is representative of a widespread current conception of realism which dispenses with its social dimension, as if realism could be other than social, and it surely points to a common ideological prejudice, namely that, history having come to an end, all appropriate novelistic materials in works of contemporary setting are inevitably of private nature: personal relationships and moral insight. This prejudice, it must be added, is by no means a prerogative of our time. In *History and Class Consciousness*, Lukács saw it as a defining characteristic of bourgeois thought, a circumstance that could be in fact extended to all hegemonic ideologies. Raymond Williams, for example, locates it in *Daniel Deronda* (1876), George Eliot's only novel set in her own time, and one which certainly evinces an attitude marked by resignation before the course of events. In this way, for Williams in that novel Eliot 'is able, conscientiously, to narrow her range because the wide-ranging community, *the daily emphasis of want*, is supposed to be past and gone with old England. All that is left is a set of personal relationships and of intellectual and moral insights, in a history that for all valuing purposes has, disastrously, ended' (Williams, 1973: 180; my italics).

It is likely, nevertheless, that Franzen's critics have been misled in this respect by his apparent renunciation to the social novel in the *Harper's* essay.[4] Indeed, it seems that Franzen cannot but be a social novelist, as befits a writer of realist inclinations. Therefore, rather than a let go of the social, what is apparent in *The Corrections* is that Franzen has found a different form, if by no means new, of including society in the texture of the

---

[4]See, for example: 'At the heart of my despair about the novel had been a conflict between a feeling that I should Address the Culture and Bring News to the Mainstream, and my desire to write about the things closest to me, to lose myself in the characters and locales I loved ... As soon as I jettisoned my perceived obligation to the chimerical mainstream, my third book began to move again' (HA 95).

novel, one in which the intended social vision is implied in the characters' interaction rather than directly conveyed in expository manner by authorial comments or digressions, as it is mostly the case in *The Twenty-Seventh City* and, especially, *Strong Motion*. In this way, in the same *Harper's* essay in which some critics read Franzen's disavowal of social criticism we can notice the following acknowledgement of its inevitability: 'I'm amazed, now, that I trusted myself so little for so long, that I'd felt such a crushing imperative to engage explicitly with all the forces impinging on the pleasure of reading and writing: as if, in peopling and arranging my own little alternate world, I could ignore the bigger social picture even if I wanted to' (Franzen, 2002: 95).

Paula Fox's short novel *Desperate Characters* (1970), a piece of fiction which Franzen has passionately praised, most notably in the *Harper's* essay, has surely been influential in persuading Franzen that the conflicts of an affluent white middle-class family were worthy of intense novelistic exploration. It seems likely that Fox's work played an important part in the modification of his approach to social description. Whereas in Franzen's previous work individual (especially family-related) and social concerns are two clear axes of interest which at times appear to point in different directions, *Desperate Characters* seems to provide him with a model of a tighter integration of both spheres of interest, a more balanced account of that dialectic duality of human beings which Lukács himself advocated. Even the structure of *The Corrections* seems inspired by *Desperate Characters*: Franzen's novel is divided into the five interrelated stories of its main characters, each one of them to some extent an independent novella which follows the model of Fox's novel. The influence of *Desperate Characters* on Franzen has been analysed by Green, who notices how in the *Harper's* essay the novelist praises 'a delicate balance between the domestic and the social novel' in Fox's book (Green, 2005: 97). Certainly, in her novel Paula Fox strikes a fine balance in the way of conveying a social vision with a minimum of narratorial comment, by way of relating the individual and social dimensions of its main characters, the Bentwoods, a Brooklyn upper-middle-class intellectual couple. In his 1999 introduction to the paperback edition of *Desperate Characters*, Franzen highlights the novelist's ability to equate 'a crisis in marital partnership with a crisis in business partnership and a crisis in American urban life' (Franzen, 1999: xiii). Such synthetic capacity often relies on symbolism and metonymy: the dread of impending social and personal disintegration that runs through the novel is represented by Sophie Bentwood being bitten by a stray cat, an apparently minor event which becomes ominously symbolic. Urban decay and class hatred are represented obliquely by means of the apparently banal intrusion of rubbish, irate drunkards and sneering rural people upon the formerly unconcerned world of the Bentwoods. Former Otto Bentwood's friend Charlie Russell very precisely describes the condition of the couple as 'drearily enslaved by introspection while the foundation of their privilege is being blasted out from under them' (Fox, 2003: 39), which summarizes the mood of liberal guilt that permeates the novel and can be easily related to political attitudes that can be found in *The Corrections*, discussed below.

The representative qualities of the Lamberts did not go unnoticed with some critics, possibly as unaccustomed in contemporary fiction. For example, in hindsight Michiko Kakutani criticized what she considered excessive symbolism in the characterization of the Lamberts, in comparison with the more individualized characters of *Freedom* (see Kakutani 2010). However, most critics agreed on the breakthrough development in characterization involved in *The Corrections*. Perhaps most conspicuously, Wood set Franzen's novel as an example against what he considered DeLillo's 'total lack of characterological depth' (Wood 2001a). In his praise of Franzen, Wood is surely overdoing his criticism of DeLillo, but there is certainly a striking, fundamental difference in the way characterization works in *The Corrections* as opposed to Franzen's first two novels. Rebein (2007: 214–18) has rightly pointed out how in *The Twenty-Seventh City* Probst's symbolic identification with the city (see, e.g. TS 216–17), which is a central motif in the novel, is based on an overt authorial act of will: it is given from the outside, and assent is compelled from the reader. In contrast, the characterization of Parkinson's disease-affected Alfred Lambert seems to come much more naturally *from within*:

'I'll leave you alone for a minute,' Denise said, 'while I get the lunch going.'

He closed his eyes and thanked her. As if waiting for a break in a downpour so that he could run from his car to the grocery store, he waited for a lull in his tremor so that he could reach out and safely eat what she'd brought him.

His affection offended his sense of ownership. These shaking hands belonged to no one but him, and yet they refused to obey him. They were like bad children. Unreasoning two-year olds in a tantrum of selfish misery. The more sternly he gave orders, the less they listened and the more miserable and out of control they got. He'd always been vulnerable to a child's recalcitrance and refusal to behave like an adult. Irresponsibility and indiscipline were the bane of his existence, and it was another instance of that Devil's logic that his own untimely affliction should consist in his body refusal to obey him. (TC 77, qtd. Rebein, 2007: 218)

Here, as we observe Alfred's efforts to control his trembling hands we are also offered an insight into his personality, into his private suffering as his old authoritarianism and self-reliance – which, it is implied, most likely were a disguise for sheer self-consciousness – are pathetically mocked by his current physical disability. Alfred's bewilderment is undoubtedly more moving than Probst's, as it is felt as more naturally arising from his circumstances – his painful attempt to steady his hands – than Probst's more arbitrary identification with the city.

Similarly, although the character of Chip is invested with an obvious representative quality, Franzen takes care of providing that generalizing impulse with a unique individualizing background. As Lukács argues:

> The typical is not to be confused with the *average* (though there are cases where this holds true), nor with the *eccentric* (though the typical does as a rule go beyond the normal). A character is typical in this technical sense, when his innermost being is determined by objective forces at work in society ... the determining factors of a particular historical phase are found in them in a concentrated form. Yet, though typical, they are never crudely 'illustrative'. (Lukács, 2006a: 122)

Thus, we understand the inner fragmentation and alienation of Chip and Gary Lambert, for example, as an effect of the alienation brought about by consumer society, but we also see the possible origin of Chip's disordered hedonism in his reaction as a child to his father's repressive puritanism. Chip's backlash is compellingly illustrated in the also individual-yet-typical scene of *the dinner of revenge*. In this way is achieved what Lukács calls the 'organic unity of profound individuality and profound typicality' (2006a: 123), which is a requirement for the characters of a realist novel. Admittedly, typicality has been one of the concepts inherent to the realist novel which have been challenged by postmodernism's anti-realist drive. As Franzen himself observes in 'Mr. Difficult', postmodernist novelists seem to have collectively assumed John Hawkes' famous dictum: 'I began to write fiction on the assumption that the true enemies of the novel were plot, character, setting and theme, and having once abandoned these familiar ways of thinking about fiction, totality of vision or structure was really all that remained' (Enck, 1965: 149). This has important implications concerning the communitarian import of the novel. In fact, typicality seems both a requirement of the realist novel and one of the main components of its capacity for the creation of community. According to J. Hillis Miller, recognizable characters make community. As the American critic argues, 'the novelist makes his particular configurations of character out of personality "traits" that are already known to his readers. They are known not as the property of this or that real person, but as general components of character that may be possessed by many persons' (Miller, 1992: 69).

Miller draws on the etymology of the word *character* (among other meanings, a character is a recognizable sign which is, in turn, made up of conventional traits or graphs that may appear in other signs) to underline its obvious social quality, akin to that of a linguistic sign or a piece of currency. For the critic, 'the characters in a novel spring to life when each has been imprinted with an assemblage chosen from common traits of character that make up the common genetic code in the community of readers for which the novel is written' (Miller, 1992: 70). Elaborating on the parallelism between linguistic signs, monetary units and fiction characters, the critic predicates a socially integrating function for the latter:

> The common possession of these little coins [recognizable characters], their free circulation within society, from readers to novelist to novel and back again to the readers, is the fund or reserve out of which the novel is conceived. This common pool guarantees the novel's function in the psychic economy of the society to which it belongs, just as all speech and all writing are made of a finite lexicon of words, out of which all sentences have to be made. (Miller, 1992: 70)

According to Miller, then, the novel performs an important part in the creation and maintenance of communities. As I discuss in the previous chapter, the American critic argues that the novel contributes to promote sympathy and break down egoism by underscoring the fundamental sameness that lays in the other, notwithstanding an irreducible core of otherness (Miller, 2001: 66). It follows, besides, from Miller's argument and from his choice of examples which illustrate it, that it is the *realist* novel that can best fulfil this function. It is hard indeed, to predicate a true community-building effect of fictions which, Lukács reminds us, by overlooking the social dimension inherent to human beings project a picture of complete, essential isolation of the individual, and present an image of society as hopelessly unintelligible. This is not to imply, of course, any superiority in literary terms, but to acknowledge an obvious set of social implications of the realist novel. It seems clear that Franzen, who has often expressed his concern with what he perceives as a loss of community in contemporary society, recognizes this sympathetic effect of the novel. In fact, he proceeds to relentlessly explore it by means of the continuous intimation of his characters' consciousness he provides throughout the novel, be it through the use of free indirect speech or by the interventions of a narratorial voice which is sometimes hard to tell apart from that of his characters. Franzen has recently recognized the development of the reader's sympathy for his characters as one of his main concerns.[5] As *The Corrections* shows, one of the most powerful ways of prompting such identification is by conveying the characters' most acute desires. In the novel, there is always something that all the main characters badly want, be it money, food, sex, recognition or one last family Christmas. In Franzen's words:

> my breakthrough, the thing I learned in writing this book if I learned nothing else, was that a good way to write a scene, a good way to write

---

[5]See 'A Rooting Interest: Edith Wharton and the Problem of Sympathy'. *The New Yorker*, 13 February 2012.

a book, is to define a character by what he or she *wants*. Sex is useful to the storyteller because the wanting can be so extreme. The wanting is so blunt and ferocious. It's a great plot device; once you take away conspiring Indians, or serendipitous earthquakes, you need something else to drive the plot ... I was also looking for a counterpoint to the relative abstraction of the cultural or political or linguistic preoccupations that drove the previous generation of big novels. Saying 'I'm hungry and I want something' is a form of correction, a correction towards more traditional and humane motives for a novel. (Antrim, 2001: n.pg.)

We have also seen that Franzen is fond of using his characters' readings to further develop them. It is significant then that at the bottom of his path of self-deterioration and irresponsibility Chip confesses to himself to not having read a novel in at least a year (TC 527). This fact, according to Franzen's logic, which is also Miller's, underscores – and in some way partly explains – the extent of the egoism and lack of sympathy achieved by Chip.

7 The end of *the era of hardware*

It is obvious that Franzen has tried to attain a synthetic, representative quality in *The Corrections* that goes beyond what can be found in his previous work. It is the five members of the Lambert family, of course, who become the means for this comprehensiveness. From a social point of view, the older Lamberts and their offspring stage the divide between two different American worldviews: the Midwestern and the Eastern, which would be safe to characterize in turn as modern and postmodern, as the differences between them seem historical rather than merely cultural. In the passages of *The Corrections* devoted to Alfred and Enid Lambert's youth in the early 1960s we can observe the heyday of American industrial society, which is to say of the American middle class. Alfred, the head of the family, is employed as an engineer by Midland Pacific, a Midwestern railway, for all of his working life. This pays for a comfortable life in a suburb characterized by an atmosphere of good neighbourliness. The autobiographical elements used by Franzen in his construction of this opposition are well known, and are interesting as they are clearly reflected in the novel. As he affirms in his interview with Antrim: 'To say that the book is thematically self-conscious is to put it mildly. I come from a kind of old-fashioned Midwest, and I live in a technocorporate, postironic, cool, late-late Eastern world. The two worlds hardly ever talk to each other but they're completely, constantly talking to one another inside me' (Antrim, 2001: n.pg.). In this way, Alfred and Enid stand for a distinctively Midwestern ethos characterized by tradition, by the austerity of those who have been through hard times, by the value conferred on hard work, thrift and communitarian bonds of neighbourliness. In the course of his inspection of the infrastructure of Erie Belt, an Ohio-based railway, young Alfred observes that such disposition is being replaced by what he sees as Eastern frivolity:

> Everywhere Alfred went in the Erie Belt's hinterland he heard young Erie Belt employees telling one another 'Take it easy!' ... The phrase seemed to Alfred an Eastern blight, a fitting epitaph for a once-great state, Ohio, that parasitic Teamsters had sucked nearly dry. On the high prairie where he'd grown up, a person who took it easy wasn't much of a man. Now came a new effeminate generation for whom 'easygoing' was a compliment. (TC 281)

But Alfred' Midwestern code is also, as Franzen is keen on showing, a mindset marked by stiff social conservatism and patriarchal attitudes, made evident in the way he tends to tyrannize his wife. In a way, Alfred, like Martin Probst in Franzen's first novel, stands for a now disappearing type of social organization which Bauman (2000) has called solid or heavy modernity – *the era of hardware* – and Beck on his part has analysed as industrial society. In this sense, we may remember that for Beck (1992: 106), industrial society has a certain feudal quality in that it is based on a fundamental distinction of roles, male and female, which are ascribed to the individual by birth. The sphere of production and wage labour is assigned to men, and the realm of family and housework to women, always in a relation of dependence and male supervision. This brings about a certain antagonism between the sexes which to an extent parallels that between classes, as the quarrels between Alfred and Enid Lambert superbly exemplify. From a different point of view, Alfred's distinctive austerity and integrity – the very qualities behind his productiveness – are shown to have their correlate in sexual repression, which is perceptible in his guilty masturbation at a hotel when away from home (TC 284) or in his refusal to Enid's advances concerning oral sex (TC 322). In this sense, it is significant to see how Alfred seems only able to repress the libidinal impulses that bedevil him when he is away from home by working even harder, in explicit illustration of Freud's famous view of sublimated sexual drives as the basis of culture: 'civilization depends upon restraint', says Alfred to the sentient turd that torments him in his dementia (TC 328).

To be sure, Alfred's job stands for a kind of manly, rewarding productive labour that has traditionally occupied a central place in American ideology, although this construction is clearly undermined by Franzen's examination of its underside. This has been noticed by Ty Hawkins (2007) in his essay on the ideological constitution of the American Dream. As Hawkins recounts, at the end of Arthur Miller's *Death of a Salesman* (1949), Biff Loman (the son of the play's protagonist Willy Loman) aspires to avoid the alienation inherent to his father's kind of job by seeking a more fulfilling and meaningful work which in his view should be related to the worker's own environment, such as farming work. Though in theory Alfred's work as a railroad engineer should meet Biff's requirements for non-alienated labour, as Hawkins remarks, it actually represents the failure of the myth of meaningful, hands-on work as an escape from alienation. Not only does the railroad finally succumb to unproductive speculation but Alfred falls to Parkinson's disease soon after he retires. Alfred's abnegation, an archetypal example of what after Weber is usually understood as Protestant work ethic (especially as regards its business-like emphasis on delayed gratification), thus comes to seem as a kind of false consciousness, an ideologically induced containment device meant to postpone, by means of sheer exhaustion, an inevitable realization of vital emptiness: 'Months were rushing him forward on their rigid track, carrying him closer to the day he'd be the father of three, the year he'd paid off his mortgage, the season of his death' (TC 285). As Colin Hutchinson has observed, 'Franzen suggests that the values of the Wroths and those of Alfred are not so very far apart and that Alfred (and therefore "old" capitalism) held within himself the seeds of his own destruction' (Hutchinson 2008: 151), something which seems to be corroborated by the degenerative character of his illness. After all, as Miller's play accurately shows, the generations of Willy Loman and Alfred Lambert preceded that of the younger Lamberts in the generalized access to gratification through technological consumerism. Although this is sometimes obscured in his fiction by Franzen's nostalgias, late capitalism is only the consequence of the development of the immanent, reifying logic of capitalism. The advent of postmodernity was then implicit in modernity, just as Alfred's dementia was inscribed in his own genes.

Franzen's work also reflects one of the processes inherent to what Beck describes as advanced modernity qua risk society, namely the *de-standardization* of work. The parts of *The Corrections* dedicated to Alfred and Enid Lambert's youth show that labour, clearly structured in solid and understandable ways, was a cornerstone of American industrial society together with its complementary institution, the nuclear family. As Beck argues, following Helmut Schelsky, at that time family and occupation still are 'the two great forms of security that had remained for people in modernity', providing people's lives with 'inner stability', as well as affording access to fundamental social experiences (Beck, 1992: 140).[6] The ascendancy of this socio-economic configuration was visible in the external

---

[6]In his interview with Antrim, he relates this circumstance to his father's working experience: 'I look at my father, who was in many ways an unhappy person, but who, not long before he got sick, said that the greatest source of satisfaction in his life had been going to work in the company of other workers. He got up every weekday morning for forty-plus years, put on a nice suit and a hat, went to this wonderfully structured environment, and did work that he perceived to be important and constructive' (Antrim, 2001: n.pg.).

prominence and inner organization of work centres. This is reflected in the novel in the description of the Midland Pacific headquarters building:

> The brain of the Midland Pacific, the temple of his soul, was a Depression-era limestone office building with rounded rooftop crenellations like the edges of a skimpy waffle. Higher-order consciousness had its cortical seat in the board-room and executive dining room on the sixteenth floor and in the offices of the more abstract departments (Operations, Legal, Public Relations) whose vice presidents were on fifteen. Down at the reptile-brain bottom of the building were billing, payroll, personnel and data storage. In between were mid-level skill functions such as Engineering, which encompassed bridges, track buildings, and signals. (TC 407)

The organic quality of the representation of the building evokes a reassuring sense of meaningfulness and functional stability. In its reflecting a *natural* order, the anthropomorphic analogy of the description reminds medieval conceptions of the body politic as analogically reflecting the hierarchically structured order of the universe. It evinces, in any case, that industrial society is characterized by what Bauman calls 'the solidity of mutual engagement' (Bauman, 2001: 42), which involves a certain feudal quality in that both employer and employee (or ruler and ruled) are bonded to a place. Of course, there is also an implication of rigid hierarchy and a disciplinary regime based on constant, direct supervision. The centralized production centres of the industrial age have traits of both fortress and prison, in contrast with the dissemination of production in advanced modernity. As Bauman has argued of society in general (2001: 41–2), in our time the enforcement of discipline does not rest in a cumbersome panopticon-style apparatus but in the uncertainty of the ruled as to what move their rulers, now exterritorial and diffuse, may make next. Therefore, as the novel shows, Midland Pacific's impressive infrastructure and its meaningful organization of material and human resources are doomed with the advent of liquid modernity (Bauman 2000), a passage marked in the history of the company by its takeover by the Wroth brothers. As Beck explains, 'The observable symptom of such a transition from the old to the new employment system would be the gradual *abandonment* of large-scale work buildings, which, like the dinosaurs of the industrial age, would more and more serve only to remind us of a dying epoch' (1992: 142–3). The abandonment of structured labour runs parallel then to the desertion of infrastructure. This relinquishment is symbolic but has very real consequences, especially concerning the status of community in the affected sites. There is more to infrastructure than just the usual phallocentric pride, as the novel shows. In this sense, Franzen's choice of Alfred's occupation is highly significant: he works for a railway which plays an important role in the maintenance of Midwestern communities ('he knew firsthand what scheduled service meant to a town's civic pride, how the whistle of a train could raise the spirits on a February morning at 41°N 101°W' [TC 79]), but which is to be dismantled by the speculative investors. The fact that Alfred's specific job at the railway is the maintenance of infrastructure recalls the way in which the latter is invested with communitarian symbolism in *Strong Motion*. Infrastructure is seen as part of that threatened pool of traditionally shared resources which Hardt and Negri (2005) refer to as *the common*,[7] and which Žižek describes as 'the shared substance of our social being' (Žižek, 2009: 428). In *The Corrections*, Franzen continues this symbolic strategy and we can find a matching passage to that of his previous novel, containing another elegy for infrastructure:

The Erie Belt was a regional system whose freight business trucks had damaged and whose passengers business private automobiles had driven into the red. Although its trunk lines were generally hale, its branches and spurs were rotting like you couldn't believe. Trains poked along at 10 mph on rails no straighter than a limp string. Mile upon mile of hopelessly buckled Belt. Alfred saw crossties better suited to mulching than to gripping spikes. Rail anchors that had lost their heads to rust, bodies wasting inside a crust of corrosion like shrimps in a shell of deep-fry. Ballast so badly washed out that ties were hanging from the rail rather than supporting it. Girders peeling and corrupted like German chocolate cake, the dark shavings, the miscellaneous crumble. (TC 281)

In *The Corrections*, again, the planned, collective vision embodied by infrastructure, even when privately owned, appears as bound to dissolution: the era of hardware is coming to an end. If in Franzen's previous novel the smell of abandoned, rotting infrastructure impregnates the city, now it is expeditiously dismantled and scraped by the Wroths for meagre though immediate profit: 'He went over to the siding and saw three fellows ripping down the wire, smashing signal boxes, coiling up anything copper ... Hired for copper salvage at fifty cents a pound'.

In contrast, the Lamberts' offspring live in a late postmodern world of cool sophistication, instant gratification by means of consumption, financial speculation and relentless individualism – a world which besides seems destined to overcome any other cultural forms in the apparently irresistible momentum towards homogenization of contemporary commercial culture. This representation of the East as 'the symbol of the corruption of American

---

[7]In *Multitude*, Hardt and Negri explain their preference for the singular form of the noun – as opposed to the more frequent plural *commons*, used among others by Žižek – as a way of highlighting its philosophical content and differentiating the concept from its older sense referring to the pre-capitalist shared productive spaces destroyed by privatization (Hardt and Negri, 2005: xv).

values', as Jesús Ángel González (2015: 15) has pointed out, places Franzen in a literary tradition that has Fitzgerald's *The Great Gatsby* (1925) as a landmark. Like their parents, the three Lambert siblings also play different representative roles. Chip, a disgraced former professor of cultural studies, occupies a central place and represents the ineffectuality of a contemporary Left which, engrossed in theoretical disquisitions, has been reduced to political irrelevance, neutralized by the system it purports to oppose after having embraced materialist culture and, last but not least important, because in the course of its anti-authoritarian struggle it has lost sight of fundamental communitarian referents. Chip is additionally deployed by Franzen in a stint in Lithuania to show first hand some of the noxious effects of globalization. Gary, the eldest brother, is a Philadelphia bank executive. He illustrates the bland materialism of the wealthy (Eastern) suburban class. The youngest sibling is Denise, a celebrity chef with a messy private life. She attests to the spiritual impoverishment and inner fragmentation entailed by the frantic lifestyle of the successful, but also embodies those problems of social skills and adaptation which characterize other Franzen's characters such as Louis Holland and Renée Seitchek. We may notice how against the solid tangibility of Alfred's work, the occupations of his offspring are characterized by a marked speculative nature. Like Martin Probst in *The Twenty-Seventh City*, Alfred Lambert hates speculation and he even refuses to take advantage of inside knowledge concerning the merger of Midland Pacific and Erie Belt, to his wife's dismay. In contrast, plain financial speculation is Gary's main activity; then (mostly ineffective) theoretical speculation is presented as a central component of Chip's academic job; and Denise's success, for all her talent, is presented as ultimately dependent on hype (the fact that her trendy Philadelphia restaurant is set in an abandoned, hollowed-out electric power plant is certainly significant, adding to that Midwest-East symbolism).

In the postmodern culture of the younger Lamberts, a neurotic form of consumerism based on the cultivation of instant gratification has substituted Protestant work ethic as a fundamental compelling force, as is exemplified by Chip's comic shoplifting scene at an upscale groceries store. Even if they are actually founded upon social exclusion, as the novel suggests, the communitarian aspects of the Lamberts' Midwestern suburban world, illustrated by relations of good neighbourliness and mutual trust, are in sharp contrast with the rampant individualism that characterizes their offspring's Eastern lives. The younger Lamberts also illustrate the ongoing decay of industrial society's conception of the nuclear family, subject to the erosion of the forces of modernization. Indeed, in the process of individualization that is characteristic of modernity and the result of the extension of the reifying logic of capitalism to all areas of life, 'the relationship between family and individual biography loosens', to use Beck's phrase (Beck, 1992: 114). In this way, it is only Gary of all three siblings who has carried through the formation of the classic family unit.

Significantly, however, his attempts to implement an improved, more up-to-date and *democratic* version of the model inherited from his parents fail pitifully. Gary tries to rescue the reassuring qualities of his parents' model of family – its 'solidity of mutual engagement', in Bauman's expression – but devoid of its older feudal and patriarchal characteristics. But Gary's family is afflicted by the individuation forces of advanced modernity, attesting to the fact that, as Beck argues, the family is the ground where the contradictions of modernization are staged. As the novel shows, the relations between the members of Gary's family are mediated by commodity fetishism and competition and, as a result, the comforts and confidence which used to be provided by true mutual commitment must be sought in the 'self-help' and pop-psychology books consumed by Gary's wife. The nuclear family seems then the object of Franzen's conflicted nostalgia regarding the industrial age as its erosion is obviously perceived as a loss. If the older Lambert's house stands for the family it used to shelter, its current cracks are analogous to the crumbling items of infrastructure sung by Franzen in *Strong Motion* and *The Corrections*: both symbolize a communitarian impoverishment.

In the representation of this dichotomy between modern and postmodern culture, as well as in the lamentation for the perceived loss involved in this cultural turn, to use Jameson's term, Franzen's views seem informed by Daniel Bell's representation of what he called the cultural contradictions of capitalism. Bell observes, and obviously regrets:

> the development of new buying habits in a high consumption economy and the resultant erosion of the Protestant Ethic and the Puritan Temper, the two codes which once sustained the traditional value system of our society. It is the breakup of this ethic and temper, owing as much to changes in the social structure as in the culture, that has undercut the beliefs and legitimations that sanctioned work and reward in American society. It is this transformation and the lack of any rooted new ethic, that is responsible, in good part, for the sense of disorientation and dismay that marks the public mood today. (Bell, 1972: 31)

The decay of the Protestant ethic is certainly a central issue in *The Corrections*, which starts by declaring that Alfred Lambert's code, 'the whole Northern religion of things [is] coming to an end' (TC 3). Franzen seems to share with Bell the sense that the causes of this 'disorientation and dismay' lay in changes in the economic structure, as we can notice in his emphasis on the transition from a productive to a speculative economy. In spite of his hostility against 1960s' counterculture, for Bell the roots of the cultural change are economic. As he quite precisely states:

> The Protestant Ethic and the Puritan Temper, as social facts, were eroded long ago, and they linger on as pale ideologies, used more by moralists to

admonish and by sociologists to mythologize than as behavioral realities. The breakup of the traditional bourgeois value system, in fact, was brought about by the bourgeois economic system – by the free market, to be precise. (Bell, 1972: 32)

The view of culture as emanating from the economic base of the mode of production is of course a tenet of classic Marxist thought. The problem in Bell's argument, a problem conspicuously shared by Franzen's political outlook, is that he does not pursue the full implications of this conception, or, to put it simply, that he does not really believe in it. Indeed, Bell begins his essay with an assertion of the independence of the realms of economics, politics and culture, and with a claim about the supremacy of the latter over the other two in terms of initiative for change (1972: 11–12).[8] On his part, in the *Boundary 2* interview Franzen argues: 'I can hear myself proving that I'm not a Marxist in my bones, because I'm proposing that politics is not the last instance. It is itself a phenomenon; it's not the driving force' (Connery and Franzen, 2009: 45). This is a significant statement on its own but is even more meaningful if we substitute 'the economic base' for 'politics'. I will be discussing the political implications of this ideological conception for Franzen's work in the following chapter. Suffice it to advance here that one outcome of a social perspective which tends to conceive of the spheres of the economy and culture as independent, obscuring then the ways in which the former conditions the latter, is arguably a propensity towards inoperative lamentation of cultural loss. A second consequence, as *Freedom* illustrates, is a clear vulnerability before the ideological campaign staged by the American Right in the so-called culture wars.

8 Problems of perspective in the postmodern scene

The characters and incidents in *The Corrections* show a clearly synthetic quality, as we have seen, but to assess the social and political scope of Franzen's realism there are other elements that must be considered. One of them is what Lukács analysed as perspective. This complex concept refers to the principle of selection and organization of the necessarily limited materials (characters, situations, etc.) which will metonymically inform a fictional construction of larger individual, social and historical implications. According to the Hungarian thinker, the validity of a writer's perspective depends on the lucidity of her social insight, so that she is able to detect

---

[8]Bruce Robbins has pointed to the contradictions of Bell's statement 'within Bell's own argument' (Robbins, 1999: 30).

and examine the most significant circumstances where social contradiction, development and change are enacted. Of course, such insight is for Lukács related to the writer's social conditions and ideology. Therefore, although the theorist praises a number of bourgeois critical realist writers – most notably Balzac and Mann (Lukács 2006a) on account of their penetrating social vision, he also argues the limitations of perspective caused by their class adscription. For Lukács, then, even in the case of the most socially insightful bourgeois novelists, their account of what he saw as the most dynamic and significant social force, that of socialism within the working class, was bound to be a description from the outside (Lukács, 2006a: 93). For the critic, 'writers will tend to present an inside picture of the class on which their own experience of society is based. All other social classes will tend to be seen from the outside' (Lukács, 2006a: 94). In *The Country and the City*, Williams argues similarly with respect to George Eliot's social portrait: although her social vision is much wider and far more penetrating than most previous English novelists, there are times when her perspective is inevitably external. In Williams' words: 'though George Eliot restores the real inhabitants of rural England to their places in what had been a socially selective landscape, she does not get much further than restoring them *as a landscape* ... But as themselves they are still only socially present, and can emerge into personal consciousness only through externally formulated attitudes and ideas' (Williams, 1973: 168).

These questions are brought to the fore when we set Franzen's aspiration to broad social and cultural description against his actual perspective. It is easy to realize that the cast of characters whose point of view he explores belong almost invariably to white upper-middle-class families throughout his work (Purity Tyler, the heroine of Franzen's latest novel is a welcome exception). As Williams might put it, Franzen's position as an observer is 'a position which is part of the community being known' (Williams, 1973: 164). It is precisely in *The Corrections*, the novel where his characters seem most representative, that their social circle is the most restricted. For a socially concerned novelist, this entails important constraints. It is certainly not the same, for example, to obliquely *imply* social oppression, which is Fox and Franzen's technique, than to actually *show* it from the point of view of the oppressed. This restriction, which contrasts with the larger scope of classic realists such as Balzac or Eliot, inevitably causes a limitation of perspective which Franzen tries to compensate for by means of narratorial comments and digressions. As I have already discussed, this is surely one drive behind the contemporary cohort of white straight, middle-class cultivators of the Systems novel. It seems clear that most contemporary white straight American writers, even those of radical persuasions, lack the knowledge and/or confidence to attempt description of social groups other than their own. This is so for a number of complex reasons which include not only the inherent limitations of class perspective on the part of the writers, but also an increased social awareness and heightened sense of belonging on the part of minority social groups. Such awareness even suggests that attempts at social description from an outsider writer are likely to be met with hostility. This deprives these writers of access to a wealth of materials, that is, specific characters and situations of significant novelistic value concerning fundamental issues such as identity development, interpersonal bonding, social group dynamics and community. As a result, white straight middle-class writers with social concerns and oppositional political stands tend to resort to the – inevitably more abstract – analysis of the workings of an impregnable system.

This withdrawal clearly involves a loss as far as the Lukácsean ideal of totality is concerned, but it also entails a substantial decrease in the kind of discursive variety defined by Bakhtin as *heteroglossia*. This certainly makes things easier for the novelist, who may thus avoid acute problems of discourse management. As Williams explains,

> A knowable community can be, as in Jane Austen, socially selected; what it then lacks in full social reference it gains in an available unity of language in all its main uses. But we have only to read a George Eliot novel to see the difficulty of the coexistence, within one form, of an analytically conscious observer of conduct with a developed analytic vocabulary, and of people represented as living and speaking in mainly customary ways ... There is a new kind of break in the texture of the novel, an evident failure of continuity between the necessary language of the novelist and the recorded language of many of the characters. (Williams, 1973: 169)

There can be little doubt that Franzen's answer to the problems described above by Williams includes a restriction in both social point of view and discourse. This brings about a certain discursive uniformity that has been noticed by critics who have pointed out at the similarity between Franzen's narratorial speech and that of his characters. This way, in *The Corrections* we can distinguish two main idioms, those of the two fundamental groups of characters: the old-fashioned accents of rigid perplexity, of stubborn Midwestern traditions exerting resistance to new cultural ways; and on the other hand the ironic, flexible voices of postmodern Eastern *cool*. The narratorial voice, on its part, tends to reproduce each character's individual discourse around his or her interventions. For example, Enid's personality, shaped by her humble Midwestern background, is correspondingly reflexed by the narrator's language in one of the scenes that take place at a cruise: 'There was no porthole. A room with a view would have cost hundreds of dollars more, and Enid had reasoned that, since a stateroom was mainly used for sleeping who needed a porthole, at that price? She might have looked through it six times on the voyage. That was fifty dollars a look' (TC 278).

In contrast, the narrator recounts Gary's expectations concerning his father's metallurgic patent in a state-of-the-art Eastern ironic speech that is in accordance with his greedy nature: 'Gary's hopes of extracting quick megabucks from Axon were withering in the absence of online hype. Feeling a bit e-weary, fighting an e-headache, he ran a word search for earl eberle ... *Forty million dollars annually* was more like it: *Forty million dollars annually* restored Gary's hopes and pissed him off all over again' (TC 195). All in all, however, it is the younger Lamberts' up-to-date irony that the narrator's own ironic voice favours through the novel. In fact, as it is also the case in the rest of Franzen's novels, the identification of the narrator with the characters' idiom and the constant use of free indirect speech often produces ambiguity as to the authorship of reflections, making them difficult to ascribe to either narrator or characters.

It is striking to see, however, how this homogeneity in speech and social point of view can be broken by an outburst of radical social alterity, of the repressed but necessary underside of the characters' world. Interestingly, these are occasions on which the liberal stand is ruthlessly tested. As we have seen, in *The Twenty-Seventh City* Barbara Probst is killed by a random effusion of violence from the ghetto, a space of dehumanization which is seen as the repressed but ultimately intractable excrescence of St Louis's system, the inevitable by-product of its socio-economic processes. In *The Corrections*, we find a similar incident in the meaningless murder of a social worker named Jordan Roth, the young daughter of a wealthy white liberal Eastern couple, at the hands of Kellye Withers, a black inhabitant of the ghetto. The fact that the only view of lower-class and marginalized groups in his novels should be thus associated with violence and crime is surely a sign of limitation in perspective on Franzen's part. But, in any case, the extreme brutality of the murder tears up the tissue of the novel's familiar world like a sudden irruption of the Real on the symbolic order, to use Lacanian terms. The story of the murder is complexly retold by the narrator from Sylvia Roth's account to Enid Lambert with a deadpan and a gradual disclosing of the horrifying details that involve a certain gruesome irony. Roth's narration is interspersed with remarks quoted from the murderer's declaration at the trial which reveal him through his speech as a black youth. His blunt interventions evince a bloodcurdling utter lack of empathy which seems to be the product of life in the ghetto: as I have observed following Bauman in my study of Franzen's first novel, the ghetto constitutes a laboratory of dehumanization (Bauman, 2001: 212). In any case, the trauma virtually undoes Sylvia Roth, torn between her lust for revenge by means of Withers' scheduled execution and her liberal persuasions and understanding of underlying social problems:

She wanted him dead despite imagining a society that provided jobs at a decent wage for young men like him (so that he would not have had to

bind the wrists and ankles of his former art therapist and bully out of her
the passwords of her bank and credit cards), a society that stanched the
flow of illegal drugs into urban neighborhoods (so that Withers could not
have spent the stolen money on crack, and would have had more mental
clarity when he returned to the apartment of his former art therapist).
(TC 352–3)

Here we may notice the tormenting suspicion on the part of Silvia Roth
that on a deep level her social class bears some kind of responsibility for
the tragedy that befell her daughter, an obvious example of that crippling
sentiment known as liberal guilt which Franzen and probably a good deal of
his readership are certainly familiar with. Actually, the naturally devastating
effect of such a trauma seems to be compounded by its impact on her
previous ideological positions: 'She wanted him dead despite knowing
her desire would please conservatives for whom the phrase "personal
responsibility" constituted permission to ignore social injustice' (TC 354).
Conflicting impulses then have left Sylvia trapped in a circular dynamics
of anger and shame that impedes the necessary course of grief: 'She was
a Sisypha who every night destroyed her own creations' (TC 348). The
passage is notable as an example of Franzen's new, more complex and subtle
way of conveying social views, in this case concerning the violence that
consumerist society inherently generates: whereas in *Strong Motion* these
reflections took the form of narratorial comments or just plain digression,
here the message is transmitted through free indirect discourse interspersed
with third-party quotations (those of Withers). In any case, the tragedy of
Sylvia Roth's daughter harks back to a previous and seemingly minor event
in the narrative whose significance is now highlighted, namely the small
electric chair that an infant Gary Lambert includes – mainly to earn his
father's approval – in the jail he has built with Popsicle sticks (TC 315).
Now we understand that at the foundations of St Judean communitarianism
Franzen finds something more than pioneering spirit. Actually, we know
that Franzen was interested in the role of prisons and the penal system as
elements of class repression which support an unjust socio-economic regime
during the process of writing *The Corrections*. This is shown in his 1995
essay 'Control Units' (included in HA), where he conducts a reportage
study of maximum security prisons in Colorado evidently influenced by
the Foucault of *Surveiller et punir*. Be it as it may, Sylvia's predicament
connects with the mood of liberal guilt and themes of political paralysis
and impotence which are so prominent in the novel. These problems, which
to some extent are Franzen's own, are clearly embodied by the character of
Chip Lambert.

The cultural and political climate of postmodernism poses further
problems of perspective for the bourgeois male novelist than those
described by Lukács. John Kucich (1988) is one of the critics who have

been more influential in examining the difficulties for white male American writers to articulate a critical position of their own, a quandary he has memorably defined as 'the plight of the white male writer'. In an essay on DeLillo's fiction, Kucich argues that postmodernism, in its rejection of any unifying political narrative, and in its acknowledgement that all political struggle is ultimately constituted by nothing but language, and language being grounded on nothing but language itself, has left the social position of the speaker as the only source of legitimation for oppositional political discourse. Many a critic, indeed, shares the opinion that along the end of the twentieth century, the Left has been disabled to some extent by the work of theorists such as Jean-François Lyotard and Jean Baudrillard with their contention that, as Colin Hutchinson has put it, 'there is effectively nothing beyond ideology at all: no "deeper" Marxist-friendly reality or teleology, and no stable codes of meaning or agreed set of values that are revealed once the dark curtain of ideology has been drawn back' (Hutchinson, 2008: 5). For Kucich, the typical 'postmodern paranoia about the ability of mainstream culture to appropriate all gestures of resistance to it' (Kucich, 1988: 333) has exacerbated distrust to the extent that 'the discourse of postmodern politics has usually demanded – much more so than in any prior form of political art – that the marginal or aggrieved social position of the speaker (and in some cases the audience) guarantee its political legitimacy' (1988: 333). This situation, which denies the possibility for an *outside* writer to create a text containing the same ideological import, in Kucich's words 'spells political death for the white male American postmodernist' (1988: 333). The critic himself illustrates the case in his essay with a scathing criticism of DeLillo's political stance, which he regards as reinforcing the state of affairs he means to oppose. This same argumentation is at the basis of much political criticism addressed to Franzen. It is the case, for example, of Catherine Toal (2003), who denies Franzen – together with Rick Moody and David Foster Wallace – the legitimacy of his critical position on the subject of contemporary preoccupation, with mental health, on the grounds of his participation in a mainstream masculine culture which is in crisis.

In *The Corrections*, the character who embodies the predicament described by Kucich is obviously Chip Lambert, whose job as a professor of cultural theory is no less symbolic than his father's. As a representative of certain theory-informed contemporary Left, the picture he presents is certainly disheartening. The professedly Foucauldean scholar criticizes corporate advertising practice without acknowledging that his own teaching is funded by those same corporations, and combines a radical political discourse with mindless absorption in consumerist culture. Chip, whose office is located in D – College's *Wroth* Hall, accurately represents a sense of impotence felt in contemporary left-wing quarters which is derived from what is widely perceived as loss of direction and complicity with the system. The difficulties posed, as far as Chip's critical position is concerned, by the current prevalence of political discourses based on social position and identity are made apparent by his perplexity before a reproof from his disdainful student Melissa Paquette, concerning the gains achieved by minority groups:

> 'This whole class', she said. 'It's just bullshit every week. It's one critic after another wringing their hands about the state of criticism. Nobody can ever say what's wrong exactly. But they all know it's evil. They all know 'corporate' is a dirty word. And if somebody's having fun or getting rich – disgusting! Evil! And it's always the death of this and the death of that ... Here things are getting better and better for women and people of color and gay men and lesbians, more and more integrated and open, and all you can think about is some stupid, lame problem with signifiers and signifieds'. (TC 50–1)

Significantly, Chip cannot answer Paquette's tirade. It is not just that the lecture comes to an end but that he feels unable to articulate any theoretical discourse against the force of the argument of empowerment of minority groups. Any objection concerning, for example, the essentialism of minority discourse, the way it tends to obscure class differences or leave untouched the economic origin of those differences. The seemingly unending capacity of the establishment for the co-optation and assimilation of critical discourse is shown in Melissa's approval of the women-targeted campaign of W – corporation that Chip presents for analysis: 'It's celebrating women in the workplace ... It's raising money for cancer research. It's encouraging us to do our self-examinations and get the help we need. It's helping women feel like we own this technology, like it's just not a guy thing' (TC 50). The problem for Chip is that there is little that he can argue against assimilation, as he is fully assimilated himself.

Interestingly, in his previous novel Franzen had adopted different types of recognizable feminist discourse and made somewhat of a martyr of its female protagonist. This could be seen as a strategic move to secure the otherwise precarious critical capacity of his authorial position. In Hutchinson's opinion, 'the use of a female protagonist is one means by which the white male left-liberal novelist is able in some measure to deflect the accusation that his proposal of a communitarian solution to his own crisis carries with it implications of patriarchal reassertion' (Hutchinson 2008: 134), which the critic exemplifies with the character of Martha Cochrane in Julian Barnes' England, England (1998). However, in The Corrections it is easy to sense some authorial antagonism in Franzen's portrait of Chip's professional rival, the feminist Vendla O'Fallon, apparently more attuned than Chip to contemporary academic trends. Kucich predicates of DeLillo's novels that they 'often strike back by trying to demonstrate that social identity is the wrong bulwark against the rational poverty of contemporary avenues of opposition' (Kucich, 1988: 339). Similarly, Toal accuses Franzen of too sympathetic a treatment of Chip, as in her opinion the novelist presents the young professor 'as a victim of the social power of women and minorities' (Toal, 2003: 315). Indeed, Chip is genuinely a mess and is rightfully expelled from his job, but O'Fallon on her part is presented as a near academic fraud, a representative of the blandest therapeutic views of culture ('Vendla's idea is that we should sit around and talk about our feelings' [TC 56]) whose popularity with students mainly stems from her not being intellectually demanding. As I advanced in the introduction, at this point it is difficult not to consider that, in his recognizable nostalgia for what we have called, following Beck, the American industrial age, Franzen might also be influenced by motives outside the aforementioned communitarian longings. After all, the industrial age was a period in which Franzen's cultural authority would have been secure.

In any case, Chip clearly embodies those 'themes of entrapment within circularities, and of resistance being undermined by ambivalent impulses', that Hutchinson discerns at the heart of *The Corrections* in his essay on Franzen (Hutchinson, 2009: 199). This entrapment is symbolized by Sylvia Roth's obsessive habit of drawing guns and especially by Chip's endless, inconclusive reworking of his film script *The Academy Purple*. Interestingly, such indecisive aimlessness may be found in numerous other left-liberal intellectual or academic characters in contemporary fiction. Jack Gladney, the consumption-prone professor founder of the field of Hitler studies in *White Noise* is a clear forebear of Chip in DeLillo's fiction, while the ineffectual *old drone* Bob Holland of *Strong Motion* is Chip's antecedent in Franzen's own work. Probably the closest forerunner of Chip, however, is Grady Tripp, novelist and teacher of creative writing in Michael Chabon's *Wonder Boys* (1995). Very much like Chip's, Tripp's private life is a mess of uncontrolled hedonistic drives and mild irresponsibility; and if Chip is struggling with his script, Tripp is unable to finish his long-awaited novel, a work forever in progress whose manuscript is over 2,000 pages long. And, of course, both characters inevitably point as well to DeLillo's Bill Gray, the reclusive writer in DeLillo's *Mao II* (1991), who after twenty-two years is unable to finish his book due to circumstances that go well beyond the merely aesthetic and are related to his own cultural marginalization. As Green has observed apropos of DeLillo's character, 'something in the culture at large, from which he has done everything possible to insulate himself, undermines his faith in the novel – the particular novel he is trying to complete, and the novel in general' (Green, 2005: 163).

These fictional novelists' inconclusive struggling with their stalled works represents the difficulty for contemporary liberal writers to arrive at a satisfactory synthetic view of social totality, mostly because of apparently insurmountable limitations in perspective. Without appropriate synthesis, a writer intent on providing a wide social view may end up stuck in a novel which, as the famous Borgesean map, is just as soul-destroying and hypertrophied as the system it purports to portray. This is, not incidentally, one the accusations Franzen aims at Gaddis in 'Mr. Difficult'. Significantly, and with a heavy dose of irony, reflecting on his unfinished screenplay Chip acknowledges that 'he'd imagined that he could remove certain hackneyed plot elements – the conspiracy, the car crash, the evil lesbians – and still tell a good story. Without these hackneyed plot elements, however, he seemed to have no story at all' (TC 104). In any case, any account of the perplexed liberal intellectuals that populate contemporary fiction should include Howard Belsey, the art history professor protagonist of Zadie Smith's *On Beauty* (2005), whose overdue deconstructionist monograph on Rembrandt has come to a hopeless standstill. The allusion is all the more pertinent as the similarity of concerns and techniques between the Smith's novel and *The Corrections* is remarkable. In the somewhat phony environment of Wellington, a fictional Ivy League college, Smith explores the contradictions and bewilderment of contemporary progressive thought as it clashes with conservative positions. Like Franzen, Smith confronts typically postmodern, theory-driven ways of approaching art with more traditional humanist views. But even more relevant is the way, arguably more successful than Franzen's, in which Smith manages to combine her focus on familial relationships with a wide, indeed global perspective. To begin with, she show us the rougher parts of Boston's Roxbury and the racially mixed, working-class neighbourhoods of Northern London. Besides, whereas Franzen resorts to more far-fetched endeavours in Lithuania, Smith has a different way of providing her story of two privileged academic families with social implication and depth: simply paying attention to the illegal Haitian immigrants who work in the wealthy community of Wellington, and by extension to their troubled mother country.

9 The search for community in post-historical times

Also in evident synthetic fashion, Chip's hedonism and anti-authoritarianism are charged with ideological implications. Hutchinson (2008), probably the critic who has examined the ideological import of Franzen's novels in a more thorough and balanced way, detects in them an indictment of the outcome of the libertarianism and individualism of the counterculture of the 1960s. For Hutchinson, who in this argument follows Patricia Waugh, such libertarianism proved to be more inclined to the satisfaction of individual appetites than to the building of true alternative communitarian bonds, and thus revealed itself amenable to dissolve into the selfish, unrestrained individualism of social Darwinism that was celebrated by the prevailing political stances during the 1980s and which seems very much to enjoy ascendancy today. For Hutchinson, the libertarian vocabulary of the rebellious movements of the 1960s was safely integrated in the language of dominant neo-liberalism and now only serves to reinforce consumerism and social stasis. From a different point of view, the success of the political Right's strategy in the ideological struggle known in the United States as culture war(s), which I discuss at length in the following chapter, may also account for the rejection by a certain contemporary Left of radical libertarian views inherited from the 1960s. According to Bruce Robbins, a testimony to the success of the Right's ideological offensive in the culture war is the development of 'the real, if badly named, phenomenon of "left conservatism"' (Robbins, 1999: 33). For the critic, 'Provoked by the success of the Right's cultural campaign, many progressives have been tempted to reply in kind; they have sought to win back cultural territory occupied by the family-values platform by appropriating carefully selected planks. Some were already "embarrassed by or actively hostile to the cultural radical legacy of the sixties"' (1999: 33). It is easy to perceive Franzen's aversion towards that legacy in the derisive portrait of Chip Lambert's radical political views (what the narrator calls his 'Foucaultian heart' [TC 511]).

Certainly, a concern with what is widely felt as a decline of community in the United States is evident in the works such as Richard Rorty's *Achieving Our Country* (1999) or Robert D. Putnam's *Bowling Alone* (2000). Amitai Etzioni has even taken the step of trying to start a communitarian movement, with *The Spirit of Community: The Reinvention of American Society* (1998) as its manifesto. It is conspicuous, nevertheless, that these authors, especially Putnam and Etzioni, do not attribute any of the social wrongs that are afflicting American communities to the inherent contradictions of capitalism. Such lack of analytical depth weakens their critical stand which at times seems limited to a set of recommendations to social agents based on mere good will. However, their identification of the period starting with the New Deal and going through the post-war decades as the high point of American communitarianism implies that it was the processes of political de-regulation and unchecking of capitalism that have been implemented since the 1970s which have brought American *Gemeinschaft* to what they see as its current critical condition.

Hutchinson (see 2008: 93) also discerns a recent 'communitarian turn' among left-liberal writers which in his opinion Franzen exemplifies, together with British novelists such as Jonathan Coe, Ian McEwan or Martin Amis. Such inflection is apparent in the recuperation of certain ideological tropes which have hitherto been associated with social and political conservatism but which now may be seen as sites of resistance against the overpowering forces of reification and fragmentation of late capitalism. And if discourse about community, public institutions, history and family may be used against the hegemony of contemporary neo-liberalism, it would be easy to infer that so can be realism. However, as Hutchinson hastens to add, using discourse and values related to conservatism – still somewhat of an embarrassment in certain left-wing quarters – requires a great deal of precaution, as 'the danger of adopting tropes that assert the importance of unity and tradition is that one also risks their less palatable associations: inflexible social hierarchies, sexism, homophobia, nationalism, racism and xenophobia' (2008: 93). Such precautions are apparent, for example, in Stephen Daldry's film *Billy Elliot* (2000), which takes care of separating commendable communitarian values of class solidarity in the miners' ideology from the more restrictive aspects of their tradition, such as homophobia and anti-intellectualism. Similarly, we have seen how Franzen's account of the Midwestern ethos of the older Lamberts acknowledges its communitarian attributes but also dwells on its authoritarian and repressive aspects. Of a similar opinion to Hutchinson is Bruce Robbins, who in a 2007 essay precisely entitled, after Franzen's suggestive phrase in *Strong Motion*, 'The Smell of Infrastructure', sees the novelist's dirge for abandoned or dismantled utilities in that novel as a communitarian plea. The critic identifies a strain of anti-utilitarianism of Romantic origin in left-wing intellectuality that has led it to abstract Foucaldean critique rather than to the actual defence of points crucial to the survival of community. In his words:

> To speak telegraphically, my point is that water is being privatized. The privatizing of water has at least as good a claim as the Panopticon to stand for what is most wrong with the world at the present time. Yet thanks to our anti- utilitarian, antigovernmental bias, we of the 'cultural left' have little if anything to say about it. (Robbins, 2007: 28)

For Robbins, like for Hardt and Negri, the commons are being enclosed without the left having been able to articulate a valid response. Indeed, the intense anomie of late capitalism has increased under the ongoing financial crisis to a pitch which seems to have bewildered many quarters of that 'cultural left', usually populated by hitherto unconcerned scholars of difference or by intellectuals grown in the safer environment of social consensus that followed the Second World War. Robbins' point is that we need to make infrastructure visible 'as a guide to the struggles of the present' (Robbins, 2007: 32). For certain critics, however, it is precisely the struggles of the present which is most painfully absent in Franzen's novels. For critics such as Annesley and even Hawkins, Franzen fails in his critical attempt not least because he does not articulate any possibility of agency and resistance. An examination of the portrait of actual left-wing or progressive movements (that is, discounting Chip's barren theoretical disquisitions) in *The Corrections* certainly renders a most unpromising picture. We are introduced to the corrupted, Mafia-connected unionism of the Teamsters and to a radical Left scene in Philadelphia characterized by short-sightedness, dogmatism, marginality and ultimately ineffectuality. There are two significant initiatives in the novel: one is the brutal aggression that a W – Corporation executive suffers at the hands of Robin Passafaro's troubled stepbrother (a darker, senseless version of the individual's struggle against the corporation that Renée embodies in *Strong Motion*). The other is the occupational farm started by Robin Passafaro in a Philadelphia slum, an isolated project which arises more from Passafaro's personal need for atonement than from any explicit, collective political vision. Tellingly, Passafaro's initiative, which is funded by the fortune her husband has obtained by selling software to W – Corporation, seems to Denise 'utopian and crackpot' (TC 461). Then, while in Franzen's previous novels we observe the exploration of the viability of political communities, that is, communities intent on some kind of social transformation (chiefly represented by the group of Indian conspirators in *The Twenty-Seventh City*, and by the small group of young questers led by Renée in *Strong Motion*), in *The Corrections* on the other hand this possibility seems to be explicitly dismissed from the outset.

Especially critical of Franzen's political stand is Annesley in his dismissal of Franzen's view of globalization as deterministic and 'un-dialectical' (Annesley, 2006: 125). For this critic, Franzen represents globalization as 'an irreducible reality that the novel is powerless to either interrogate or resist' (Annesley, 2006: 124). In his essay, Annesley proceeds with an argumentation which has become remarkably influential in Franzen's critical assessment: with his characters deprived of agency, and his 'hegemonic and incontestable' (2006: 125) depiction of globalization, Franzen is actually reinforcing the process he is trying to criticize. In my view, although Annesley's critique contains valuable insight into Franzen's work, it is unfortunately overdone and shows an evident moralistic and condescending tone that works against its intended effect. Earlier in this chapter, I observed the transitional, hybrid character of *The Corrections*. In a way, then, we could describe the novel as a take on globalization from a formal point of view which is still close to the essentially static Systems novel. I have argued above that globalization has produced a renewed interest in totalizing thought and in the workings of the global capitalist system. It should be taken into account, in this sense, that between the writing of *The Corrections* and Annesley's essay important works appeared that collectively have undeniably shaped general opinions about that process. Perhaps most notably, Hardt and Negri's fundamental *Empire* (2000) has contributed to spread dialectic views of globalization which both acknowledge its oppressive aspects and discern the new possibilities for emancipation it offers, much in the way Marx and Engels saw capitalism in *The Communist Manifesto* as presenting more opportunities for liberation than previous modes of production.

Admittedly, Annesley and other critics of Franzen have a point in signalling to his refrain from the representation of viable agency and progressive social change, but they do not really account for the formal and ideological reasons behind this withdrawal or the symbolic compensations that his novels offer to make up for that renunciation. In any case, the end of *The Corrections*, despite its allusion to the cyclic crises of capitalism, is actually characterized by the same suggestions of end of history as his previous novels: '*The correction*, when it finally came, was not an overnight bursting of bubble but a much more gentle letdown, a year-long leakage of value from key financial markets, a contraction too gradual to generate headlines and too predictable to seriously hurt anybody but fools and the working poor' (TC 647, Franzen's italics).

Certainly, after the tremendous burst of the financial bubble we have more recently attended to and the new awareness brought about by it, this passage seems curiously dated and a manifestation of what Lukács would surely perceive as defective historical perspective. Although it is all too easy to be overly critical with the benefit of hindsight, we may observe that in this respect Franzen's fiction deviates significantly from Auerbach's concept of realism. We know that the German critic considered a historical view of the present and an adequate representation of the social forces conducive to historical change as necessary components of the realist vision; and though Franzen usually traces the origins of social situations and families back to their historical roots (be it the decay of St Louis, the environmental transformation of New England by capitalism or the Depression background of the Lambert family), there is no sight in his fiction so far of any serious factors of social change. Of course, a blocked historical vision is a sign of our time, as Jameson has famously argued, an incapability to imagine future social developments that are not strictly eventless repetitions of an eternal present. As Hardt and Negri put it, 'Empire presents itself not as a historical regime originating in conquest, but rather as an order that effectively suspends history and thereby fixes the existing states of affair for eternity' (2001: xiv). The force of such perception of immutability – which would by the way have seemed most strange to the founding fathers (and mothers) of the realist novel – is certainly one reason behind the decline of the social novel along the last decades of the twentieth century and since. But this vision of triumphant, limitless capitalism has also brought about what Annesley (1998) has defined as a whole new subgenre, that of 'blank fiction', represented by the production, among others, of Bret Easton Ellis, Susanna Moore or Chuck Palahniuk. According to Annesley, such fiction, characterized by its complete immersion in consumerist society and utter lack of any ethical grounding, has come to take over the Systems novel as a reference in contemporary narrative. What is Franzen's way then in the middle of such harsh landscape? How does he cope with the perceived sociopolitical dead end he finds himself at by the end of *The Twenty-Seventh City*?

As I already advanced, from his second novel on Franzen resorts to narratives of personal salvation which involve a strategy of displacement of conflicts from the social to the personal domain. The first and last sentences of the novel's epilogue constitute an unequivocal index of this symbolic substitution of the private for the social. In the previous quotation we have seen that the last section of the novel begins with yet another confirmation of the persistence of the status quo, a jaded acknowledgement of the hopeless repetitiveness of pseudo-events in the public sphere. However, the last line is on a contrasting note: 'She was seventy-five and she was going to make some changes in her life' (TC 653). The shift of attention from an irredeemable realm to another where the future can still be envisaged with hope is obvious. If we believe, with Fredric Jameson, that all narratives enact symbolical resolutions of unsolvable social contradictions, we may observe that, faced with the perceived impossibility of social transformation, Franzen and his characters take the road of self-amelioration. To this end, the novelist directs his characters on a path of self-abasement and deterioration which leads to dejection or, more specifically, depression, until a cathartic personal event awakens their sense of sympathy and orients them towards community understood as a commitment to the closest other. The obvious implication here is that before you may think of helping others you must be able to help yourself. This is certainly the trajectory of Chip Lambert in *The Corrections* and Louis Holland in *Strong Motion*. We have seen how the latter is degraded by his unfair, dominance-seeking treatment of Renée Seitchek until she is grievously shot. From that point on, he lovingly dedicates himself to her care. In a similar way, Chip goes through a descendent curve of self-degradation and inner fragmentation and is tainted by self-deception, irresponsibility and selfishness (it is surely not incidental that during this time his occupation evolves from the teaching of cultural studies to wire fraud, which obviously suggests a common ground to both activities). As Franzen declares in his interview with Burn, self-deception was a significant concern for him during the writing of *The Corrections*. The novelist refers to its use as a driving force for the narrative and a source of comedy:

> I am indeed interested in self-deception. Realist fiction presupposes that the author has access to the truth. It implies a superiority of the author to his or her comically blundering characters. *The Corrections* was written as a comedy, a somewhat angry comedy, and so the self-deception model worked perfectly. Self-deception is funny, and the writer gets to aggressively inflict painful knowledge on one character after another. (Burn, 2010: 66)

In fact, it could be said that all the members of the Lambert family are afflicted by self-deception. Chip thinks himself a subversive intellectual and a prospective filmmaker who is simply undergoing a spell of bad luck; and his mother Enid insists on denying the reality of the fragmentation of her family and her husband's mind. At any rate, Chip is presented as lost to himself: 'He'd lost track of what he wanted, and since who a person was was what a person wanted, you could say he'd lost track of himself' (TC 620). Chip finally hits the bottom during his pitiful escape from Lithuania. Parallel to what happens to Louis in *Strong Motion* when Renée is shot, this is an epiphany-like moment of self-recognition for Chip, coincident with his vital lowest point, in which he is taught humility and abandons his previous pretension and self-deceiving. The final recognition of the reality of his situation is linked to the recognition of his true self and opens the way for his salvation and attainment of peace and happiness. Salvation is completed by the aforementioned necessary ethical commitment, or the acceptance of the ethical demand placed by the other upon the self, to use Critchley's formulation. Thus, Chip devotes himself to taking care of his sick father and having lost enough of his egoism he is able to find a stable, satisfactory love relationship. In contrast, the possibility of self-recognition and then salvation is denied to Denise and Gary, who at the end of the novel are still in the grip of erroneous notions of themselves.

These narratives resemble Franzen's own account of his vital and literary evolution, which he has presented in his non-fiction – most notably in the *Harper's* essay – in terms of a misguided downwards path, namely that of the practice of literary postmodernism and radical, grand-scale sociopolitical critique, which led him to a dead end and actual depression, followed by epiphany-like rediscovery of his own literary self. Insofar as these stories culminate in personal salvation, they perform an obvious legitimating function of Franzen's *conversion*. The ethical commitment they stage has led critics to discern a communitarian turn at the end of *The Corrections*, and accordingly to qualify their otherwise rather harsh criticism of Franzen's sociopolitical stance. For example, Hawkins argues: 'If this is a long journey for Chip, it is likewise a long journey for Franzen, one that carries him through the end of the twentieth century and deposits him squarely on the brink of a metavision of community that could anchor the twenty-first-century social novel which effectively challenges the hegemony of self-interest' (Hawkins, 2010: 82).

We should bear in mind, however, that the community towards which these characters head for is ultimately the *Ur*-community of family and/or the community of lovers, for which the community of readers proposed by Franzen in the *Harper's* essay can be seen as a substitute. Indeed, it is not hard to interpret Franzen's vision of family as that of the last line of defence against the fragmenting forces of individuation which characterize advanced modernity. In his novels the family is the symbolic site where, as in a traditional romance, the inveterate structural narrative function of reconciliation takes place, bringing to the readers the reassuring, comforting effect of narrative closure in a pattern which recurs in all of Franzen's novels, except *The Twenty-Seventh City*, and that will attain culmination in *Freedom*.

5

How to close
a (meta)narrative: *Freedom*

*The final belief is to believe in a fiction, which you know to be
a fiction, there being nothing else. The exquisite truth is to know
that it is a fiction and that you believe in it willingly.*

WALLACE STEVENS

1 Introduction: *Freedom* as a destination

One of the tenets of this book is that all artistic forms have an inherent
ideological message. Accordingly, the key question about Franzen's transition
is that it is not only stylistic but political. In this sense, Franzen's evolution has
involved the disavowal of previous and more radical stylistic and political
approaches. For a novelist to turn his fiction over time to more conservative
grounds is certainly not uncommon, but Franzen's case seems unique in the
way he has been able to integrate a complex case into a meaningful narrative,
vigorously arguing through outspoken pieces of non-fiction. But perhaps
what is most striking is the manner in which he has inscribed a justification
for his evolution in his works of fiction. From *Strong Motion* on, Franzen
has articulated his novels around plots of personal salvation that in one
way or other resemble Franzen's own narrative of conversion, acting thus as
disguised apologies of Franzen's own stylistic and ideological evolution. In
this chapter, I will analyse the ways in which *Freedom* constitutes the final
buttress to support that construction.

We have seen that in *The Corrections* Franzen's narrative wager involves
a symbolical substitution of private for public concerns, a move that has
been taken by certain critics (e.g. Green 2005) as a retreat from the political.
After this seeming abdication, it is remarkable to notice how the possibility
of activism is raised so vividly in *Freedom*, embodied by the characters of
Walter Berglund and Lalitha. This chapter aims to probe the actual substance

of this engagement: its ideological assumptions and its socially antagonistic dimension; the significance of the fact that it is the ecology that is offered, exclusively, as the central object of reformist concern. Of course, I examine the fact that their initiative fails spectacularly, faced with the public's incomprehension and mired by inevitable compromise with the system. At the same time, I also observe and interrogate the implications of Franzen's ideological shift from the more radical positions of his early work to the critical liberalism that prevails in his fourth novel, a political stance that he has elsewhere presented as inherent to the novelistic form and which he evidently uses to support the aforementioned narrative of conversion. In the study of Franzen's rhetorical and ideological strategies of self-justification, as well as in the assessment of the actual depth and significance of his critical insight in *Freedom*, especially as regards the potentialities and limitations of his chosen novelistic form, I rely on the theoretical constructions of Fredric Jameson and Franco Moretti, whose shared conception of the novel as a symbolic artefact and as such a problem-solving device, both from a social and psychological point of view, are especially relevant to Franzen's narrative endeavour. Particularly, I will be concerned with the ways in which *Freedom* re-enacts literary procedures dating back to the classical *Bildungsroman*, which is not surprising when we bear in mind that Franzen's career makes for a *Künstlerroman* in its own way.

2 Guilty (liberal) pleasures

As in his previous novels, with the exception of *The Corrections*, Franzen places an urban account at a prominent place at the beginning of *Freedom*. Perhaps surprisingly, given the grim pictures of apparently unstoppable urban degradation and the ensuing loss of community that abound in Franzen's previous fiction, *Freedom* starts on a contrasting note: in the first pages of the novel we witness the regeneration of Ramsey Hill, an inner-city slum in St Paul, Minnesota,[1] by young, left-leaning couples like the Berglunds, 'the first college grads to buy a house on Barrier Street since the old heart of St Paul had fallen on hard times three decades earlier' (F 3). As in *The Corrections*, we find again that the novel is articulated around a Midwestern family invested with representative qualities. This synthetic character of the novel's protagonists – one of the marks of classic realism – is not as pronounced as in the case of the Lamberts, whose two generations seemed to embody two American worldviews, but was nevertheless perceived

---

[1] As undoubtedly Franzen knows, nearby Summit Avenue is the site of the house where Francis Scott Fitzgerald grew up, a connection that is reminiscent of the allusions to St Louis' native T. S. Eliot in *The Twenty-Seventh City*. Another example, like Franzen himself, of a novelist who fled the Midwest to find recognition in the East.

by some critics. For example, Sacks observed that 'The Berglunds' personal crises are thus framed as a microcosm of a national obsession with freedom and global pre-eminence' (Sacks, 2010: n.pg.).

As the narrator informs us, the neighbourhood's new settlers, those latter-day Midwestern pioneers, strive to 'relearn certain life-skills that your own parents had fled to the suburbs specifically to unlearn' (F 3), a phrase loaded with suggestions of filial rebellion and community building that inevitably recall the alternative cultural movements of the 1960s. At any rate, the lines recall Franzen's praise of city life (as opposed to life in the suburbs) in his 1995 essay 'First City'. In that piece, Franzen commends the way the urban experience endows citizens with a set of skills regarding how to share the public space while retaining a reasonable amount of privacy. In his opinion, true privacy 'depends not on the pseudoparental expedients of isolated houses and controlled shopping environments but on modes of adult behaviour best learned in public spaces like the sidewalk' (HA 193–4). The initiative of Ramsey Hill's young settlers then appears at first sight as an attempt at reversing the phenomenon of white flight that has ravaged so many inner-city districts in the United States and which was a central theme in *The Twenty-Seventh City*. This way, instead of the recurrent images of emptiness and urban de-textualization into meaninglessness that we find in Franzen's previous novels, *Freedom* starts by staging the opposite movement: the re-knitting of social fabric by the new dwellers of the district. In contrast with the allusions to T. S. Eliot's *Waste Land* of Franzen's first novel, young Patty Berglund's everyday interaction is aptly depicted with an environmental image of fertility: 'For all queries, Patty Berglund was a resource, a sunny carrier of sociocultural pollen, an affable bee' (F 5). However, as the reader soon realizes, the utopian edge of Ramsey Hill's regeneration is inevitably impaired: the community formed by the regenerators of Ramsey Hill proves to be built upon the same opposition as society at large: the one between the included and the excluded.

It is obvious that every process of settlement tends to produce antagonism between original inhabitants and newcomers, and this is certainly the case with gentrification, as Franzen's first novel sharply illustrates. One then might have expected Franzen to exploit the inevitable tensions between widely different social groups in the benefit of the novel's social insight, very much in the way Paula Fox uses the awkward coexistence of the protagonist couple, the well-off Bentwoods and their poorer neighbours in her novel. Strikingly, however, in *Freedom* the perspective of the impoverished original citizens of Ramsey Hill is reduced to a few conspicuously passing, ironic references. This anticipates the fact that the novel's perspective is, once again, unequivocally white liberal, upper-middle class. In this way, in the middle of a page-long comic enumeration of life skills required by the district, which includes, for instance, the proper maintenance of Volvo cars, we can find 'how to respond when a poor person of color accused you of

destroying her neighborhood' (F 4). It could be argued that this reference
to the loser side of gentrification, together with other related brief allusions
mentioning panhandlers and public schools abandoned by the middle class,
being all of them embedded in a long list of petty-bourgeois banal concerns,
would serve a corrosive intention as to exposing the selfish insularity
of the new inhabitants of Ramsey Hill, and by extension of their bland
liberalism, were it not for the fact that, as it turns out, this is the last time
that these disagreeable issues are discussed in the novel. It would seem that
with these allusions Franzen is just acknowledging the existence – and the
unfairness – of such situations in as quick as possible a way before he can
turn to something else. That being, of course, the story of the Berglunds,
which unfolds against a cultural and political portrait of the troubled years
of the George W. Bush administration and is accompanied by a somewhat
cumbersome environmentalist plea. Furthermore, any expectations as to
the possibility that the novel is presenting a communitarian or progressive
initiative of any consequence in its rendering of Ramsey Hill's refurbishing,
or alternatively providing a serious exercise in social critique are rapidly
dismissed by the general tone of mild, affectionate irony and blatant middle-
class perspective of its introductory chapter 'Good Neighbors'. Indeed,
here the reminiscence of John Updike's *Couples* (1968) is obvious from
the very outset. The Hanemas' first liner and their subsequent chatter in
Updike's novel ('What did you make of the new couple?') resound heavily
through *Freedom*'s introduction, especially when the narration conveys the
discussion of the Berglunds by the Paulsens, a gossipy neighbour couple.
Perhaps less becoming, though clearly perceptible as well, is the reminiscence
of contemporary mass-culture products such as the TV series *Desperate
Housewives* or *Sex and the City* and their voiceover introductions to each
show. After all, the first chapter performs very much the same function of
a film trailer: a narrator of limited knowledge teases the audience with the
intriguing skeleton of the tale of the Berglunds as seen from the point of
view of their neighbours.

3 Beaten up by rednecks: Class discourse and ideology

As will have become already apparent, the concept of social class is a
fundamental one in this chapter. This notion, of course, is not self-explanatory
but rather a permanent source of a heavily ideologized sociological debate
in which not only the character of society's stratification into classes but the
very existence of classes as well is questioned. Although Marx discusses the
concept of class only briefly in *Capital*, the idea is central in Marxist theory.
Within that tradition, the division of society into classes is determined by

position within the process of production. A succinct definition of class was proposed in 1919 by Lenin, for whom

> Classes are large groups of people differing from each other by the place they occupy in a historically determined system of social production, by their relation (in most cases fixed and formulated by law) to the means of production, by their role in the social organization of labor, and, consequently, by the dimensions of the share of social wealth of which they dispose and the mode of acquiring it. Classes are groups of people one of which can appropriate the labor of another owing to the different places they occupy in a definite system of social economy. (Lenin, 1965: 421)

Also relevant for the purpose of this book is Max Weber's influential notion of status group, which both contrasts and partially overlaps with the traditional Marxist concept of class. In contrast with the Marxist tradition, for Weber social stratification is not ultimately economically determined – which under capitalism means market organized. In his view, a political community is not only constituted by an 'economic group' but must perforce also entail the construction of 'value systems', in accordance to which the community constituents have more or less legitimacy or prestige (Weber, 1978: 902). This accounts for a variety of relations between economic position and actual status since classes and status groups may and frequently do coexist, and in theory classes may develop into status groups and vice versa (see Weber, 1978: 932).

The crucial introduction of the ambiguous element of *honour* as a non-economically determined factor to account for social stratification opens the way for moral considerations that can be used to legitimize social inequality or advocate any kind of social leadership. In this chapter, I argue that Franzen shows a position implicitly informed by Weber's thought in *Freedom* as part of the legitimation strategy for his own social outlook. This view becomes clearer when we replace the archaic concept of honour used by Weber with the more modern notions of *dignity* and *intellectual enlightenment*, characteristics which for Franzen differentiate certain characters belonging to a class, according to mere economic criteria, from the rest of the members of that class. This is apparent in his treatment of the Berglunds, who, like the Probsts or the Lamberts, are presented in a much more favourable way than other characters theoretically belonging to the same class but lacking their legitimizing dignity – a moral stance which is shown as the result of having achieved their current social position through adherence to traditional Protestant work ethics. In consistence with this approach, Franzen downplays the shaping role of the mode of production but emphasizes cultural differences when he confronts characters belonging to different social classes.

As it may be readily noticed, *Freedom* is characterized by quite apparent displays of social antagonism. One of the main objects of confrontation does already appear in the first chapter, namely working-class, right-wing populism as embodied in the character of Blake, the new boyfriend of Carol Monaghan, one of Ramsey Hill's older neighbours. Blake disturbs the neighbourhood's apparently Arcadian left-liberalism with his glaring Republicanism (which includes an 'I'M WHITE AND I VOTE' bumper sticker in his truck) and, perhaps even worse, with his alien cultural coordinates and coarse taste. It should be noted that while Franzen's perspective has certainly been middle class throughout his work, he seems to have driven that stance one step beyond in *Freedom*, the novel where we find his middle-class vision most unremittingly deployed and his social perspective most constricted. In this respect, we may remember how in *The Twenty-Seventh City* Martin Probst's outlook is unequivocally middle class too, despite his wealth and status as a successful contractor, and how his worldview and values are vindicated against those of the corrupt and selfish ruling class of St Louis. Nevertheless, in Franzen's first novel there are the Indian conspirators brought in from the outskirts of capitalism, the satiric insight into the city's power machinery, and the scandal of the derelict human refuse of East St Louis, a symptomatic reminder of the social consequences of capitalism; all of which elements overrule the Probsts' narrower field of vision. In *Strong Motion*, there is a resort to the critical power of Marxism and feminism. In *The Corrections*, the perspective certainly gets narrower, but this is to some extent made up for by its global concerns and its contrasting of two different world views: the Midwestern modern of the Lamberts and the Eastern postmodern of their offspring. In *Freedom*, however, every social perspective that is brought to bear only seems to be proving its fundamental wrongness as compared to Franzen's middle-class ideal. From a Marxist point of view, this kind of oppositional stand is inherent to any class discourse. As Jameson has put it:

> the very content of a class ideology is relational, in the sense that its 'values' are always actively in situation with respect to the opposing class, and defined against the latter: normally, a ruling class ideology will explore various strategies of the legitimation of its own power position, while an oppositional culture or ideology will often, in covert and disguised strategies, seek to contest and undermine the dominant 'value system'.
>
> This is the sense in which we say, following Mikhail Bakhtin, that within this horizon class discourse ... is essentially *dialogical* in its structure. (Jameson, 2002: 69)

The upper-middle-class, enlightened left-liberalism of the Berglunds confronts basically two antagonist social perspectives in *Freedom*. In the first place, we find working-class right-wing populism. The concept of populism is certainly a controversial one in at least two ways: in the disagreement among theorists as to its characterization and in its being frequently utilized in political struggle as a derogatory adjective against adversaries who threaten a specific hegemonic consensus. This is certainly not the place to conduct an exploration of a complex idea which would inevitably take us far from our way. In order to arrive at a working concept let us state that the notion of populism assumed by this book is not the typically pejorative one that can be found in much liberal thought but rather follows Laclau's more neutral description of it as a political logic inherent to processes of social change. This logic governs the articulation into equivalence of a variety of social differences involving different demands. For Laclau, 'the equivalential moment presupposes the constitution of a global political subject bringing together a plurality of social demands. This in turn involves ... the construction of internal frontiers and the identification of an institutionalized "other"' (Laclau, 2005: 117). The fact that populism operates over what Laclau has termed 'empty signifiers' entails that its referents are indeterminate until they are *filled in* by the hegemonic process. As a result, populism is multivalent and lends itself to very different political causes. According to the novel, the political stance of large segments of the working class is characterized by a particular form of right-wing populism which is apparent in a reductionist and intensely confrontational political outlook obviously hegemonized by the ruling classes. This ideological stance is represented by Blake, by the stubborn West Virginian Coyle Mathis and their associates and, last but not least, by Walter Berglund's own father and siblings. It should be noted that in the novel their confrontation is not abstract but very real – they are actually and explicitly the Berglunds' antagonists, what prevents them from attaining their perceived life goals. As Laclau and Mouffe argue, antagonism is that relation in which 'the presence of the Other prevents me from being totally myself' (Laclau and Mouffe, 2001: 125). In this way, we realize that Blake stands in the way of Patty's relationship with her own son, and Mathis and his group of rednecks are an obstacle to Walter's environmental scheme. Not to mention the way young Walter is tormented by his father and siblings. Indeed, the portrait of Walter's father, the truly obnoxious Gene Berglund, deserves special attention: 'He was belligerently populist, defiantly proud of his *un*specialness, and attracted therefore, to the dark side of right-wing politics' (F 446). Through an interminable series of consistently poor business decisions, Gene drives his family into a precarious financial situation (the fact that he alone is responsible for his economic misfortunes is not, of course, without ideological implications: Franzen's antagonistic strategy of self-legitimation is evidently at work here) and then cultivates a bitter anti-bourgeois, and most importantly for Franzen, anti-intellectual resentment: 'To Gene, this was just more evidence that his siblings looked down on him, considered themselves too fancy for his motel, and generally belonged to that privileged class of Americans which it was becoming his great pleasure to revile and reject' (F 447).

As if this were not enough, as an interracial couple Walter and Lalitha are the object of the aggressive racism of a rural West Virginian at a restaurant. Working-class characters in *Freedom*, especially when rural, are invariably depicted as anti-intellectual, anti-liberal, disdainful of environmental issues, and even prone to racism and physical violence, as is proved by the beating Walter receives at the hands of Mathis and his followers. Soon it becomes obvious that in his construction of working-class characters, Franzen is drawing from, as well as contributing to, a well-known repertoire of disparaging fictional types – the narrow-minded, the coarse, the redneck: 'He felt conspicuous enough already, felt glaringly urban, sitting with a girl of a different race amid the two varieties of rural West Virginians, the overweight kind and the really skinny kind' (F 307).

It is also noticeable that, in his representation of lower-class hostility towards the liberal gentry embodied by the novel's main characters, Franzen is following again the model provided by *Desperate Characters*. In this sense in Fox's novella, for example, the liberal Bentwoods make a trip to the countryside holiday farmhouse they own to find that it has been broken in and viciously wrecked in the inside. When they question the rural working-class locals who are supposed to look after the house about the incident, they are met with barely concealed derision. The evident antagonism exasperates Otto Bentwood: 'I wonder if those Haynes cretins had something to do with it. How they hate us! Did you see how gratified they were by this trouble of ours? Everything in that kitchen ... it all said one thing to me. It said, *die*' (Fox, 2003: 140).[2]

However, while Fox is cold and ambiguously detached in her presentation of the Bentwoods, and usually deploys a narratorial deadpan that compels the reader to assess the Bentwoods' moral and psychological positions in his or her own terms, Franzen's approach is rather, as it was in *The Corrections*, the opposite: warm, affectionate empathy, frequently realized in exhaustive – and sometimes even redundant – renderings of the characters' thoughts in which the narrator's speech is often hard to tell from that of the characters. Franzen's sympathy then, which he has claimed as a key attribute of a novelist,[3] is evidently selective and founded on a kind of partial identification with his characters.

---

[2]The passage from *Desperate Characters* has a quite literal echo in *Freedom*, in what seems a tribute to Paula Fox. In Franzen's novel, Richard Katz experiences the hostility of Washington D.C. in the same terms: 'The whole city was a monosyllabic imperative directed at Katz in his beat-up biker jacket. Saying: die' (F 350). The formula reappears some pages later, this time reflecting with considerable bitterness the intergenerational divide between Katz and the younger attendants to Conor Oberst's concert: 'They gathered not in anger but in celebration of their having found, as a generation, a gentler and more respectful way of being. A way, not incidentally, more in harmony with consuming. And so said to him: die' (F 369).

[3]See 'A Rooting Interest. Edith Wharton and the Problem of Sympathy'. *The New Yorker*, 13 and 20 February 2012.

The way in which Franzen characterizes working-class people is also revealing as it involves not only political or moral discredit but cultural embarrassment as well. In the presentation of those characters, Franzen deftly strings together apparently casual details of what contemporary educated upper-middle-class people would consider unforgivable bad taste: Blake's 'great room' with its beer keg and foosball, Carol Monaghan's 'tarty' clothes and excessive make-up, Walter's brother's favouring of 'anthem rock', all of which are in sharp contrast with the Berglunds' 'excellent urban-gentry taste' (F 350). These references are aimed at an audience that will recognize them as a vindication of their own taste, which at times suggests that *Freedom* is fundamentally intended for a specific demographic group, that of its main characters. Just as in *The Corrections* Franzen showed his adeptness at highlighting the status-marker function of *refined* consumption patterns, in *Freedom* he seems to be proving Pierre Bourdieu's remarks as to the fact that 'art and cultural consumption are predisposed, consciously and deliberately or not, to fulfil a social function of legitimating social differences' (Bourdieu, 1984: 7).

4 Franzen and the *culture wars*

Franzen's harsh portrait of working-class characters and his rather unconcealed display of antagonism might at first sight appear as curiously un-liberal, as it apparently contradicts what Hutchinson has described as 'the tendency for contemporary left-liberals to attempt to reconcile, synthesize or transcend opposing views rather than to assert one view over another in the manner most frequently associated with political radicalism' (Hutchinson, 2008: 5). As Laclau and Mouffe argue, 'the notion of antagonism has been erased from the political discourse of the Left' (Laclau and Mouffe, 2001: xiv), which has brought a 'sacralisation of consensus' (2001: xv). Why then this antagonism towards working-class characters, which seems ill at ease with traditional progressive visions of social harmony?[4] Part of this

---

[4] In *The Eighteenth Brumaire*, Marx explains social-democracy's proverbial pursuit of social harmony in terms of limitation of perspective, or, more exactly, of the (mis)application of one limited class perspective to society as a whole: 'The peculiar character of social-democracy is epitomised in the fact that democratic-republican institutions are demanded as a means, not of doing away with two extremes, capital and wage labour, but of weakening their antagonism and transforming it into harmony. However different the means proposed for the attainment of this end may be, however much it may be trimmed with more or less revolutionary notions, the content remains the same. This content is the transformation of society in a democratic way, but a transformation within the bounds of the petty bourgeoisie. Only one must not form the narrow-minded notion that the petty bourgeoisie, on principle, wishes to enforce an egoistic class interest. Rather, it believes that the special conditions of its emancipation are the general conditions within which alone modern society can be saved and the class struggle avoided'. (Marx, 2001: 50)

animosity probably constitutes a symptomatic manifestation – in the way of self-justification – of what is usually known as liberal guilt: the shameful realization of the basic unfairness at the root of one's privilege. In this sense, the novel's early, seemingly pre-emptive denial of such guilt in the Berglunds reads as a kind of *excusatio non petita*: 'To Seth Paulsen ... the Berglunds were the super-guilty sort of liberals who needed to forgive everybody so their own good fortune could be forgiven; who lacked the courage of their privilege. One problem with Seth's theory was that the Berglunds weren't all that privileged; their only known asset was their house, which they'd rebuilt with their own hands' (F 7).

But the ultimate cause of Franzen's hostility is surely to be found in an ongoing sociocultural phenomenon taking place in the United States, namely the widespread ideological polarization of American society over a number of perceived key issues such as reproductive rights, conceptions of family, sexual morals, education, the relationship with the sacred, the morals of art, certain civil rights and freedoms, the attributes and functions of the government, or the size and competences of the welfare state. This ideological battle, popularly known as culture war(s) has been famously analysed by James Davison Hunter (1991), who accurately discerns a struggle for power in the current fight for 'the definition of America'. The perception as to which side is leading in this fight may vary in accordance to the ideological perspective, but it is clear that liberals tend to think that they have been losing the ground before the conservatives for a long time. Walter does not mince words voicing that opinion: '"Listen Richard," Walter said. "The conservatives won. They turn the Democrats into a center-right party. They got the entire country singing *God Bless America*, stress on *God*, at every single major-league baseball game. They won on every fucking front, but they especially won culturally and *especially* regarding babies"' (F 221).

For many observers indeed, the antagonism provoked by that ideological cleavage, which has been widening since at least the 1960s, probably reached a peak during the first decade of the twenty-first century. From a left-liberal point of view, it is probably political analyst Thomas Frank who has made the most influential contribution to this debate. In his partisan volume, he caustically decries the ideological dominance of what he calls 'the great backlash', a conservative reaction whose origin he explains as a response to the moral and political upheaving of the 1960s. Frank's thesis is that conservative leaders have been able to ideologically trick the American working classes through a form of 'tragically inverted class consciousness' (Frank, 2004: 259) into supporting political stances that are against their own interest. According to Frank, the contemporary American political scenario is one of 'sturdy blue-collar patriots reciting the Pledge while they strangle their own life chances' (2004: 10). For the analyst, the Democratic Party is itself to blame for having squandered its traditional allegiance with the working class by focusing on technocracy, dropping class language and ceasing to address people on the losing end of the free-market system. In turn, while certainly less publicized, Bruce Robbins' view of the issue seems the most perceptive. For Robbins (1999), the ongoing controversy over culture rests upon the ideological perception of an illusory separation of the economic and cultural realms, which he already discerns, as we have seen in the previous chapter, in the thought of theorists such as Daniel Bell. Robbins follows Habermas in stating that this disjunction – which is in contradiction of Marxist views of culture as emanating from the mode of production – turns culture into a sort of scapegoat as it allows the less desirable consequences of capitalist modernization to be burdened on it. According to Robbins, this disjunction of realms, which protects capitalism from radical critique, has been successfully exploited by the Right to achieve an apparently contradictory political hegemony:

> From the perspective of economics, it means that the victims of capitalism are enlisted in support of capitalism. From the perspective of culture, it means that the Republicans can support family values while encouraging social conditions under which family values will be unlivable – conditions under which, as Marx put it, everything solid melts into air. This self-contradiction is veiled from sight by the disjunction of culture and economics, which thus serves as the glue fastening together the victim/victimizer coalition. (Robbins, 1999: 32–3)

In understanding this kind of seemingly contradictory political investment, the theory of political hegemony developed by Laclau and Mouffe (2001) under Gramsci's influence is certainly relevant. From their point of view, it could be argued that American neo-conservatives have succeeded in constructing a hegemonic articulation through a system of equivalences, unifying multiple subject positions (or social groups) around certain individualistic definitions of individual rights and negative conceptions of liberty which act as nodal points or master-signifiers, and whose definition is in the benefit of the ruling elite.

The contradictory political landscape depicted in *Freedom* may also be interpreted, in terms which are not incompatible with those of Laclau and Mouffe, in the light of Žižek's views of ideology. One of the manifestations of ideology is the gap between one's actual best interest and the real effect of the political stand one defends. Such gap has become very wide indeed in the case of the conservative populism that has taken root among the American lower and working classes. An explanation for this kind of ideological blindness can be found in a generalized libidinal investment in what could be described as a series of ideological fetishes, which is particularly entrenched in American society due to its specific historical configuration. For Žižek, the function of ideology in modern societies has come to rely mainly on fetishism. As he has put it,

> In our allegedly 'post-ideological' era, ideology functions more and more in a *fetishistic* mode as opposed to its traditional *symptomal* mode. In the latter mode, the ideological lie which structures our perception of reality is threatened by symptoms *qua* 'returns of the repressed' – cracks in the fabric of the ideological lie – while the fetish is effectively a kind of *envers* of the symptom. That is to say, the symptom is the exception which disturbs the surface of the false appearance, the point at which the repressed Other scene erupts, while the fetish is the embodiment of the Lie which enables us to sustain the unbearable truth ... fetishists are not dreamers lost in their private worlds, they are thoroughgoing 'realists', able to accept the way things are because by clinging to their fetish they are able to mitigate the full impact of reality. (Žižek, 2009: 65)

It is clear that Franzen is aware of the working of this kind of ideological fetishism and he sets about exposing it in the novel. In his *Time* magazine interview following the release of the novel he argues in this direction: 'It seemed to me that if we were going to be elevating freedom to the defining principle of what we're about as a culture and a nation, we ought to take a careful look at what freedom in practice brings' (Grossman, 2010: n.pg.). In particular, he is keen on laying bare the fetishized concept of freedom that pervades American political discourse, which in his view poses a fatal hindrance to the public discussion of key issues in rational, scientifically enlightened terms of common good:

> 'It's all circling around the same problem of personal liberties', Walter said. 'People came to this country for either money or freedom. If you don't have the money, you cling to your freedoms all the more angrily. Even if smoking kills you, even if you cannot afford to feed your kids, even if your kids are getting shot down by maniacs with assault rifles. You may be poor, but the one thing nobody can take away from you is the freedom to fuck up your life whatever way you want to.' (F 361)

Significantly, we may notice that here the lower and working classes are specifically singled out as the prototypical prey to the ideological power of fetishized freedom. It is difficult, however, not to feel that there is something too simplistic, too flattering for the middle classes in this picture of lower and working classes in the grip of ideology and manipulated by a ruthless ruling class, while the urban gentry of *New York Times* readers remains relatively non-alienated. Žižek has been concerned with the ideological struggle outlined by Walter, taking it beyond the usual liberal self-centred expression of victimhood or despair at the dreadful backwardness of the lower and working classes. He acknowledges that the ruling class hypocritically mobilizes a populist moral agenda with which it ultimately is not concerned, tolerating, in his words, this 'moral war as a means of keeping the lower classes in check, that is, enabling them to articulate their fury without disturbing their economic interests' (Žižek, 2009: 360).[5] For Žižek then the culture war spells more than liberals will acknowledge: '*culture war is class war* in a displaced mode' (2009: 360). A class war which, needless to say, would pose a threat to the liberal gentry's privilege too, were it to take full form. Besides, as the Slovenian thinker argues, 'it takes two to fight a culture war' (2009: 360). For him, liberals' consecration of certain issues (the fight against sexism, racism and fundamentalism, the defence of multicultural tolerance) as central in the political debate covertly serves a hegemonic purpose in subduing the lower class: 'while professing solidarity with the poor, liberals encode culture war with an opposed class message: more often than not, their fight for multicultural tolerance and women's rights marks the counterposition to the alleged intolerance, fundamentalism and patriarchal sexism of the "lower classes"' (2009: 361). It is obvious that environmentalism, the central political issue offered by the novel, belongs in the list of liberal concerns mentioned above and is then also susceptible of being strategically used as an instrument of opposition to a rival class. In this sense, it is telling that two working-class characters in the novel, namely Blake, the Berglunds' Republican neighbour in Ramsey Hill, and Walter's elder brother are depicted as notorious, prompt fellers of trees.

5 Enlightened elites and fear of populism

It is in the context of this embittered political atmosphere, one in which left-liberal influence is widely perceived to be steadily declining, that Franzen's disparaging show of working-class types is best understood, as it is evident that for the novelist the popular classes have been hopelessly colonized by the political Right and therefore stand as one of the greatest obstacles for the

---

[5] Although he may overlook its ultimate ideological implications in the benefit of his own political stand, Franzen is of course aware of the fundamental phoniness of the culture war scenario, of its function as ideological distraction for the naïve across the mainstream ideological spectrum. For example, apropos of the Republican leaders' hypocritical endorsement of the conservative moral agenda, Richard Katz points out to Zachary, a liberal teenager: 'Do you think George Bush actually hates gay people? Do you think he personally gives a shit about abortion? Do you think Dick Cheney really believes Saddam Hussein engineered 9/11?' (F 202)

realization of any progressive reformist agenda. Franzen's response to this state of affairs seems to be the same perplexed frustration that currently afflicts many left-liberals in the United States. In this sense, Simon Critchley sees a disabling weakness in the political vision of much of today's American Left: they do not understand the essentially adversarial character of politics. For Critchley, the Republican leaders show a clear, Carl Schmitt-influenced understanding of the adversarial nature of the political, which they conceal under a moralizing and apparently depoliticized discourse – a hypocritical but effective stance.[6] In contrast, for Critchley, the Democrats

> want to bring healing and reconciliation to the divided body politic. ... They need to study their Carl Schmitt and more importantly, Gramsci on common sense, hegemony, religion, ideology and collective will formation ... the sine qua non of oppositional politics lies in an understanding of populism, what Gramsci used to call the 'national-popular'. What needs to be politically articulated at this historical conjuncture is, in my view, a leftist populism. (Critchley, 2012: 143–4)

As I will be discussing below, Franzen's final political vision is aimed towards reconciliation, rather than determined oppositional politics, and certainly there is not much in the novel that is attuned to the articulation of the leftist populism proposed by Critchley. On the contrary, apparently for Franzen the impulse for social amelioration can only come from a scientifically enlightened elite (which is not to be confused with the basically self-serving Republican ruling class). This implies a rejection of populism which from Laclau's point of view amounts to a dismissal of the political as such: 'the assertion that the management of community is the concern of an administrative power whose source of legitimacy is the proper knowledge of what a 'good' community is' (Laclau, 2005: x). In this sense, we may notice that Walter does believe in progressive change but in the way of reform led by influent progressive circles. As he exemplifies it: 'Positive social change works top-down ... The surgeon general issues his report, educated people read it, bright kids start to realize that smoking is stupid, not cool, and national smoking rates go down' (F 362). In the same way, the declared aim of Walter and Lalitha's projected summer activities is to gain 'rich college kids' for the cause of population control, in an implicit acknowledgement, but also an

---

[6]In *The Concept of the Political*, first published in 1932 (the year before he joined the Nazi party), Schmitt conducts a sharp critique of liberalism on the grounds that its inherent tendency towards compromise and procedure instead of struggle when conflict is envisaged, as well as its propensity to diverge the latter into the abstract realms of ethics and economy inevitably entail an impoverishment of the political. For Schmitt, the departing point of politics lies in the friend–enemy distinction. In his words: 'Political thought and political insight prove themselves theoretically and practically in the ability to distinguish friend and enemy. The high points of politics are simultaneously the moments in which the enemy is, in concrete clarity, recognized as the enemy' (Schmitt, 1996: 67).

endorsement, of the classist character of (what is left of) the public sphere. At this point, we may notice again that the credit given to experimental science in Franzen's novels is remarkable. Renée Seitchek, the heroine who uncovers Sweeting-Aldren's corporate malfeasance in *Strong Motion*, is a scientist using scientific methods of enquiry. Significantly as well, what makes Walter's collaboration with the coal industry in his environmental project acceptable, even though it entails the practice of mountain-top removing (a procedure usually considered ecologically harmful), is the fact that the latter is to be followed by 'science-based reclamation' of the mined areas. Franzen's apparent trust of experimental science acquires interesting connotations in *The Corrections*, where the productiveness and communitarian benefits of Alfred Lambert's work, as a railroad engineer who in his free time conducts metallurgic research in a home laboratory, are contrasted with the sterility and phoniness of his son Chip's labour as a professor of cultural theory. This faith in experimental science seems one more of Franzen's characteristic nostalgias (i.e. those evoked by the city, the public sphere, industrial society, the social novel), as it is to be surely more characteristic of traditional industrial society than of the ongoing advanced phase of late capitalism that Beck has described as reflexive modernity or risk society. Indeed, the current validity of science as a socially acknowledged epistemological foundation could be not much higher than that of Chip's critical theory. We have already seen, following Beck, that in advanced modernity the relentless process of *scientization* of society has also brought a critique of science, which has become reflexive, taking itself as its own main subject. As a result, scientific discourse has been rendered ambiguous, suspect indeed of being subservient to spurious interests, disabled thus as a basis for a universally acknowledged truth.

Walter's favouring of reform advanced by enlightened elite also brings to the fore the issue of philanthropy, which has a prominent place in the novel. Indeed, Walter's environmental schemes are in all respects philanthropic except paradoxically – given the etymology of the term – in their not having *people* as their primary beneficiaries. Significantly, Jameson has included the philanthropic project, understood as an individual (that is, crucially, *not collective*) attempt to solve the dilemmas of totality, among the strategies of containment used by realist writers to hold in check everything that may threaten the ontological status of the world created by their work. As the American theorist puts it, 'everything which is not-being, desire, hope, and transformational praxis' must be folded back into the status of nature. According to Jameson, 'these impulses toward the future and toward radical change must systematically be reified, transformed into "feelings" and psychological attributes, the properties and accidents of "characters" now grasped as organisms and forms of being' (Jameson, 2002: 181). The philanthropic project then 'stands at the very fault line of such narrative strategies, and is best renaturalized as quixotic altruism, eccentricity, or harmless mania' (2002: 181). As Jameson has noticed, following Lukács, the deployment of the philanthropic endeavour as a novelistic theme involves positing ethical abstraction as a central motivation for a character. This circumstance, given that the proper raw material for narrative is the empirical rather than abstraction, inevitably leads to what Lukács calls 'a demonic narrowing of the soul', which manifests itself only negatively, by the hero having to abandon everything he achieves because '[reality] is never what he wants, because it is broader, more empirical, more life-like than what his soul set out to seek' (Lukács, 2006b: 110). This is, quite precisely, the case of Walter, whose demonic disposition, together with the divergence between his 'abstract idealism', to use Lukács expression, and the non-compliant empirical reality, are made dramatically manifest in his inflamed 'cancer on the planet' speech at the inauguration act for the environmental reserve he has promoted. The novel even contains an explicit piece of praise of philanthropy: although he makes fun of rock celebrity Bono's commercialized persona, Richard Katz – somewhat improbably – acknowledges his integrity in 'trying to do some actual hands-on good in Africa. Like: be a man, suck it up, admit that you like being part of the ruling class, and that you believe in the ruling class, and that you'll do whatever it takes to consolidate your position in it' (F 204).

6 The insidious charm of the ruling class

At the other end of the scale of social antagonists, according to Franzen's upper-middle-class perspective, is what we may call the ruling class, formed by members of the corporate and political elite (which in the novelist's perspective is usually associated to the Republican Party). In *Freedom*, this class is mainly represented by two characters: Vin Haven, the energy tycoon who finances Walter's environmental plan for his own profit-making ends and who finally betrays the spirit of the project; and Howard (whose family name Franzen conspicuously never provides), the founder of a conservative think tank dedicated to produce arguments to support American military intervention in Iraq and elsewhere. Both characters bolster the upward trajectories of Walter and his undergraduate son Joey, respectively. Furthermore, as if in a classical *Bildungsroman*, both characters act as the devious mentors of the upstart hero. Significantly, however, for both Berglunds such association eventually only leads to their entanglement in different webs of corruption from which they have to extricate themselves after sobering disappointment. For Franzen then the games played by the ruling class are essentially debased and there is no way of playing them without getting sullied. In this respect, the coherence in Franzen's outlook throughout his work is remarkable: again, obscure and far-reaching corporations or lobbies, powerful enough to turn the political power into an instrument of their interest, reveal themselves as the true villains of the story. This was the case, we may remember, with the lobbies of corporate interest that indirectly ruled St Louis for their own benefit in *The Twenty-Seventh City*. The pattern is confirmed with Sweeting-Aldren, the rogue corporation that causes earthquakes in *Strong Motion*, and with the Wroth brothers, the speculative investors who buy and subsequently dismantle the Midland-Pacific railroad – as well as public assets around the world – in *The Corrections*. We may observe as well that, as befits a realist writer, Franzen eschews again the paranoia-inducing, undecidable conspiracies of a certain kind of postmodernist fiction. In *Freedom*, the real conspiracy is the collusion of corporate and political interest that leads to that gigantic scam which is the American intervention in Iraq. The actual evil-doers are also visible and unambiguous: George W. Bush, Dick Cheney, Richard Perle and the rest of conservative leaders who control the government. A special mention is deserved in this respect by Howard, the neocon thinker who, with rhetoric borrowed from Leo Strauss, defends the legitimacy of the lies told by the government to justify the war, embodying thus the blunt ideological cynicism that sustains the privilege of the ruling elite. Howard exemplifies the kind of hypocritical but clear-sighted political vision attributed by Critchley to Republican leadership. The depiction of his Jewishness is also interesting. As Franzen makes clear, Howard is too much of a pragmatic cynic to be a real believer. Nevertheless, he is able to turn Jewish cultural heritage into a convenient, consumer-friendly tool for self-help:

'We have the most marvelous and durable tradition in the world', he said. 'I think for a young person today it ought to have a particular appeal, because it's all about personal choice. Nobody tells a Jew what he has to believe. You get to decide all that by yourself. You can choose your very own apps and friends, so to speak'. (F 269)

To this bland depiction of Judaism we can apply Žižek's remarks on so-called Western Buddhism, which he describes as an ideological fetish that helps the *user* through any unsavoury act of cynicism or compromise she may be obliged to perform: 'It enables you to fully participate in the frantic capitalist game while sustaining the perception that you are not really in it, that you are well aware how worthless the whole spectacle is, since what really matters is the peace of the inner Self to which you know you can always withdraw' (Žižek, 2009: 66).

One consequence of this individualistic approach to religion is that it can hardly lead to substantial forms of community since there is obviously little coincidence of interest between a member of the ruling elite associated to the Republican Party such as Howard and, say, a Queens middle-class Jew. But there is an additional and important political implication to the forms of Jewishness presented in *Freedom*, one that reflects Franzen's own antagonism towards identity-based political dynamics which undermine his critical authority as a white straight male intellectual. As Franzen presents it, Judaism becomes a form of empowerment since by invoking it one instantly becomes a member of a (vertical) minority community and this way acquires a better position in the politico-economic competition of American society. This is highlighted by an incident in the last part of the novel. We learn that Edgar, Patty's younger brother and a ruined former stock-market broker, has joined an ultra-orthodox Jewish congregation whose support he relies on to feed his family, and is considering moving with his family to a settlement in Palestine funded by an American Zionist group (which of course involves dispossession of Palestinian citizens). He has become, out of mere material convenience, a *professional* member of a minority. This criticism of identity politics seems to be confirmed by Patty, who, although theoretically a Jew by birth according to Jewish tradition, dismisses any religious or cultural affiliation:

> 'You see,' she said, 'I think, when it comes to religion, you're only what you say you are. Nobody else can say it for you.'
> 'But you don't have *any* religion.'
> 'Exactly my point. That was one of the few things that my parents and I agreed on, bless their hearts. That religion is stoopid.' (F 265)

Patty's parents, the snobbish Emersons, certainly belong to the upper class as well, although on a lower tier than Howard, and therefore bear their own share of guilt in Franzen's social picture. However, their culpability is of a different type and occurs in a different realm: the private sphere of the family. Joyce Emerson is a prominent Democrat politician in New York State and the venality of political activity is more than once alluded to in the novel, but in that public domain the Emersons are redeemed to an extent by Joyce's successful husband Ray and his *pro-bono* work as a lawyer in favour of the socially disadvantaged. What Patty, through whose vision we approach the Emersons, cannot forgive is their parenting. Not only was she always disregarded in favour of her spoiled sister. As she recounts in her autobiographic text, when as a teenager she is date-raped by the young son of an influential, politically allied family, her parents react, appallingly, with calculating tepidness. In the description of the Emersons, *Freedom* repeats the model of family relationship that appears in *Strong Motion*: children neglected by withdrawn, ineffectual fathers and self-absorbed, un-motherly mothers. The Emersons are therefore disabled as providers of what for Franzen is the fundamental communitarian sphere: the family.

7 *Aurea mediocritas*: Franzen's middle-class ideal

Against this range of reactionary and antagonistic social positions Franzen posits his own particular ideal of middle class, which is ultimately an ideal of class reconciliation, as we will see. Franzen's proposed middle-class model is embodied by Walter and Patty Berglund, with whom the reader is invited to sympathize throughout the novel by means of traditional narrative devices such as free-indirect-discourse explorations of consciousness by a sympathetic narrator, and, needless to say, by the emotional response elicited by their painful melodramatic vicissitudes. Like the Probsts in *The Twenty-Seventh City* and the Lamberts in *The Corrections*, the Berglunds are characterized by one circumstance that sets them apart from *regular* middle-class families like, for instance, the Paulsens in *Freedom*, namely the *legitimacy of original hardship* or, to put it another way, the exemption from the original sin of privilege. In this sense, Franzen is again noticeably consistent throughout his work: we may remember how the wealthy Martin Probst is a self-made man who grew up in the Depression era, just like Enid and Alfred Lambert (who, as we know from interviews and Franzen's memoir *The Discomfort Zone*, are modelled to a certain extent on his own parents). All three are examples of social and economic success through reliance on traditional Protestant work ethic. It seems clear that for Franzen the class affiliation of these characters is not the mechanic result of the deterministic workings of the economy but a circumstance loaded with legitimating moral and symbolic values that grant them a distinctive kind of dignity. These characters are then presented not as mere constituents of a class but rather as *honoured* members of a sort of Weberean status group. This receives further confirmation by the way Walter manages to escape the poverty and oppression of his unsupportive and reactionary working-class family by means of sheer abnegation. Particularly, the fact that Walter is able to acquire a notable amount of *cultural capital*, to use Bourdieu's term, getting himself a good education and a remarkably wide range of cultural interest amid the intellectual squalor of his family is part of the general strategy of legitimation of his political and moral stand in the novel. In fact, it may be argued that what legitimizes Walter's gentry membership is precisely this early acquired cultural capital and the distinction it entails. Interestingly, here we can also find another act of justification of Franzen's own career inscribed in the novel: Walter's commendable cultural achievement makes for a refutation of accusations of elitism sometimes addressed to intellectual circles (criticism of the kind sometimes received by Franzen himself, as he acknowledges in 'Mr. Difficult' in the wake of his dispute with Oprah Winfrey in 2001).[7] The ground for such rejection of charges would be, of course, that even if the community of readers often advocated by Franzen in his essays is effectively an elite, membership is self-appointed, as Walter's case shows. A sceptic observer of Walter's upward social mobility might argue, however, that the novel takes it too much for granted, as his trajectory from college to lawyer for the corporation 3M and subsequent senior work for Natural Conservancy is presented as nothing but straightforward. Be it as it may, the difficult circumstances of Walter's formation obviously make a difference for Franzen, who is, for example, keen on making clear that the wealthy neocon consultant Howard *inherited* most of his riches.

8 Beyond the war: Salvation and reconciliation

Status-group legitimacy in terms of *honourable* origin of wealth (according to Franzen's own standard) is only one part of the ideal of middle class proposed by the novel. Equally important is a certain measure of ideological enlightenment, which includes, of course, environmental awareness. This is something that disqualifies the rural, uneducated families led by Coyle Mathis, whose new income, now that they are employed by LBI in its body-armour plant, enables them to instantly and effortlessly join the middle class. In the semi-drunken, unmistakably Franzenesque rant which Walter addresses to them, the novelist seems to vent his exasperation with a middle class that he sees as completely abducted by consumerism. Here, the Franzen of *Strong Motion*, the slightly misanthropist practitioner of systemic, global critique reappears:

> Welcome to the middle class! That's what I want to say ... because it's a wonderful thing, our American middle class. It's the mainstay

---

[7]On 24 September it was announced that *The Corrections* had been selected for the hugely popular Book Club hosted by presenter Oprah Winfrey in her show. According to Burn, 'Winfrey had evidently called Franzen on the afternoon of 31 August to reveal that *The Corrections* would be selected by her powerful book club ... Farrar, Strauss and Giroux apparently printed 500,000 more copies on the strength of her choice' (Burn 2008: 45–6). However, a few weeks after agreeing to appear in the show, Franzen, then in the middle of a sixteen-city promotional tour, began to express his misgivings about his participation in Oprah's Book Club in different interviews to local media. On repeated occasions, he expressed his dislike of a great part of Winfrey's previous choices as well as of her treatment of them, both of which he seemed to regard as, so to speak, middlebrow. Similarly, he declared his uneasiness about the fact that the new volumes of *The Corrections* were to be printed with the Oprah's Book Club logo in their covers. Eventually, Winfrey withdrew her invitation to the show (though not her recommendation of the book). The dispute immediately turned into a national media affair which filled countless pages and minutes on air and attracted numerous accusations of ingratitude, elitism and snobbism upon Franzen. As respects *The Corrections*, however, the controversy apparently only added to its popularity.

of economies all around the globe! ... And now that you've got these jobs at this body-armor plant', he continued, 'you're going to be able to participate in those economies. You, too, can help denude every last scrap of native habitat in Asia, Africa, and South America! You, too, can buy six-foot-wide plasma TV screens that consume unbelievable amounts of energy, even when they are not turned on! ... It's a perfect system, because as long as you've got your six-foot-wide plasma TV, and the electricity to run it, you don't have to think about any of the consequences. You can watch *Survivor: Indonesia* till there's no more Indonesia! (F 483)

The allusion to television in Walter's irate speech reminds us that in previous novels Franzen has shown a remarkable awareness of the conforming effect of the ideological output produced by the media. Most notably, in *Strong Motion* the unremitting use of clichés by the media contributes decisively to deactivate the politically destabilizing potential of the earthquake. In the last chapter of *Freedom* there's an overview image of the newly built Canterbridge Estates by what used to be the relatively unspoiled Nameless Lake.[8] Significantly, Franzen shows us through the windows of each house the flickering of large TV screens telling their viewers 'whatever the world believed was happening to it tonight' (F 557). It is in contact with this un-enlightened middle class, environmentally unfriendly, ideologically alienated by consumerist culture (a middle class, last but not least, whose free-ranging cats are murdering American songbirds), that Walter's innate misanthropy reaches a peak. At this point, the novel's net of antagonisms gets to a deadlock. The system, symbolized by American suburban expansion, reveals itself intractable again, immune to enlightenment and change. This is the kind of social impasse that we may observe in Franzen's early novels, especially in *The Twenty-Seventh City*, and would have surely meant the collapse of the novel's plot, at the hands of the impossibly non-compliant determinism inherent to realism, were it not for the romance-like message of reconciliation brought by rescuing Patty, which is a key element in the ideological message of the novel. In sight of the romantic excess of the memorable *mise-en-scène* of Patty and Walter's reconciliation, with the former determined to let herself die in the cold unless she is rescued by the very person she is actually rescuing from dejection, we may remember

---

[8]Walter's retirement in search of solitude to his modest dwelling by a small lake; his living, quite literally, in contemplation of nature; his conflicts with neighbours he sees as alienated by the uses of society; all this cannot but recall Thoreau's account of his life by Walden's pond (1854). Thoreau's book, which Walter had actually taken to the house as a teenager (F 454), is a classic reminder of the individual's urge, so often told by American literature, to leave behind a society which is seen as irremediably corrupt – an impulse that is inevitably associated with misanthropy. Walter's solitude, however, besides being made impossible by exurban expansion has a contemporary quality to it, as his cottage is equipped with a connection to the Internet.

with Jameson the liberating effects of romance on the stifling confinement to the existent which is characteristic of realism. There is in romance a principle of transformation of reality that transcends realism's commitment to what is (Jameson, 2002: 90–1). From the point of view of Laclau and Mouffe we could argue that, if antagonism represents the experience of the limits of the social, of its ultimate impossibility (Laclau and Mouffe, 2001: 84), that is one impossibility which may be overrun by the magic of romance and melodrama. It is easy now to understand Franzen's choice of *Freedom*'s opening epigraph: 'I, an old Turtle,/Will wing me to some withered bough, and there/My mate, that's never to be found again,/lament till I am lost'. The lines are taken from a climactic scene of reencounter in *The Winter's Tale*, the best known of Shakespeare's final plays, which together constitute a fundamental codification of the architecture of romance in modern literature.

For a contrast, if we look back at Franzen's first novel we may notice that in true realistic logic, that is to say, in absence of the salvational perspectives brought by romance or melodrama, a conspiracy intending to radically subvert the status quo of an American city cannot but fail leaving behind a suffocating sense of despair at an oppressive system. This is obviously not the feeling evoked by *Freedom*, whose ending carefully works to leave each character – and reader – therapeutically satisfied. Indeed, a simple look at the plot of the novel reveals the important presence of melodramatic elements. This is acknowledged by Patty in her autobiographic text, where she refers to the vital trajectory of *Freedom*'s main characters as 'some bizarre pathological sequence of events'. As she rightly wonders, 'What were the chances of all that happening?' (F 139) Chances are certainly few, but as in *Jane Eyre* or the humblest of soap operas, the constantly high emotional temperature enhances suspension of disbelief and we are carried away by the sheer momentum of events in a tale filled with turning-point events or, to use Barthes' terms, a heavily *kernel-driven* narrative.[9] According to Brooks, melodrama infused the realist novel with 'a sense of memorability and significance' (Brooks, 1976: 13) of which the novel was in need. After all, as Brooks persuasively puts it, melodrama belongs to those narrative 'modes which insist that reality can be exciting, can be equal

---

[9]Patty's text, an autobiography entitled *Mistakes Were Made*, 'composed at her therapist's suggestion' (F 27–187), fulfils a fundamental double role: an external one as it provides the reader with an important part of the story of the Berglunds told from Patty's point of view, and an internal one as its discovery by Walter starts a chain of events that drive the novel forward. It is significant that this textual element takes the novel farther away from canonical realism: Franzen does not create an independent narrative voice for Patty that is actually different from that of the rest of the novel (which would have been the *realistic* thing to do), and the passage seems a modern version of the 'discovered manuscript topos' which Michael McKeon sees as characteristic of romance (McKeon: 2002: 57) or, perhaps more precisely, the textual strategy of the 'secret memoir' with which, according to the critic, seventeenth-century romance defended itself against new 'anti-romance' stands (McKeon: 2002: 55).

to the demands of the imagination' (Brooks, 1976: 6). The excitement of theatricality notwithstanding, perhaps the greatest service paid to *Freedom* by its melodramatic component is related to its structural configuration. In absence of conspiracies to set a plot in motion and bring it to its ultimate consequences, melodrama can be a convenient generator of narrative. Of particular importance, to this effect, is its capacity to provide meaningful, satisfying – even if often catastrophic – closure. In Jameson's words: 'emptied of its content and traditional meaning, melodrama ... is also an empty form, which survives to supply the structure of narrative and in particular that by which it can be set in motion and that with which it can find closure' (Jameson, 2013: 160). We should note, nevertheless, that while melodrama – which in any case is a recognizable usual component of the nineteenth-century novel as well – may in a way compensate for the ontological limitations of realism, it also involves its own rigidities, as most generic discourse does. In fact, for Moretti melodrama is the necessary, stabilizing counterbalance to the characteristic irony which he sees as consubstantial to the novel and which always threatens to corrode and undermine its own discourse (Moretti: 2000: 99).

9 Keeping it in the family

To complete Franzen's implicit proposal for social reconciliation we should also notice that just as Walter leaves behind the reactionary, alienated working class, Patty cuts off her ties with the condescending and morally compromised upper-class Emersons, renouncing material benefits to carve the decencies of middle-class life from scratch with Walter. In this way, by means of *déclassement*, the Berglunds become a kind of new social synthesis that carries within itself a potentiality for social reconciliation. This view is consistent with Moretti's claim that 'the novel is founded on the assumption that social relationships are representable through the filter of *personalization*' (Moretti, 2000: 54). This book is dependent on Jameson's claim that all narrative is the manifestation of a political unconscious in the sense that it tries to present a symbolic resolution of an unsolvable social problem. A similar case is made by Moretti regarding the social function of the novel. In his words, 'Symbolic forms are fundamentally problem-solving devices: ... they are the means through which the cultural tensions and paradoxes produced by social conflict and historical change are disentangled (or at least reduced). Here lies the so-called social function of literature, with its so-called aesthetic pleasure: solving problems is useful and sweet' (Moretti, 2000: 243–4).

I have already stated that Franzen's wager, from *Strong Motion* on, is a displacement of political reformist concerns by individual stories of self-amelioration, a retreat from a hopeless public sphere into the private world of the family, where salvation – albeit certainly not without suffering and due expiatory penance – is still possible. This may seem a grim prospect for a reformist at first sight but it shows an evident Utopian drive in the sense Jameson uses the term. If, after all the misery and pain inflicted, Walter and Patty, Chip Lambert and his parents, Louis Holland and Renée Seitchek may all reconcile, surely there might still be some hope for us all at the end of the day. It should be noted that the model of reconciliation proposed by the novel is not one that solves the causes of the conflict, in the familial as in the social realm, but rather one that teaches us to live with them. The conflict between Patty and Walter is the inevitable consequence of her contradictory love for both him and Richard Katz. Patty's infidelity cannot be made not to have happened and innocence cannot be restored, but, as the novel shows, one should be able to move on and leave some of all that suffering behind. In the same way, the causes for the social and ideological antagonisms described in the novel are not really going away, as they are inherent to the capitalist system, but there is always the possibility of mitigation, gradual improvement or damage control, those archetypical liberal goals.[10] In displacing conflicts from the social sphere to the familial then Franzen is opening up a space in which deplored socio-historical facts are 'no longer quite so irreparable, no longer quite so definitive', to quote Jameson in his discussion of Balzac's *La Vieille Fille* (Jameson, 2002: 151). Needless to say, this is not to imply that Franzen envisages family as some Arcadian realm in any way. On the contrary, for the novelist the communities of family and lovers are veritable battlefields fraught with horrors whose exploration Franzen presents as his fiction's overt objective. However, they seem to be the only realms where actual truth can be generated and, thanks to the power of romance, they form the sphere where redemption is always possible.

It is obvious that this kind of arrangement does not constitute a realist synthesis in any way, but rather a *compromise*, which is, according to Moretti, 'the novel's most celebrated theme' (Moretti, 2000: 10). It is this which the *Bildungsroman*-like form employed by Franzen encourages us to pursue. As Moretti puts it, in this favouring of compromise the classical novel of formation shows its adaptation, as a kind of narrative embodiment of the reality principle, to a modern bourgeois culture that is characterized by ideological pliancy and contradiction:

> When we remember that the *Bildungsroman* – the symbolic form that more than any other has portrayed and promoted modern socialization – is also the most *contradictory* of modern symbolic forms, we realize that

---

[10]As Lalitha remarks to the more radical Richard, 'we're a pragmatic organization. We're not trying to overthrow the whole system, we're just trying to mitigate. We're trying to help the cultural conversation catch up with the crisis before it's too late' (F 362).

in our world socialization itself consists first of all in the interiorization of a contradiction. The next step being not to 'solve' the contradiction, but rather to learn to live with it, and even transform it into a tool for survival. (Moretti, 2000: 10)

Franzen is then, to use Žižek's expression, translating 'a historical Real in terms of a family narrative', an ideological operation whereby 'the conflict of larger social forces (classes and so forth) is framed into the coordinates of a family drama' (Žižek, 2008: 52). This undertaking ultimately implies proposing the family as a social model. Such ideological strategy, of course, is hardly new in the history of the novel. As Moretti shows, in the classical *Bildungsroman* the family is often the metaphor for a possible social pact. In his words, 'it is not a question of retreating within the family to pursue there those ends which the public sphere tends to frustrate, but of irradiating outside the family that notion of inner harmony and trustful acceptance of bonds that are its most salient features' (2000: 24). The articulation of an adequate mechanism of social advancement, together with the restoration of social harmony, were, as Moretti has argued, recurrent objectives of the nineteenth-century novel, since both novelists and their audience were eager to see the healing of the breaches brought about by the French Revolution and its aftermath. As the Italian critic puts it, the classical *Bildungsroman* narrates 'how the French Revolution could have been avoided' (2000: 64). In a similar way, once its ideal of enlightened, progressive middle class has been asserted, at the end of *Freedom* movements of conciliation abound. Walter reconciles with his son, with his working-class brothers, and even, thanks to Patty's help, with his *regular* middle-class neighbours in the Canterbridge Estates (the ones previously presented as alienated cat-owners and TV-viewers), in whom he instils the seed of environmental consciousness granting them access to the bird sanctuary into which he turns his property by the lake. Even reconciliation with his former best friend Richard Katz is suggested. On her part, Patty makes peace with her son Joey, with her parents and even sets about assuaging the financial disputes within the Emerson family. Needless to say, the reconciliation of Walter and Patty after their estrangement is the true event of the novel, the cathartic culmination towards which it is structurally directed. This rhetorical strategy corresponds to the type of narrative textual configuration which Moretti, following Yuri Lotman, describes as 'classification principle'. As the Italian theorist argues, although in varying proportions, both the classification principle and a transformation principle are present in all narratives, and the pre-eminence of one over the other has important ideological implications. In his words:

Where classification is strongest – as in the English 'family romance' and in the classical *Bildungsroman* – narrative transformations have meaning in so far as they lead to a particularly marked ending: one that establishes a classification different from the initial one but nonetheless perfectly clear and stable ... This teleological rhetoric – the meaning of events lies in their finality – is the narrative equivalent of Hegelian thought, with which it shares a strong *normative* vocation: events acquire meaning when they led to *one* ending and one only. (Moretti, 2000: 7)

All these acts of reconciliation in *Freedom*, among others, are actantial or proairetic schemata – to use Greimas' and Barthes' terms, respectively – inherited from the classic nineteenth-century novel and as such, as Jameson has shown, constitute narrative *ideologemes* that continue to emit their ideological message 'like a shell or exoskeleton ... long after the extinction of his host', to use the American critic's memorable phrase (Jameson, 2002: 137). In a way then, if for Moretti much of the nineteenth-century novel tries to convey the notion that the revolution never took place, it may be argued that *Freedom* evinces a longing for a return to the height of the liberal consensus more than forty years ago, that is, as if the culture wars had never taken place. This is, to be sure, a wish for reconciliation in one's own terms.

There can be little doubt that an aspiration as the one described above has little use for the classic Marxist vision of society divided into antagonistic classes created by the blind forces of the economic base and vying for hegemony. In contrast, Weber's vision of society structured by different status groups whose respective ideological stance may be assessed on intellectual, moral and even *aesthetic* grounds becomes a valuable support for Franzen's implicit Utopian vision: a harmonic, unequal but organic society where an enlightened elite, self-appointed and meritocratic, rationally and benevolently leads the way towards the common good. This is a kind of communitarian potential that Arrighi, Hopkins and Wallerstein seem to discern in Weber's theory:

A status group-structuring of the distribution of power, because the constituent groups are arrayed honorifically by rank, confers on each other more or less prestige and pride, and through that, the solidarity and capacity to act collectively in relation with one another. A class structuring of this distribution of power, in contrast, because of the market principle – which in its operations for Weber, either eliminates all consideration of honor from its relations or is constrained in its working by them – provides its constituent classes with no necessary solidarity in their relations with one another, and hence no necessary capacity for collective action in or on this relations, In short ... status groups are constituents of and therefore carriers of a moral order, in Durkheim's sense. Classes are not. (Arrighi et al., 1989: 17)

10 The politics of environmentalism: Failure and salvation

After examining the novel's general ideological stance, it is time to analyse in depth its professed political commitment. We have seen that environmental concerns are a constant in Franzen's novels and non-fiction. Whereas in *The Corrections* environmental preoccupations recede to the background, in *Freedom* they become, at least on a conscious level, the overriding political issue. This environmental consciousness in *Freedom* is represented by Walter (who is introduced in the novel's first page as 'greener than Greenpeace') and his young assistant – and eventually also lover – from Bengali origin, Lalitha. Their conservationist project, developed in quite a Faustian way thanks to the copious funding of a questionable sponsor, the aforementioned energy magnate Vin Haven, is twofold. In the first place it involves the creation of a stronghold for a relatively endangered migratory songbird, the cerulean warbler.[11] Here the motif of the creation of a pure, secluded natural space devoid of any human presence reappears. The misanthropic hints of such aspiration are highlighted by the fact that the scheme requires the displacement of dozens of poor rural families – the ones led by Coyle Mathis – from their ancestral homes in a backward West Virginian county. The classist implications of the move are so obvious that the reader is tempted to interpret it as ironic, that is, as an acerbic criticism of the kind of liberal-progressive approach to social problems which is disabled by its coldly intellectual character and its seemingly unbridgeable psychological distance from the actual people on which it is to act – a political stance which ultimately only leads to lower and working-class people embracing all the more readily the ideological decoys offered by the ruling class (just as Mathis' people are bound to become supporters of the Republican-biased politico-corporate complex that will employ them). Walter's project cannot but raise the question as to why the possibility of promoting sustainable, *songbird-friendly* development for that community is never even considered. Again, as in the initial passing allusion to poor black people intruding into the banalities of Ramsey Hill's gentrifiers, it is evoked the possibility of a social and political criticism which would attain real depth insofar as it would be first and foremost a piece of *self*-criticism. However, the novel is clear in its sympathies and these are granted to Walter and Lalitha not only with the traditional resources of the realist novel, such as point of view or exploration of consciousness, but also with the full power of melodrama's capacity for eliciting the emotional identification of the reader.

---

[11]Franzen's indefatigable dedication to bird watching is documented in 'My Bird Problem', included in his memoir *The Discomfort Zone* (2006). In 'The Ugly Mediterranean', included in FA, the novelist recounts his activism in favour of migratory songbirds in Cyprus.

The second part of Walter and Lalitha's environmental scheme is a campaign to raise awareness of the need for global population control, on account of overpopulation being the most acute environmental threat to the planet. According to the two campaigners, since the 1970s, the time when that issue was allegedly an assumed part of the political debate, support for the cause of population control has all but disappeared, in what Walter regards as another manifestation of the culture war through which the political Right has eroded liberal influence: 'In my own way', Walter said, 'I guess it was part of a larger popular shift that was happening in the eighties and nineties. Overpopulation was definitely part of the public conversation in the seventies, with Paul Ehrlich, and the Club of Rome, and ZPG. And then suddenly it was gone. It became just unmentionable' (F 220).

A glimpse at the intellectual references from the late 1960s and 1970s evoked by Walter reveals that they are characterized again by unpleasant detachment and all but entomologist-like indifference to the actual people concerned.[12] Evidently aware of this, Franzen provides a *humane* root to Lalitha's unmovable commitment to the cause: her belief developed as a result of the shock of the vision of overpopulated Calcutta's squalor as a teenager (F 315). The justification mimics Paul Ehrlich's appalling description of Delhi at the beginning of his (discredited) catastrophist classic *The Population Bomb* (Ehrlich, 1968: 1) and inevitably reads as *ad hoc*. However, in spite of Walter and Lalitha's passionate commitment, Franzen's endorsement of Ehrlich's views seems unlikely. Given that in *Strong Motion*, Franzen draws heavily upon the respectable work of the environmental historian William Cronon, it is difficult indeed to explain the poor quality of Walter's theoretical equipment in this particular issue, unless it is because Franzen does intend to portray Walter and Lalitha as 'crackpots', to use his frequent expression. Thus, their exalted, narrow-minded approach contrasts with the author's more comprehensive and tolerant vision. This certainly would justify the novel's subsequent sobering course of events understood as a manifestation of Franzen's currently more moderate stand. By the end of the novel, Walter's vision is both wider and more temperate. To be sure he is – thanks to Patty's quintessentially novelistic intervention, which is to say, thanks to the sympathy-enhancing properties of the novelistic form – more sympathetic and less prone to be judgemental. The implication here is that, until the end of the novel, the author is wiser and less radical than his characters because he has already been through what his characters still

---

[12]Paul Erhlich, co-founder of the Zero Population Growth organization, is an entomologist and professor of population studies. He is the author of the best-selling – and much criticized – *The Population Bomb* (1968), in which he strongly advocates governmental intervention into population control. In that volume, Ehrlich makes a series of catastrophist predictions regarding overpopulation which have proved to be wrong. Like Walter in the novel, in his analysis Ehrlich completely disregards questions of social inequality or the relations of production.

have to endure. Any reader acquainted to the *Harper's* essay will recognize the striking similarity of concerns and pathos between Walter and the Franzen of the early nineties as described by the novelist himself – social disintegration and entropy, erosion of the public sphere, irrelevance of art, commercialization of culture, loss of community:

> 'This was what was keeping me awake at night,' Walter said. 'This fragmentation. Because it's the same problem everywhere. It's like the internet, or cable TV – There's never any center, no communal agreement, there's just a trillion bits of distracting noise. We can't never sit down and have any kind of sustained conversation. All the real things, the authentic things, the honest things are dying off. Intellectually and culturally, we just bounce about like random billiard balls, reacting to the latest random stimuli.' (F 218)

This is probably the novel's fundamental contribution to Franzen's own narrative of conversion. The parallelism of Walter's turmoil with Franzen's avowed state of dejection and despair during the early 1990s is evident: 'He was aware, of course, that it was wrong to feel this way ... He was aware of the intimate connection between anger and depression, aware that it was mentally unhealthy to be so exclusively obsessed with apocalyptic scenarios, aware of how, in his case, the obsession was feeding on frustration with his wife and disappointment with his son' (F 315).

The words used by Franzen to describe himself during the early nineties as 'a very angry and theory-minded person' (HA 4) can easily apply to Walter. As Richard Katz puts it, Walter is 'an *angry* crank' (F 218). This (which, incidentally, is a variation on the well-known novelistic theme of the revolutionary whose ideological ardour derives from frustration and resentment, one of realism's naturalization strategies of Utopian impulses analysed by Jameson) relates the novel to *Strong Motion* as well, where anger and its concomitant depression are key concerns, as illustrated by the character of Louis Holland. In any case, as Franzen confesses in the *Harper's* essay, 'If you are depressed you will sooner or later surrender and say: I just don't want to feel so bad anymore' (HA 93). Then, if we are to believe Franzen's metanarrative, the novelist, for the sake of the continuity of his work, which seemed in great peril, and ultimately for the sake of his own sanity, abandoned postmodernism's more radical approaches to the novelistic form, together with his previous, also radical pretentions of large-scale, systemic social critique. In a way, with this act a Freudian reality principle asserted itself. What Franzen's metanarrative and Walter's story share is that confronted with the impossibility of social amelioration, the only viable alternative they envisage is self-betterment to thus achieve some kind of emotional redemption. In other words, salvation can only be individual. Correspondingly, Walter abandons his grand environmentalist (that is, *political*) schemes to settle for a small scale, local actuation (the modest bird shelter into which he turns his house by the lake), which furthermore at the end of the novel he leaves behind to try and regain domestic, everyday happiness in the domain of the family. The move, like Franzen's, is presented as legitimized by the intensity of the pain he has hitherto endured. Suffering (and the basic human necessity, embodied by the Ego, to stop suffering) is indeed a fundamental source of legitimacy in Franzen's work. It justifies Walter's abandonment of his grand-scale environmentalist approach in *Freedom* as well as Franzen's notorious stylistic and political disavowal within the frame of the narrative the novelist has devised for himself. The suffering of a character is, after all, a basic resource to elicit sympathy and emotional identification in the audience of any narrative. And pain, meticulously described by the omniscient narrator, is what ultimately ennobles the Berglunds' tale of social and emotional dysfunction. In her 2003 essay, Toal already identifies Franzen's use of depression as a source of legitimation for his abandonment of the perspective of progressive social reform (see Toal, 2003: 314). Indeed, it is safe to argue that Franzen has sought legitimation in unhappiness and pain, both for his characters as for himself, all the way from *Strong Motion* and the *Harper's* essay through his recent commencement address at Kenyon College entitled 'Pain Won't Kill You' (Franzen 2012).[13]

But Franzen's self-justification strategy in *Freedom* is not only deployed through Walter's experience: an important part is played by Joey's own narrative. In this sense, it may be argued that while Walter and Patty's story shows important elements derived from the *Bildungsroman*'s tradition, Joey's subplot constitutes a novella of formation in its own right. Joey's narrative has a clear antecedent in Franzen's previous novel, as there is an evident parallelism between Joey's story and that of Chip Lambert, whose life trajectory already constitutes the main expression of Franzen's metanarrative in *The Corrections*. Both characters are defined by their initial anti-parental revolt; both achieve an economic position above their respective merit through the intervention of unsavoury mentors who back their participation

---

[13]In fact, Franzen has used unhappiness as a legitimation strategy so often that we may well consider him an apologist of pain. I shall briefly mention that in the *Harper's* essay, Franzen advocates a 'tragic realism', characterized by its concern with a primordial, inescapable existential pain that he refers to as 'the Ache'. As we have seen, in *Strong Motion* depression and anger are central concerns and are even granted an oppositional import when a depressed Louis Holland clings to his inner 'lump of sorrow' against an unfair state of affairs (SM 503). In the aforementioned commencement address, Franzen argues that 'when you consider the alternative – an anesthetized dream of self-sufficiency, abetted by technology – pain emerges as the natural product and natural indicator of being alive in a resistant world' (FA 11). One of the arguments whereby unhappiness affords Franzen legitimation is that for him it leads to the creation of better art. For example, we may compare the dark, tormented artist Richard Katz, who turns 'his ungratified desire into art' (F 349), with the tepidness of the younger and better-adjusted Conor Oberst. There is also a measure of intergenerational grudge: As the novel informs us, 'his [Richard's] perception of the world as a hostile adversary, worthy of his anger – had made him more interesting than these young paragons of self-esteem' (F 348).

in a dishonest enterprise. The correlate is also noticeable in the salvational character of the account of their moral evolution: both characters undergo a process of self-degradation which is the result of their selfish disposition until they hit the bottom in catastrophic failure. They are subsequently redeemed by self-discovery and assumption of their actual selves, which involves letting go of externally imposed, alien narratives and a commitment to the other within the realms of family and the 'two-person world' (F 476) of a community of lovers. In the case of Joey, the quasi-allegorical move includes renouncing the flashy but insubstantial Jenna, assuming his commitment to his unsophisticated girlfriend Connie, and returning to his so-far disdained family. Last but not least, he gives up his lucrative but immoral job to take up a community-favourable and environmentally friendly work as a broker of shade-grown coffee – a final token of the way in which, as in a classical *Bildungsroman*, his coming of age is associated to his true and honourable social integration. The comic context of the scene notwithstanding, Joey's self-discovery is also presented as a kind of epiphany:

> He could see this person so clearly, it was like standing outside himself. He was the person who'd handled his own shit to get his wedding ring back. This wasn't the person he'd thought he was, or would have chosen to be if he'd been free to choose, but there was something comforting and liberating about being an actual definite someone, rather than a collection of contradictory potential someones. (F 432)

Here we are reminded again that Franzen's metanarrative is also markedly salvational: after a long period of disorientation and ever deeper dejection that results from following self-imposed corrupt and alien literary ways, there is an epiphany-like moment in which the novelist rethinks the nature of his literary calling and decides to listen to his own true self as a writer. Common to Franzen's salvational narratives (those of his characters and his own) is the crucial end of self-deception. Joey stops pretending he can be a 'bad news' character, that is, ruthless in business and in his dealing with women, like some of his successful Young Republican acquaintances, and must settle for his actually being an ordinary decent person. Chip, whose most evident show of self-deception is perhaps his endless retouching of his unviable film script, stops postponing the dreaded coming to terms with the moral contradictions that beset him. Walter is forced to realize the unbearable (though sensed) truth about his marriage, and he must confront the real outcome of his collaboration with Vince Haven. In the same way, according to Franzen's metanarrative, after writing his second novel there is a time when he is unable to continue pretending he is a middle-aged postmodernist writer, the mask that he has donned to avoid confronting the deep personal conflicts that afflict him. A realm of painful personal experience from which, however, its truest writing will flow once the mask has been shed.

The parallelism between the characters of Chip and Joey is also noticeable at another structural level: both are used in order to illustrate an important critical point that Franzen wishes to make. Chip is sent to Lithuania so that *The Corrections* may show from the field the deleterious effects of unchecked capitalism and economic globalization. Joey becomes a Young Republican so that we may observe from within the stark hypocrisy of the neocon ideologists and the ruthless pursuit of self-benefit of the Republican elite. Subsequently, he becomes a contractor for the U.S. military so that we can watch from the inside the true character of American intervention in Iraq: a colossal scramble for spoils and profit, such as described by Naomi Klein (2004). Joey's story is therefore one of the novel's entry points for world history in its proper domain of everyday life – a universal history which, according to Moretti, is 'funneled' and reshaped through the viewpoint of everyday life to amplify and enrich the life of the individual (Moretti, 2000: 35).

11 The elephant in the room

There is another important aspect of Walter's environmentalist commitment that requires discussion here, namely the degree to which it displaces other social concerns. This is especially conspicuous regarding his concern with overpopulation, which Walter heatedly presents as a kind of source of all evils, while on the other hand population control is proposed as a universal instrument of damage mitigation:

> Think about how crowded the exurbs are already, think about the traffic and the sprawl and the environmental degradation and the dependence on foreign oil ... And then think about global carbon emissions, and genocide and famine in Africa, and the radicalized dead-end underclass in the Arab world, and overfishing the oceans, illegal Israeli settlements, the Han Chinese overrunning Tibet, a hundred million poor people in nuclear Pakistan: there's hardly a problem in the world that wouldn't be solved or at least tremendously alleviated by fewer people ... Any little things we might do now to try to save some nature and preserve some kind of quality of life are going to get overwhelmed by the sheer numbers, because people can change their consumption habits – it takes time and effort, but it can be done – but if the population keeps increasing, nothing else we do is going to matter. And yet *nobody* is talking about the matter publicly. It's the elephant in the room, and it's killing us. (F 220)

Overpopulation may well be the elephant in the room of the public debate nowadays, but, as this excerpt shows, there is a voluminous bulk negatively defined at the heart of Walter's discourse too, namely the absence of any reference whatsoever to social emancipation, neither regarding its necessity nor its conditions of possibility or potentiality. In the novel, the politically enlightened, ideologically aware Walter takes existing social and political structures for granted and never gives a thought to issues of social inequality, never considers crucial questions such as the current relations of production, nor even to weigh their environmental consequences. Certainly, we should be wary when assessing Franzen's actual endorsement of Walter's views. We know that for the most part of the novel Franzen emphasizes the exalted elements in Walter's discourse only to demand assent from the audience when this discourse loses its radical edge. Franzen is interested in making his characters appear narrow-minded so as to highlight his own enlarged, sympathetic vision and in doing so he is inscribing an inescapable element of ideological ambiguity in the novel. However, it is Franzen who is using Walter as a mirror and an instrument of self-justification and therefore it seems reasonable to infer a substantial degree of sanction to Walter's stand. We already know that Franzen's novels tend to deny the possibility of collective emancipatory action (although in some cases, like in the first two novels, the possibility is first suggestively evoked and then cancelled), but in *Freedom* its absence is made more patent by the sheer elaborateness of Walter's scheme, and by the cumbersome arguments he has to bring to bear to support it. Indeed, what Franzen's procedure recalls more than anything here are the well-known psycholinguistic strategies of avoidance and substitution. As he recounts in the *Harper's* essay, his head 'had been turned by Marxism' in college (HA 61–2), but now he seems at pains to conceal it. In this sense, it is not difficult to see Walter's environmentalist passion as part of a fetishistic disavowal, a kind of *Verleugnung* involving, to use Žižek's words, 'the elevation into the principal Cause of some fetishistic ersatz of the class struggle as 'the last thing which we see' prior to confronting the class antagonism' (Žižek, 2008: 339). Relatedly, this treatment of a fetishized environmentalism is consistent with Jameson's unmasking of the philanthropic drive as a deactivation of Utopian impulses, discussed above. Here we are once again reminded of Macherey's injunction to the critic to explore not what is in the object of study but rather that which is not: 'the silences, the denials and the resistance in the object – not that compliant implied discourse which offers itself to discovery, but that condition which makes the work possible, which precedes the work so absolutely that it cannot be found in the work' (Macherey, 1989: 150). From this point of view we can consider class struggle and emancipatory fight in the novel as the '*absence* without which it would not exist' (Macherey, 1989: 85).

At times, the conversion of social issues into environmental problems is so obvious that it would look ironic – and as such ambiguous – if, once again, the ironic interpretation were not against the overall rhetorical structure of the novel. In this way, strikingly enough, in the *Harper's* essay Franzen complains about social and cultural fragmentation in the United States and roughly fifteen years later Walter bemoans the fragmentation of the habitat of songbirds in *Freedom*:

> I wasn't accomplishing anything systemic in Minnesota. We were just gathering little bits of disconnected prettiness. There are approximately six hundred breeding bird species in North America, and maybe a third of them are getting clobbered by fragmentation. Vin's idea was that if two hundred really rich people would each pick up one species, and try to stop the fragmentation of their strongholds, we might be able to save them all. (F 218)

We may note, incidentally, once again the eulogy of philanthropy, the idea of progressive change as necessarily promoted by a social or cultural elite. In contrast, the events organized by Free Space, the activist movement for population control created by Walter and Lalitha, soon develop into anarchic, menacing concentrations of radicals, 'the sort of discontents who hit the streets in ski masks to riot against the WTO' (F 494). In good liberal fashion, Walter laments the current national mood of political anger that shows up in meetings sponsored by Free Space: 'His father had been enraged like that, of course, but in a much more liberal era. And the conservative rage had engendered a left-wing counter-rage that practically scorched off his eyebrows at the Free-Space events in Los Angeles and San Francisco' (F 493). The main Free Space gathering in West Virginia turns into an uncontrollable, muddy mixture of Woodstock festival and anti-globalization riot, the crowd certainly closer to an angry mob than to what Hardt and Negri would call a *multitude*. As a horrified Lalitha tells Walter, 'everybody's stoned and spread out over ten acres, and there's no leadership, it's totally amorphous' (F 500). For Hardt and Negri, the multitude is the emerging new model of de-centred, non-hierarchical and pluralistic configuration of singularities acting in common. Although they never provide a tight definition of it, in the trilogy beginning with *Empire* (2000) Hardt and Negri rely heavily on this concept derived from Spinoza's philosophy. For these theorists, the multitude has replaced older sociopolitical groups such as the working class or the proletariat as the main element of democratic resistance in a contemporary global system which they call Empire. In *Multitude*, Hardt and Negri refer to the incomprehension or even downright rejection that contemporary, spontaneous, horizontal movements of protest tend to elicit in the mainstream Left, usually more interested in a nostalgic revival of older communitarian institutions – a response that is evidently shared by Lalitha and Walter:

> Even when something that resembles the people does emerge in the social scene in the United States, Europe and elsewhere, it appears to the leaders of the institutional Left as something deformed and threatening. The new movements that have arisen in the last decades – from the queer politics

of ACT-UP and Queer Nation to the globalization demonstrations at Seattle and Genoa – are incomprehensible and threatening to them, and thus monstrous. (Hardt and Negri, 2005: 191–2)

The picture of deranged progressive action presented by *Freedom* brings to mind the fact that previous depictions of activism in Franzen's work are rather dismal. Most conspicuously, in *The Corrections* we may find the isolated, 'crackpot' individual initiative of Robin Passafaro and her occupational urban garden for slum teenagers in Philadelphia; the mindless and counterproductive brutality of her brother's attack on a W – Corporation executive; and the corruption of the Teamsters' unionism.

Against this sombre scene regarding progressive action, *Freedom* seems to offer environmentalism as the most important reformist field, which brings us to the crucial question of the real critical import of environmentalism in Franzen's proposal. From the point of view of Laclau and Mouffe, environmentalism is just one of the multiple contemporary subject positions which can be included in a hegemonic articulation. However, its meaning cannot be defined *a priori*. As they claim: 'The political meaning of a local community movement, of an ecological struggle, of a sexual minority movement, is not given from the beginning: it crucially depends upon its hegemonic articulation with other struggles and demands' (Laclau and Mouffe, 2001: 87). In this sense, Badiou has observed that, in our time, any perspectives of radical political change are bound to develop as different forms of local collective experimentation (Badiou, 2013: 37). But for the French thinker, 'This experimentation must be guided by ideological norms … It's a question of whether what one does in a particular situation goes in the direction of equality, elaborating a vision that is opposed to the absolute domination of private property and of the political and social organization that depends on this' (2013: 37).

It may be argued, following Žižek, that from a progressive point of view – which is how Franzen presents his proposition – the key question about environmentalism, in the same way as about multiculturalism, feminism, or any other specific or minority concern movement, is whether it can be integrated in a broader chain of progressive struggle for emancipation. The likelihood of this circumstance should be tested against the basic social antagonism underwriting the existing variety of social difference: that between the Included and the Excluded. For the Slovenian thinker, this antagonism is the fundamental one, the point of reference for all others and the source of their subversive edge (Žižek, 2008: 430). For Žižek, only a certain type of environmental activism would qualify as part of the aforementioned emancipatory alliance: 'only those ecologists are included who do not use ecology to legitimize the oppression of the "polluting" poor, trying to discipline the Third World countries' (2008: 428). This is so because, according to Žižek, 'one can sincerely fight for ecology … while not questioning the antagonism between the Included and the Excluded – what is more, one can even formulate some of these struggles in terms of the Included threatened by the polluting Excluded' (2008: 430). Furthermore, as the theorist argues, the overlooking of the mentioned social opposition may lead to an exaltation of philanthropy such as which afflicts Walter. As he puts it: 'In short, without the antagonism between the Included and the Excluded, we may find ourselves in a world in which Bill Gates is the greatest humanitarian fighting against poverty and diseases, and Rupert Murdoch is the greatest environmentalist mobilizing hundreds of millions through his media empire' (2008: 430). In this sense, for example, it is striking to notice that Franzen's frequent allusions to the journeys of migratory birds disturbingly call to mind the hazardous circumstances of migrant people, a pressing issue that is never addressed by the novel.

From these considerations, it should be clear that Walter's political stance, characterized by a peculiar mixture of cold abstractness, rage, intellectual elitism, fetishizing of ecology, and a focus that virtually turns away from the actual sources of social inequality and social antagonism, is no example of 'subversive edge'. Actually, it could be argued that it is only Walter's anger and misanthropy that tells his ecologist devotion apart from environmentalism understood as 'the safest of liberal concerns', as Anis Shivani calls it in his censorious review of the novel (Shivani, 2011: n.pg.). This, of course, is hardly surprising and consistent with the psychological function that the novel performs for its author – a function which is easy to see, following Moretti, as that of protection of the Ego which he predicates of the classical *Bildungsroman*. We have seen that according to the critic, the genre is characterized by an avoidance of threats for the Ego and obstacles for its compromises (see Moretti, 2000: 12). In the case of *Freedom*, that protection of the Ego would be given by the extent to which it contributes to Franzen's own metanarrative (a protection also extensible to readers sharing a similar perspective). In this sense, we know from essays such as 'My Bird Problem' (Franzen, 2006) and 'The Ugly Mediterranean' (Franzen 2012) that Franzen largely shares Walter's environmental concerns, except for the overpopulation issue, which is all but absent from his non-fiction work.[14] It is Walter's ardent concern for population control which stands for the radicalism that Franzen has abandoned in his stylistic and political approach to the novel – the radicalism which, because of the self-justifying function of his narrative of conversion, is open to censure and rejection in *Freedom*. Therefore, in strictly structural terms as regards that symbolic function in Franzen's metanarrative, Walter's zeal for population control would be

---

[14]The population control policies enforced by Chinese governments are briefly and uncritically mentioned by Franzen in 'The Chinese Puffin', a 2008 reportage article on the environmental effects of industrial development in China included in the compilation *Farther Away* (FA: 206).

interchangeable for any other political passion that could be presented as hopelessly utopian. Certainly, consciously formulated utopias have been traditionally ill-treated by the novelistic genre. To use Moretti's argument once more, conscious utopias, like revolutionary rupture, make visible 'all too clearly the abstract one-sidedness of the great forces at the heart of every civilization, forces which any novel tries to exorcise through mediation and compromise' (Moretti, 2000: 54). Now it is pertinent to recall that Franzen has praised the novel's capacity to promote sympathy, a quality which for him seems associated with liberalism and compromise:

> When Jane Smiley uses the phrase 'the liberal novel', she basically means 'the novel, period'. The form is well suited to expanding sympathy, to seeing both sides. Good novels have a lot of the same attributes of good liberal politics. But I'm not sure it goes much further than liberalism. Once you go over to the radical, a line has been crossed, and the writer begins to serve a different master. (Connery and Franzen, 2009: 46–7)

Even the character of Richard Katz seems to support Franzen's apology of compromise by way of negative example: his relentlessly uncompromising attitude has earned him admiration and a street credibility which is his main asset. However, Katz, who is significantly shown in the novel reading Pynchon's *V* and expressing his desire to see the system overthrown, tends to see the world as meaningless and is prone to bouts of self-destructive nihilism. Katz then stands as a symbol of the dead end and destructive potential involved by radicalness. It is in the light of this embracement of sympathy and compromise that one of Franzen's great disavowals that have marked his career, the rejection of critical theory, is best understood, as nothing represents abstract radicalism – and thus threatens compromise – like critical theory. In point of fact, critical theory stands as a symbolic token of Franzen's *conversion*: from initial false faith to abjuration.

Of course, the emphasis put by this book on the *Bildungsroman*'s tendency towards compromise, and on Franzen's readiness to profit from it, cannot but raise the question of the motives behind the environmental (which, I insist, stands for *political*) commitment offered by the novel or, in other words, the question as to why show commitment at all. Discussing in biographical terms the reasons and drives behind Franzen's felt need to write socially engaged fiction would be probably futile, but there are nevertheless certain circumstances particular to contemporary American society that are worth bearing in mind as they are relevant to the ways in which Franzen's social engagement is shaped and expressed. I have already discussed how the rise of identity politics in the United States and elsewhere has badly undermined the cultural authority of white straight male writers. Given the fact that in the contemporary scene the authority of an intellectual's stand is greatly increased by its having an oppositional character, there are compelling incentives for a writer to articulate such a position. In this sense, Joan Didion's memorable words, written in 1965, on intellectuals' need for social engagement are entirely relevant to the understanding of Walter, Franzen's partial alter ego: 'There's something facile going on, some self-indulgence at work. Of course we would all like to "believe" in something, like to assuage our private guilt in public causes, like to lose our tiresome selves; like, perhaps, to transform the white flag of defeat at home into the brave white banner of battle away from home' (Didion, 2008: 162).

The question for a writer such as Franzen is how to substantiate a critical position from the mainstream, with no minority or underprivileged group to rely on, even more when potentially critical subgenres such as the Systems novel have been discarded and political utopias are out of the question. In this sense, environmentalism may afford a much-needed critical position for the novelist. However, we should bear in mind that the same non-specific character which makes environmentalism available for any novelist as an instrument of critical leverage, in practice undermines its actual power as such, unless it is deployed in the way proposed by Žižek, mentioned above. Which is, as we have seen, not Franzen's case.

12 The ring of life: *How to Live. What to Do*

There is another important way in which the novelistic form chosen by Franzen performs that Ego-protective function analysed by Moretti. This strategy is once again related to Franzen's metanarrative and relies on the almost uncanny capacity for narrative to provide meaning and purpose, to impose order and connection on essentially meaningless circumstances and events by providing an inner thread, or *plot*, that connects them, as if sequence somehow engendered causality and purpose. This meaning-conferring capacity is conveyed by Michael J. Toolan's succinct but compelling definition of narrative: 'a perceived sequence of non-randomly connected events' (Toolan, 1988: 7). As Toolan argues, a mere juxtaposition of events does not constitute a narrative. The fact that events are perceived as 'non-random' implies 'a connectedness that is taken to be *motivated* and *significant*' (Toolan, 1988: 7, my emphasis). In Frank Kermode's expression, narrative allows us to 'experience that concordance of beginning, middle, and end which is the essence of our explanatory fictions' (Kermode, 2000: 35–6). A concordance which, in the critic's view, we need all the more acutely in our sceptic times to make sense of the world. This capacity, although inherent to all narrative, seems to reach a formal peak in the classical *Bildungsroman*, in all likelihood as a result of its vocation for harmonizing individual development and social integration. As Terry Eagleton puts it, 'Narrative orders the world into a shape which seems to emerge spontaneously from it'

(Eagleton, 2005: 16). Moretti (2000: 18) illustrates this ordering capacity of the novel with two excerpts from *Wilhelm Meister*:

> I lost myself in deep meditation and after this discovery I was more restful and more restless than before. After I had learnt something it seemed to me as though I knew nothing, and I was right: for I did not see the connection of things [*Zusammenhang*], and yet everything is a question of that. (*Wilhelm Meister*, I, 4)
>
> The presence of the ancient well-known works of art attracted and repelled him. He could grasp nothing of what surrounded him, nor leave it alone; everything reminded him of everything. He overlooked the whole ring of his life; only, alas, it lay broken in pieces in front of him, and seemed never to want to unite again. (*Wilhelm Meister*, VIII, 7)

These passages find a clear echo in Franzen's presentation of Walter's existential disorientation and sense of meaninglessness:

> He let the phone slip from his hand and lay crying for a while, silently, shaking the cheap bed. He didn't know what to do, he didn't know how to live. Each new thing he encountered in life impelled him in a direction that fully convinced him of its rightness, but then the next new thing loomed up and impelled him in the opposite direction, which also felt right. *There was no controlling narrative*: he seemed to himself a purely reactive pinball in a game whose only object was to stay alive for staying alive's sake. (F 318, my emphasis)[15]

There is an evident parallelism between Wilhelm's lack of *Zusammenhang* and Walter's longing for a 'master narrative'. As Moretti argues, the German term used by Goethe is revealing, in its double meaning, of the narrative logic of the classical *Bildungsroman*. As the Italian theorist puts it, it tells us that 'a life is meaningful if the *internal* interconnections of individual temporality ("the plot of all life") imply at the same time an opening up to the *outside*, an ever wider and thicker network of external relationships with "human things"' (2000: 18). In this way, plot as a chronological sequence 'is transfigured into a system of relationships' (2000: 19). In the classical *Bildungsroman* then, the processes of the hero's socialization and the achievement of maturity go hand in hand, and completeness of the individual is achieved in community. As Moretti puts it, 'One must learn first and foremost, like Wilhelm, to direct "the plot of [his own] life" so that each moment strengthens one's sense of belonging to a wider community' (2000: 19). Then, once the process is completed, the narration can conclude.

---

[15]In the passage Franzen seems to be alluding to an early poem by Wallace Stevens precisely entitled *How to Live. What to Do.*

In turn, in invoking *narrative* as an ordering principle, Walter is making basically the same plea as Wilhelm, as narrative is a privately originated activity which also opens up to the social outside. Narrative works indeed simultaneously as an inner sense-making procedure that strings events in a thread of causality and as a social, performative speech act intended to cause an effect in an audience. As Macherey put it, the logic of narrative 'compels' both its producer and its receiver (Macherey, 1989: 43). For Walter, narrative is ultimately the instrument required to reconnect with society and escape the prison-house of misanthropy. The difference between the heroes of classical *Bildungsroman* and Walter – and the rest of Franzen's perplexed creatures for that matter – is the sense of what lies in that outside. For Franzen, the target community for the maturing hero can only be that of family, or even its core, the community of lovers, 'a couple united as a front against the world' (F 476) – that 'two-person world' to which he frequently alludes in his work, since larger communities have been discarded as impossible in a world marked by fragmentation. Actually, as Franzen famously bemoaned in the *Harper's* essay, in the contemporary cultural climate even the performative character of narrative would seem dubious, as its audience inexorably dwindles and blurs, were it not for the community of readers whose existence the novelist has recurrently argued through several essays.[16] In any case, it is only when eventually Walter and Patty arrive at a true, secure version of this 'two-person world', authenticated by all their previous suffering, that they achieve true maturity and stability – the final stage towards which the plot of the novel has been directed. Reconciliation is thus accomplished and the narration, as salvational as the narrative of Franzen's conversion, can finally close. This is, by all standards, a far cry from realism. Realism is rather calculated contingency, the 'meaningful meaninglessness' – to use Moretti's phrase – of Barbara Probst's absurd death and Martin's perplexity at the end of *The Twenty-Seventh City* – curiously the novel which is usually considered the least realist among Franzen's. A rapid comparison with Lalitha's death in *Freedom* is revealing: Lalitha's untimely death is tragic, but *meaningful*, or, to put it another way, her death is given meaning by the narrative insofar as it brings about a great deal of things that *need* to happen so that the novel achieves its meaningful closure: Walter's abandonment of his over-ambitious activism, his hermit-like retirement to his house by the pond, sympathetic identification with his grief on the part of readers and other characters alike, and, ultimately, his rescue by Patty and subsequent reconciliation which constitute the climax of the novel. What we find then with increasing clarity through Franzen's novels from *Strong*

---

[16]In his 2012 essay 'On Autobiographical Fiction', compiled in *Farther Away*, while recalling the compositional process of the *Harper's* essay, the novelist restates his belief in a community of readers and writers: 'I became aware of belonging not just to the two-person team of me and my wife but to a much larger and still vital community of readers and writers. To whom, as I discovered, crucially, I also had responsibilities and owed loyalty' (FA 133).

Motion on until its culmination in *Freedom* is a kind of happy ending which, although common in classic realist novels, actually inheres in romance. This makes for the curious paradox that Franzen's first novel, usually considered the most clearly postmodernist one, actually contains a realist ingredient which is weakened in Franzen's subsequent more 'realist' fiction. There is, at any rate, little room for salvation in true realism. In fact, the truth is quite the opposite, since for a truly realist narrative an unhappy ending is all but compulsory. In contrast, it is easy to see how the narrative strategy of the happy ending contributes to Franzen's metanarrative: the recurrent happy endings we can find in Franzen's novels from *Strong Motion* represent quite literally its sanction. Happy endings, as the teleological culmination of the narrative, reinforce the sense of meaningfulness provided by the narrative form by elevating it to the category of immanent. As Moretti describes it, 'Time is transfigured by the meaning it has helped to establish, and the latter is in turn immanent to the world we find at the work's end' (2000: 118). And the happiness that reigns at the end of *Freedom* certifies that yielding to the reality principle which brought about Franzen's and Walter's respective disavowals was the right thing to do. Here we can conclude, with Moretti, that the reality principle, rather than the antagonist of the pleasure principle as is usually assumed, is actually an extension of the latter, which, by modifying and extending it, makes its fulfilment possible. After all, if the basic aim of the Ego is to avoid unhappiness, it is by being led by the reality principle that it manages to be at ease in the world. Stopping suffering, avoiding unhappiness, being at ease in the world. 'If you are depressed you will sooner or later surrender and say: I just don't want to feel so bad anymore.' This is certainly a life goal one can relate to, and one which for the novelist is worth a whole narrative of salvation.

6

Recapitulation: What's in an ending?

Closings are the keystone of Franzen's romance-like narratives, and *Freedom*'s finale is so resonant that it seems fit to end not only a narrative but also a metanarrative, the one that ideologically sustains most of Franzen's fiction. Still under the spell of that ending, it is appropriate to sharpen our focus on the evolution of Franzen's way of providing a closure for his novels, as it is revealing of the gradual development of his textual strategies of legitimation. As we have seen, Franzen has resorted to the salvational teleology of romance ever since *Strong Motion*. But there is a qualitative difference between *Freedom* and the previous novels, which arises from the respective different degrees of formal and emotional emphasis with which salvational closure is asserted. To be sure, *Strong Motion*'s happy end was in sharp contrast with the bleakness of *The Twenty-Seventh City*, but it looks certainly cautious and restrained with hindsight after the impact of *Freedom*'s ending. It almost looks like a last-minute change of mind on Franzen's part. Even though the airiness of *Strong Motion*'s ending is reinforced by the enumeration of three weddings of secondary characters, in an obvious celebration of family bonds, there is a tentative quality to the way Franzen presents the prospective life in common of Louis and Renée. The narrative ends soon after their reconciliation with an ambiguous note: the last thing we see from them is a minor argument. The possibility of childbearing has been hinted at, but for all we know their relationship might as well be finished the next day. What we have is Louis's invitation for Renée to walk with him:

> 'Oh, what's wrong, what's wrong?'
> 'Nothing's wrong. I swear to you. I just have to walk now. Walk with me, come on. We have to keep walking.' (SM 508)

Four years later, the *Harper's* essay clearly shows Franzen using a salvational narrative pattern to reconcile personal contradictions: through recognition of his true writing self and dedication to his proposed community of readers he is able to escape depression and is reborn as a novelist. The pathos of the closing lines of the essay is actually not unlike that of *Strong Motion*'s ending: hopeful but not quite wholeheartedly affirmative: 'A generation ago, by paying close attention, Paula Fox could discern in a broken ink bottle both perdition and salvation. The world was ending then, it's ending still, and I'm happy to belong to it again' (HA 97).

With *The Corrections*, Franzen certainly goes one step beyond in the spirited assertiveness of its ending: the epilogue informs us that Chip finds love and stability with his father's neurologist and becomes the father of twins. It is also suggested that Chip is well received by the family of his new Jewish wife. And, certainly, there is the novel's last line conveying Enid's sense of liberation after Alfred's death: 'She was seventy-five and she was going to make some changes in her life'. Still, this information is provided in summarized way in a semi-comic, anti-climactic epilogue completely devoid of the emotional intensity of the previous scene led by Chip and his sick father at the hospital. The power of *Freedom*'s ending is definitely on a higher level and is the product of the melodramatic intensity of Walter and Patty's reconciliation: its carefully staged theatricality realized in Patty's apparent decision to let herself die of cold, without uttering a word, rather than going away from Walter again; her seeming last-resort rescue by the latter; the immense relief – for characters and readers – at the realization, pointed out by the narrator, that the unbearable heaviness of all their previous suffering, of all their mutually inflicted wounds, has come to equal the weight of a feather. In fact, Patty and Walter's encounter is invested by Franzen with the mysticism of *communion*:

And so he stopped looking at her eyes and started looking into them, returning their look before it was too late, before this connection between life and what came after life was lost, and let her see all the vileness inside him, all the hatreds of two thousand solitary nights, while the two of them were still in touch with the void in which the sum of everything they'd said or done, every pain they'd inflicted, every joy they'd shared, would weigh less than the smallest feather on the wind.
'It's me,' she said. 'Just me.'
'I know,' he said, and kissed her. (F 559)

This climax is also followed by an epilogue where the loose ends of the narrative and characters are tied up and reconciliation triumphs, but this time we are left in no doubt as to the actuality of Walter and Patty's ensuing happiness together. Likewise, as in a classical *Bildungsroman*, Franzen is clearer about the balance achieved by Walter between his always unsatisfied individuality and the necessity of social integration.

We find an eloquent defence for his unabashed deployment of narrative closure in Franzen's interview with Burn. When the critic observes the contrast between the open character of the endings in Franzen's first two novels and the more tightly resolved endings of *The Corrections* and *Freedom*, the novelist uses a rhetoric which is reminiscent of his polemic essay 'Mr Difficult'. It is significant that Franzen also relates happy endings to *meaning* – a match which ultimately lacks a rational justification but which is revealing once again of the protective psychological function performed by the kind of fiction practised by Franzen:

> I can see that lack of resolution as a young writer's move. You find that you have talent as a novelist, you understand a lot more about the world than many other people your age do, and yet you haven't lived enough – certainly I hadn't – to really have something to say. Everything is still guessed at, every conclusion is provisional. And this came to be my gripe at postmodern aversion to closure. It's like, Grow up already! Take some responsibility for your narrative! I'm not looking for *the* meaning, but I'm looking for *a* meaning, and you're denying me a vital element of making sense of any story, which is its ending! Aversion to closure can be refreshing at certain historical moments, when ossified cultural narratives need to be challenged. But it loses its subversive bite in a culture that celebrates eternal adolescence. It becomes part of the problem. (Burn: 2010: 70)

In *Reading for the Plot*, Peter Brooks reminds us that the relationship between ending and meaning has been a constant in much thought on narrative from Aristotle on. Brooks follows Barthes in identifying the reader's desire for meaning with a desire for the end of the narrative (Brooks, 1984: 92). But one does not need to wait until the end to experience the power of an ending to generate meaning. For Brooks, the sense of a beginning is already determined by the sense of an ending. Even more, the sense of an ending actually structures the narrative at any given point. As the critic puts it: 'we are able to read present moments – in literature and, by extension, in life – as endowed with narrative meaning only because we read them in anticipation of the structuring power of those endings that will retrospectively give them order and significance of plot' (1984: 94). Accordingly, one of the effects of *Freedom*'s climax and ensuing closure is that the previous events of the narrative, even the most painful ones, instantly become teleological, that is, conducive to this very result. They become, so to speak, justified. Therefore we can see that Walter's attempts to act upon the public sphere on a grand scale, that is, his schemes to create a vast, untouched natural reserve for the cerulean warbler first and, then – even more ambitious – to organize a large, influential NGO in favour of population control, are destined to fail with a backlash of pain and tragedy for Walter. Quite simply put, Walter's experience shows that trying to change the world leads to failure and depression. It should be noted that Walter's plans are presented as radical measures fuelled by radical theories and ultimately by deep personal frustration of familial origin. In contrast, humble recognition of one's limitations, which includes the abandonment of illusions of grandeur and the rejection of over-ambitious abstract theory, allows Walter to open up his shut-off self to the demands placed upon him by his closest others – his family. In this way, the Berglund family, a small community which was in a shambles, is regenerated, and in turn will act as a mediator to allow Walter's integration into larger social communities, as is proved by Patty's deft mediation between the misanthropic Walter and his neighbours at Canterbridge Estates. Large-scale reforms have been discarded then, but substantial benefits, even if more limited in scale have been achieved. 'You must be the change you wish to see in the world', says a famous aphorism attributed to Gandhi, and the modest bird sanctuary by the lake left by Walter to that community becomes a symbolic reminder of what the world could become if everyone lived by that principle.

It is surely not necessary to insist on the similarities between this biographical trajectory – or that of Chip Lambert, for that matter – and Franzen's personal *Künstlerroman*, started in the *Harper's* essay and subsequently echoed by critics. Notorious disavowals of previous professions such as Walter's, and drastic, publicized shifts in literary and ideological stances such as Franzen's usually require some kind of justification or legitimation on the part of the subject, especially if they imply the retreat to a zone of ideological comfort. No doubt an effective one is to present them as a way out of intolerable suffering or, even better, to cast them as the traditional structural element of *recognition* (including both self-recognition and recognition of the closest other) in a romance-like narrative culminated by ethical or amorous commitment. Thus, in the *Harper's* essay and 'Mr Difficult' we are made to know that Franzen's self-imposed burden led him to sheer depression and how he could only escape from it *in extremis* by letting go of that weary and misguided load, coming to terms with his true literary self, and embracing a narrative mode that would allow him to concentrate in small (familial) communities that were emotionally and experientially close to him. In this way, the novelist came to serve that family-like community of readers he had just come to recognize and to which he is now committed. It is only a small conceptual leap that allows us to grasp how, drawing on the teleology of narrative and the sentimental power of romance and melodrama, Franzen's stance is justified by Walter's, as it had previously been by Chip's and, still in a tentative way, by Louis's.

It is not hard to see that all these formal decisions on Franzen's part are ideological; that is, they imply an assessment of social situations and an implicit evaluation of different possible courses of political action. There is certainly a difference between showing examples of resistance and displaying social assimilation. Pursuing social conflicts to their roots through an open-ended, contingent world, as Franzen tries to do in his first novel, is one thing, while protecting the Ego by means of ideological compromise is an altogether different one. Showing individual amelioration as the only way to improve society is a decision which has a political significance. Symbolically deactivating persistent social and political contradictions by transporting them to the more amenable sphere of the family, a domain where they can be solved by the wish-fulfilment power of romance and melodrama, involves an ideological move. And it is one, I should say, that seems scarcely possible outside one particular world-view, namely that of liberalism. The only one in which, as Jameson has put it, 'the political and the ideological are mere secondary or "public" adjuncts to the content of a real "private" life, which alone is authentic and genuine' (Jameson, 2002: 279). Franzen's position then implies (and thus supports) a typically liberal separation between the realms of private life and politics which, according to Jameson, would not be possible 'for any world-view – whether conservative or radical and revolutionary – that takes politics seriously' (2002: 279).

It should be clear that Franzen's formal and thematic choices are ideological not only in the more obvious, common-sense meaning of the term, that is, in the sense that they support the liberal ideology. They are profoundly ideological in that – like most cultural products at any historical moment for that matter – they work to, in Jameson's terms, 'manage' and 'defuse' potentially dangerous political impulses conducive to change which are instead rechanneled and offered different 'non-political' objectives of a 'private' nature. But we should not forget either that, as Jameson has argued following Bloch, there is a dialectical relation between ideology and the Utopian impulse. In the course of the very process whereby cultural products deactivate potentially destabilizing political or proto-political impulses, these same drives must perforce be evoked, which in a way keeps them alive. As has been shown, this circumstance is particularly visible in *The Twenty-Seventh City* and *Strong Motion*, where the final assertion of the immutability of the status quo, which I have interpreted as a product of a specific ideological climate, cannot conceal the intense underlying Utopian yearnings. In these two novels, hopes of change are frustrated, but the wishes for a true Event and for the sense of fulfilment afforded by commitment to a community of activists have been inscribed. But there is yet another aspect of the relation between the ideological and the Utopian to be considered in relation to Franzen's work. We have seen that Franzen's novels incorporate rhetorical artefacts of ideological legitimation which support not only his particular political and literary evolution, but much larger perspectives of social antagonism in ongoing disputes for cultural and political hegemony in the United States and elsewhere. As Jameson shows (2002: 277–8), this kind of devices, like all genuine hegemonic attempts, cannot perform their function by sheer force. Rather, they must compel assent through persuasion, that is, by offering their receivers different types of incentives and gratification. Again, this can be perceived in Franzen's work. The abandonment of perspectives of change in the public sphere, the relinquishment of public intervention, the desertion of the idea of collective emancipatory action that are symbolically staged in *The Corrections* and *Freedom* require powerful ways of compensation for both writer and readers. These can be found – by means of the elation produced by the reader's sympathetic identification with characters, which as we know has become a central preoccupation for Franzen – in the absorbing quality of melodramatic vicissitudes within families, in the compelling force of personal narratives of salvation. As Bloch realized, the gratification of Utopian impulses is a fundamental incentive in the process of ideological persuasion and legitimation. In this sense, it is not difficult to notice that *The Corrections* and *Freedom* still harbour Utopian longings only now at a deeper level, confined within a more manageable domain. After all, the fact that the novelist is proposing family as a sort of last refuge from the ruthless anomie of late capitalism constitutes of itself a Utopian statement. Like Franzen's characters, surrounded by a bitingly cold environment, we are still in sore need for the warmth of communion and community, and in his novels Franzen provides us with them within the small world of the family or the 'world of two' of the community of lovers.

Before this recapitulation comes to its end, there is still a last methodological aspect to be addressed. The attention devoted to Franzen's use of the teleological quality of narrative for self-legitimating highlights the fact that this study has also told its own story: that of the linear development of Franzen's formal and ideological strategies of self-legitimation. Inevitably then this book has made use of some of the very same meaning-conferring properties of narrative exploited by the novelist: the capacity to originate connectedness, to turn sequence into causality. In fact, it is not difficult to realize that this book contains a metanarrative on a metanarrative. This circumstance does not invalidate its claims: it might well be that all criticism with a diachronic perspective actually resorts to the properties of storytelling. Not to mention that there is a distinctive teleological thread joining usual structural elements such as the introduction and the conclusion of any text.

7

Epilogue: *Purity* and hope

When pain and danger press too nearby, they are incapable of giving any delight, and are simply terrible; but at certain distances, and with certain modifications, they may be, and they are delightful, as we every day experience.

EDMUND BURKE

1 Romance and narrative desire

It is surely a fortunate circumstance that Jonathan Franzen's latest novel is not organized around the same salvational metanarrative I have discussed in the previous chapters. Certainly, another novel built upon the same structural pattern would have become redundant and with *Purity* Franzen proves his ability to explore new narrative territories. But this is not to say that the same old fundamental ideologico-formal nodes that have previously articulated Franzen's narrative are absent here. On the contrary, in *Purity* the familiar perspectives of salvation and redemption are as intensely felt as anywhere else in Franzen's work, while the use of narrative elements taken from the romance tradition is arguably taken to new heights. This is easily shown by the mere enunciation of the novel's plot, which is probably best discussed right at the outset. This is the tempestuous sequence of events:

Purity (Pip) Tyler is a young graduate who shares a squat in Oakland, California, with a group of people that includes a variety of social misfits, radical political activists and a Hispanic immigrant with a cognitive disability. She has a precarious job as a telemarketing phone operator for a semi-fraudulent energy distribution business that cashes in on the environmental concerns of its customers. Pip is in constant financial trouble as she is burdened by an $180,000 student debt. Pip's mother, who works as a supermarket checker in Santa Cruz, is emotionally dependent on her daughter. It is the case that, for reasons unknown at the beginning of the novel, she had left Pip's father and assumed a new identity before Pip was born. Much to Pip's vexation, her mother stubbornly refuses to reveal the name of her father and even keeps the secret of her own identity and previous life.

Increasingly distressed after a series of painful romantic setbacks, Pip quits her job and is recruited for an internship in the Bolivian headquarters of The Sunlight Project, an organization devoted to leaking confidential information concerning the malfeasance of corporations and governments. There she meets the Project's charismatic leader, the German Andreas Wolf, a Julian Assange-like figure with whom she engages in an intense but unsuccessful relationship. It is Pip's hope that Wolf will help her find his father's identity.

The next section of the novel is concerned with the personal trajectory of Andreas Wolf in the Democratic Republic of Germany during the 1970s and 1980s. Andreas is the son of a professor of English Studies. He was conceived outside his mother's marriage but was recognized by her mother's husband, a respected member of the Central Committee. He is therefore a member of the Republic's elite. Andreas has a brilliant mind but is tormented by a life-long problematic relationship, suggestive of an unresolved Oedipal situation, with his emotionally unstable mother. This familial conflict has made Andreas into an angry, cynic person, unfit for the rigid sociopolitical environment of East Germany and disinclined to love relationships. He is disgraced after he publishes a satirical poem on socialism. Protected by his influential parents, he takes refuge in a Protestant church where he works as a counsellor for young people at social risk while he indulges in constant womanizing. One day he meets Annagret, a teenage girl who is being sexually attacked by her stepfather. The latter is a Stasi informant who takes advantage of the perilous position of Annagret's mother (a nurse secretly addicted to drugs) to prevent his stepdaughter to act against him. Andreas, who has fallen in love with the girl, convinces Annagret to let him kill her stepfather, which he does with her help. Affected by remorse and the fear of being caught, Andreas and Annagret become estranged for ten years. In 1989, during the last days of the socialist regime, Andreas has the chance to get into the Stasi general archive and smuggle out his personal file, where he presumes he is held as suspect for the murder. As he is running out of the building he is filmed by a television crew and thus achieves international fame. Soon he turns into a global celebrity activist, chased by governments around the world as he develops his leak-hosting organization. Nevertheless, Wolf is increasingly beset by depression and psychic fragmentation and ends up committing suicide by throwing himself off a cliff near his Bolivian headquarters.

In the months before his death, Wolf talks Pip into working with Tom Aberant, the director of an online news service based in Denver with whom Wolf had unsuccessfully tried to cultivate a friendship. Crucially, not only is Aberant aware of Wolf's crime but he had even helped him move the hidden corpse of Annagret's stepfather to a safer location in 1989. Wolf has found that Aberant is Pip's father (a circumstance unknown to Tom) and is acting mostly out of spite, trying to damage their future relationship. Eventually, Wolf illuminates Pip with the truth about her origin by sending her an autobiographical text which he has illegally extracted from Tom's computer. Through this document, Pip learns about the turbulent love relationship between their parents and, notably, she discovers that her mother is in fact Anabel Laird, a former feminist artist who had forsaken her family, one of the richest in America, before disappearing and changing her identity. Pip also finds out that her mother is the heiress to a fabulous amount of wealth which she refuses to claim.

Some months come by in the course of which Pip comes to terms with the truth about her family. She goes back to Oakland and takes a job at a coffee shop. She is reconciled with Jason, a young math graduate with whom she builds a satisfactory love relationship. With his help she arranges an encounter for her parents in the hope that they can be in at least civilized terms.

As we can see, this markedly kernel-driven narrative includes distinctively romance-like situations such as disguised identities that are eventually disclosed; far-fetched and life-changing coincidences; peripeteian changes of fortune which include the inheritance of vast sums of money; emotionally super-charged recognitions. Perhaps above all, the heroine's evolution through the story has all the elements of a *quest*. From a structural point of view, the initial situation that brings about the movement of the narrative is distinctively romance-like: a situation of lack, an imbalance in the state of affairs. In the previous chapter, we have seen that any narrative is moved by *desire* – a desire for meaning which is ultimately fulfilled by an ending. At the beginning of *Purity*, Pip's state of mind is marked by deep dissatisfaction. She is in sore financial and social need, but above all she is beset by a strong yearning: she wishes to know the identity of her father – adamantly withheld by her mother – and by the same token her own. This want produces a state of 'narratability' in the text which is described by Peter Brooks in erotic terms: 'a tension, a kind of irritation, which demands narration ... a condition of tumescence, appetency, ambition, quest' (Brooks, 1984: 103). A similar desire, according to the critic, lies at the heart of our desire for narrative plots. These concepts are part of a suggestive analogy drawn by Brooks between the workings of narrative and the account of human life provided by Freud in his essay *Beyond the Pleasure Principle* (1920) – a comparison which shall prove relevant for my analysis of the novel.

We have seen that the conspiracies of Franzen's early fiction were convenient narrative resources with which to generate *narratable* events in a socio-historical situation perceived as essentially eventless. Similarly, I have already pointed, following Jameson and Moretti, at melodrama's capacity to bring about narration-worthy events or, to put it other way, to invest daily life with a sense of memorability. In the same way, there is no doubt that the almost *sexual* proliferation of plot afforded by a romance-like configuration also offers substantial rewards for the contemporary novelist. For the

South Korean – born German philosopher Byung-Chul Han (2015), we live in a 'society of transparency' (*Transparenzgesellschaft*), where principles of *selection* are replaced by mere *addition*. This means that the drive towards the inert accumulation of information has become dominant in contemporary culture. For Han, this situation entails a semantic impoverishment in the first place but also a loss of 'narrativity'. To exist at all, Han argues, narration requires selection, and this implies a measure of *negativity*, tension and resistance which are all but absent in a culture dominated by an excess of *positivity*. In this wider context, Franzen's choice of romance is best understood. The realist novel, with its built-in ontological conservatism, seems more vulnerable than romance-like fiction to this kind of narrative stagnation. In contrast, the idea of adventure, so dear to romance, is related to what is to come (*ad-venire*), as Brooks reminds us (Brooks, 1984: 93), and is therefore filled with a narrative promise. Certainly, as regards *Purity*, Pip goes through vicissitudes that can be seen as nothing short of an adventure.

It is interesting to notice that Franzen is today generally taken as a straightforward realist writer. However, on a different, deeper level of analysis we could argue that his liberal use of the literary past as a catalogue of narrative resources is arguably so deeply postmodern we no longer even notice it. This nominalist debate is not, in any case, my main interest here. Besides, the articulation of more or less realist novels upon romance-like narrative structures is hardly new. As Bakhtin observed, the novel – and particularly the *realist* novel – is a protean, destructive genre that in the course of its historical development has eroded other related narrative forms but has nevertheless been able to incorporate them. Another way of putting it is that realism's opposition to these forms is somehow internal. As Jameson claims, 'realism is opposed to romance only because it carries it within itself and must somehow dissolve it in order to become its antithesis' (Jameson, 2013: 139). Therefore, for example, the blueprint of romance is certainly visible, even if transformed, in many of the landmarks of the nineteenth-century British novel. Numerous writers incorporated non-realist elements from romance or melodrama into their novels, attesting to the inclusiveness of the genre. As an example that can be related to *Purity*, two major works of the nineteenth-century realist novel, George Eliot's *Daniel Deronda* and Henry James's *The Princess Casamassima* show characters in search of a father. For Eagleton, this suggests that novels are in essence romances that have adapted to a new environment:

> Novels are romances – but romances which have to negotiate the prosaic world of modern civilization. They retain their romantic heroes and villains, wish fulfilments and fairy-tale endings, but now these things have to be worked out in terms of sex and property, money and marriage, social mobility and the nuclear family. ... In the Brontës, George Eliot, Hardy and Henry James, you can find vestiges of 'premodern' forms such as

myth, fable, folk-tale and romance, mixed with 'modern' ones like realism, reportage, philological investigation and the like. (Eagleton, 2005: 2–3)

Moretti (200) has discussed the reliance on romance shown by the English novel from its inception as a sign of the political stability achieved by England prior to the totalizing intellectual systematization brought by the Enlightenment. Duncan, however, has dismissed Moretti's arguments as simplistic. For Duncan, the generalized presence of romance elements in the nineteenth-century English novel does not denote an archaic character, but rather attests to its modernity (Duncan, 1992: 5–6), particularly as it is related to its ability to transcend generic boundaries and its resistance to the polarization between 'high' and 'low' literature. Though not acknowledged by Duncan, another trait that distinctively relates Victorian fiction to our culture is the propensity to use sentimentality to cut through the contradictions of an impossibly complex world – a world which, rapidly transformed by industrial revolution and a veritable globalization, was perhaps in some respects not so distant from our own.

The considerations above will allow us to readily recognize that the influence of the nineteenth-century English novelistic tradition, which was already perceivable in *The Corrections*, is paramount in *Purity*, as Franzen acknowledges with the nickname of the novel's heroine, taken from Dickens's *Great Expectations*. In turn, other narrative modes and genres previously dominant are downplayed now. It is the case of *Bildungsroman*, which was central in *The Corrections* and *Freedom*, but also of the classic novel of social analysis and panoramic scope. This is not to say that Franzen has altogether abandoned *synthetic* realism in *Purity* but rather that he has opted for an apparently more restricted focus and a less *allegorical* way of reflecting the times in his fiction. This entails less reliance on symbolically representative characters than was the case in *The Corrections* and *Freedom*. Likewise, the amount of text overly devoted to explicit social analysis is strikingly small if we compare it with Franzen's previous novels. Once again, he has brought to bear Paula Fox's *Desperate Characters* as an inspiration. We may notice as well that Stendhal's old notion of the novel as a mirror of what is most significant in the world is still patent in Franzen's argumentation:

One of the characteristics of dreams is that, as long as they last, they feel like they're taking place in a complete world. And this is very substantially paradoxical, because the dreamer tends to be focused on a small number of intensely meaningful objects, rather than on the world around them. If there's a trick to recreating this paradox in a novel, it's one I learned from reading and rereading Paula Fox's novel *Desperate Characters*: if you pay careful enough attention to a character's inner life, it turns out to be a marvelously detailed mirror of the character's outer world. (Franzen, 2015b: n.pg.)

Melodrama, another *para-realist* generic component of Franzen's fiction which was liberally used in *Freedom*, is also present in *Purity*. Franzen openly acknowledges it making Andreas's biological father write a supposedly autobiographical novel entitled *The Crime of Love*. The genre's influence is most notably perceivable in the tormented love relationship between Tom Aberant and Anabel Laird. Significantly, their story is told in a private confessional text narrated – for the first time in Franzen's fiction – in first-person form by Tom. This digital file, which is surreptitiously stolen by Wolf and subsequently sent to Pip, constitutes a modern-day version of the classic romance *topos* of the found manuscript (McKeon, 2002: 57), very much in the same way as Patty's autobiographical text in *Freedom*. As in the case of Patty's document, Tom's narrative performs a double function: it conveys new, enlightening biographical information about the characters and is the cause of new events after being read by one of them. Be that as it may, Tom and Anabel's relationship reaches heights of dysfunctionality, bitterness and agony that surpass those of the turbulent story of Walter and Patty Berglund. Tom thus recalls his last moments with Annabel:

> 'Give me a baby. Leave me with something.'
> 'No way.'
> 'I think it could happen tonight. I have a sense for these things.'
> 'I think I'd sooner kill myself than sign on for that.'
> 'You hate me.'
> 'I hate you.'
> She was still in love with me. I could see it in her eyes, the love and the pure inconsolable disappointment of a child. I had all the power, and so she did the only thing still available to her to stab me in the heart, which was to roll over submissively and raise the skirt of her robe and say, 'All right, do it.' (P 436)

What follows the excerpt above, told in in narrative ellipsis, is anal sex between Anabel and Tom. This is probably more sensational than other comparable scenes in Franzen's fiction but, as I will be discussing in the following section, the difference is not only a matter of degree.

2 *A Touch of Evil*: *Purity* and the Gothic

Melodramatic excess takes on a new, distinctive quality in *Purity*. Melodrama is here deliberately tinged with the eerie flavour of the Gothic in an attempt to invest it with a measure of the latter's own sublimity and transcendence. With this move, Franzen incorporates a new influence which widens his generic scope and connects with a vigorous American literary tradition, that of the American Gothic. In particular, *Purity* recalls at times the long lineage of American narratives recounting the fate of decaying families afflicted by secret sins, a prolific line running at least from Nathaniel Hawthorne and Edgar Allan Poe through William Faulkner. Some other times, it is the claustrophobic, unhealthy quality of exalted love relationships that bears the mark of the Gothic. The fact is that in *Purity* Franzen infuses his usual domestic domain of family relationships with a new unfamiliarity: the same kind of *unhomeliness* that Sigmund Freud examines in *The Uncanny* (1919). Freud's essay focuses on the German term *Unheimliche*, considered to be untranslatable but generally rendered as *uncanny* in English. In this text, often invoked in the analysis of Gothic and fantastic fiction, Freud looks into different ways in which familiar situations acquire a disturbingly unfamiliar (not necessarily supernatural) quality. A closer look at certain narrative themes present in the novel should clarify my point here. Anabel and Tom are not merely divorced. She abruptly disappears from Tom's life without leaving a trace and twenty-five years after he is still 'haunted' by her, to the dismay of Tom's current partner, journalist Leila Helou ('Do you have any idea ... What's it like to live with a man still haunted by a woman he hasn't seen in twenty-five years?' [P 233]). Anabel has become a metaphysical presence that impinges on Tom's mind. At the end of his confessional narrative, Tom is quite explicit about it: 'I never stopped wondering where Anabel is and whether she's alive ... I remain convinced that I'll see her again someday, even if I never see her again. She's eternal in me. Only once, and only because I was very young, could I have merged my identity with another person's, and singularities like this are where you find eternity' (P 443). This way, just as the moon brings dreams of long-dead Annabel Lee to his lover in Poe's famous poem, the ghostly sadness of lost Anabel recurrently visits Tom's 'nighttime dreams' (P 443).

In fact, Franzen's generic choice should not surprise us as it is related to his favouring of romance-like narratives: the Gothic started as a variation of romance and both genres are logically related. Duncan points at several characteristics of 'Gothic romance' that can be related to *Purity*: 'The eighteenth-century Gothic romances themselves insistently thematize the structure of a dislocated origin: in the obsession with fragmented and contaminated genealogies, in plots that turn upon usurped patrimony, incest, lost relations; in characterizations of psychological repression' (Duncan, 1992: 23). All these *topoi* survive in the American Gothic tradition and can be traced, to some extent or other, in the biographies of the novel's central characters. Like Faulkner's Southern families, Anabel's family seems doomed under the curse of its immense and questionably obtained wealth, as the behaviour of her debased brothers suggests. She has severed all bonds with them, depriving thus her daughter not only of the knowledge of her family background but also of the inheritance to which she is entitled. On his part, Andreas's real father is an ex-graduate student incarcerated by the socialist regime. Destitute and angry, he stalks teenage Andreas to burden him with censure of his mother, very much an apparition from the past as the ghost of Hamlet's father (Franzen makes the reference explicit in a truly uncanny scene). For Duncan, the Gothic novel also describes 'the malign equation between an origin we have lost and an alien force that invades our borders, haunts our mansions, possesses our souls' (Duncan, 1992: 23). There is indeed a time when terror and fear of death – emotions which Edmund Burke (1757) signalled as distinctive features of the sublime – assume centrality in the novel. There is an ominous quality in the pages leading to the carefully planned murder of Annagret's stepfather that is wholly new in Franzen's fiction, with Dostoevsky as a not-so-distant reference. This crime intensifies Andreas's social isolation much in a way that recalls how Hawthorne's characters are sometimes alienated from their communities by the force of secret guilt. We must also bear in mind that, even if his crime might be viewed as an act for love for the helpless Annagret, in Andreas's mind there lurks a dark, amoral side of his personality, referred to in the novel as 'the Killer', which sometimes compels him to hurt other people and himself. Eventually, Andreas goes through a true dissociation: one part of his mind is crying for help, but, as in a veritable possession, he is in the grip of the Killer. In the most spectacular scene of the novel, this sinister force makes him jump off a cliff after he has tried to hurt Tom in the basest of ways. In fact, Andreas's split personality can be seen as a variation of the motif of the *Doppelgänger*, identified by Freud (2003: 141) as a distinctively uncanny theme, and a classic of Gothic fiction.[1]

Fear of incest is also a characteristic concern of the Gothic novel – including the American Gothic novel – ever since Horace Walpole's *The Castle of Otranto* (1764), commonly taken as the founding work of the genre. Such dread is evoked in *Purity* as well. There are Oedipal implications in the relationship between Andreas and his troubled mother, Katya. She is as much an ineradicable, not so alien presence encroaching upon Andreas's self as Anabel is for Tom. According to Freud, the uncanny is usually characterized by a disquieting uncertainty about its ontological status. In the same way, Franzen never completely lifts a certain veil of ambiguity over the subject of Andreas's relationship with his mother. The fact is, however, that Andreas constantly blames her for having psychologically damaged

---

[1] It is noticeable how Franzen's account of his year in Berlin in the grip of literary obsessions, familial hang-ups and an isolation broken mainly by tortuous correspondence with his Anabel-like fiancé gradually takes on a certain Gothic quality in *The Kraus Project*. Along the volume's extensive footnotes, Franzen manages to provide a report of the period and a Freudian analysis of his twenty-two-year-old self. The culminating scene is one in which he suffers a small mental breakdown that is described in somewhat Gothic terms as 'the thing in control of me':

> At this point I went literally crazy for about fifteen minutes ... Some shadow thing in me, some thing that my conscious self could never see clearly but was no less *me* than my conscious self was, had momentarily got the upper hand. (KP 230)

him by inordinately doting on him since he was a child. Not to mention that he tells Pip that his mother showed him her genitals when he was seven (P 65), and that he sleeps with the actress who plays his mother in a film being made about him. In fact, before Pip's identity is actually disclosed, fear of unwitting incest also hovers over the relationship between her and Tom.[2] According to David Morris, incest is 'the visible or secret or absent center of forbidden desire to which terror always, ultimately, returns' (Morris, 2004: 56). But incest is also perhaps the clearest symbol of the danger of untimely end that, according to Brooks, always threatens the flow of a narrative. As he puts it, drawing upon the Freudian concept of *death drive*, 'Incest is only the exemplary version of a temptation of short-circuit from which the protagonist and the text must be led away, into detour, into the cure that prolongs narrative' (Brooks, 1984: 109). After all, according to Todorov, the essence of narrative is *transformation* (Todorov, 1977: 233), that is, a dynamic combination of resemblance and difference. This would entail that incest, which in a way comes to stand for the embracement of *sameness*, cannot mean but untimely death. It is surely significant that Pip, who has dodged the danger of incest, makes it to the *natural* end of her narrative, while Andreas's is short-circuited by suicide.

The Gothic becomes a convenient narrative tool for Franzen in *Purity* in several manners. One of them is that it provides him with a means to *ennoble* certain painful ways in love relationships by claiming a kind of aesthetic sublimity for them. Some of these conflicts will sound familiar for readers of Franzen's non-fiction. In his autobiographical essay 'My Bird Problem', included in *The Discomfort Zone*, the novelist analyses his relationship with his wife during the 1980s and early 1990s.[3] As Franzen recounts, he and his wife were an isolated couple, deeply 'absorbed in each other' (DZ 165) for years on end: 'For a long time, back in the eighties, my wife and I lived on our own little planet. We spent thrilling, superhuman amounts of time by ourselves' (DZ 165–6). This situation, which as could be expected brought suffering and a painful end for the couple, reappears in *Purity* in

---

[2]We should note, drawing on David Morris's elaboration (Morris, 2004: 56) that the fear of incest between Pip and Tom is of a different kind than that between Andreas and Katya. In the case of the latter danger arises, in truly Gothic fashion, from repressed desire. However, for Pip and Tom the perils are those of mere coincidence or imprudence, as in the case, mentioned by Norris, of two romance-influenced novels: *Moll Flanders* and *Tom Jones*.

[3]In *The Kraus Project*, Franzen recounts the beginnings of the relationship with his wife to be. Given its relevance to *Purity*, this is possibly the place to briefly comment on the main features of this decidedly odd work. The text is a bilingual compilation of Franzen's translation— assisted by Paul Reitter and Daniel Kehlmann—of three essays and a poem by the now obscure Austrian thinker Karl Kraus (1874–1936). The most distinctive characteristic of the *Project* is the astonishing disproportion of the footnotes with the original text. Some of the notes are intended for the better understanding of Kraus and his context, but the better part of them are devoted to Franzen's critique of contemporary technological culture (extrapolating from Kraus's similar concerns), and an account of the year he spent in Berlin on a Fulbright grant in 1982.

the relationship between Tom and Anabel, now invested with a mystic, visionary intensity which obviously aims at the perverse sublimity of the Gothic. In this way, in the up and downs of their life together Tom perceives 'a dissolution of the boundaries of our selves' (P 379). This produces an elation that is reminiscent of the rush of intoxicating substances: 'All drugs are an escape from the self, and throwing myself away for Anabel, doing something *obviously wrong* to make her feel better, and then reaping the ecstasy of her renewed enthusiasm for me, was my drug' (P 382). Tom, who is from Denver, Colorado, represents a classic American innocence that in his previous novels Franzen has embodied in Midwestern characters. He is nevertheless bewitched by the dark allure of the well-nigh daimonic Anabel: 'The ring on her finger had magical powers. I was fucking my *betrothed*, there was a new dimension to the joy of it, an immeasurably deeper chasm into which to throw myself, and no end to the falling' (P 393). Tom and Anabel's relationship follows the logic of addiction down to the bitter end: 'Now I was experiencing her psychic pain directly as my own. The heaven of soul-merging was a hell' (P 399).[4] It is easy to sense here the traits that Vijay Mishra attributed to the Gothic sublime, 'always an overglutted sign, an excess/abscess, that produces an atmosphere of toxic breathlessness' (Mishra, 1994: 19). To continue with the analogy between narrative and human life taken from Freud and Brooks, we may remember that narratives are driven by a kind of desire which from a structural point of view necessarily requires some degree of difference and imbalance. In keeping with that, eventually sexual activity between Tom and Anabel dwindles to almost nothing, not only, as Tom puts it, because of 'typical marital boredom', but because 'our souls were merged' (P 403). It may well be that the use of melodrama, with its high emotional temperature, and the Gothic, with its reliance on the lurid and supernatural, is the only way of making the *merging of two souls* interesting from a strictly narrative point of view. Then we could see the Gothic as the perversely appealing emanation from the corruption of two narrative flows that have become stagnant.

3 What lies beneath: *Purity* and repetition

At this point, it will surely be clear that the reasons for *Purity* to follow the twisted logic of the Gothic are in many respects reasons concerning the ways the Gothic has of unearthing what lies hidden, buried deep within our past, our family, our social community, our own mind. In his essay on that elusive subject, Freud recalls that for Schelling the uncanny is 'something that

---

[4]In *The Kraus Project*, Franzen recalls his troubled relationship with his ex-wife in similar terms: 'It's dangerous and ultimately impossible to wholly hand over the self to the Other' (KP 229).

should have remained hidden and has come into the open' (Freud, 2003: 148). Similarly, in Mishra's words, the Gothic sublime is 'a moment of entry into the unconscious, the *unplumbable*' (1994: 19). Certainly, the Gothic novel has frequently elicited a variety of psychoanalytical approaches. In the same way, what *Purity* has of Gothic also seems to call for a Freudian reading that goes beyond the Oedipal implications evoked by Andreas and his mother. Once again, here we may confidently follow Peter Brooks to grasp the parallelisms between narratives and some of Freud's theories. Previously I have referred to the way in which Franzen's characters are drawn to patterns of compulsive repetition in their relationships with family and lovers. Nowhere in his fiction is this tendency clearer than in *Purity*. What in previous novels is suggested about the origins of these recurrent situations is made explicit now. Significantly, in 'My Bird Problem' Franzen explains that the repetition of marital quarrels that followed a similar pattern was a constant in his marriage. As he puts it, 'I had old journals containing transcripts of early fights which read word-for-word like the fights we were having ten years later' (DZ 169). According to Franzen, the frustrations of conjugal life found alleviation in bird watching, which in his account takes the form of a rather compulsive and repetitive activity too. This recurrence also reappears as a narrative element in *Purity*. Tom and Anabel's relationship is marked by the repetition of quarrels that doggedly follow the same pattern: disputes generally started by Anabel, usually revolving around subtle questions of moral choice and semantic nuance. Whereas in previous novels, Franzen's characteristic scenes narrating conjugal skirmishes followed Hegelian dynamics of *Lordship and Bondage*, as I discussed in my analysis of *Strong Motion*, in *Purity* the emphasis is rather on hopeless repetition:

> Pleasure was low on the list of what either of us was after. ... My love was like the engine of a hundred-dollar car that had no business starting up and yet kept starting up. The murder and suicide I imagined weren't figurative. I would keep going back, and it would be worse each time, until finally we were driven to the violence that released our love to the eternity it belonged to. (P 436–7)

And indeed there seems to be no remedy for them: at the end of the novel they continue to argue for hours in the reconciliatory meeting organized by Pip for them. Appropriately, we are offered only incomplete and decontextualized fragments of that argument. This emphasizes its quality of meaningless repetition, to the extent that Anabel and Tom end up sounding like an angry version of Vladimir and Estragon in Beckett's *Waiting for Godot*.

Compulsive repetition is especially visible in Andreas Wolf's life. He indulges, we are told, in inordinately frequent masturbation during his teenage years. Then he manages to make his meetings with his mother invariably painful for both. As Weinstein has pointed out, Franzen summarizes Andreas's relationship with Katya in a single compelling phrase: 'Hated her and needed her and hated her and needed her' (Weinstein, 2015: 2008). Most notably, he cannot stop seducing the young girls he gets to know through his counselling job, a tendency he continues when he becomes a world celebrity. His success does not prevent him from becoming addicted to online pornography with the advent of the Internet era.

In *Beyond the Pleasure Principle*, Freud is concerned with the drive to repeat unpleasant experiences, an impulse in apparent contradiction with the universal pleasure principle he postulates. Compulsive repetition is an obscure, ambiguous phenomenon and Freud identifies different sides of it in his also ambiguous essay. His inquiry becomes particularly relevant for the analysis of Franzen's novels when he ascribes the compulsion to repeat in adults to unconscious repressed material harking back to infantile life:

> The patient cannot remember the whole of what is repressed in him ... He is obliged to *repeat* the repressed material as a contemporary experience instead of, as the physician would prefer to see, *remembering* it as something belonging to the past. These reproductions, which emerge with such unwished-for exactitude, always have at their subject some portion of infantile sexual life – of the Oedipus complex, that is and its derivatives. (Freud, 1955: 18)

According to Freud, the origin of this dysfunction lies in the sense of abandonment and failure experienced by the child when her first sexual efflorescence – directed towards her parents – is abruptly put to an end by reality. This loss is experienced by the child as the product of her personal inadequacy. In some cases, as Freud puts it, 'Loss of love and failure leave behind them a permanent injury to self-regard in the form of a narcissistic scar ... which contributes more than anything to the "sense of inferiority" which is so common in neurotics' (1955: 20). We have seen that a low self-esteem which is presented as the product of a deficit of parental recognition is a frequent feature of Franzen's protagonists. It is certainly the case of Louis and Renée, Walter and Patty, Pip and her mother Anabel. In general, Franzen's novels teem with adult characters stuck in childlike situations who compulsively re-experience childhood scenarios. This psychological entrapment is ritually symbolized in each of Franzen's novels from *Strong Motion* on by the characters' troubled return to their childhood bed in their parents' home. That same childhood bed is invoked with despair by Andreas, the most damaged of Franzen's protagonists: 'Eventually he determined that what had depressed him was his childhood bed, the bed itself, in the Müggelsee house, and the feeling that he'd never left it: that the more he rebelled against his parents and the more he made his life a reproach to theirs, the more deeply he rooted himself in the same childish relation to them' (P 85).

This unfulfilled infantile need for recognition finds its way to the world of adult relationships. In these cases, compulsion to repeat becomes an attempt to rewrite history. The person afflicted by it tries time after time to retrospectively satisfy her frustrated infantile needs through amorous relationships with other people – and more often than not with people who are precisely the least likely to do so: people bearing some kind of resemblance with the neglecting parent. This is clearly the case of Andreas. He exemplifies what Freud describes as 'the lover each of whose love affairs with a woman passes through the same phases and reaches the same conclusion' (1955: 22). But here Franzen draws a clear difference between Pip and the rest of the characters. Perhaps not surprisingly, Franzen never shows us Pip's immediate reaction to the shocking news about her family. We never get to know about the process of coming to terms with the truth. Several months have elapsed when we meet her again after the revelation and she seems well adjusted enough. This kind of authorial swiping would have been problematic in a truly realist novel, but not in *Purity*. Franzen has let the power of the romance quest perform the proverbial cathartic function of psychoanalytic treatment. In other words, the subject Pip has attained the object she was after: she has found the identity of her father (and mother) and in doing so she has gained access to her true self. Now she is free. And although she had been seeking a father figure in previous relationships, as is shown by her desperate craving for Stephen, her much older housemate, by the end of the novel she has built a satisfactory relationship with the lovely, non-conflicted Jason. In this way, unlike her parents, she manages to escape the tormenting cycle of repetition. From the point of view of Brooks' narratological reading of Freud, it would seem that the initial 'irritation of plot', which was the product of a romance-like design, has finally achieved the quiescence of narrative closure embodied by the resulting harmony between Pip and Jason.

It is important to notice, however, that the novel's final amorous equilibrium is presented as provisional and is limited to the young lovers. With this restriction of the scope of bliss in the novel, Franzen is obviously making a point on love relationships – one that tells *Purity* apart from his previous fiction. Franzen's idea concerns the possibilities and consequences of the communion of lovers, a theme which is recurrent in his work. We have seen that in *Strong Motion* Louis resents not being able to achieve such closeness with Renée even during sexual intercourse. In contrast, as was discussed in the previous chapter, Franzen implies the possibility of this kind of mystic union in the climactic moment of the reconciliation between Walter and Patty in *Freedom*. In *Purity*, a metaphysical 'merger of souls' is attributed to Anabel and Tom. Franzen even brings in John Donne's poem *The Ecstasy* to illustrate his idea. In *Purity*, Franzen overly warns us against the dangers of pursuing such ideal of union, which amounts to implicitly argue for its potential existence. However, as we have seen, the writer is also strategically using the idea of communion of souls to heighten the intensity and interest of his novelistic materials, which throws some ambiguity on his own ideas on the subject.[5]

4 Franzen and the *Great American Rant*

There is yet another aspect of the compulsion to repetition studied by Freud in *Beyond the Pleasure Principle* that is relevant to our novel, especially as concerns Franzen's social views. Clinical evidence compels Freud to theorize the existence of a force 'more primitive, more elementary, more instinctual than the pleasure principle which it over-rides' (1955: 23), namely the death drive. With this proposition, Freud goes against the common conception of instincts as impulses conducing the living being towards change. Rather, for the Viennese thinker an instinct is 'a tendency innate in living organic matter impelling it towards the reinstatement of an earlier condition, one which it had to abandon under the influence of external disturbing forces' (1955: 36). The death drive would then be the impulse driving organisms to return to inorganic form in their own immanent ways. In the larger picture, according to Freud, the pleasure principle, which seeks to keep the amount of excitation in the mental apparatus to a minimum through its discharge (1955: 62), would be subservient to the universal instinct to return to quiescence. Significantly for my analysis of *Purity*, Freud argues that repetition compulsion is a manifestation of that same desire to return to an earlier (ultimately inorganic) state of things. Franzen's perspective on contemporary experience of the digital world seems influenced by Freud's thought and his views are quite obviously dramatized through Andreas. This character's experience in the digital sphere is marked by compulsive repetition, that is, by revisiting behaviours known to be harmful. Pornography is the evident symbol of that:

> It was only much later, when the Internet had come to signify *death* to him, that he realized he'd also been glimpsing *death* in online porn. Every compulsion, certainly his own viewing of digital images of sex, which quickly became day-devouringly compulsive, smacked of death in its short-circuiting of the brain, its reduction of personhood to a closed loop of stimulus and response. (P 465)

---

[5]From the point of view of Nancy's philosophy, such community of lovers would be a mystification based on an impossible notion of absolute immanence. In Nancy's words, community 'is not a communion that fuses the *egos* into an *Ego* or higher *We*' (Nancy, 1991: 15).

As was also visible in *Strong Motion*, Franzen seems to discern here a dismal horizon in the culture, perhaps in human life at large. It is conceivable, nevertheless, that for the liberal humanist in Franzen the full consequences of Freud's arguments on instinctual life may be appalling. Admittedly, there have been characters in Franzen's novels that have harboured an obvious death wish: the suicidal Andreas, of course, and also Alfred Lambert in *The Corrections*. However, in both cases, the desire for death was presented as the specific product of depression and psychic fragmentation. Freud's insight goes far beyond. There is a radically anti-humanist, anti-Romantic quality in Freud's conclusions: 'It would be counter to the conservative nature of instinct if the goal of life were a state never hitherto reached ... *The goal of all life is death*' (1955: 38). This is in utter contradiction with Franzen's avowed vision of human beings as creatures aspiring for the infinite, the divine – a vision which is at the foundation of his own novelistic practice, theorized by the writer himself in the *Harper's* essay as *tragic realism*. This notion recurs in Franzen's fiction. In *The Corrections*, for example, the narrating voice reflects that the human animal contains 'a brain capable of conceiving the infinite and wishing to be infinite itself' (TC 537). In turn, in *Purity* human life is described as 'endless desire with limited supplies' (P 102). Again, here we find the sublimity of excess as a source of consolation. Horror at deeper and darker intuitions would be traceable in the shrill tone with which Franzen extrapolates Andreas's ordeal to the culture at large. For the novelist, the Internet is responsible for 'the characteristic annihilation of the distinction between private and public ... the dissolution of the individual in the mass. The brain reduced by machine to feedback loops, the private personality to a public generality: a person might as well been already dead' (P 465).

Previously to the publishing of *Purity*, Franzen had similarly taken issue with contemporary digital culture in some of the amazingly copious footnotes of *The Kraus Project*. In one of them, for example, Franzen proclaims: 'The actual substance of our daily life is total electronic distraction' (KP 14). These cultural remarks take us to the central sociocultural issue tackled by Franzen in *Purity*, namely the consequences of the digital revolution. The portion of text explicitly committed to this kind of critique is clearly smaller than in Franzen's previous novels, possibly because he had had the opportunity to express his opinions at length in *The Kraus Project* (see, for example, KP 274–5). Be that as it may, his aim is certainly far-reaching. Along a couple of remarkable pages conveying Andreas's thought in loose free indirect speech, Franzen energetically draws a parallelism between life in the Democratic Republic of Germany and contemporary culture. In these passages he argues a totalitarian character for the latter, marked by the omnipresence of the Internet. Curiously enough, here we witness the return of the same Foucault-influenced vision of a pervading, inescapable system that in

Strong Motion brought about the bitterest social comment in Franzen's fiction. A partial retake, in sum, of the Systems novel:

> Before he'd quit doing interviews, the previous fall, he'd taken to dropping the world *totalitarian* ... In fact, he simply meant a system that was impossible to opt out of. You could cooperate with the system or you could oppose it, but the one thing you could never do, whether you were enjoying a secure and pleasant life or sitting in prison, was not to be in relation to it. If you substituted *networks* for *socialism*, you got the internet. Its competing platforms were united in their ambition to define every term of your existence. (P 447–48)

The comparison may strike us as exaggerated but is compellingly put. For Franzen, the omnipresence of the Internet, with the ensuing machinization of the mind and abolition of the public/private divide, spells death for the individual. It is hard, however, not to feel that positing the Web and its ubiquity as what is most wrong with the world today is an ideological act with a marked class bias. In a nutshell, it is to dismiss and drive out of focus a variety of social and political problems. In *Purity*, Franzen is tacitly proposing a *third way* between socialist dictatorship and contemporary digitized society, that of enlightened liberal humanism. But, as we have seen in this book, this stance requires that an intractable Real of violence, exploitation and social inequality is kept in the underside. Not to mention that Franzen's is a position ultimately dependent on capitalism, which is itself a system not a bit less pervasive than the German socialist regime, and which also tends to define every term of our existence. Franzen goes on to deny the character of a true revolution to both the socialist revolution and the digital expansion. In his reasoning we can perceive the same abhorrence of radical social change which, as we have seen, Moretti identified as essentially novelistic. Here we may also notice that Franzen's reliance on science as a transcendent discursive foundation, which I have discussed in previous chapters, is intact. For the novelist, science rather than politics provides the model for any true revolution: 'The mark of a legitimate revolution – the scientific, for example – was that it didn't brag about its revolutionariness but simply occurred' (P 448). Franzen is especially mordant when he compares the new digital moguls with the leaders of the socialist regime: 'Like the old politburos, the new politburo styled itself as the enemy of the elite and the friend of the masses, dedicated to *giving consumers what they wanted*' (P 449). And what consumers living in the anomie of liquid modernity want is often the consolation of belonging afforded by commodified pseudo-communities. Indeed, a prominent aspect of Franzen's critique is his censure of the commercialization of contemporary communitarian longings: 'The New Regime even recycled the old's Republic's buzzwords, *collective, collaborative*' (P 449).

The considerations above are related to another angle of Franzen's critique of digital society in *Purity*, namely the permanent exposition of the individual in social media, where a particular blend of narcissism and need for recognition runs rampant. This condition has become a defining characteristic of our transparent society according to Byung-Chul Han, whose social views in this respect bear a strong resemblance to Franzen's. For the German thinker, permanent, deliberate exposition defines contemporary culture, a *pornographic* society where every subject is the object of its own advertisement and 'everything is measured by its exhibition value' (Han, 2015: 11). Han coincides with Franzen in attributing a certain totalitarian character to contemporary culture. For Han, the society of unveiling is also a society of total control by virtue of the sort of inverted panopticon conformed by social media and total exposition.

In contrast with this social trend, Franzen argues for secrecy. It seems fitting that Andreas, who has thrived on the revelation of other people's secrets, is aware of their fundamental part in the constitution of identity: 'How do you know that you're a person, distinct from other people? By keeping certain things to yourself. You guard them inside you, because, if you don't, there's no distinction between inside and outside. A radical exhibitionist is someone who has forfeited his identity' (P 275). Secrets, according to Andreas, also play a necessary role in the establishment of human relationships that aim to go beyond the narcissistic play of the social media: 'To have an identity, you have to believe that other identities equally exist. You need closeness with other people. And how is closeness built? By sharing secrets' (P 275).

There are more aspects in which Franzen's social views coincide with Han's. Throughout the novel, Franzen is decidedly belligerent with contemporary positions in favour of total transparency regarding sensitive political and corporate information. Such positions are represented by Andreas Wolf, whose organization The Sunlight Project receives and uploads massive amounts of leaked data. In keeping with Franzen's invariably derogatory depictions of political communities and activism, Wolf's Project is presented as a sort of cult where adoring young women compete for the attention of the alpha male. What is more, Franzen does not fail to point out that Wolf's activism, in its being dependent on platforms such as Google, ultimately serves to reinforce the 'Regime' he is out to attack. Therefore, 'fearing what Google could do to him', Wolf is compelled to decline the release of inside information he is offered concerning the corporation's malpractice: 'Can't do it. I need Google on my side' (P 450).

5 Journalism, fiction and hope for the public sphere

More important from a symbolical point of view, however, is the antagonistic dichotomy drawn by the novel between leakers and true journalists, an opposition where we may clearly identify a self-legitimating intention on Franzen's part. Journalism is represented in the novel by Tom Aberant – Franzen's partial alter ego – and his current partner, the Pulitzer Prize-winner Leila Helou.[6] The novelist opposes the mere acritical accumulation of information that he attributes to leakers with the procedures of investigation, interpretation and synthesis characteristic of journalism. As Leila puts it in an interview:

> The leakers just spew. It takes a journalist to collate and condense and contextualize what they spew. We may not always have the best of motives, but at least we have some investment in civilization. ... The leakers are more like savages ... they have this savage naïveté, like the kid who thinks adults are hypocrites for filtering what comes out of their mouths. (P 493)

In other words, as Han puts it, 'more information and communication alone do not illuminate the world ... the mass of information produces no truth' (Han: 2015: 41). It is hard not to feel here that, with his defence of the principles of good journalism, Franzen is also vindicating his own position as a novelist. A realist novel, after all, is also based on social investigation, selection of relevant, representative features, and careful edition. Not to mention that both journalist and Franzen's ideal novelist are equally bonded to the reader by a tacit pledge, or 'Contract', such as the one posited by Franzen in his essay 'Mr Difficult': an agreement whereby the reader expects the writer to provide her with something true, useful and (if at all possible) enjoyable. A time-honoured expectation already codified by Horatio in his *Ars Poetica* as *prodesse et delectare*. There is of course something paradoxical about Franzen's stance, given that *Purity* can hardly be considered a true realist novel, but it attests to the writer's unfaltering antagonistic disposition. Once again, Franzen confronts an old, familiar foe: the same kind of *maximalist* novel[7] bloated with information that *The Corrections* (whose protagonist, as we have seen, was initially meant to be named Andy Aberant) seemed destined to become previously to Franzen's *conversion*. This impression is reinforced by the portrait of one of Pip's housemates, Dreyfuss. A highly intelligent young man deprived

---

[6]There is a clear parallelism between the characters of Leila and Lalitha in *Freedom*. In both novels, a cumbersome subplot is organized around them, which inevitably lends them a subservient character. Lalitha's subplot was the vehicle for Franzen's environmentalist views in *Freedom*. In the case of *Purity*, Leila's investigation of the temporary loss of a nuclear warhead in a military base in Amarillo, Texas, becomes an illustration of the possibilities of on-the-ground investigative journalism.

[7]The term has been proposed by Stefano Ercolino (2014) to define a typically postmodernist subgenre of fiction characterized, among other features, by its disproportionate inclusiveness regarding information. In a perhaps questionable choice, Ercolino posits *The Corrections* as an example of that kind of novel, along with others such as *Infinite Jest* or *Gravity's Rainbow*.

of social skills, Dreyfuss is also characterized by an inability to select and synthesize: when he is to be evicted, he presents a 300,000-word list of charges to support his case against the foreclosing bank. The evocation of certain contemporary novelists of the 'Status' kind posited by Franzen in 'Mr Difficult' is inevitable. The bulk of David Foster Wallace – the revered author of the gigantic *The Infinite Jest*, ambiguously discussed by Franzen in that essay – also looms here.

A similar analogy obtains between Anabel, an uncompromising experimental filmmaker, and Tom, who is not only a journalist but also a would-be writer of fiction. After years of excruciating work, Anabel presents the result of her (unfinishable) project. 'The resulting twenty-four-minute film was radically repellent, a full-scale assault on the visual cortex, but you could also see genius in it if you looked at it right' (P 384–5). Significantly, against this unmistakable example of 'Status' art, Franzen sets *Doctor Zhivago*, Tom's mother all-time favourite film. The fact that it is based on a novel built upon the same general principles defended by Franzen is surely not coincidental.

But not only is Anabel an emotional and artistic extremist – she is also a political one. The treatment of Anabel's feminism, which often falls into caricature, is certainly another aspect of Franzen's anti-radicalism. Long gone are the days when, in *Strong Motion*, the novelist sought political legitimation and critical thrust in feminism. Certainly, Franzen's commitment was not rock-solid then. Ecofeminist tenets, for example, were evoked in that novel mainly to provide an aesthetic resonance by drawing analogies between its heroine Renée Seitchek and the earth. In *Purity*, however, the display of ecofeminist concerns is obviously satirical. Anabel, who is also a strict vegetarian, has her menstrual periods and sexual appetites in perfect, invariable synchrony with the phases of the moon. More importantly though, the way she resorts to women's status as social victims in her recurrent dialectical battles with Tom is unequivocally presented as unreasonable. In his memoir, Tom reflects with irony how his 'male vileness' was 'an impediment to our union of souls' (P381). All in all, Franzen's professed political stance is embodied by Tom's *middle way*:

'What if you could start your own magazine? What would you do with it?'

I said I would try to serve the truth in its full complexity. I told her about the politically polarized house I'd grown up in, my father's blind progressivism, my mother's faith in corporations, and how effectively the two of them could poke holes in each other politics.

'I could tell your mother a thing or two about corporations', Anabel said darkly.

'But the alternative doesn't work, either. You get the Soviet Union, you get the housing projects, you get the Teamsters union. The truth is somewhere in the tension between the two sides, and that's where the journalist is supposed to live, in that tension. It's like I *had* to be a journalist, growing up in that house.' (P 365)

What is remarkable in *Purity* is that investigative journalism is presented as viable in our time and a cause worth fighting for. Even the heroine Pip becomes a proficient journalist. Undeniably, this stance in favour of journalism entails hope for the public sphere, since both are indissolubly related. Journalism, like public opinion, was part of the same broad cultural revolution that brought into being the public sphere in the eighteenth century. The same public sphere, indeed, whose decay Franzen has lamented through novels and essays. How can this hope be reconciled with as bleak a vision of contemporary culture as that expressed by Franzen in *Purity*? The answer surely lies in the constitutional optimism of romance. It is impossible to compose a depressing romance. There is also the fact that Franzen provides the novel with the powerful figure of the scapegoat. Andreas Wolf is the only protagonist in Franzen's fiction that is not saved ever since *Strong Motion*. When Wolf, the most daimonic character ever created by Franzen jumps off the cliff, he is symbolically taking with him all the insanity and misery which according to Franzen we inflict on ourselves in our engagement with the digital world. Apart from that, in the symbolic landscape of the novel, journalism could even be seen as part of the good cause in the perennial fight between good and evil consubstantial to romance. Good journalism is a form of serving the community – a larger community that now goes beyond the narrow limits of the family to which Franzen's previous novels had staged a retreat. And if good journalism serves the larger community, surely this must also be the case of good fiction. Franzen's novels often illustrate the need to keep infrastructure in good shape. In a similar way, through its enhancement of sympathy and critical consciousness, good fiction would contribute to the maintenance of the emotional and political infrastructure of the community. What is often harder to acknowledge, of course, is that this stance also entails supporting a particular ideological infrastructure with social implications that may not be wholly palatable for both author and readership.

6 The perks of limited closure

The social hopes identified above, however, are too wide and diffuse, too abstract to really become the textual foundation of the Utopian investment of a romance-like narrative. The theatre where the intoxicating perspective of future happiness is symbolically asserted must remain the family. So is the case with *Purity*. Once again, reconciliation is paramount in Franzen's fiction. Pip, with her characteristic *pure* heart, acts as an active catalyst for forgiveness in her family. Inevitably, again, the reconciliation promoted by

Pip transcends the particular to acquire larger symbolic implications: peace and forgiveness between Tom and Anabel would amount to a well-nigh miraculous reconciliation of liberal and radical politics. That would surely be pushing the neatness of closure too far. It is no wonder then that this time Franzen discards a tightly knitted ending such as the one in *Freedom*, and elegantly opts instead for *deferred* hope in a less conclusive ending. As I have advanced above, whatever hopes there may be for a better future, they are entrusted to the younger generation, that of Pip and Jason, who are deemed still unaccountable for the evils of the world. This is in sharp contrast with the grudge perceivable in *Freedom* against the allegedly better-adjusted younger generations and their excessive sense of entitlement. It is also a gesture of trust that partly overrides the apocalyptic tone of Franzen's previous criticism of the dominance of social media—platforms which are, precisely, massively used by young people. In the final scene of the novel, Pip literally shuts the door on the unending repetition of her parents' disputes – whose previous sublimity of excess and darkness is now nonchalantly softened by a touch of comedy – and takes Jason's hand. Hope is perhaps not conclusive, but she is comforted by Jason and the community of independent spirits she has achieved with him (as opposed to the destructive merger of souls of her parents), as well as by benevolent nature:

> Pip shut the door again, to block out the words, but even with the door closed she could hear the fighting. The people who'd bequeathed a broken world to her were shouting at each other viciously. Jason sighed and took her hand. She held it tightly. It had to be possible to do better than her parents, but she wasn't sure she would. Only when the skies opened again, the rain from the immense dark western ocean pounding on the car roof, the sound of love drowning out the other sound, did she believe that she might. (P 563)

At this point, in a typical romance-like narrative, the object of the quest would have been attained. Harmony would have been restored in the realm of the family which is, as usually, symbolic of the body social. Now we may clearly realize some of the ideological implications of this kind of closing. At the beginning of the novel Pip is besieged by a crippling student debt, dismal job prospects and, in general, actual poverty. She is in fact an apt representative of a generation of young people in developed countries that in all likeliness will not achieve the living standards of their parents. But these problems, which have deep and complex social, historical and political causes, are symbolically solved by the magical powers of romance, now materialized as inherited money. As Duncan puts it apropos of Walter Scott, 'the romance tends to iterate its final status as an artificial exclusion from historical process, in the topos of domestic idyll' (Duncan, 1992: 15).

However, we know – Franzen makes no effort to conceal it – that what has been attained in *Purity* is not true harmony. In contrast with *The Corrections* and *Freedom*, the ending of *Purity* stages an imperfect and thus, at least at first sight, a less romance-like closure. The possibility that Pip and Jason should end up repeating the same mistakes as their elders is openly acknowledged, as we have seen. The continuing hostility between Anabel and Tom stands as a recalcitrant source of negativity in the novel, unamenable to the smoothing power of narrative closure. It is perhaps a potential cause for the 'irritation of plot' discussed above which might spawn yet another narrative. In any case, if we follow our premise of the socially symbolic character of narrative, it is easy to argue that such irreparable relationship stands for a core of intractable social conflict which will remain refractory to the most enlightened and well-meaning attempts at social reform. Harmony, the novel shows, cannot be complete. Paradoxically, rather than curtailing the power of romance-like closure, this acknowledgement of limitedness may work to enhance it in our cultural context because it brings the form closer to the readers' own experience of a world where narrative closure is hard to come by. Then it might well be that imperfect romance-like narratives disguised as realist novels such as Franzen's can become a suitable, well-received vehicle to articulate our perennial concern with the fate of community in the disconcerting anomie of our world.

WORKS CITED

Adorno, Theodor W. ([1991] 2001), *The Culture Industry: Selected Essays on Mass Culture*, London and New York: Verso.

Althusser, Louis (2008), *On Ideology*, London and New York: Verso.

Annesley, James (1998), *Blank Fictions: Consumerism, Culture and the Contemporary American Novel*, London: Pluto Press.

Annesley, James (2006), 'Market Corrections: Jonathan Franzen and the "Novel of Globalization"', *Journal of Modern Literature*, 29 (2): 111–28.

Antrim, Donald (2010), 'Interview with Jonathan Franzen', *Bomb* 77: n.pg. Available online: http://www.bombsite.com/franzen/franzen.html (accessed 24 October 2011).

Armstrong, Nancy (2005), *How Novels Think: The Limits of individualism 1719-1900*. New York: Columbia University Press.

Arrighi, Giovanni, Hopkins, Terence K. and Wallerstein, Immanuel (1989), *Anti-Systemic Movements*, London: Verso.

Atwood, Margaret ([1972] 2008), *Surfacing*, London: Virago.

Auerbach, Erich ([1955] 2003), *Mimesis: The Representation of Reality in Western Literature*, Princeton: Princeton University Press.

Bachelard, Gaston ([1964] 1994), *The Poetics of Space*, trans. M. Jolas. Boston: Beacon Press.

Badiou, Alain (2001), *Ethics: An Essay on the Understanding of Evil*, trans. P. Hallward, London and New York: Verso.

Badiou, Alain and Tarby, Fabien (2013), *Philosophy and the Event*, trans. L. Burchill, Cambridge: Polity Press.

Bakhtin, Mikhail M. (1981), *The Dialogic Imagination: Four Essays*, ed. Michael Holquist, trans. Caryl Emerson and Michael Holquist, Austin: University of Texas Press.

Barthes, Roland (1974), *S/Z*, trans. R. Miller, Malden, MA and Oxford: Blackwell.

Bauman, Zygmunt (1997), *Postmoderniy and its Discontents*, New York: New York University Press.

Bauman, Zygmunt (2000), *Liquid Modernity*, Cambridge: Polity Press.

Bauman, Zygmunt (2001), *Community. Seeking Safety in an Insecure World*, Cambridge: Polity Press.

Beck, Ulrich (1992), *Risk Society: Towards a New Modernity*, trans. M. Ritter. London, etc.: SAGE.

Bell, Daniel (1972), 'The Cultural Contradictions of Capitalism', *Journal of Aesthetic Education*, 6 (1/2): 11–38.

Beuka, Robert (2004), *SuburbiaNation*, New York: Palgrave Macmillan.

Billy Elliot (2000), [Film] Dir. Stephen Daldry, UK: BBC Films et al.

Blanchot, Maurice (1988), *The Unavowable Community*, trans. P. Joris, Barrytown, NY: Station Hill Press.

Bloom, Harold ([1973] 1997), *The Anxiety of Influence: A Theory of Poetry*, Oxford: Oxford University Press.

Bourdieu, Pierre (1984), *Distinction: A Social Critique of the Judgement of Taste*, Cambridge, MA: Harvard University Press.

Bowlby, Rachel (2010), 'Foreword', in M. Beaumont (ed.), *A Concise Companion to Realism*, xiv–xxi, Chichester: Wiley-Blackwell.

Brooks, Peter (1976), *The Melodramatic Imagination: Balzac, Henry James, Melodrama and the Mode of Excess*, New Haven: Yale University Press.

Brooks, Peter (1984), *Reading for the Plot*, Cambridge, MA: Harvard University Press.

Brooks, Peter (2005), *Realist Vision*, New Haven and London: Yale University Press.

Burke, Edmund ([1757] 1998), *A Philosophical Enquiry into the Origin of our Ideas of the Sublime and Beautiful*, New York: Oxford University press.

Burn, Stephen J. (2008), *Jonathan Franzen at the End of Postmodernism*, London: Continuum.

Burn, Stephen J. (2010), 'The Art of Fiction 207: Jonathan Franzen', *Paris Review* 195: 38–79.

Butler, Judith and Salih, Sara, eds (2004), *The Judith Butler Reader*, Malden, MA: Blackwell.

Byung-Chul, Han (2012), *Transparenzgesellschaft*, Berlin. Matthes & Seitz.

Calvino, Italo (1972), *Le Città invisibili*, Milan: Mondadori.

Chabon, Michael ([1988] 2005), *The Mysteries of Pittsburgh*, New York: Harper Collins.

Chabon, Michael ([1995] 2008), *Wonder Boys*, London: Fourth Estate.

Cixous, Hélène (1976), 'The Laugh of the Medusa', trans. K. Cohen and P. Cohen, *Signs* 1 (4): 875–93.

Connery, Christopher and Franzen, Jonathan (2009), 'The Liberal Form: An Interview with Jonathan Franzen', *Boundary 2* 36 (2): 31–54.

Critchley, Simon (2012), *Infinitely Demanding: Ethics of Commitment, Politics of Resistance*, London: Verso.

Cronon, William (1983), *Changes in the Land: Indians, Colonists, and the Ecology of New England*, New York: Hill and Wang.

Debord, Guy ([1967] 2009), *Society of the Spectacle*, trans. K. Knabb, Eastbourne, UK: Soul Bay Press.

Defoe, Daniel ([1722] 1994), *The Journal of the Plague Year*, London: Everyman.

DeLillo, Don (1986), *White Noise*, Penguin: New York, etc.

DeLillo, Don (1991), *Mao II*, New York: Viking.

DeLillo, Don (1997), 'The Power of History', *The New York Times*, 7 September: n.pg. Available online: http://www.nytimes.com/library/books/090797article3.html (accessed 10 March 2014).

DeLillo, Don ([1997] 1999), *Underworld*, London: Picador.

Denith, Simon (2010), 'Realist Synthesis in the Nineteenth Century Novel', in M. Beaumont (ed.), *A Concise Companion to Realism*, 33–49, Chichester: Wiley-Blackwell.

Duncan, Ian (1992), *Modern Romance and Transformations of the Novel: The Gothic, Scott, Dickens*, Cambridge: Cambridge University Press.

Eagleton, Terry ([1983] 1996), *Literary Theory: An Introduction*, 2nd edn, Malden, MA: Blackwell.

Eagleton, Terry ([1976] 2002), *Marxist and Literary Criticism*, London and New York: Routledge.

Eagleton, Terry (2003), 'Porkchops and Pineapples', *London Review of Books*, 25 (20): 17–19. Available online: http://www.lrb.co.uk/v25/n20/terry-eagleton/pork-chops-and-pineapples.

Eagleton, Terry (2005), *The English Novel. An Introduction*, Malden, MA: Blackwell.

Eliot, T. S. ([1922] 1990), *The Waste Land and Other Poems*, London: Faber and Faber.

Ercolino, Stefano (2014), *The Maximalist Novel: From Thomas Pynchon's Gravity's Rainbow to Roberto Bolano's 2666*, New York: Bloomsbury Academic.

Etzioni, Amitai (1994), *The Spirit of Community: The Reinvention of American Society*, New York: Touchtone.

Eugenides, Jeffrey ([1993] 2002), *The Virgin Suicides*, London: Bloomsbury.

Fox, Paula ([1970] 2003), *Desperate Characters*, London: Flamingo.

Frank, Thomas (2004), *What's the Matter with Kansas? How Conservatives Won the Heart of America*, New York: Henry Holt.

Franzen, Jonathan (1996), 'Perchance to Dream: In the Age of Images, a Reason to Write Novels', *Harper's Magazine*, 1996 April: 35–54.

Franzen, Jonathan (2002a), *How to Be Alone*, London: Fourth Estate.

Franzen, Jonathan (2002b), 'Mr. Difficult: William Gaddis and the Problem of Hard-to-Read Books', *The New Yorker*, September 20: n.pg. Available online: http://www.newyorker.com/magazine/2002/09/30/Mr.-difficult (accessed 24 November 2011).

Franzen, Jonathan (2006), *The Discomfort Zone: A Personal History*, London, etc.: Harper Perennial.

Franzen, Jonathan ([1992] 2007), *Strong Motion*, New York: Picador-Farrar.

Franzen, Jonathan ([1988] 2010a), *The Twenty-Seventh City*, New York: Noonday-Farrar.

Franzen, Jonathan ([2001] 2010b), *The Corrections*, New York: Picador-Farrar.

Franzen, Jonathan (2010c), *Freedom*. London: Fourth Estate.

Franzen, Jonathan (2012a), *Farther Away*. London: Fourth State.

Franzen, Jonathan (2012b), 'A Rooting Interest: Edith Wharton and the Problem of Sympathy', *The New Yorker*, 13 February: n.pg. Available online: http://www.newyorker.com/magazine/2012/02/13/a-rooting-interest (accessed 5 March 2014).

Franzen, Jonathan (2013), *The Kraus Project*, London: Fourth Estate.

Franzen, Jonathan (2015a), *Purity*, London: Fourth Estate.

Franzen, Jonathan (2015b), 'Modern Life Has Become Extremely Distracting', *The Guardian*, 2 October: npg. Available online: http://www.theguardian.com/books/2015/oct/02/jonathan-franzen-writing-freedom (accessed 30 October 2015).

Franzen, Jonathan and Smith Rakoff, Joana (2001), 'Making the Corrections: An Interview with Jonathan Franzen', *Poets and Writers* 29 (5): 27–33.

Freud, Sigmund ([1920] 1955), *The Standard Edition of the Complete Psychological Works, Volume XVIII*, London: The Hogarth Press.

Freud, Sigmund ([1919] 2003), *The Uncanny*, trans. David McClintock, London: Penguin.

Frye, Northrop ([1957] 1971), *Anatomy of Criticism: Four Essays*, Princeton, NJ: Princeton University Press.

Frye, Northrop (1976), *The Secular Structure: A Study of the Structure of Romance*, Cambridge, MA: Harvard University Press.

Fukuyama, Francis (1992), *The End of History and the Last Man*, London: Hamish Hamilton.

Giddens, Anthony (1991), *The Consequences of Modernity*, Cambridge: Polity Press.

González, Jesús Ángel (2015), 'Eastern and Western Promises in Jonathan Franzen's *Freedom*', *Atlantis* 37 (1): 11–29.

Grand Torino (2008), [Film] Dir. Clint Eastwood, USA: Malpaso Productions et al.

Green, Jeremy (2005), *Late Postmodernism: American Fiction at the Millennium*, Gordonsville, VA: Palgrave Macmillan.

Greimas, A.-J. (1966), *Semantique Structurale: Recherche de Méthode*, Paris: Larousse.

Grossman, Lev (2010), 'Great American Novelist: Interview with Jonathan Franzen', *Time*, 12 August: n.pg. Available online: http://content.time.com/time/magazine/article/0,9171,2010185,00.html (accessed 22 October 2011).

Habermas, Jürgen ([1962] 1991), *The Structural Transformation of the Public Sphere: An Inquiry into a Category of Bourgeois Society*, trans. T. Burger, Cambridge, MA: MIT Press.

Hardt, Michael and Negri, Antonio (2001), *Empire*, Cambridge, MA and London: Harvard University Press.

Hardt, Michael and Negri, Antonio (2005), *Multitude: War and Democracy in the Age of Empire*, London: Penguin Books.

Hardt, Michael and Weeks, Kathi, eds (2000), *The Jameson Reader*, Malden, MA: Blackwell.

Harvey, David (2012), *Rebel Cities: From the Right to the City to the Urban Revolution*, London and New York: Verso.

Hassan, Ihab (1981), 'Cities of Mind, Urban Words: The Dematerialization of Metropolis in Contemporary America Fiction', in M. C. Jave and A. C. Watts (eds), *Literature and the American Urban Experience: Essays on the City and Literature*, 93–112, New Brunswick, NJ: Rutgers University Press.

Hawkins, Ty (2007), *A Smile and a Shoeshine*: From F. Scott Fitzgerald to Jonathan Franzen by Way of Arthur Miller. The American Dream in *The Great Gatsby*, *Death of a Salesman* and *The Corrections*', *Arthur Miller Journal* 2 (1): 49–68.

Hawkins, Ty (2010), 'Assessing the Promise of Jonathan Franzen's First Three Novels: A Rejection of *Refuge*', *College Literature* 37 (4): 61–87.

Hunter, James Davison (1991), *Culture Wars: The Struggle to Define America*, New York: Basic Books.

Hutcheon, Linda (1988), *A Poetics of Postmodernism: History, Theory, Fiction*, London and New York: Routledge.

Hutcheon, Linda (1994), *Irony's Edge: The Theory and Politics of Irony*, London and New York: Routledge.

Hutchinson, Colin (2008), *Reaganism, Thatcherism and the Social Novel*, New York: Palgrave Macmillan.

Hutchinson, Colin (2009), 'Jonathan Franzen and the Politics of Disengagement', *Critique*, 50 (2): 191–205.

Irigaray, Luce ([1974] 1985), *Speculum of the Other Woman*, trans. G. C. Gill, Ithaca, NY: Cornell University Press.

Jameson, Fredric ([1971] 1974), *Marxism and Form: Twentieth-Century Dialectical Theories of Literature*, Princeton, NJ: Princeton University Press.

Jameson, Fredric (1984), 'Review of Don DeLillo's *The Names* and Sol Yurick's *Richard A*', *Minnesota Review*, 22: 116–22.

Jameson, Fredric (1991), *Postmodernism, or, The Cultural Logic of Late Capitalism*, London and New York: Verso.

Jameson, Fredric (1994), *The Seeds of Time*, New York: Columbia University Press.

Jameson, Fredric ([1981] 2002), *The Political Unconscious: Narrative as a Socially Symbolic Act*, London and New York: Routledge, 2002.

Jameson, Fredric ([1998] 2009), *The Cultural Turn: Selected Writings on the Postmodern 1983-1998*, London and New York: Verso.

Jameson, Fredric (2013), *The Antinomies of Realism*, London and New York: Verso.

Jiménez Heffernan, Julián (2007), *De Mostración: Ensayos sobre descompensación narrativa*, Madrid: Antonio Machado Libros.

Jiménez Heffernan, Julián (2013), 'Introduction: Togetherness and Its Discontents', in J. Jiménez Heffernan, P. Martín Salván and G. Rodríguez Salas (eds), *Community in Twentieth-Century Fiction*, 1–47, London: Palgrave, 2013.

Jurca, Catherine (2001), *White Diaspora*, Princeton, NJ: Princeton University Press.

Kakutani, Michiko (2001), 'A Family Portrait as Metaphor for the 90s', *New York Times*, 4 September: n.pg. Available online: http://www.nytimes.com/2001/09/04/books/books-of-the-times-a-family-portrait-as-metaphor-for-the-90-s.html (accessed 24 September 2011).

Kakutani, Michiko (2010), 'A Family Full of Unhappiness, Hoping for Transcendence', *The New York Times*, 15 August: n.pg. Available online: http://www.nytimes.com/2010/08/16/books/16book.html (accessed 21 November 2011).

Kermode, Frank ([1967] 2000), *The Sense of an Ending: Studies in the Theory of Fiction*, New York: Oxford University Press.

Klein, Naomi (2004), 'Baghdad Year Zero: Pillaging Iraq in Pursuit of a Neocon Utopia', *Harper's Magazine* September: 43–53.

Klepp, L. S. (1992), Review of *Strong Motion*, by Jonathan Franzen, *Entertainment Weekly*, 14 February: n.pg. Available online: http://www.ew.com/article/1992/02/14/strong-motion (accessed 5 October 2011).

Knight, Peter (2002), 'Introduction', in P. Knight (ed.), *Conspiracy Nation: The Politics of Paranoia in Postwar America*, 1–17, New York: New York University Press.

Kucich, John (1988), 'Postmodern Politics: Don DeLillo and the Plight of the White Male Writer', *Michigan Quarterly* 27: 328–40.

Lacan, Jacques (1991), *Le Séminaire. Livre XVII: L'envers de la psychanalyse*, ed. J.-A. Miller, Paris: Seuil.

Lacayo, Richard (2001), 'Great Expectations', *Time*, 10 September: n.pg. Available Online: http://content.time.com/time/magazine/article/0,9171,1000729,00.html (accessed 10 October 2011).

Laclau, Ernesto (2005), *On Populist Reason*, London and New York: Verso.

Laclau, Ernesto and Mouffe, Chantal (2001), *Hegemony and Socialist Strategy: Towards a Radical Democratic Politics*, London and New York.

LeClair, Tom (1987), *In the Loop: Don DeLillo and the Systems Novel*, Urbana, IL: University of Illinois Press.

Lefebvre, Henry (1996), 'The Right to the City.' *Writings on Cities*, trans. and ed. E. Kofman and E. Lebas, Oxford: Blackwell.

Lenin, Vladimir Ilych (1965), *Collected Works: Vol. 29*, Moscow: Progress Publishers.

Lorca, Federico García ([1940] 2002), *Poet in New York*, trans. G. Simon, S. F. White and C. Maurier, ed. C. Maurier, London: Penguin.

Lukács, György ([1920] 2006a), *The Theory of the Novel*, trans. A. Bostock, Monmouth: Merlin Press.

Lukács, György ([1955] 2006b), *The Meaning of Contemporary Realism*, trans. John and N. Mander, Monmouth: Merlin Press.

Lukács, György ([1938] 2007), 'Realism in the Balance', trans. R. Livingstone, in R. Taylor (ed.), *Aesthetics and Politics*, 28–59, London and New York: Verso.

Lynch, Kevin (1960), *The Image of the City*, Cambridge, MA: MIT Press.

Lyotard, Jean-François (1979), *La Condition Postmoderne: Rapport sur le Savoir*, Paris: Minuit.

Macherey, Pierre ([1966] 1989), *A Theory of Literary Production*, trans. G. Wall, London and New York: Routledge.

Marcuse, Herbert (1964), *One-Dimensional Man: Studies in the Ideology of Advanced Industrial Society*, Boston: Beacon Press.

Martín Salván, Paula (2006), 'Introduction: Postmodernism, or the Problematics of a Figure of Belatedness', in J. Gascueña Gahete and P. Martín Salván (eds), *Figures of Belatedness: Postmodernist Fiction in English*, 15–36, Córdoba: Servicio de Publicaciones de la Universidad de Córdoba.

Martín Salván, Paula (2009), *Don DeLillo: Tropologías de la Postmodernidad*, Córdoba: Servicio de Publicaciones de la Universidad de Córdoba.

Marx, Karl ([1842] 2001), *18th Brumaire of Louis Bonaparte*, London: Electric BookCompany.

Marx, Karl and Engels, Friedrich ([1848] 2010), *The Communist Manifesto*, London: Arcturus.

McHale, Brian (1987), *Postmodernist Fiction*, London and New York: Routledge.

McKeon, Michael ([1987] 2002), *The Origins of the English Novel, 1600-1740*, Baltimore: John Hopkins University Press.

McLaughlin, Robert L. (2004), 'Post-Postmodern Discontent: Contemporary Fiction and the Social World', *Symploke*, 12 (1–2): 53–68.

Miller, J. Hillis (1992), *Ariadne's Thread: Story Lines*, New Haven and London: Yale University Press.

Miller, J. Hillis (1995), *Topographies*, Stanford, CA: Stanford University Press.

Miller, J. Hillis (2001), *Others*, Princeton, NJ: Princeton University Press.

Mishra, Vijay (1994), *The Gothic Sublime*, Albany: State University of New York Press.

Moody, Rick (1994), *The Ice Storm*, London: Abacus.

Moretti, Franco ([1987] 2000), *The Way of the World: The Bildungsroman in European Culture*, trans. A. Sbragia, London and New York: Verso.

Moretti, Franco ([1983] 2005), *Signs Taken for Wonders: On the Sociology of literary Forms*, trans. S. Fischer, D. Forgacs and D. Miller, London and New York: Verso.

Morris, David ([1985] 2004), *Gothic Sublimity*, in F. Botting and D. Townshend (eds), *Gothic: Critical Concepts in Literary and Cultural Studies, Vol. 2*, 50–68, London and New York: Routledge.

Nancy, Jean-Luc (1991), *The Inoperative Community*, trans. P. Connor, Lisa Garbus, Michael Holland and Simona Sawhney, Minneapolis: University of Minnesota Press.

Nash, Christopher (1993), *World Postmodern Fiction: A Guide*, London and New York: Longman.

Parrish, Timothy (2010), 'Tribal Politics and the Postmodern Product', *American Literary History* 22 (3): 645–56.

Passaro, Vince (1991), 'Dangerous Don DeLillo', *The New York Times* 19 May: n.pg. Available online: https://www.nytimes.com/books/97/03/16/lifetimes/del-v-dangerous.html (accessed 5 February 2014).

Propp, Vladimir Iakovlevich ([1928] 1968), *Morphology of the Folktale*, 2nd edn, trans. L. Scott, Austin: University of Texas Press.

Putnam, Robert D. (2000), *Bowling Alone: The Collapse and Revival of American Community*, New York: Simon and Shuster.

Pynchon, Thomas ([1966] 2000), *The Crying of Lot 49*, London: Vintage.

Rebein, Robert (2007), 'Turncoat: Why Jonathan Franzen Finally Said 'No' to Po-Mo', in N. Brooks and J. Toth (eds), *The Mourning After: Attending the Wake of Postmodernism*, 201–21, Amsterdam: Rodopi.

Ribbat, Christoph (2002), 'Handling the Media, Surviving *The Corrections*: Jonathan Franzen and the Fate of the Author', *Amerikastudien/American Studies* 47 (4): 555–66.

Robbins, Bruce (1999), 'Disjoining the Left: Cultural Contradictions of Anticapitalism', *Boundary 2* 26 (3): 29–38.

Robbins, Bruce (2007), 'The Smell of Infrastructure: Notes Toward an Archive', *Boundary 2*, 34 (1): 25–33.

Rohr, Susanne (2004), 'The Tyranny of the Probable: Crackpot Realism and Jonathan Franzen's *The Corrections*', *Amerikastudien/American Studies* 49 (1): 91–105.

Rorty, Richard (1999), *Achieving Our Country: Leftist Thought in Twentieth-Century America*, Cambridge, MA: Harvard University Press.

Rubins, Josh (1992), 'How Capitalism Causes Earthquakes', *The New York Times*, 16 February: n.pg. Available online: http://www.nytimes.com/1992/02/16/books/how-capitalism-causes-earthquakes.html (accessed 24 September 2011).

Ruland, Richard and Bradbury, Malcolm (1991), *From Puritanism to Postmodernism: A History of American Literature*, Penguin: New York, 1991.

Sacks, Sam (2010), 'Power Struggles, Family Style', *The Wall Street Journal*, 20 August: n.pg. Available online: http://www.wsj.com/articles/SB10001424052748703649004575437761339795700 (accessed 21 November 2011).

Schmitt, Carl ([1927] 1996), *The Concept of the Political*, trans. G. Shwab, Chicago: University of Chicago Press.

Shivani, Anis (2011), 'Why Jonathan Franzen's *Freedom* Is the Most Overrated Recent Novel', *Huffington Post*, 2 July: n.pg. Available online: http://www.huffingtonpost.com/anis-shivani/jonathan-franzen-freedom-overrated_b_819103.html (accessed 21 November 2011).

Smith, Zadie (2005), *On Beauty*, London: Penguin.

Smollett, Tobias ([1771] 1983), *The Expedition of Humphrey Clinker*, ed. J. L. Thorson, London and New York: Norton.

Stern, J. P. (1973), *On Realism*, London and Boston: Routledge and Kegan Paul, 1973.

Tanenhaus, Sam (2010), 'Peace and War', *The New York Times*, 19 August: n.pg. Available online: http://www.nytimes.com/2010/08/29/books/review/Tanenhaus-t.html?_r=0 (accessed 24 November 2011).

Toal, Catherine (2003), 'Corrections: Contemporary American Melancholy', *Journal of European Studies*, 33: 305–22.

Todorov, Tzvetan (1969a), *Grammaire du Décameron*, The Hague: Mouton.

Todorov, Tzvetan (1969b), 'Structural Analysis of Narrative', trans. A. Weinstein, *Novel: A Forum on Fiction*, 3 (1): 70–6.

Todorov, Tzvetan (1977), *The Poetics of Prose*, Oxford: Blackwell.

Toolan, Michael J. (1988), *Narrative: A Critical Linguistic Introduction*, London and New York: Routledge.

Updike, John ([1968] 2012), *Couples*, Random House: New York.

Varsava, Jerry (2003), 'The Quest for Community in American Postmodern Fiction', *International Fiction Review*, 30 (1/2): n.ag. Available online: http://journals.hil.unb.ca/index.php/IFR/article/view/7735/8792 (accessed 10 June 2013).

Weber, Max ([1922] 1978), *Economy and Society: An outline of Interpretive Sociology*, Berkeley and Los Angeles: University of California Press. Available online: https://archive.org/details/MaxWeberEconomyAndSociety (accessed 1 November 2013).

Weinstein, Philip (2015), *Jonathan Franzen: The Comedy of Rage*, New York and London: Bloomsbury Academic.

Weston, Jessie L. ([1920] 1997), *From Ritual to Romance*, Mineola, NY: Dover.

Williams, Raymond (1973), *The Country and the City*, New York: Oxford University Press.

Williams, Raymond (1977), *Marxism and Literature*, Oxford: Oxford University Press.

Williams, Raymond (2005), *Culture and Materialism*, London: Verso.

The Wire (2002–8), [TV programme], created by David Simon, USA: HBO.

Wood, James (2001a), 'Abhorring a Vacuum', *The New Republic Online*, 18 October: n.pg. Available online: http://www.newrepublic.com/article/books-and-arts/76988/abhorring-vacuum (accessed October 2011).

Wood, James (2001b), 'What the Dickens', *The Guardian*, 9 November: n.pg. Available online: http://www.theguardian.com/books/2001/nov/09/fiction.reviews (accessed 10 November 2011).

Wood, William ([1634] 1977), *New England's Prospect*, ed. A. T. Vaughan, Amherst: University of Massachusetts Press, 1977.

Yardley, Jonathan (1992), 'Whole Lot of Shakin'', *The Washington Post Book World*, 22 (2), 12 January: 3. Available online: http://www.bookrags.com/criticism/jonathan-franzen-crit/4/#gsc.tab=0 (accessed 25 May, 2015).

Žižek, Slavoj (1989), *The Sublime Object of Ideology*, London and New York: Verso.

Žižek, Slavoj (2002), *Welcome to the Desert of the Real! Five Essays on September 11 and Related Dates*, London and New York: Verso.

Žižek, Slavoj (2008), *In Defense of Lost Causes*, Verso: London and New York.

Žižek, Slavoj (2009), *First as Tragedy, Then as Farce*, Verso: London and New York.

INDEX